Building & Renovating Schools

- *Design*
- *Construction Management*
- *Cost Control*

Drummey Rosane Anderson, Inc., *Architects*

and
Joseph Macaluso
David J. Lewek
Brian C. Murphy

RSMeans

Building & Renovating Schools

- Design
- Construction Management
- Cost Control

 Reed Construction Data

Copyright ©2004
Reed Construction Data, Inc.
Construction Publishers & Consultants
63 Smiths Lane
Kingston, MA 02364-0800
781-422-5000
www.rsmeans.com
RS**Means** is a product line of Reed Construction Data

Reed Construction Data, Inc., and its authors, editors and engineers, endeavor to apply diligence and judgment in locating and using reliable sources for the information published herein. **However, Reed Construction Data makes no express or implied representation, warranty or guarantee in connection with the content of the information contained herein, including the accuracy, correctness, value, sufficiency, or completeness of the data, methods and other information contained herein. Reed Construction Data makes no express or implied warranty of merchantability or fitness for a particular purpose.** Reed Construction Data shall have no liability to any customer or other party for any loss, expense, or damages, whether direct or indirect, including consequential, incidental, special or punitive damages, including lost profits or lost revenue, caused directly or indirectly by any error or omission, or arising out of, or in connection with, the information contained herein.

No part of this publication may be reproduced, stored in a retrieval system, or transmitted in any form or by any means without prior written permission of Reed Construction Data.

The editor for this book was Andrea St. Ours. The managing editor was Mary Greene. The production manager was Michael Kokernak. The production coordinator was Marion Schofield. The electronic publishing specialist was Paula Reale-Camelio. The proofreader was Robin Richardson. The book and cover were designed by Norman R. Forgit. The cover photographs are copyright Greg Premru Photography, Inc. The cover image is copyright Drummey Rosane Anderson, Inc.

Printed in the United States of America

10 9 8 7 6 5 4 3 2 1

Library of Congress Catalog Number Pending

ISBN 0-87629-740-8

Table of Contents

Acknowledgments

This book was written by a team of experts, with input from a number of other individuals and organizations. The primary and contributing authors and the reviewers are listed in the "About the Authors and Contributors" section following these acknowledgments. Others who provided assistance are listed below.

We would like to thank Greg Premru of Greg Premru Photography for granting permission to feature his photographs on the cover and in Chapters 1-5. We are grateful to David Castelli, Vice President of DC&D Technologies, Inc., for allowing us to reprint school case studies that originally appeared in the magazine *Design Cost Data*. In addition, we would like to acknowledge John Wiethorn, who reviewed and provided helpful comments on the "Performing Arts Centers" section of Chapter 5, and Thomas D. Thacher II, President and CEO of Thacher Associates LLC, who contributed information and insight used in the preparation of Chapter 8.

Drummey Rosane Anderson, Inc., authors of Chapters 1-5 of this book, would like to acknowledge the following contributors: Peter Vanderwarker for his photographs and Terry Cracknell for his illustrations featured throughout Part I; Progressive Architecture Engineering (Grand Rapids, MI) and Moseley Architects (Morrisville, NC) for their case studies on green design in Chapter 2; David Stephens of High Tech High for providing assistance and for permission to use photographs of the school in Chapter 3 and for the "Project Room" case study in Chapter 5; and Michael DiBari of Systems, Software, Support, Inc., 3SINET, Inc., for advice and use of graphics for the "Computer Labs and Training Rooms" section of Chapter 5. DRA would also like to thank Dr. Carolyn Markuson of biblioTECH Corporation for providing information for the "Libraries/Media Center" section of Chapter 5.

About the Authors and Contributors

Part I

"Planning & Design," Part I, was authored by members of **Drummey Rosane Anderson, Inc. (DRA)**, an architectural firm that has specialized in the design of educational facilities for over 80 years. Recognized as a leader in the field, DRA is the recipient of numerous design awards and citations and is a regular contributor to educational journals and conferences. Headquartered in Newton, Massachusetts, their Web site is www.DRAarchitects.com. Individual DRA authors and contributors are noted below.

Carl R. Franceschi, AIA, co-author of Chapter 2, "Green Design," and reviewer of the Part I chapters, is President of DRA. He holds a Bachelor of Architecture degree from Cornell University and is a registered architect in Massachusetts and several other northeast states. Mr. Franceschi has completed more than 60 primary and secondary school design projects, totaling over six million square feet, several of which have received national recognition. Mr. Franceschi maintains professional affiliations with the American Institute of Architects (AIA), Boston Society of Architects (BSA), National Council of Architectural Registration Boards (NCARB), Council of Educational Facility Planners International (CEFPI), and the National Middle School Association (NMSA). He is a lifetime honorary member of the Boston Architectural Center, where he has participated as a design studio instructor and thesis advisor, and where he currently serves on the faculty with the Practice Curriculum Committee.

Owen Beenhouwer, AIA, contributor to the Part I chapters, is a principal and past president of DRA. Mr. Beenhouwer holds an M.S. in Conservation of Natural Resources from Yale University, and a Master of Architecture degree from Columbia University School of Architecture. He is a registered architect in New York, Connecticut, New Jersey, and Massachusetts and maintains professional affiliations with the American

Institute of Architects, Boston Society of Architects Educational Facilities Committee, NCARB, Society for Preservation of NE Antiquities, and National Trust for Historic Preservation. Mr. Beenhouwer has been responsible for the design of more than 50 educational facilities, including the nationally recognized Remington-Jefferson K-8 School in Franklin, MA and the Athol-Royalston Middle School in Athol, MA.

Pao-Chung Chi, AIA, author of Chapters 3, "Integration of Technology" and 4, "Integration of Security," and reviewer of Chapters 1, 2, and 5, is a principal of DRA with oversight responsibility for practice management, technology development, and quality assurance. Mr. Chi has over 25 years of professional experience in the field of architecture and is a registered architect in New Hampshire, New York, Pennsylvania, and Connecticut. He holds a Bachelor of Architecture degree from Tunghai University in Taiwan and a Master of Architecture in Urban Design from Harvard University Graduate School of Design. Mr. Chi maintains professional affiliations with the American Institute of Architects, the Boston Society of Architects, the Construction Specifications Institute, and the International Code Council. His practice covers projects in both public and private sectors with a focus on primary and secondary school planning and design.

James A. Barrett, AIA, also contributed to the Part I chapters. He is a principal of DRA with primary responsibility for managing educational projects. Mr. Barrett is a registered architect with more than 20 years of professional experience and is NCARB-certified with active registrations in Massachusetts, Connecticut, Pennsylvania, New Jersey, Ohio, and Virginia. He is currently a member of the American Institute of Architects, Boston Society of Architects, U.S. Green Building Council, Society for College and University Planning, Council of Educational and Facility Planners International, and Boston Society of Architects Healthcare Committee, has participated as a Boston Architectural Center faculty member, and currently serves on the Boston Architectural Center Alumni Board of Directors. Mr. Barrett is a frequent contributor to educational conferences and has presented on such topics as green schools and the history of classroom design. He holds a Bachelor of Science degree in Interior Design, Design Resource Management from the University of Connecticut, and a Bachelor of Architecture degree from the Boston Architectural Center.

D. Paul Moore, AIA, co-author of Chapter 1, "Programming and Pre-Design," and Chapter 5, "Specialty Spaces," is an associate with DRA specializing in programming and conceptual design of educational facilities. Mr. Moore is NCARB-certified, and is a registered architect in Massachusetts and Michigan. He maintains professional affiliations with the American Institute of Architects and the Boston Society of Architects. Mr. Moore has completed numerous feasibility studies incorporating master planning, site evaluation, and community involvement. He is also a faculty member at the Boston Architectural Center, specializing in 2-D and 3-D CAD software applications and architecture.

Donald Nelson, AICP, co-editor of Part I and co-author of Chapters 1 and 5, "Programming and Pre-Design" and "Specialty Spaces," is a facilities planner and project manager with DRA, responsible for master planning, needs assessment, and facilities programming for both the public and private sectors. He holds a Bachelor of Architecture degree from Rensselaer Polytechnic Institute, as well as a Master of City and Regional Planning from Rutgers University. Mr. Nelson maintains professional affiliations with the American Institute of Certified Planners, the Boston Society of Architects, and the Society for College and University Planning. He has significant planning experience and has been responsible for over 50 facilities projects and planning studies for a wide range of building types. His current work at DRA includes strategic planning studies for school facility construction projects in New England.

Paul Brown, AIA, co-author of Chapter 2, "Green Design," is a LEED-certified architect and project manager with DRA, where he is involved with numerous educational facilities projects. He is a registered architect in Massachusetts and Maine and maintains professional affiliations with the American Institute of Architects, the Boston Society of Architects, and the U.S. Green Building Council. Mr. Brown has also had significant experience with medical facilities and historic preservation.

Alana J. Wiens, co-editor of Part I and contributor to Chapters 1 and 5, is Marketing Director at DRA with responsibilities including business development, proposal writing, community relations, and strategic planning. Ms. Wiens' background includes numerous political and public education campaigns, in which she directed communications and public information efforts. Her academic background includes a Master of Arts in Political Science from Acadia University.

Matthew Roberts, co-author of Chapter 5, "Specialty Spaces," is a designer and job captain for several K-12 educational projects with DRA. He is currently a candidate for a Master of Architecture degree at the Boston Architectural Center. Mr. Roberts' design background includes residential, commercial, and retail projects, in addition to educational facilities.

Part II

Part II, "The Construction Process," was written by three authors who represent the different aspects of a school project's construction phase.

David J. Lewek, author of Chapter 9, "The Importance of Project Management," is founder and president of TPJ Associates in Hanson, Massachusetts, a construction project management firm specializing in large public school projects and the training of construction professionals. Prior to the start of his tenure at TPJ Associates in 1993, Mr. Lewek worked at RSMeans as Director of Construction Services. Previously, he was Manager of Construction and Facilities for Child World, Inc., and Construction Manager for ten years with Chas. T. Main Engineers. A Senior Lecturer at Northeastern University in Boston since

1980, Mr. Lewek has taught a number of management courses and has guest-lectured at Boston University, MIT, NYU, and Johnson & Wales University. He has also delivered seminars in Russia, Saudi Arabia, and across the United States on a variety of project management topics. Mr. Lewek holds a Master of Business Administration degree from Rensselaer Polytechnic Institute.

Joseph Macaluso, author of Chapters 6, 7, and 8, ("Cost Estimating," "Scheduling a School Construction Project," and "Types of Contracts and Contractor Selection") and reviewer of the other chapters in this publication, is a Certified Cost Consultant and a member of the Association for the Advancement of Cost Engineering International, where he is chair of the Government and Public Works Special Interest Group. Mr. Macaluso works as a construction cost estimator for Empire State Development Corporation, New York State's economic development agency, which provides financial and technical assistance to businesses, local governments, and community-based, not-for-profit corporations for economic development and large-scale real estate projects.

Over the past 20 years, Mr. Macaluso has prepared construction cost estimates and schedules, reviewed construction budgets, and negotiated change orders for major public works and public/private collaborative projects. He has worked for the NYC School Construction Authority, NYC Transit Authority, and NYC Health and Hospitals Corporation. Mr. Macaluso has prepared numerous construction cost estimates for new schools and major renovation projects and was instrumental in automating the construction cost estimating/tracking process and initiating a construction cost database. He has taught cost estimating at Long Island University and LaGuardia Community College and has published many articles on the subject.

Brian C. Murphy, author of Chapter 10, "Managing the School Construction/Renovation Process," is a Development Manager at The Beck Group in Tampa, Florida, which offers expertise in development, planning, architecture, interior design, and construction services for owners and investors. Mr. Murphy has extensive experience in project management, including many educational facilities. He has managed multiple school construction projects simultaneously. Recently, Mr. Murphy led a team that completed a new middle school while full operations continued uninterrupted at the former school on the same site. A licensed general contractor and real estate broker, he has a Bachelor of Science degree in Building Construction from the University of Florida, where he is currently a candidate for an MBA.

Other Contributors

James Armstrong, CPE, CEM, reviewer of this publication, is an Account Executive at NSTAR Electric and Gas in Westwood, Massachusetts, and former Program Manager of Energy Conservation Programs for municipal, state, federal, and industrial agencies. Prior to his work with NSTAR, Mr. Armstrong was a Senior Project/Application Engineer at Shooshanian Engineering and Trigen Boston Energy Corporation. He also served as Utilities Manager and Property Manager at the Devens

Commerce Center (formally Fort Devens), and as Facilities Manager at Colby Sawyer College and the Museum of Science in Boston. Mr. Armstrong is a contributing author and editor of *Preventive Maintenance Guidelines for School Facilities* and *Green Building: Project Planning & Cost Estimating,* among other publications. He is a graduate of Calhoon MEBA Engineering School, Baltimore, MD, and a retired U.S. Marine Engineer and Lieutenant U.S. Navy Reserve Engineering Officer. Mr. Armstrong also serves as an elected school committee member of the Whitman-Hanson regional school system in Massachusetts and Chairman of the high school building committee. Mr. Armstrong was recently appointed by the Massachusetts Department of Education to the state's Green Schools Certification Task Force.

Barbara Balboni, AIA, reviewer of this book and editor of Part IV, *"School Construction Costs,"* is a Construction Cost Engineer/Editor at RSMeans, a product line of Reed Construction Data in Kingston, Massachusetts. She is the Senior Editor of Means *Square Foot Costs, Assemblies Cost Data*, and *Interior Cost Data* publications, and maintains several components of the Means cost database. Ms. Balboni also conducts seminars on square foot and unit price estimating and conducts market research and consulting projects in construction cost estimating. Prior to her tenure at Reed Construction Data, she was a member of the Kingston School Committee for 15 years, where she was involved in several construction projects. Ms. Balboni also worked as Designer/Project Manager for the architectural firms Lowrey and Blanchard, Blanchard Architectural Associates, Inc., and the McKenna Group, Ltd. She has been responsible for all phases of architectural projects from programming and schematic design through construction. Ms. Balboni is a member of the American Institute of Architects and the Boston Society of Architects.

R. Lee Derr, reviewer of this publication, is a project manager with Rogers-O'Brien Construction in Dallas, Texas. In 18 years of construction management, he has worked on projects in Massachusetts, Maryland, Virginia, Washington, D.C., and multiple urban areas of Texas. Mr. Derr has served as project manager on sixteen school projects for four different school districts in Texas. His other projects have included a corporate campus, hotel and conference center, courthouse, museum, power retail center, and nuclear plant.

Waller S. Poage, AIA, CSI, CVS, reviewer and contributor to Chapter 8, "Types of Contracts and Contractor Selection," is an architect with offices in Alexandria, Virginia. Over the past 35 years, Mr. Poage has gained national recognition for his work in regional and urban planning and corrections architecture, cellular telecommunications, and value engineering. He has served as a member of the faculty of the School of Art and Design at the University of Texas at San Antonio, and is the recipient of numerous professional awards. He is the author of *The Building Professional's Guide to Contract Documents, Third Edition,* also published by RSMeans.

Introduction

Aging school facilities, changing demographics, and the need for new technologies have made school projects one of the construction industry's strongest markets. As projects become more complex, and as time, money, and quality issues create higher demands for school districts, project team members need to clearly understand one another's roles and responsibilities in the planning, design, budgeting, and construction process.

The training of school administrators is naturally focused on providing the best possible educational experience to students, not on managing construction projects. Given that most school districts undertake major building projects only once every 20-40 years, it is not realistic to expect school board members, school building committees, the principal, or other administrators to possess the expertise necessary to manage design and construction on a multi-million-dollar scale.

Architects, engineers, and contractors seeking work on school projects also need to bring themselves up to speed on the concerns of school administrators. They must allow time for important communications with teachers, parent groups, and community members who have a stake in the project and whose activities are directly affected by the ultimate design—and the construction process.

This book addresses the planning, design, and construction phases—whether for a new building, renovation, or expansion. Part I, **Planning & Design** written by an architectural firm specializing in educational facilities, describes the activities that should occur in this phase. The first chapter focuses on planning studies, procurement of professional design services, approvals, and funding. These tasks must be completed early to provide a solid foundation for the project and to avoid budget and schedule overruns and strained community relations. Subsequent chapters in Part I provide technical and economic guidance on some timely issues: green design; computer technology and security/safety requirements; and the special design issues of dedicated spaces such as performing arts centers, gymnasiums, pool facilities, and libraries.

Part II, **The Construction Process**, describes the activities that occur, for the most part, after the planning is complete and the design finalized. Topics include the types of construction contracts and contractor selection, how preliminary and detailed cost estimates are prepared, and the scheduling methods that are used to keep the project on track. Part II also covers the services of project management consultants and the workings of the project team—owner, architect/engineer, and contractor. The last chapter addresses key items (such as construction phasing and safety measures) that the contractor must control to meet student/staff needs and ensure timely project delivery.

The **Case Studies** in Part III provide ideas and inspiration from recently built schools. They describe the projects' goals, such as enhanced learning, support spaces for new curricula, and energy efficiencies. Each case study includes challenges, solutions, and final costs: both construction and General Requirements items such as coordination, quality control, commissioning, and close-out.

Part IV, **School Construction Costs**, is cost data that can be used for budgeting during the planning phase. This information is in the form of square foot costs for "generic" building models for high schools, junior high schools, and elementary schools, as well as free-standing school buildings such as athletic facilities, auditoriums, and libraries. These national-average costs have been compiled by RSMeans and can be adjusted to over 900 locations in the United States and Canada, using the Location Factors provided.

The construction of any building is a complex process. The construction of a school is among the most complex due to the number of constituencies that need to be satisfied, the high visibility of most projects, and the strict schedule and budget limitations. School administrators, members of the school building team, the school board, parent and teacher groups, and others have a huge advantage if they are familiar with the planning, design, and construction processes *before* the project gets under way. Likewise, design professionals and contractors who are interested in this burgeoning market, but not experienced in school projects, need to be well-versed in school construction's special requirements, particularly those items that need attention in the early stages. If neglected, they can cause enormous schedule and budget problems, not to mention poor public relations. This book is designed to provide that information advantage—and to help all project team members reach their goals.

Note on Terminology: Some of the terms used in this book may have different meanings or applications for the different project team members—and in different schools and school districts. The term, "project manager," for example, may be used by all three of the major project team members—owner, architect, and contractor—to refer to an individual assigned by each of them to oversee their team's role in the project. The term may also refer (as in Chapter 9) to a consultant hired to represent the school and communicate with the architect and contractor throughout the project.

Similarly, the entity that represents the school's interests throughout design and construction and communicates regularly with the architect and contractor may be a school building committee (a group of citizens appointed by the local government to legally represent the town, as owner), an individual on the school staff (such as the school principal or facility manager), or a project management consultant as described above. Each school has its own special requirements and procedures, and sometimes terminology—whether evolved over time or imposed by the state, the county, the district, or (in the case of private schools), its own board of directors or similar group.

Part I

Planning & Design

Fundamental changes are occurring in the planning and design of school facilities. This evolution is tied to societal developments that are influencing educational philosophy, requirements for technology and security, and the overall relationship of schools to the community. Part I of this book addresses many of these changes and how they are reflected in school design.

Chapter 1, "Programming and Pre-Design," is an overview of the planning process, including why a planning study may be needed, the various types of studies, how professional design and planning services are procured, and what to expect at each step. This chapter

describes why planning is such an important part of school design and construction, why changes in education philosophy and teaching requirements need to be addressed at this stage, and why good communication and community participation are essential. The chapter also shows how to implement the recommended plan, including necessary approvals and funding.

Chapter 2, "Green Design," explains the importance of "green," or sustainable, design in terms of energy and cost savings and a healthier indoor and outdoor environment; economic issues to consider; and the steps needed during implementation to ensure green building systems operate as planned. This chapter also provides a review of green design technologies currently available for school facilities.

Chapter 3, "Integration of Technology," addresses a number of issues that affect the planning of computer technology in schools. While it cannot substitute for teachers, advancing technological applications have unquestionably had a major impact on the educational philosophy of schools, including the movement to more project-based learning. This chapter describes currently available and evolving technology, and how to integrate it successfully into the school building design. A mini-glossary of computer systems terminology is provided at the end of the chapter for non-IT professionals.

Chapter 4, "Integration of Security," examines recent changes in security issues that affect the planning and design of school facilities. Security is a complex topic involving policies, procedures, design, technologies, and intervention. Furthermore, each school will have unique security requirements. This chapter describes security design strategies, including an assessment of school needs, appropriate environmental solutions, and integrated technological solutions. It also considers the effect that major security measures have on staff and students, and the need to strike an appropriate balance between safety and a welcoming environment for learning.

Chapter 5, "Specialty Spaces," addresses the requirements of components found in most schools. These include traditional school spaces, such as libraries/media centers, athletic facilities, and auditoriums, as well as those that support particular programs, such as performing arts centers and vocational-technical areas. The new project rooms, which are a direct outgrowth of project-based learning, are also covered. This chapter discusses the unique features and requirements of each of these specialty spaces, and provides examples of design solutions.

Chapter 1

Programming and Pre-Design

Drummey Rosane Anderson, Inc.

The design of a school facility requires considerable background research and planning to ensure that the final outcome will fully meet the needs of the school community. It is during the programming and pre-design phase that these activities take place. This chapter will explore the key issues involved in planning a new school facility, including:

- How to prepare for the planning process
- What can be expected from a planning team
- How much time the planning process will take

Also included is a case study of a facility planning effort, which illustrates the approach of a design team, as well as the issues affecting the outcome.

The number and variety of studies and technical reports to be prepared at this stage can seem a bit overwhelming. In reality, this is the research phase of the project. The process is similar to purchasing a car after compiling information on various models and comparing the features with one's actual needs. A study for a school building project will look at the existing facilities, other existing schools of a similar type, the specific needs of the school, the schedule, and the budget. All of these factors will help determine the optimum choices for a school district or private school entity. By understanding the programming and pre-design process in advance, school representatives will be able to work with school facilities planners and/or architects to create a document that will guide building committee decisions, justify the project to the community and state or board (in the case of private school construction), and build a solid project foundation.

Several types of studies are commonly conducted for school building projects. This chapter will clarify the steps involved in each type of study, what to expect, and the design and support benefits of community participation. The chapter will also outline the typical process used to hire an architect. This information will prepare participants for the planning process—with an overall understanding of this phase of the project, as well as technical terminology and tips for avoiding problems.

The Need for Programming and Pre-Design

Programming and pre-design, often referred to as *planning* or *facility planning*, are the early action stages of a school design project. These activities normally establish the guidelines and parameters of the project, providing a sound basis for subsequent architectural design solutions and construction. Programming and pre-design studies are conducted when there is a problem or need—either existing or anticipated—concerning a specific school or school system. Such issues include changes in enrollment resulting in school overcrowding or under-use, lack of appropriate facilities for current or future anticipated teaching needs, deteriorating building systems, and a need to accommodate new or future technologies. Planning studies should provide a framework for solving immediate problems and a direction for long-term solutions.

Types of Studies

The many types of planning studies serve various purposes and range in size and complexity depending on the school's needs and resources. Studies can be system-wide *comprehensive master plans* for school districts, or *facility master plans* for individual schools (new stand-alone facilities, renovation or addition to existing, or a combination). *Program studies* may also be included to determine future space needs. *Feasibility studies* may be needed to determine initial project need, direction, and cost for planning purposes. *Site selection studies* may be required to determine the best locations for future school construction. Other specialized studies that may be necessary to support the primary planning study include land use, open space, environmental impact, parking, traffic and access, and energy studies, to name just a few.

Procurement of Facilities Planning and Architectural Services

The school building committee must first determine the scope of services desired. Facilities planning and architectural design are two different services, although some architects can offer both. *Facilities planning* is the process of determining the needs of the building users; *architectural design* provides answers to these needs. Once the needs of a facility have been determined during the planning process, the architect develops options and helps the school building committee measure them against the needs. Successful architectural design will satisfy the functional requirements of a building and achieve meaningful and enduring results for the school district and community. The final design should reflect the goals and vision of the project, schedule requirements, and budget limitations.

The design firm that is selected should have the ability to:

- Facilitate a process of informed decision-making.
- Advise the building committee on financial and other implications of each decision.

- Develop and establish guidelines for the entire project.
- Produce a plan that meets the needs of students, teachers, and staff.

If the project continues past the study stage, the firm should have the capability of continuing the project through design, construction, and occupancy.

A school district may also choose to hire one firm to perform the planning phase and another for the architectural phase. In fact, some jurisdictions may *require* that different firms complete each of the two phases. Other jurisdictions may allow one firm to perform both phases, but with separate negotiations and contract for each phase. The school district may also consider hiring a planning specialist, depending on specific needs, such as preparing enrollment projections, detailed site surveys, or real estate analysis.

It should be noted that many larger school districts and some private schools have their own in-house facilities (planning and design) departments. Depending on the size of the project, these facilities departments may do much or all of the programming, pre-design, and design work themselves or contract the work to an outside consultant. *(See the section on "Selection of a K-12 Facility Design Team: Architect and Engineers" later in this chapter.)*

Study Process

The planning process is a time of discovery and decision-making about the mission, purpose, and intent of the school project. There is no one, step-by-step process for preparing all planning studies. Each is unique in the issues/problems it addresses. Each has different goals to achieve, information available, and information that must be collected. An experienced facility planning consultant will be sensitive to the many and diverse demands on the decision-making body that is responsible for finding appropriate solutions within budget constraints.

Planning is not a linear process. It involves carefully integrating an enormous amount of data and making calculated decisions in the areas of space needs, site suitability, engineering, technology, security, sustainable design, finances, and many other areas. The consultant should facilitate a process of informed decision-making.

The planning consultant should seek input from all appropriate user groups. Community participation programs,

Terminology

Program/space program: *A comprehensive list identifying every space required within the facility. Normally includes current space needs, as well as projected needs (often five to ten years, depending on the scope of the project). Depending on the complexity and stage of the project, the program will identify the requirements of each space, including its required size and configuration, number of users, special electrical and mechanical requirements, special servicing needs, security issues, public and private access requirements, adjacency requirements (see below), and other special needs.*

Adjacency requirements: *The key proximity requirement of each space in the facility. It is the ideal or required relationship of one space to another. Some spaces may need to be side-by-side for operational efficiency; others may need only a convenient proximity; others may have no relationship; and still others may need to be some distance apart for acoustic, security, or other reasons. These adjacency requirements will be a major influence in determining the overall facility organization.*

discussed in the following section, can make a significant difference in the success of the planning effort.

Although every planning study is unique, many of the following study components are typical of the planning process. The scope and complexity of these steps will vary.

- Develop a project understanding
  — Collect base school administration and project information
  — Develop evaluation criteria (goals, objectives, mission)
- Develop a facility space program (determination of need)
  — Determine enrollment projections
  — Develop space program
    — Administration spaces
    — Support spaces
    — Teaching spaces
    — Athletic spaces
    — Multi-purpose spaces
    — Community use functions
    — Site-related spaces and developments
    — Technology and communications
    — Building systems
    — Storage
    — Circulation (corridors and stairs, etc.)
  — Determine adjacency requirements (proximity of and access from one space to another)
  — Determine public access requirements
  — Determine service and special equipment requirements
- Analyze existing conditions, to include:
  — Description of the school system or individual school
  — Site analyses
  — Existing building conditions analysis
  — Cost analysis of needed upgrades, maintenance, and repairs
  — Preparation of an information base for planning and design
- Develop planning solutions (solving the need)
  — Develop a planning approach
  — Confirm and expand evaluation criteria
  — Develop concept options: Arrange the spaces in relationship to one another
  — Develop a cost estimate for new construction/renovation
  — Evaluate and rank options

— Select a recommended option

— Refine the recommended option

• Prepare a final facility planning document, to include:

— Recommendations with cost analysis

— Implementation plan with scheduling and phasing

Implementation of the recommendations may directly follow the completion of the planning study. This will depend on the project findings, project goals, available funding, and other factors.

Community Participation

Involving the community throughout the planning and design process has proven to be worthwhile for many school districts. Early community buy-in is *critical* if there is to be a vote on a bond issue. By encouraging active community participation, two things happen: useful and exciting ideas are brought forward, discussed, and acted-on; and the participants benefit from a sense of trust that results from being included in the planning process.

Community participation sessions at the planning and design stage are held for two main purposes:

• Project input
• Public information

The *project input sessions* occur early in the process and allow parents, neighbors, and other community members (as well as trustees/board members and potential donors in the case of private schools) to express their views of the project and raise issues that others on the design team may not have considered. Longer public input sessions (sometimes referred to as *design charettes*) may involve actual design work—including sketches and diagrams that can be made during the meeting.

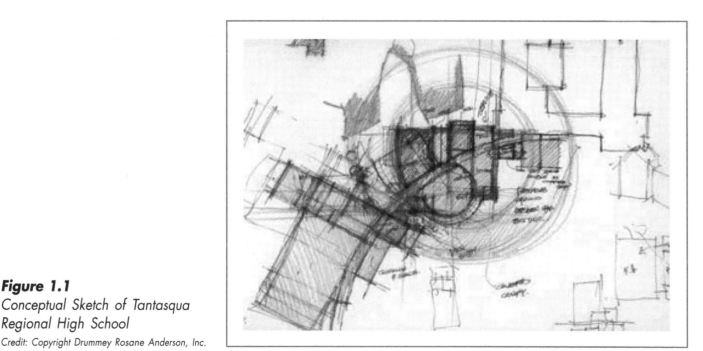

Figure 1.1
Conceptual Sketch of Tantasqua Regional High School
Credit: Copyright Drummey Rosane Anderson, Inc.

One strategy that often works well is to divide the larger group into smaller teams to tackle specific questions. Each of these teams can be equipped with the tools they need to express their ideas in notes and sketches. Individual efforts can be discussed and reviewed when the larger group comes back together. A well-planned community/design session may be an all-day event, with designated breaks for food and informal discussions. Small teams can spend an hour or two on a particular task, take a break, and then tackle another issue. Several teams can discuss important questions independently and then compare results. The moderators can move freely among the teams to facilitate discussions.

Public information sessions generally take place later in the process and allow the school administration and project architects to present the design concept/schematic designs to the school community and answer any questions. These information sessions can help avoid rumors and diffuse tension in the community. In communities where voting is required in order to fund the project, public information sessions may be numerous.

Publicity is crucial for public meetings. The design team may assist by designing and mailing informational flyers, making public appearances, setting up a Web site, appearing on local television, or meeting with special interest groups. A well-prepared community-team planning session requires careful consideration of the invitation process, a clear agenda, a skilled moderator, and achievable goals. Various individuals may share the role of moderator. At the beginning of the session, local elected officials may wish to introduce the team and speak generally

Figure 1.2
Architect Conducting a Community Workshop
The community workshop fosters two-way communication between the public and the planning team.
Photo Credit: Drummey Rosane Anderson, Inc.

about the goals and agenda. It may then be best to hand off the process to the lead architect to actually conduct the "work" of the planning session. This will ensure that the individual who needs the information, the designer, is directing the collection of that information. This will also enable the desires of the community to flow directly through the architect into the actual plans for the building.

As the community/team planning session proceeds, whether a short evening session or an all-day workshop, participants often gain a sense of mutual trust as ideas are fairly evaluated. This results in a sense of understanding and depth of appreciation of the design process, which will pay back dividends later in the process. Even when a particular "favorite" idea cannot be accommodated, its advocates can better understand the reasons why it has been set aside, and should appreciate the value of alternative ideas that have been included.

The primary objective of good community participation is to ensure that the future building provides for the needs of those who will use it, and those who will be asked to support the project. A building that fails to serve the needs of the community, failure of a bond issue vote, or the lack of a donation to a building fund are all unhappy outcomes for everyone, but relatively easy to avoid.

The Planning Study

This section provides a more detailed review of the steps normally required in a facility planning study. While every planning study is unique, the following guidelines may be helpful to those embarking on this process. The guidelines include a framework for the appropriate steps and an approach that will be needed from the initial project inception through to the final report.

Development of Key Project Parameters

This is the basic information that will be required by the facility planning consultant in order to conduct the planning study. Most of these items should be readily available. The consultant should be able to work with the school building committee to develop or gather the remaining information. All of the following items should be discussed at the kick-off meeting (project initiation meeting), or as soon as possible thereafter. The kick-off/project initiation meeting is the first formal meeting between the design team and the client and is the first step of the planning effort. A wide range of issues are discussed, providing both the client and design team with a clear understanding of the intent and direction of the process, the goals and criteria of the project, the appropriate lines of communication, information that is available, and the overall timeline.

Client Description: The consultant needs to know the name of the individuals on the school building committee who will be making decisions, along with their contact information, and whom to report to, if these individuals are not from the school building committee. The constituency that will influence decisions [school board (board of trustees in a private school), administrators, faculty, planning group, community liaison, other interested parties] should also be described. Specific lines of communication should be developed between the school building committee and the consultant.

Project Identification/Description: The consultant and the building committee must have a clear understanding of the project need and what drives that need (enrollment changes, population shifts, overcrowding or under-use, poor structural/environmental conditions, technological needs, new educational programs, or other issues).

Planning Horizon: This is the planning period, based on the school building committee's need and the information available. Normally, larger, system-wide studies would consider long-range and possibly phased solutions.

Type of Planning Study: What type of planning study will this be? Will this be a long-term, comprehensive planning strategy for the school district (taking six months or longer to complete), or a fairly quick measure (taking one to three months) to solve a specific, immediate problem? The consultant can work with the school administration to determine the most appropriate type of study to meet the school's needs, whether it is a feasibility study, programming study, or some other specialized study.

Project Vision: This is the overall project direction that the school administration may desire. It could include such issues as school size and organization (small schools, neighborhood schools, schools within schools, academies, or clusters), department organizations, the need for new programs and program changes, and goals for "green design." The project vision should include a technology vision, with goals based on the level of technology desired in the facility. Finally, the vision should include the level of security required or desired by the building committee.

Evaluation Criteria: The building committee and consultant should collaborate to define the specific goals, objectives, and mission of the project. These criteria should include quantitative sustainability performance goals that, for example, may include a desired Leadership in Energy and Environmental Design (LEED) level rating. The building committee and consultant should commit to these evaluation criteria and use them on a continuing basis for evaluating planning options. *(See Chapter 2 for more on energy savings and environmental design.)*

Planning Standards: The building committee should provide any specific planning or design standards that are required by the school district or private school, to supplement state and other local requirements. In areas where there are no applicable legislated standards, standards will need to be developed by the consultant, in collaboration with the school district.

Information Sources: The building committee should provide the consultant with all available information, including enrollment/demographic studies, existing site and building conditions, surveys, other relevant information, and sources for information not readily at hand.

Project Budget: The building committee should describe the proposed budget and its limitations. The study may work within an existing budget or help determine budget needs if the budget has not yet been established. The educational funding process must be described.

(Note: A State-By-State Index, provided in the Resources section of this book, includes contact information for each state's Board of Education, as well as for statewide educational planning, design, and funding agencies.)

Development of a Facility Space Program

The space programming process should begin soon after the initial project kick-off meeting and should include the following steps.

Enrollment Projections

Enrollment projections are an essential consideration when planning a new school facility. Depending on the school district, this information may or may not be readily available. Some districts may update enrollment figures on an ongoing basis, while others may depend on data provided by their state Department of Education. Still others may hire an enrollment consultant to produce projections with an independent viewpoint, removed from political influences. Whatever the source, projections should be renewed annually to enhance their validity and to update any unusual regional demographic trends that may influence the data.

From the designer's perspective, reliable enrollment information is essential immediately following the initial project kick-off meeting, as it is the foundation for the entire programming effort. It is important for the project team to understand that the design process is directly dependent on the quality, timeliness, and accuracy of the preliminary enrollment projections. While a certain amount of flexibility can be built into a design to accommodate reasonable enrollment variations, no design can properly respond to unlimited variables. Enrollment projections must include a defined margin of error based on statistical "bell-curve" calculation methods.

Enrollment projections for private schools serve a different purpose. The private school decides how many additional seats to offer to the population they serve, based on balancing the costs for staffing, facilities, and marketing with the income from increased tuition. Population projections seek to match the projected need with the proposed changes to the number of seats being offered.

Space Programming Process

School programming and design is based on the synthesis of information from many sources, as well as state and local requirements to meet enrollment projection needs and anticipated changes in the educational program. The project team should meet initially with the school building committee to review specific programming and planning objectives.

These may include:

- Establishing planning criteria and assumptions for the overall facility plan and design
- Understanding the primary functions and activities of all departments and education programs to be included in the facility
- Verifying the current education program
- Finalizing population and enrollment projections
- Determining appropriate and available space standards or the need to develop them
- Confirming the goals, objectives, and evaluation criteria

In addition, the consultant should also meet with the school principal(s) and other appropriate staff members to learn of their observations and concerns about the existing school building(s) and site(s).

User interviews should be held with appropriate personnel (administrators, department heads, faculty), students, and community liaison to determine space, operational, and adjacency requirements. The school building committee, with the guidance of the planning consultant, should determine the list of interviewees. A questionnaire (normally prepared by the consultant with collaboration and approval of the school building committee) is a useful tool during the interview process, as it helps to maintain consistency.

The starting point for projecting space needs includes an analysis of present staff and an assessment of the adequacy of existing space. Detailed information will be collected, including space requirements, adjacencies, and access requirements; security; support needs; special HVAC and electrical requirements; and documentation of users' energy needs. Representatives of the school building committee should attend all of the user interviews and review the data before it is incorporated into the program. Additional meetings should be held with local agencies and organizations such as the city or town's Finance Committee, Conservation Commission, Historical Commission, Fire Department, Police Department, Building Commission, Parents' and Teachers' Association, and so forth.

During programming, regularly scheduled meetings with key building committee representatives should be planned, with their comments integrated into the space programming process. In addition, the planning team should ideally attend public forums to receive input from local residents. In the case of private schools, meetings should be held with trustees, development and fund-raising staff, and potential donors. Information from all resources should be integrated into the final building program.

Once the interviews are complete, and all of the data has been collected and verified, a database of total space needs (existing and future) will be formulated. In addition to space requirements, this database will include adjacencies, access and operational issues, anticipated technological change, and other key information needed for subsequent planning.

Analysis of Existing Conditions of School Facilities

The space planning process should culminate in a Space Program Summary Report documenting future space, adjacency, and operation requirements. Depending on the scope of the study, this may be a stand-alone document or could become a division or chapter in a larger document that includes the facility program, existing conditions survey, development and evaluation of planning options, selection of a recommended option, cost analyses, and an implementation plan.

This task should begin soon after the initial project kick-off meeting. It can run concurrently with the development of the facility program and may include some or all of the following components.

Description of the School System or Individual School

This will include information such as the total enrollment, grade-level breakdown, and number and size of classrooms. In addition, the description will include the number and location of individual buildings and enrollment, by each school, within the entire school system.

Site Analyses

A good site analysis of one or more existing sites (such as Figure 1.3) includes the following:

- Site description (location, size, parking and circulation, recreation areas)
- Zoning
- Environmental concerns
- Site utilities (current condition and capacities)
- Topography
- Wetlands
- Geotechnical (soil) conditions
- View corridors (uninterrupted line of sight to and from the building)
- Neighborhood context
- Site survey, as required

A site analysis of other potential (owned and non-owned) sites may include additional factors such as:

- Ownership. Are the sites under the control of the school district, or are they available for purchase?
- Relationship to school population need.
- Site analysis (as previously described, but with fewer factors for preliminary screening of sites, and more detailed factors for final screening of sites).
- Evaluation matrix to determine best candidate sites.

Existing Building Conditions Analysis

An analysis of existing school buildings should include the following components, as applicable to the scope of the project:

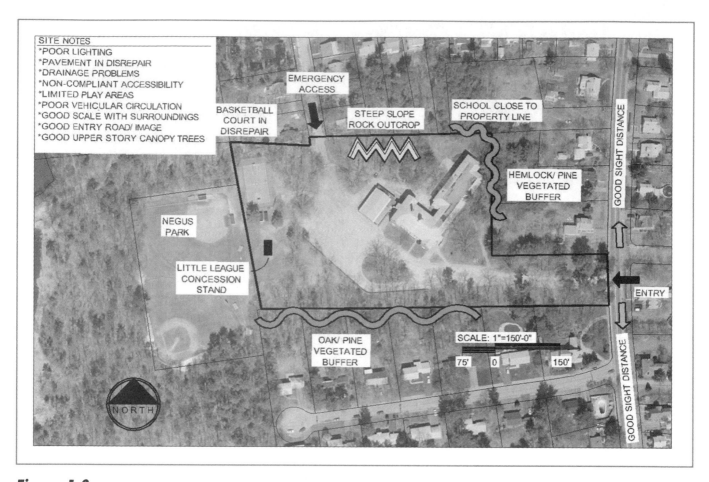

Figure 1.3

Existing Site Conditions

The site analysis describes existing conditions outside of the building, including landscape, accessibility, space, and parking issues.

Credit: Copyright Drummey Rosane Anderson, Inc.

(See Figure 1.4.)

- Building size (net and gross square feet)
- Building organization (Does current building organization/layout work? Is it flexible? Is there expansion potential?)
- Existing space analysis (on a room-by-room basis compared to minimum standards)
  — Summary of inadequate spaces
  — Key accessibility issues
  — Efficiency of existing space
- Building exterior description (adequacy, upgrade requirements)
- Structural description (adequacy, upgrade requirements)
  — Planning implications [example: low ceilings and structural members may limit mechanical, electrical, and plumbing (MEP) upgrades]

— Seismic upgrades may be required to meet current code requirements

- Heating, ventilation, and air conditioning (adequacy, upgrade requirements)
  — Planning implications (Longer school year/community use may require air conditioning.)
  — Asbestos covering heating lines, hot water lines, and boilers often an issue
- Plumbing (adequacy, upgrade requirements)
  — Planning implications (Many, if not all, older fixtures may be inefficient and will not meet accessibility and other code requirements.)
- Fire protection (adequacy, upgrade requirements)
  — Planning implications (may not meet current code requirements, and may not exist in many older facilities)
- Electrical systems (adequacy, upgrade requirements)
  — Planning implications (Major upgrades may be needed for additional technology, new code requirements.)
- Lighting (adequacy, upgrade requirements)
  — Planning implications (Older lighting systems may be inefficient, may not meet today's code requirements, and may contain hazardous materials.)
- Vertical transportation (adequacy, upgrade requirements)
  — Planning implications (Older multi-floor schools often have no elevators, which are required by current accessibility standards.)
- Data and technology systems (computers)
- Communications systems (adequacy and upgrade requirements for phones and intercoms)
- Emergency and security systems (adequacy, upgrade requirements)
- Code compliance (overall deficiencies based on current applicable codes, including building, energy, seismic)
- Americans with Disabilities Act (ADA) compliance (overall deficiencies based on current accessibility standards)
- Environmental analysis [type, location, and estimated quantities of known and assumed asbestos-containing building materials (ACBM) mercury, lead, PCBs, and other hazardous materials]
- Indoor air quality
- Observations of specific interior spaces
- Current and anticipated maintenance and operating costs
- Overall security deficiencies

Figures 1.4 and 1.5 are typical of what might be expected as part of an existing buildings conditions analysis. Figure 1.4 is an *Existing Conditions Survey* drawing indicating areas of significant concern in the building. Such an illustration is typically followed by accompanying text describing the building conditions in detail. Figure 1.5 shows a *Key Accessibility Issues* graphic, also followed by text describing in detail the areas of concern indicated on the drawing.

As with the space program, a summary report of existing conditions should be produced documenting existing site and buildings conditions, as well as existing space occupied by each department. This may also be a stand-alone document or become a part of a larger study document.

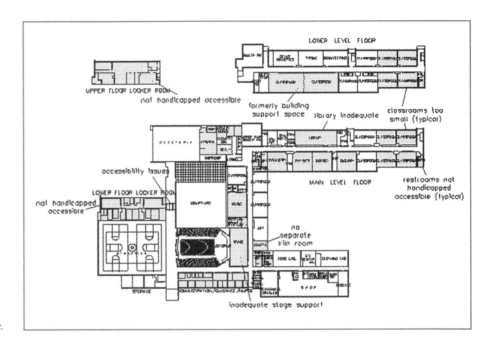

Figure 1.4
Existing Condition Survey
Note: Shaded spaces in this plan are undersized relative to space standards for schools.

Credit: Copyright Drummey Rosane Anderson, Inc.

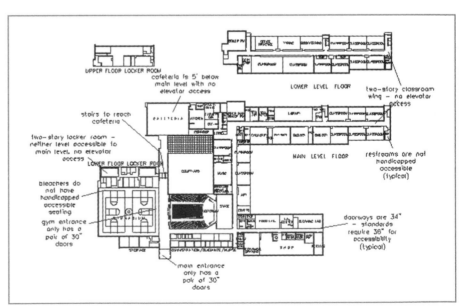

Figure 1.5
Key Accessibility Issues
This plan shows where the existing building fails to provide handicapped accessibility.

Credit: Copyright Drummey Rosane Anderson, Inc.

Preparing an Information Database for Planning

The planning consultant must compare existing space assignments to projected space requirements (from the facility space program) over the designated planning timeline. This comparison will illustrate the current space shortages and will generate total square footage requirements for renovation/relocation or new construction, assuming optimal reuse of existing space. A database will be prepared during the planning period to document existing space occupancy, existing and future space requirements, and additional space required.

Development of Planning Solutions

Develop a Planning Approach

The building committee and consultant will need to collaborate on a basic approach to the project. This approach will involve choices about the rehabilitation or expansion of existing facilities, demolition of buildings that cannot be reused, and locations of new, stand-alone buildings. The characteristics of existing facilities and buildings should be assessed against future space requirements and maintenance and operational costs to determine the viability of rehabilitating and expanding these structures versus other action.

Renovation Versus New Construction

Whether to renovate a school or build new is perhaps the most important fundamental question of the early planning stages for many projects. There are advantages and disadvantages to each choice particular to the special circumstances of every planned school, and these must be considered carefully. How is the renovation versus new construction question answered? What factors need to be considered?

The cost of renovating an older facility versus building a new one is often the first question that arises on many projects. If land is not available for a new building, then the question may be moot. However, when space is available, the cost of each approach needs to be considered. There is usually no simple answer. On a relatively new existing building that requires little more than new technology resources and a "face-lift," renovation should be less costly than building new. For an older building that was constructed before the implementation of current codes, renovation costs can increase dramatically, particularly if an effort is being made to accurately restore historic features. Hazardous materials may need to be abated, accessibility upgrades for the physically challenged may need to be addressed, and structural reinforcement and energy-use upgrades of building shells may be required to resist wind and earthquake forces and meet current construction standards.

There are other factors in addition to cost to be considered in the renovation versus new construction debate. Parents and teachers are becoming increasingly concerned about indoor air quality and healthy building environments. In many cases, people equate "healthy" with "new," and are wary of renovating an older building. In other cases, people may mistrust new higher-technology building materials, as well as express a preference for the known environment of an older building.

One of the key concerns for a renovation project is maintaining a completely dry environment during the construction process. Mold and mildew have become major health (and insurance) concerns for buildings. These organisms propagate in a moist environment, and a building under renovation is particularly vulnerable to moisture problems.

Green design is another topic that should be considered in each approach. Many proponents of green, or sustainable, design feel that it is better to recycle an older building for these reasons: it reduces the use of new building components that must be manufactured from raw materials, keeps construction debris out of the waste stream, and preserves open space by reconstructing instead of developing unused land.

Green advocates may also support new construction, particularly when it is combined with renovation of existing facilities. New construction can also offer the advantage of providing a facility with good air quality, which is another major goal of the green design movement. Some green building benefits can, for the most part, be achieved *only* through new construction. These include: optimal siting of the building, maximum use of daylighting, MEP (mechanical, electrical, and plumbing) efficiencies, structural accommodation of solar and other green systems, and maximum use of green building materials.

In many cases, local historic agencies will have the final word in the renovation versus new construction debate. Many older school buildings are beautiful structures that are highly valued by those who want to protect our built environment. Historic preservation agencies may dictate what can and cannot be done at a particular school building project site. Even when the governing regulations are not enough to prevent demolition of an older school building, public opinion and local activist organizations can make a strong case for preservation and renovation. The challenges of renovating a building while honoring its historic value may prove to have unexpected benefits. Although direct government contributions to historic preservation building projects have declined in recent years, private contributions have increased. The same activist agencies that influence the decision to renovate may also serve as resources to assist with financing such a project.

Location of New Facilities (Smaller Multi-Site Facilities/Larger Single-Site Facility)

For community-wide, multi-school projects, a decision may need to be made as to the allocation of space to be constructed. Alternatives may range from a large facility on a single site to construction of smaller facilities (such as neighborhood schools) on two or more sites. Many factors, including community and administrative issues, must be taken into consideration. Broader issues such as "smart growth" versus "suburban sprawl" are outside the scope of this book. Following are some of the advantages and disadvantages of various approaches to space allocation.

Single-site projects have the advantage of centralization. Functions such as administration, the library/media center, the nurse's office, and food service are not duplicated. Classroom flexibility is maximized—enrollment shifts from one section of the school district to another are more easily absorbed. Communication among administration and faculty may be faster, and face-to-face meetings are easier to arrange. Custodial maintenance is sometimes easier *and less costly* at a centralized site as well. Deliveries are easier to control, and material inventories easier to monitor. Perhaps most importantly, one building's mechanical and electrical systems are almost certainly easier to maintain than those in multiple facilities. In addition, the surface area of one large building will usually be less than that of multiple smaller buildings, reducing overall energy needs. It should be noted that a significant negative aspect of a centralized school is the distance it may be from many neighborhoods and the resultant need for busing.

Multiple sites also have unique advantages. Administration and staff may appreciate the flexibility and responsiveness afforded by being able to "run their own ship." Parents may feel that a smaller staff is more responsive to their own families' individual needs, resulting in a better educational program. Neighborhood schools will typically be closer to the students they serve, reducing the need for busing. Large-scale community spaces, such as auditoriums, may not be as practical with multiple sites; but having more, smaller meeting and performance spaces can offer more scheduling flexibility. In addition, recreation areas associated with the schools will be closer to individual neighborhoods. Finally, although maintenance of a single facility is easier, multiple facilities offer the benefit of redundancy; for example, if a pipe bursts and damages meeting rooms at one school, meetings can be rescheduled at another school.

Single Sites Divided into Multiple "Schools" offer a way to achieve the advantages of both smaller schools and a single site. The concept is a "school within a school" (also called a "house" or "cluster") approach. This is essentially a larger facility, subdivided into a number of smaller schools or clusters. Students and teachers spend most of their time in their individual "cluster," which can be the size of a small school. The library/media center, cafeteria, and other shared functions can be centrally located between the clusters. This approach has the advantage of providing students with the feel of a small school, while still allowing for an economy of scale. The one disadvantage is that this school would not be at the neighborhood level, and would most likely require busing. The case study later in this chapter examines this approach. *(See Figure 1.6.)*

The Movement to Smaller Schools: It should be noted that a relatively new movement in the U.S. encourages the return to smaller, neighborhood schools, even at the high school level. For example, the

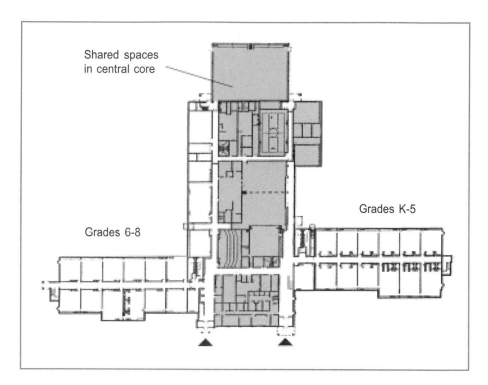

Shared spaces
in central core

Grades K-5

Grades 6-8

Figure 1.6
Combined Elementary and Middle School on a Single Site
Although the K-5 and 6-8 grade levels are separate, they are both served by a common central core.
Credit: Copyright Drummey Rosane Anderson, Inc.

Bill & Melinda Gates Foundation has established an educational grant program that encourages smaller, highly focused high schools. The foundation's goal is to improve high school and college graduation rates by creating stronger, more personalized, and ultimately more effective schools. Since 1994, the foundation has provided nearly 500 million dollars in grants to support smaller schools in school systems of all sizes throughout the country. Just a few examples of recent grants:

- The Gates foundation is currently partnering with the New York City Department of Education and has awarded it a grant of 51 million dollars to support up to 67 new smaller high schools.
- Kansas City, Missouri has received a grant of over 6 million dollars to reorganize its high schools into smaller facilities of no more than 350 students, each with a unique theme.
- A 17 million dollar grant will enable Milwaukee, Wisconsin to redesign 7 large high schools and create 40 new small high schools, providing personalized attention and a variety of learning options.
- Boston has received a 13.6 million dollar grant to create small high schools that will provide personalized attention in a supportive atmosphere. It is expected that within 4 years, up to 30% of all Boston high school students will be enrolled in these schools.

(See the Resources section at the end of the book for contact information for the Gates and other foundations.)

Constructing an Addition for Swing Space

Swing space is a concept that is being used more frequently when a project involves both the addition of new space and renovation of existing space. The swing space approach includes the initial construction of a new addition(s) with the subsequent relocation of the school operations into the new space while the renovation of the existing space is conducted. This approach aims for uninterrupted school operations during the construction process. The construction team is able to proceed with minimal disruption to their work (caused by coordinating with school activities) that would otherwise occur. Students, faculty, and parents do not have the inconvenience of temporarily relocating to a completely different site.

Potential disadvantages to the swing space approach include the longer length of time needed to complete the entire project, as well as possible design complexities. Adequate teaching space needs to be part of the first phase of construction, so that teaching programs can continue uninterrupted during the secondary renovation phase. These provisions may not always match the program objectives of the proposed project, since the facility may not have a need to construct new classroom space. Thus, the swing-space concept sometimes requires an expansion of the project's program, and/or greater expense. However, these expenses can sometimes be justified, since cost factors for such things as temporary transportation, relocation, or leasing of temporary space may be avoided. *(For additional information, see the case study at the end of this chapter.)*

Use of Temporary Classrooms

Temporary classrooms may be required as a stopgap measure to meet enrollment needs before construction or expansion can be completed. These facilities may also be used in a phasing strategy for expansion projects, or on constricted sites where a swing space addition may not be appropriate.

The quality of temporary classrooms has improved over recent years, and the delivery of such space has become more "streamlined." Vendors have learned how to target "packaged" classroom systems for school use and provide all of the planning, permitting, and financing services needed for a "turn-key" installation. The downside of this approach is that it tends to be very expensive. Individual projected budgets and total project costs should be verified when considering this solution. *(See Chapter 6 for more on cost considerations of temporary structures.)*

A community that is facing a multi-year, multi-school, system-wide project may find the temporary structure solution advantageous. Exercising lease-to-own options on the temporary units can meet financial and operational needs. Temporary spaces can be arranged at each facility in accordance with specific needs. At the end of the process, the community may choose to keep or store (if space is available) the temporary unit for use in case of unexpected events such as: a sudden change in enrollment; a natural disaster; or long-term evacuation of a building due to an operational accident.

Confirm and Expand Evaluation Criteria

Evaluation criteria are needed to weigh all proposed planning options. Initial criteria were developed in the first phases of the project based on the goals, objectives, and mission of the project. Additional criteria may include such factors as available space, required renovation and expansion, location, pedestrian and service access, functionality, adjacencies, and capital and operating cost factors. The evaluation criteria will be used to determine which facilities, building, or site options would be most suitable.

Develop Concept Options

Synthesis of information on existing conditions and future space needs forms the foundation to produce a number (often three) of concept options. *(See Figure 1.8.)* Large, comprehensive projects may involve an initial analysis of many sites before specific site and building planning can begin for one or more recommended sites. Smaller-scaled projects may involve the placement of a building on a single, new site or the location of an addition to an existing facility.

The facility space planning consultant should explore alternative designs for the project, including preliminary cost estimates (normally based on a cost per square foot at this stage) of the most promising solutions. All options must meet each department's space, operational, and adjacency needs. Each option will be described in terms of building and site

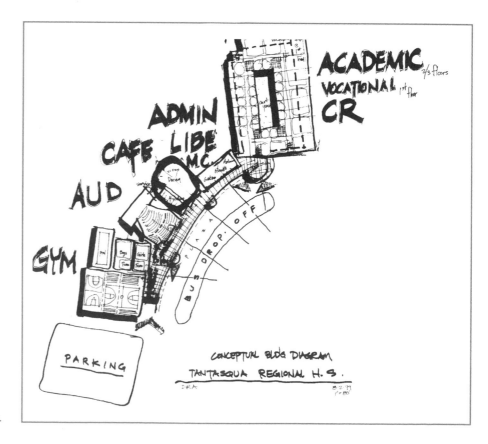

Figure 1.7
Early Concept Option Sketch, Tantasqua Regional High School, Sturbridge, MA
This concept sketch explores the relationship between the main corridor and major blocks of building space.

Credit: Copyright Drummey Rosane Anderson, Inc.

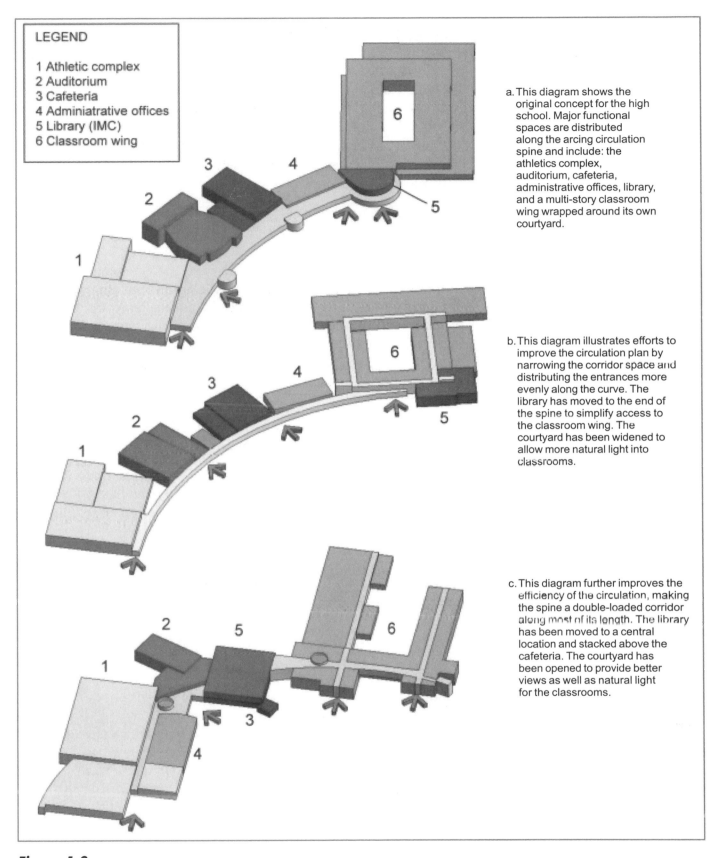

LEGEND

1 Athletic complex
2 Auditorium
3 Cafeteria
4 Adminiatrative offices
5 Library (IMC)
6 Classroom wing

a. This diagram shows the original concept for the high school. Major functional spaces are distributed along the arcing circulation spine and include: the athletics complex, auditorium, cafeteria, administrative offices, library, and a multi-story classroom wing wrapped around its own courtyard.

b. This diagram illustrates efforts to improve the circulation plan by narrowing the corridor space and distributing the entrances more evenly along the curve. The library has moved to the end of the spine to simplify access to the classroom wing. The courtyard has been widened to allow more natural light into classrooms.

c. This diagram further improves the efficiency of the circulation, making the spine a double-loaded corridor along most of its length. The library has been moved to a central location and stacked above the cafeteria. The courtyard has been opened to provide better views as well as natural light for the classrooms.

Figure 1.8

Development Sequence of a Concept Option, Tantasqua Regional High School, Sturbridge, MA

Credit: Copyright Drummey Rosane Anderson, Inc.

utilization, the functional relationship of various program elements, and a strategy for re-use of existing spaces (as required). An economic analysis of each option will establish comparative capital and operating costs for the rehabilitation, expansion, and continued operation of existing facilities and the construction and operation of new stand-alone facilities.

The consultant should incorporate planning and design features as specified by the school building committee, accommodating and/or raising for discussion such issues as:

- Approved educational and athletic programs
- Accommodations for voice/data/video technology
- Flexible spaces for changes in the curriculum
- Work space requirements of teachers and administrators
- Potential community use of facilities—auditorium, gymnasium, cafeteria, etc.
- Potential year-round use of facilities
- Suitability of additions to existing internal circulation
- The possibility for future building expansion
- Site circulation options to minimize traffic congestion, maximize safety, and provide adequate parking
- Compliance with life-safety code, seismic, and handicapped access legislation
- Budget constraints
- Compatibility of exterior design with existing buildings and nearby structures
- Construction phasing that minimizes impact on adjacent ongoing educational occupancy

The consultant should attend public forums to collect input from local residents and parents regarding the school project. All of this information may be used to formulate the building's organization, as well as its exterior and interior appearance.

Evaluate Options

An evaluation matrix is a tool often used to help the school building committee reach consensus when considering several conceptual options. In the sample matrix in Figure 1.9, the architect and committee worked together to define the criteria shown in the left column. The top row of the matrix lists the options or schemes being compared. For each option, the architect will first evaluate how well it satisfies each consideration and will then verify the ranking through discussions with the committee. Often this cycle is repeated, with new options added to the mix, incorporating the most successful parts of previous options. In the end, the evaluation matrix can summarize many hours of discussions about priorities and trade-offs that are at the heart of conceptual design decisions.

High School
Site Matrix — DRA Architects, Inc.

SCHEME	3A	3B	3C	3D
VISUAL IMPACTS				
Impact of building on 'top' of the hill	5	5	2	3
Proximity to abutters property	5	5	3	1
Shadow impact on abutters	5	4	1	1
New building competes with existing building	4	5	2	3
PROGRAM RELATIONSHIPS				
Central arrival point	1	1	1	1
Clear access to main entry / administration	1	1	1	1
Visitor parking	2	1	1	1
Classroom proximity to athletic fields	1	1	1	3
Locker room proximity to athletic fields	5	5	1	2
Internal building circulation	4	1	2	4
SITE CIRCULATION				
Potential for off street bus queueing	5	5	1	1
Separation of bus / vehicle traffic	5	5	1	1
Potential for an east / west traffic connector	1	1	3	1
Efficient parking	1	1	1	1
Potential for increase parking	1	3	5	1
Reuse of existing parking infrastructure	5	5	1	5
Ease of servicing building	1	2	1	1
Parking distribution around building	3	3	3	2
PHASING				
Functionality of site during construction	3	3	3	5
Availability of fields and parking during construction	5	5	1	5
Reliance on temporary building structures	3	2	2	4
RANKING overall score	66	64	37	47

Most Favorable 1 / 2 / 3 / 4 / 5 Least Favorable

Figure 1.9
Sample Evaluation Matrix
The evaluation matrix lists criteria along the left edge and rates how well each option satisfies these criteria in the columns on the right.
Credit: Copyright Drummey Rosane Anderson, Inc.

Refinement of the Recommended Option

Once a recommended option has been identified, the consultant will develop and refine it to a level required by the scope of the study. The final recommendation should consider the evaluation criteria, the school building committee's recommendations, and input from the community and other interested parties. The consultant should prepare.

- Plans/diagrams of the site(s), including adaptation of the site to parking, access, and circulation, as required by new or renovated facilities

- Schematic/occupancy plans of the new/renovated facilities
- A priority list of construction projects (if applicable)
- Phasing strategy
- An implementation plan
- Capital and operating cost analyses

See Figures 1.10–1.12 for examples of final recommended design options. Figure 1.13 shows the completed school.

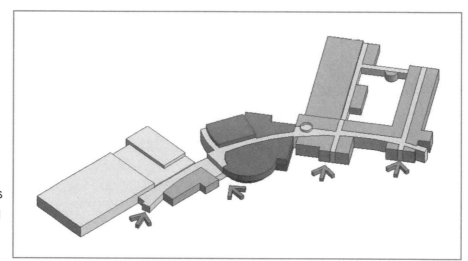

Figure 1.10
Recommended Option—Tantasqua Regional High School, Sturbridge, MA
The final plan evolved from previous concepts (Figure 1.8), incorporating their best features.
Credit: Copyright Drummey Rosane Anderson, Inc.

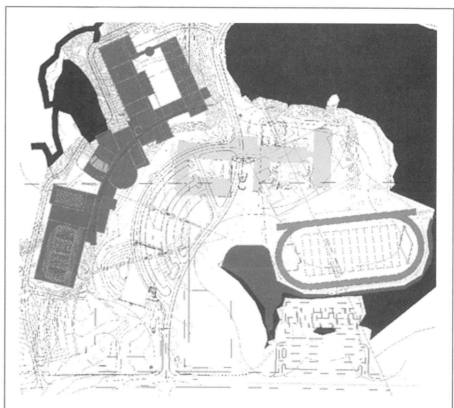

Figure 1.11
Recommended Option—Tantasqua Regional High School, Sturbridge, MA
The Tantasqua site plan illustrates the new building (dark gray) and the existing building (light gray). The dark shapes wrapping around the buildings and athletic fields are wetlands that had to be preserved.
Credit: Copyright Drummey Rosane Anderson, Inc.

Figure 1.12
Recommended Option—Elevation,
Tantasqua Regional High School,
Sturbridge, MA
Conceptual sketch of the front elevation showing possible window patterns and building materials.
Credit: Copyright Drummey Rosane Anderson, Inc.

Figure 1.13
Main Entrance and Plaza,
Tantasqua Regional High School,
Sturbridge, MA
The final design grew out of a combination of conceptual design discussions, budget estimates, and practical construction details.
Photo Credit: Greg Premru Photography

Preparation of a Facility Planning Document

A detailed report will need to document all of the information collected and the decisions made during the planning process. The report will be filed for historic records and distributed to decision-makers. Depending on the scope of the project, the following elements may be included: the facility program, existing conditions survey, development and evaluation of planning options, selection of a recommended option, cost analyses, and an implementation plan. Following is a typical outline of a detailed planning study.

- Executive Summary
- Introduction
  - Project Background
  - Methodology
  - Development of Evaluation Criteria
- Facility Program
  - Programming Process
  - Program Scope
  - Space Standards
  - Enrollment Projections
  - Space Program Summary
  - Detailed Space Program
  - Adjacency Requirements
  - Design and Operational Guidelines
- Existing Conditions Survey
  - Site(s)
  - Building(s)/Space Description
  - Existing Space Analysis
- Development of Planning Solutions
  - Approach
  - Evaluation Criteria
  - Option Development
  - Selection of Preferred Option
- Final Master Plan (Recommendations)
  - Plan/Diagrams of the Site(s)
  - Occupancy Plans of the New/Renovated Facilities
  - Priority List of Construction Projects (if applicable)
  - Phasing Strategy
  - Implementation Plan
  - Cost Analyses (capital and operating)

Project Timeline

A timeline helps everyone involved in the project understand the activities to be completed and how they relate to one another. The example below summarizes an entire project, from its feasibility study through the design process, concluding with construction and occupancy. Activities are listed in the left column, and time is measured across the top of the grid, proceeding from left to right. *(See Figure 1.14.)*

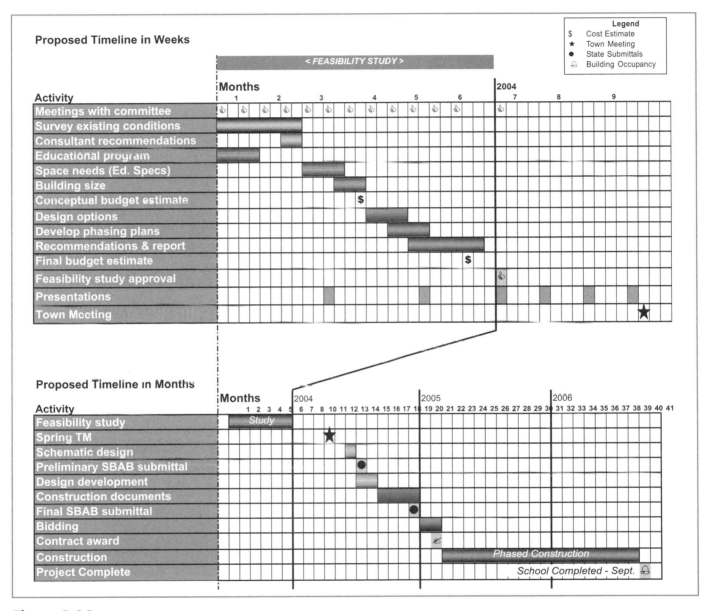

Figure 1.14
A Sample Project Timeline
Credit: Copyright Drummey Rosane Anderson, Inc.

Implementation

Once the facility plan is in place, what are the next steps?

The Approval Process

The variations of local approval processes are nearly infinite. However, they all include these key points:

- Approval of the pre-design/programming effort
- Approval of the projected project schedule
- Approval of funding

If community involvement has been active, and the response of the project design team has been genuine, the approval process can be smooth. Nevertheless, it is an undeniable reality that some people simply do not pay attention until they are asked to commit to paying for something. For this reason, it is imperative that good public records are kept of preceding work and prior intermediate approvals.

A certain amount of anxiety is natural when embarking on a large-scale and expensive building project. A well-documented design process that includes community input and buy-in is the best means to alleviate fears and build enthusiasm within a community. An objection to a particular design feature may in some cases be a way of thwarting funding of a project, no matter what the design. If this happens, the project team needs to clearly demonstrate the design alternatives that were considered and the reasoning behind decisions that were made. A reasoned response to an objection to an aspect of design can also serve to calm the fears of an individual or community.

If a public presentation will be part of an approval process, it is necessary to rehearse beforehand. A "dry-run" by the design project team should include representatives of the school administration and community, with designated individuals playing the role of the questioning public. This is an excellent way to anticipate and prepare for the unexpected. Again, a calm, organized, and clear presentation is invaluable as a means of alleviating the natural fears of those who have not participated actively in the design process.

Funding Process

Funding methods and protocols tend to be highly localized, with each school having its own project funding mechanisms. However, the following general principles should be considered:

First Things First

Determine the source of the funding and the criteria necessary to qualify for funding. If this is a public project, determine the mood of the electorate and what is needed to obtain support. Ensure that funding will be adequate to meet the project goals. *Then*, proceed.

Do Your Homework

Prepare, prepare, prepare. Examine all potential pitfalls to securing funding. Find out who the key stakeholders are in the funding process. Have all the questions been answered? Is the implementation plan clear?

Can the data be supported? Communications will be very important during this process.

Leave No Stone Unturned

Funding can be time-consuming. Cover the known channels first, but then keep looking. There are often other opportunities available. State grants may support specific program content and the spaces that support those programs. Utility rebates may support specific technological aspects of building systems that save energy. Some states have established quasi-public agencies to advance green design by offering grants for advanced design systems and renewable energy equipment. Perhaps most often overlooked is private funding for public school projects, although these sources do require compliance with applicable regulations. Private donors may contribute substantial sums to support construction of excellent schools within their community. In private schools, development staff will normally be responsible for donor funding—both for capital projects and program development.

Case Study

Davis Elementary School
Bedford, MA

Overview:

Drummey Rosane Anderson, Inc., was initially commissioned to prepare a study to assess town-wide space needs. One of the key results of this year-long study included the recommendation that the existing Davis Elementary School be replaced by a new, larger building on the same site, housing up to 560 students. Two major issues resulted in this decision: the existing facility was a 1950s structure with significant overcrowding; and the existing building layout did not support the school's progressive team teaching program. The mission of the project was to create a large school that would be proportionate in scale to young students and support the teaching methods used in the school.

The planning and design process for the school demonstrated how stakeholders can work together in an open process that produces a sense of ownership and pride in the final design. Throughout the process, bi-weekly meetings were held with the architect and the school building committee (parents, administration, and community members). The architect also hosted a community forum offering workshops on site planning, building design, "friendly" school atmosphere, and a student workshop. Publicity for this event included a panel discussion video (broadcast on local cable) featuring members of the design team and building committee. The overall design concept evolved from many community suggestions, such as designing the school as a "village," with the library as a main focal point.

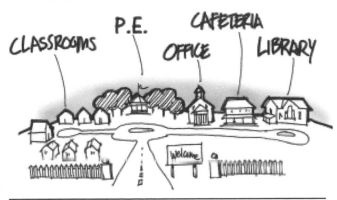

Educational Village Concept

Credit: Copyright Drummey Rosane Anderson, Inc.

continued

Features:

Completed 1999
78,000 Square Feet
560 Pupils, K-2
$10,049,786 Construction Cost
$12,907,000 Total Project Cost

Project Goals:

The project design goals included:

- Flexibility to handle changing needs
- Attractive and exciting educational spaces
- Smaller "educational communities" within the school (clusters/school within a school)
- Flexible common space in each cluster for educationalenrichment
- Centrally located library/media center
- A gymnasium large enough to accommodate school andrecreation department use with after-hours communityaccess
- Infrastructure to support computing and technical needs
- A design that allows for future expansion

Early Concept Diagram of Village Arrangement, Davis Elementary School, Bedford, MA
Classroom clusters are on the left of the plan, with shared spaces on the right, including the cafeteria, library, and gym.

Credit: Copyright Drummey Rosane Anderson, Inc.

Challenges:

A major concern of the stakeholders was that the large size of this new school might be intimidating to young children. Members of the community initially suggested that a "spoke" concept be implemented, using the library as a hub. A number of schemes were developed in an attempt to break down the scale of the school, while still providing a central location for key functions.

The recommended solution organized the facility as a "village" arrangement around multi-grade classroom cluster groups. Team classrooms are grouped around cluster spaces for multi-class group project work and team teaching. The space is wired so that technology used in the classrooms can also be used in the cluster areas. The cluster spaces contain shared resources for the teachers in the team and are joined together by a "Main Street" that leads to core spaces, such as the library and gymnasium.

The village concept also carries over to the exterior of the school with towers, rotundas, and entry kiosks. The layered masonry helps break down the scale of the school to make it less intimidating for its small users. Additionally, each cluster is color-coded, and the colors repeated in way-finding and signage throughout the school.

Stakeholders also wanted the new facility to be an integral part of the community. This affected the program and raised access and security issues. The community use issue was accommodated in several ways. The gymnasium was high-school-sized to allow for community athletic group use. The cafetorium could also be used for community meetings. Each of these areas has an exterior entrance to allow the remainder of the school to be sealed for added security.

The new building is located on the site of the existing school, which remained operational during construction and was later demolished. This presented the design challenges of working around the existing school and wetlands on the site. In addition, site safety issues were a challenge, as young students attended the existing school during construction.

continued

The design of the new Davis School addresses the initial hesitancy of parents and community members who were concerned about the move from small neighborhood schools to a larger facility. The success of the school is due in large part to the ongoing involvement of the school principal, teachers, and the community throughout the planning, design, and construction process.

Teachers and administrators from many surrounding communities visit the Davis School in order to implement many of its concepts into their own school projects. The Davis School was awarded first place in the first annual BuildSmart School Design Contest conducted by the Council of Educational Facility Planners International (CEFPI) in 2002.

Architect: Drummey Rosane Anderson, Inc.

Shared Cluster Space, Davis Elementary School, Bedford, MA

The common space is flexible, with moveable furniture and storage in brightly colored step shaped storage units.

Photo Credit: Greg Premru Photography

Detail of Cluster Concept Showing Shared Common Space, Davis Elementary School, Bedford, MA

Common space immediately outside the doors of the classrooms in each cluster is used by all of the students in this cluster.

Credit: Copyright Drummey Rosane Anderson, Inc.

Davis Elementary School Main Entrance, Bedford, MA

The entry courtyard uses window patterns, brick details, sloped roofs, and lighting to scale down the building and appear welcoming to the elementary school students.

Photo Credit: Greg Premru Photography

Selection of a Design Team: Architect and Engineers

As with the planning and design process itself, early research can prove beneficial in the architectural selection process. Information on architectural firms and the work they do can be obtained in many ways: by speaking with architects at conferences; by speaking with stakeholders in other districts that have recently completed building projects; by reviewing school facilities magazines (such as *American School & University* and *School Construction News*) for similar projects; and by checking with organizations such as the American Institute of Architects (AIA), the Committee on Architecture for Education (CAE) within the AIA, the Council of Educational Facility Planners (CEFPI), the American Association of School Administrators (AASA), the National Association of State Boards of Education (NASBE), and the National School Boards Association (NSBA), who are familiar with educational design specialists in the particular area.

For public projects, state education departments and school construction offices can offer additional guidance on two main points:

- The steps to be completed prior to the hiring of the architect to ensure project funding.
- Legal requirements of the selection process. It is important to note that many states require that available contracts be publicly advertised. Skipping this step may result in formal protests, lawsuits, or restarting the selection process.

Types of Architectural Firms

In selecting an architect, consider the various types of firms and the advantages each brings to the design process.

Sole Practitioner: These firms handle small projects locally and are generally restricted to repair or small renovation projects.

Generalist Architects: These firms design many types of buildings, usually within a specific geographical area. If there are no architectural firms specializing in educational facilities in a particular area, a local generalist may be a good choice because their proximity allows them to provide a higher level of service during the construction administration phase.

Educational Design Specialists: These firms specialize in the design of educational environments and often have educational programmers on staff. The depth of their experience means they have knowledge of building materials and furnishings suitable to schools. The main disadvantage of hiring a specialist firm is that they may lack geographic proximity. However, their teaming with a local firm can often mitigate this issue.

Architectural Firm: This may be a generalist or specialist firm that will provide a team of outside consultants for each project. These may include landscape architects, mechanical, electrical, structural, civil and environmental engineers. When evaluating a pure architecture firm, check the firm's experience working with the proposed consultant team.

Architectural/Engineering Firm (A/E): This may also be a generalist or specialist firm. However, an architectural/engineering firm may have their own in-house engineering departments, most likely mechanical and electrical, and/or structural. Remember to check which disciplines they have in-house and which will be outside consultants. The references for each department should be checked.

A comprehensive list of an architect's basic services can be found in American Institute of Architects (AIA) Document B141-1997. This is the *Standard Form of Agreement Between Owner and Architect with Standard Form of Architect's Services.* This document provides a chart that lists 68 professional services grouped into six categories, including: Project Administration Services, Planning and Evaluation Services (including programming and schematic design), Design Services, Construction Procurement Services, Contract Administration Services, and Facility Operation Services. This list is intended as a guide to all of the parties involved in identifying the scope of professional services required for the specific project. Not all of the listed services may be required, and other non-listed specialized services such as building commissioning, energy analysis, value engineering, sustainability surveys of building materials, and others may be needed. An architect may also typically employ consultants for engineering, landscape design, site surveys, environmental analyses, historic preservation, and cost estimating if the firm does not offer these services in-house.

Procurement Process

The procurement process for design services is often established by the local jurisdiction (town, city, school board, or board of trustees in the case of private schools). Issuing a Request for Proposals (RFP) or a Request for Qualifications (RFQ) is normally the first step in the procurement process. An RFP normally requests a fee proposal, but an RFQ does not.

Each state differs in its methods for regulating the procurement process and advertising RFPs/RFQs. Although projects may be publicly funded, the procurement process may vary from a centralized listing of available projects to an invited list of architectural firms. The Department of Education in each state can provide information on the requirements for each district/town/city to follow in the selection of an architect.

Every RFP/RFQ is slightly different, and many municipalities and school districts have their own requirements. However, there are certain common items that should appear in each, and certain principles should be followed. In general, an RFP/RFQ should include the following sections:

- A call for proposals
- The history of the project
- The scope of services
- Qualifications required
- Experience requested
- Evaluation criteria
- Any changes to the standard architect/client contract and forms

Providing a thorough history of the project and scope of services will help architectural firms self-screen before applying. Some states allow clients to request fee proposals in the response period. (Note that this practice is not legal in many states.) An accurate scope of services will help the responding firms provide an accurate estimate of their fees.

To invite more competitors and to generate more interest, there should be a pre-proposal briefing meeting to allow interested firms to meet with key individuals in the process, ask questions, and tour the facilities or the site. This saves time and ensures that all interested firms receive exactly the same information.

The following information should be considered for inclusion in the RFP/RFQ:

- Firm qualifications.
- Examples of recent, similar projects that are similar in size, cost, and complexity.
- List of references: Asking for school committee, school administrator, facility manager, consultant, general contractor, and project manager references will create a more in-depth picture of the firm's ability in this area.
- History of legal issues: Firms that work primarily with public projects are often involved in various lawsuits. Obtaining this history early in the process will allow the building committee to evaluate the seriousness, frequency, and type of issues the firm has faced, and to talk to others involved in the project.
- Assurance of financial stability: It is important to make sure the firm has the resources to be able to complete the whole project. *(See Chapter 8 for more on evaluating a firm.)*
- Design vision/project approach: In discussing the design approach, the firm should state the steps it will take to lead the building committee through the process. This will provide some insight in to the style of the firm, as well as generating questions that might be posed to the firm's references.
- Design ideas: Many towns/cities/districts will request that the architect provide them with design ideas for their project. This may be helpful for non-technical evaluators to see the unique perspective each firm will bring to the project. However, a caution with this approach is that firms will be designing with no input from users, and pre-conceived ideas may end up hurting the overall design of the school. Note also that the AIA discourages providing these types of "free design services," and many firms will be reluctant to give away their design ideas (as proprietary information) without having a contract.
- Specific forms: Almost every RFP/RFQ includes a set of forms. Check with the local municipality, county, or state as to which forms may be required for public instruction projects. These may include non-collusion forms, tax payment forms or state professional service

forms. For private schools, the selection committee or board to trustees should provide information as to what, if any, forms are required.

(See Chapter 8 for more on RFPs and RFQs.)

Depending on the type of project, the building committee may be inundated with proposals. A selection committee should be established early in the process so that an efficient evaluation procedure can be implemented for reviewing multiple proposals. This committee should normally consist of no more than seven to nine people. It may include members of the school building committee, school administrators, town administrators, and citizen, parent, teacher, and legal representatives.

One of the first steps will be to select a scoring process, possibly utilizing an evaluation matrix. To ensure fairness in the process, the following tips may be helpful:

- Ask several committee members to review each proposal and rank it. This will help the process be less subjective.
- Evaluate the experience of the key team members. While the firm itself may have the experience needed, the design team assigned may not. Conversely, a team member may have rich experience, but the firm itself may not have completed many similar projects.
- If a fee proposal has been requested, if permitted by law, examine the scope of services to ensure that any comparison is of apples to apples.
- Keep notes during the review process. An architect or the public may ask for an explanation or feedback that will require follow-up action. The notes will be useful for remembering certain aspects of that one of 25 reviewed proposals.

Once a short list has been created (usually 3-5 firms), the next step is to start interviewing firms and checking references. Interviews generally run 45 minutes to an hour each, depending on the project's size and complexity. The length of the interview generally determines the depth of the presentation. It is important to keep in mind that the school building committee and firm will be working together for three to five years, so it is advantageous to take all the time necessary to get to know each other. The goal of the interview should be to determine the chemistry between the committee and design team. To that end, it may be helpful to request that day-to-day contact people be part of the interview team. Many districts also write into the contract the names of the key individuals on the team to ensure that members are not switched after the design contract is awarded. Some districts choose to use a set list of questions for each firm, while others prefer to ask questions based on the presentation or background research.

The interview process and reference checks will allow the selection committee to make an informed evaluation and decision. Contractual arrangements with the selected team can begin shortly after the selection has been made.

Conclusion

The design process for educational facilities is step-by-step. Programming and pre-design are the first steps—establishing the direction, guidelines, and parameters of the overall project. The process involves the careful integration of an enormous amount of data and calculated decisions in many areas. The overview in this chapter includes:

- Selection of the design team
- The need for a programming and pre-design study
- Description of types of studies and why they are needed
- The need for both user and community participation
- Procurement of facility planning services
- The planning process
- Implementation of recommendations

The programming and pre-design phase is the foundation for all other phases of the school design project. As such, this phase must respond to the enormous changes that are taking place in education today—changes in both curriculum and facility requirements. Although changes in educational curriculum and philosophy are not the focus of this book, they have a significant impact on the physical needs of schools. One example is the movement to project-based learning, and another is an increased trend toward schools becoming a center of community life. Vocational education has been pushed in new directions as a result of available technology and the need to train students for the business world. Government mandates resulting in more special education spaces, the growing educational emphasis on small group learning, and the need for spaces for tutoring students in small groups have all changed the space needs of schools. These changes must be addressed during programming and pre-design.

Several other recent and ongoing trends in school facility design are addressed in the upcoming chapters. The increasing awareness of the need to preserve our environment is leading to an acceptance of high performance buildings *(Chapter 2)*. The integration of technology into the educational experience has changed the infrastructure requirements, lighting needs, class size requirements, and equipment needs *(Chapter 3)*. School designs are responding to security considerations in terms of layout, equipment, and policies and procedures *(Chapter 4)*. New courses have created the need for new specialized spaces *(Chapter 5)*. In addition, there are numerous new regulations and building code requirements regarding fire protection, energy use, seismic safety, the Americans with Disabilities Act (ADA), environmental regulation, and historic preservation that are influencing overall school design. All of these issues should begin to be addressed in the programming and pre-design phase.

Chapter 2

Green Design

Drummey Rosane Anderson, Inc.

Green design is a relatively new concept that is rapidly gaining favor in the planning and design of educational facilities. It is attention to environmental concerns in all aspects of design and construction to create a building that is healthier and energy- and resource-efficient. In the words of Greg L. Roberts, AIA, a leader in the green design movement, "Green design is a holistic process; it is not merely slipping in green materials here and there. Green design requires much more pre-planning and research, with a closer collaboration between design and engineering, to achieve 'living machines' more precisely engineered than conventional buildings."[1]

This chapter will address:

- The history of the green design movement
- The importance of green design for schools
- Terminology and standards for green design
- The economics of green design
- How to implement green design in a school project
- Some basic green design technologies and principles
- Resources for further information

The History of Green Design

Until the early 1970s, most Americans were generally unconcerned about the earth's limited resources. Materials were taken from the environment, used once, and then disposed of. Oil and other energy resources were seemingly plentiful, and people were not fully conscious of the impact that their own use and disposal practices were having on natural ecosystems. Architectural and engineering design did not emphasize energy efficiency, since it was not perceived as a need. Although buildings were insulated, there was little emphasis on research into energy-efficient materials and systems.

The energy crisis that resulted from the first oil embargo in 1973 was a major catalyst for change in attitude and design. Facility designers and many other professionals reacted quickly to reduce the energy demands of buildings, cars, and industries. Energy-efficient building design was in its infancy, and some early attempts were not completely successful. For example, many buildings were completely sealed up to prevent air infiltration and heat loss, which (while increasing energy efficiency) reduced fresh air within the building, resulting in increased respiratory problems. In addition, some people developed serious sensitivity reactions to toxins that built up inside their homes and workplaces. In schools, the teachers, administrators, and students all felt effects of poor air quality and suffered increased numbers of sick days and interrupted learning plans. During this same period, many school systems also reduced or eliminated operable windows in classrooms, increasing energy efficiency, but further reducing access to fresh air and natural light. The result was increased drowsiness and decreased learning potential in students and fewer opportunities for passive solar heating.

Indoor air quality and daylighting problems became a major force behind the current interest in green design. One of the primary goals of green design is to provide healthy indoor air, while minimizing energy use and using natural resources wisely. From this core concept, the green design movement has evolved to become multi-faceted. In addition to concerns about indoor air quality (IAQ) and energy conservation, green design is an attempt to address issues of resource allocation and preservation of natural environments.

The Importance of Green Design for Schools

Green design is particularly applicable to the design of today's schools, with newly mandated requirements for energy efficiency and a healthful environment for children. Following are some of the most important reasons for building a "green" school.

Improved Health

No other single environmental factor has more of an impact on the health of children than the quality of the indoor environments where they spend most of their time—home and school. "Clean" buildings, properly operated and maintained, give children the best chance to stay healthy. Improved health conditions also help to reduce the school's liability risks, particularly concerning indoor air quality.

Improved Learning

Children may actually learn more in a green school than in a conventional school. Improved air quality has been proven to keep students more awake and alert. Most people would agree that an alert child learns more than a listless one. Studies have also shown a direct correlation between daylighting and academic performance.

Financial Advantages

In the long term, green design costs less than conventional design. As explained later in this chapter in the "Economics of Green Design" section, long-term life cycle costs are generally calculated to be less for green buildings, due to the reduced energy use, reduced maintenance, and extended benefits of healthy environments, such as low absenteeism.

Green schools also have more options for initial capital funding. In the private sector, donors are often more willing to contribute to a building that they feel is innovative and invigorating, and grants and tax incentives are sometimes available. In the public sector, direct grants, rebates, and matching funds are often available from a variety of sources to support the particular "green" or "high-performance" aspects of a project design. Utility companies will often take an active role in evaluating and financing various energy conservation aspects of school building construction, as it helps them to avoid the costs of increased energy production.

Recruitment/Retention

Green schools are considered to be more attractive to both faculty and parents of students because of the healthier, enhanced-learning environment they provide. In the private sector, this means that it is easier to attract students and skilled teachers by maintaining a competitive position in the marketplace. In the public sector, while recruitment of students is not generally an issue (since they are normally required to attend school by law), retention of skilled faculty is easier in a green environment. Green schools that reflect a community's shared values and concerns will also increase parent and community involvement and support.

Learning Opportunities – The Classroom as the Lesson Plan

Lastly, but perhaps most important, the green school has the potential to become part of the lesson plan for the school curriculum. The physical structure of the school and the associated green technologies can actually be an enhancement to the overall program of studies, particularly science. The green school can become a launching pad for a whole generation of environmentally-aware scientists, engineers, architects, builders, writers, artists, community leaders, and citizens. Innovative building control and operating systems can provide Web-based hookups to school classrooms, where energy use can be monitored, and future use can be predicted. Special building equipment can be made visible and understandable with properly placed vision panels.

For example, at Newton South High School in Massachusetts, a graywater system will be used as an educational tool. *(See Figure 2.1.)* One section of drainpipe from a rooftop collection system will be made of glass, with lighting and a viewing panel. Text and graphics will explain that the water collected from the roof will be used later to flush the school's

Figure 2.1

Site: Aerial View, Newton South High School, Newton, MA

New classroom wing in foreground. New athletic facility in background.

Roof of athletic facility collects rainwater for re-use.

Photo Credit: Larson Associates, Inc.

toilets. A creative teacher can tie this into the environmental sciences, or math problems, or any other subject. Instead of learning only from books, young people can learn from the *experience* of being inside a green building.

Terminology

"Green design" is the most widely used and recognized term to refer to sustainable construction. It has a broad definition commonly understood to include a variety of design principles, sometimes called *energy-efficient design, high-performance design, sustainable design,* and *holistic design.* What do these terms mean, and what are the important distinctions?

- **Energy-efficient design** emphasizes a combination of highly effective space conditioning equipment and controls with a tight building envelope and an efficiently designed ventilation system. Since the introduction of ASHRAE 90.1, the amount of ventilation air required has tripled. The importance of a "tight" building has decreased, and *energy recovery ventilation* or *demand-controlled ventilation* systems (both green technologies) have proven to save more energy than insulation.

- **High-performance design** is an integrated design approach that emphasizes the latest technologies to achieve optimal performance. High-performance design requires thinking "outside of the box" to create a facility that meets its intended uses and operations while conserving resources and minimizing energy usage.

- **Sustainable design** addresses the long-term concerns of selecting the most appropriate technologies and materials and using them in a manner that avoids depleting the earth's resources. Sustainable design requires the designer to take into consideration material durability and sustainability, which involves not only the energy and environmental costs to replace the material, but its availability and rate of regeneration. In today's "throwaway" society, sustainability is a shift in thinking to make decisions based on "total cost," including health and protection of the environment, not just strict economic factors.

- A new favorite is the term **holistic design**, which emphasizes the functional relationship between the various building parts and the whole facility. Holistic design can include protection of the earth's resources, as well as an element of spirituality, aiming to create spaces that enrich the quality of the environment *and* the lives of those who use the building.

Standards

The two most widely recognized sets of standards for green design in schools are the Collaborative for High Performance Schools (CHPS) and the Leadership in Energy and Environmental Design (LEED) standards. Both organizations have functional Web sites with detailed information on their missions, structure, and publications. (*See the Resources at the end of this book for contact information.*) LEED is developing a set of guidelines specifically for schools, and it is recognized as the industry standard in general green building type classifications.

These guidelines recognize the fact that no two buildings are exactly alike, and the systems provide a "menu" approach for judging the building's sustainability and efficiency. Both CHPS and LEED guidelines offer a reference point from which to judge the degree of "greenness" of a proposed design. Both standards award points for meeting certain design objectives, such as reducing the amount of water consumed in the building. The points are totaled after the complete review of all possible "credit" categories, and the "score" determines the result. Under the CHPS standards, a school building must achieve a minimum score of 28 points in order to be certified as a High-Performance School. LEED awards various levels of achievement, such as "Certified," "Silver," and "Gold."

Other organizations also contribute to the establishment of standards for green design. For example, the Sustainable Buildings Industry Council (SBIC) has developed a public awareness campaign for High Performance School Buildings (HPSB). This council's efforts are supported by a collaboration of important public federal agencies, including the Department of Education, the Department of Energy, and the Environmental Protection Agency. More information regarding the HPSB campaign can be found on their Web site, listed in the Resources at the end of this book.

Economics of Green Design

One of the first questions asked by school administrators and taxpayers alike is, "Does it cost more to build green?" The answer is both "yes" and "no."

Short-Term Capital Costs

Yes, it often costs more to construct green buildings, when one considers the "up-front," or initial costs only. New technologies and cutting-edge design and construction services are likely to be more expensive than traditional tools and methods. For example, a hydronic heating system with energy-efficient variable speed drives (VSD) on the circulating pumps costs more to design and install than the same system with constant velocity drives. The equipment is more sophisticated, the design necessarily more exact, and the installation more complicated. However, the long-term costs will be more advantageous. The additional costs of the equipment may be in the range of 5%-10% above "typical" initial costs.

Long-Term Costs

No, it often costs less to construct a green school, when one considers total life cycle costs. Green buildings *save* money in operations and maintenance costs when evaluated over time. Consider the hydronic heating system with the VSD noted above. The VSD slows down the pumps when the design-temperature is achieved in the spaces it serves. This reduces wear and tear on the equipment and significantly reduces energy demands. The end result is lower costs over the life of the building, or lower "life cycle costs." (*See Chapter 8 for more on life cycle costing.*) In the long run, adding a variable speed drive costs much less than the same system with a constant speed delivery. The energy savings are so significant that many local utility companies will grant a rebate to the customer to offset the higher cost of purchasing this equipment. (The utility companies are willing to do this because it reduces the need to purchase expensive power to meet peak demands.) Operating costs decrease as well when pumps run slower and require less maintenance.

In addition to extended equipment life, the green approach of using more durable (as well as energy-efficient) materials can benefit schools and other owner-occupied facilities. White roof systems, for example, have proven to reduce the net cooling requirements of a facility by as much as 20%. These systems also tend to have a significantly longer life span than typical roof systems. A slight increase in initial cost may have a significant savings in life cycle cost when replacement cost is included in the calculation.

Again quoting Greg L. Roberts, on the subject of the "myth" that green buildings cost more than conventional buildings:

> *"Innovative green-building designs have demonstrated that cost-efficiency is not sacrificed for environmental stewardship. On the contrary, achievement of sustainability through an integrated balance of materials and systems has shown that sustainability can be as cost-effective as conventional projects. The real challenge is for owners and architects to think long-term, rather*

than first-cost. When we factor in energy savings over time, or increased durability, or enhanced worker productivity, green design features and materials become much easier to justify."[2]

Environmental Benefits vs. Costs

There are secondary societal benefits that accrue as a result of energy demand reduction. For example, as energy demand lessens, fewer power plants are needed, pollution caused by power generation is reduced, and utility rates stabilize. Less power production results in an improvement in outdoor air quality, with associated health benefits.

Also, consider the impact that conventional building practices have on limited water supplies. Many people view water as an unlimited resource. The following information, however, helps to put the true situation in perspective: "Ninety-seven percent of Earth's water is contained within the oceans, a little over two percent is held by ice caps and glaciers, and, of the remaining portion, a third of one percent is groundwater within a half-mile of the surface."[3] Understanding the scarcity of clean, useable groundwater, the environmental benefits of water conservation can be seen to be tremendously important, even if the direct economic benefits are limited. A gallon of water that is not needed to flush a toilet is a gallon of water that does not need to be taken out of the earth. Less water consumption means fewer wells, and a more stable water table.

It can be seen that the benefits of green design are far-reaching with a broad impact. There is a "ripple effect" of green design, as demonstrated by the examples above. Formal studies have been conducted, which have attempted to quantify these broader societal benefits. These studies help to bolster the case for green design.

Recycling

The building industry accounts for a large percentage of the material that enters the solid waste stream. Recycling building materials provides a significant positive benefit for the environment, as well as real dollar savings. More recycling and reuse of construction products results in smaller landfills, lower disposal costs, and reduced pollution of the natural ecosystems. Recycling reduces production cost, as less refinement of raw materials (and corresponding energy use) is needed.

How to Implement Green Design

Once a project team is aware of green design principles and comfortable with the preliminary economics, the next step is to develop a work plan. Following is a suggested outline for the process of starting a green school project. These are the steps that should be taken once a decision has been made to "go green":

1. Establish a clear set of goals for the project.
2. Select an appropriate team of design professionals.
3. Monitor the progress as the project evolves.

Establish Project Goals

To be successful, any project needs a clear set of achievable goals. Setting goals creates a target that the team can focus on. Goals may need to be adjusted as the project evolves and as the team learns more about its resources and objectives. The process of establishing goals will also serve to knit the team together, solidifying support for the project.

Project goals for a green school may be different than those for a conventional school. For example, cost targets may need to be adjusted, balancing higher short-term capital costs against the longer-term goals for reduction in energy usage and reduced maintenance costs. Other goals for the green school may be a reduction in the time lost due to student and faculty illnesses, increasing the school's ability to attract students, maintaining higher-quality staff, boosting parental and alumnae (in private schools) support, or contributing toward students' higher standardized test scores. One of the most important goals might be to involve the local community in the design process, as a tool to reach out for community support.

Again, Greg L. Roberts states:

> *"Green buildings begin with a commitment from the owner to build to a higher standard and require a close collaboration among all participants. The design team must be educated and oriented to the goals, costs, and benefits of green building. Stakeholders, including users, operators, builders, designers, and owners, need to work together to define requirements and identify sustainable opportunities."*[4]

Specific goals for a green design project can be subdivided into categories, including the following:

- LEED certification
- Site design
- Building envelope
- Mechanical, electrical, plumbing, and fire protection systems
- Building operations and performance
- Indoor air quality
- Materials selection
- Construction

Expertise can be sought within the community to help establish project goals. Goals should be re-evaluated during the project, and adjusted as needed to reflect the learning that has taken place among team members. Goals should be reviewed again at the end of the project, and the knowledge gained should be passed on to those operating and maintaining the facility, and to school administrators who may be involved in similar future projects.

For help setting specific project goals, it might be useful to consult the LEED standards. Targets can be set for the number of points that the team wants to achieve in each of several credit categories.

LEED Certification

The school must determine whether is it an important goal to be LEED-certified, or to achieve designation as a High-Performance School under the CHPS standards. This is a project goal that needs to be discussed and considered fully by the project team. In some communities, these standards are now a requirement of local building regulations. In other areas, achieving LEED or CHPS certification may be a valued goal, but the costs to do so may be viewed negatively. Some people feel that the administrative costs incurred to achieve LEED certification would be better spent on further green features in the school, or in curriculum development programs related to green design. There are no direct benefits of LEED certification at this time, other than possible rebates or grants that may be tied to successful certification, and the recognition of this achievement. Increasingly, tax incentives may also hinge on proven documentation from an organization like CHPS or LEED.

Site Design Goals

A green school must, at a minimum, meet local requirements for zoning and environmental compliance. Examples of green design goals for the site may include a reduction in water run-off, protection of natural site features, and perhaps no net increase in parking, offset by other transportation alternatives. Another example might be to site the building so as to minimize undesired heat gain during the summer months, while maximizing heat gain during the winter.

Building Envelope Goals

A major target in the design of the building envelope is an overall reduction in energy usage. One goal may be the aim to surpass the efficiency requirements of the local building code by a minimum of 20%, or even 40%. Another goal might be to allow the use of operable windows, while effectively managing potential conflicts with the mechanical ventilation systems. The use of a reflective white roof and high-performance window glazing to reduce the net cooling requirements are other ways in which the building envelope can reduce the facility's energy usage. A second goal of the building envelope is to maintain a healthful indoor environment by effectively protecting the occupants from aspects of the outdoor environment. Proper material selection and construction detailing will enhance indoor air quality and reduce the moisture infiltration that can produce mold and mildew. (It is important that moisture be allowed to evaporate. Molds and mildew will not propagate in a dry environment.) *(See Figure 2.2.)*

Mechanical, Electrical, Plumbing, and Fire Protection Systems Goals

A major goal in the design of the green building's mechanical and electrical systems is an increase in energy efficiency, as a result of more efficient equipment (same output, but with less input). Another goal may

Figure 2.2
Building Envelope Under Construction
New classroom wing at Newton South High School, Newton, MA.

Photo Credit: Drummey Rosane Anderson, Inc., (Contractor: Mello Construction, Inc.)

be to feature the mechanics of these systems in the buildings, with clear explanations of their functions, so that they can become part of the learning curriculum. Water conservation is the goal of green plumbing systems.

HVAC Systems: The highest priority when designing an energy-efficient HVAC system is reactivity, or the system's ability to automatically react, without human intervention, to the changes in space conditions. For example, the ventilation rate of a space can be automatically linked to the CO_2 level within the space (exhaled air). This is called *demand-controlled ventilation*. Another goal for HVAC design might be to have fail-safe overrides on occupant-controlled settings. For example, automatic windows can be programmed to close when the temperature of the space reaches certain pre-established setpoints, and the space is unoccupied.

Electrical Systems: A goal for electrical systems might be to have automatic occupancy-sensing devices that save energy by turning off lights when the space is unoccupied. Another goal might even be to produce more electricity on-site (via wind turbines, PV, or fuel cells) than is consumed on-site, to be a net producer of electricity.

Fire Protection and Plumbing Systems: These systems have specific goals regarding both water conservation and other performance parameters. A goal for the plumbing system design might be to not allow *any* water to be used only once, before being discharged back into the environment. Fire protection systems can use swimming pools as reserve capacity, and avoid expensive upgrades to underground utility services.

Building Operations and Performance Goals

Closely linked to system performance goals should be a similar set of goals for operations and maintenance. The people responsible for the maintenance and operation of the building should be consulted in the development of goal statements for this aspect of the work. Mechanical/electrical systems should also have clear and intuitive procedures for those who will operate and maintain the building systems, so that proper operation is not dependent on one individual's personal experience level.

Indoor Air Quality Goals

Specific goals can be set for the protection and maintenance of indoor air quality. Testing for air quality is straightforward, and goals should be written with an understanding of the verification needed to demonstrate their achievement. As previously stated, goals for this aspect of the project might include fewer absences for teachers, staff, and students due to health-related issues.

Materials Selection Goals

Materials selection can be considered a performance goal in the sense that it affects indoor air quality, as well as meeting overall recycling objectives, cost goals, and other project parameters. Goals for materials selection might include the prevention of any measurable off-gassing of harmful compounds beyond three months after the building has been completed. Another goal might be to meet a prescribed percentage of recycled content for the entire building, as measured by the weight or volume of all construction materials used. Yet another goal might be to use no materials that are produced more than 300 miles from the building site, to avoid the costs and energy consumption of transportation, and to support local economies.

Construction Phase Goals

Goals for the project construction should include specific, performance-based standards for operational procedures—for protection of the environment, individual worker safety, and cleanliness of the site. Recycling of construction waste material is a virtual prerequisite for green school construction, and can actually help lower costs for the contractor by reducing waste removal fees and quantities of new materials.

Selecting the Green Design Project Team

The Designers

After drafting the project goals, it is time to select the professionals who will bring those goals into reality. The project goals should be discussed with prospective designers during the selection process. The ability of these individuals to speak clearly about specific project goals will reveal much about their interest, experience, and qualifications in green design. Be aware that this is an exciting new area of design, and professionals are quick to learn the buzzwords they need to know in order to get through a preliminary selection process. As one digs deeper into actual experience with green building projects, however, specific questions should be asked about the process and technologies they have used on prior projects. It is important to focus on experience, and not to judge imperfect solutions too harshly. A designer who attempted something innovative on a previous project, with somewhat less than optimal results, probably now knows how to do the job more effectively. Such is the nature of working on the cutting edge of new design principles.

The Builder

The contractor or construction consultant can play an important role in the integrated design process, and should participate fully in the early stages of the project design when possible. Consider the form of construction contract delivery carefully. For those who can do so, a partnered approach to design and construction might be advantageous for a green building project, as opposed to the traditional design-bid-build approach. Even when bidding laws for public construction require the traditional bid approach, consider hiring a separate contractor or project manager during the design period as a consultant to review the documents and comment on constructability issues. This is particularly important for projects with a green emphasis.

Many school owners and administrators understand the need to hire the best-qualified professionals to design their buildings, but do not fully appreciate the importance of the builder's qualifications. Many teams hastily select builders on the basis of lowest cost, without a thorough consideration of their qualifications. For a green school project, this can be a recipe for disappointment. Green construction is innovative, and creative thinking and enthusiastic problem-solving are often needed during the construction process. Many aspects of the systems being installed in a green school may be new to the people performing the installation. A truly innovative design may feature systems that have *never* been installed before in exactly the same way. Today's green construction team needs to be highly educated, creative, and committed to the goals of the project. They should be brought into the process early during design, and partnered with the entire project team.

Commissioning Agent

Critical to the success of the team is the commissioning agent. A relatively new position on the project staff, the role of the commissioning agent is to help ensure the proper installation and operation of technical building systems. This professional should be hired directly by the owner, and work independently of both the designer and contractor. The commissioning agent will help to bridge the gap between goals and implementation. He or she should be involved in the project from the beginning, and especially when the construction phase accelerates towards completion. As a multitude of details are coming together between various trades, the commissioning agent will test operations, observe installation methods, and help to prevent errors that could negate the benefits of a sophisticated design. Following completion of the project, the commissioning agent may participate in a post-occupancy evaluation of building performance to verify that systems are operating as intended.

The Owner's Representative

In addition to the team of qualified professionals, it is important to have a qualified owner's representative on the project team. If the owner is a school district, building committee, or other bureaucratic entity, it is advantageous to select an individual or entity to act as an owner's representative, particularly during the construction process when time is of the essence in order to keep a project moving. The owner's representative should have the authority to make decisions consistent with the owner's goals. This person or entity therefore needs a clear understanding of the project's green design goals and a familiarity with the construction process.

Evaluate Progress as the Project Advances

Feedback is critical to understanding project progress and achieving success. As the project advances, it is important to take the time and effort to assess progress towards the achievement of the established green goals. If a point system was used to establish the goals, then periodic evaluation becomes a simple process of reviewing the points achieved by the current design. The entire project team must understand the reasons for adjustments, if needed, so that misunderstandings are avoided in the final outcome.

Green Design Technologies

Having made a decision to build a "green school" and having established and selected the project team, it is important to have a basic understanding of some of the more common practices in green design. Following are some of the specific technologies being used in green schools today.

Site Design

Water Use

It is important to manage both the volume and quality of water run-off from the site. A good strategy is to collect and re-use graywater and roof drainage water for some beneficial purpose before directly recharging it into the local water table. A sophisticated water management plan might include the diversion and filtration of roof rain run-off to a storage tank to be used for showers in athletic locker rooms. After showering, water can pass through a settlement tank and finally into infiltration units underground. Such infiltration units are designed to directly recharge the local aquifer, rather than sending water further downstream, where it can contribute to flooding. Or, even better, graywater can be used (after settlement) to irrigate playing fields and planting beds. It is important to note that parking lot run-off needs to be separated from roof run-off. Run-off from vehicular surfaces must be treated for the removal of oils and road salts before returning it to the environment, whereas roof run-off requires only simple filtration for certain types of re-use.

A basic water management system design might also include a series of retention ponds, neatly landscaped with appropriate wetland vegetation. (The Environmental Science class will not need to travel for their field trips!) Wetland environments function as "living machines" to purify water before returning it to sub-surface aquifers. Proper design of the retention pond system can accelerate this process and make it more effective.

Ornamental Plantings

Vegetative plantings should be selected with care for durability in the natural local environment, without supplemental watering. The practice of using drought-tolerant, slow-growing native species of plants has been termed "xeriscaping," based on the Greek word for "dry." This practice can conserve water, minimize pest and disease problems, reduce or eliminate fertilization requirements, and reduce maintenance.

Deciduous plants can also be selected and placed so as to provide shade when it is wanted (to minimize solar gain) yet allow penetration of the sun's rays in winter, when more direct heat gain is desired. Where supplemental watering may be required, newly developed drip irrigation systems are most efficient by precisely delivering water only where and when it is needed, and lessening wasted water through evaporation.

Building Orientation

Orienting the building on the site to take advantage of views, sun, and breezes, is an important green design strategy. On a particular site, with a prevailing winter wind from one direction, and a prevailing summer breeze from a different direction, careful placement of the building and orientation of operable windows could go far toward minimizing energy use while maximizing occupant comfort. In an urban setting, mapping the shadows of adjacent structures could be an important technology to consider for proper orientation of the new structure.

Building Envelope

Significant research is underway in the area of green building envelope design. For example, as part of product design, experts are assembling building materials under carefully monitored conditions to record data on heat and moisture migration, as well as other parameters. New products are being developed as breakthroughs are sought in low-cost sustainable materials. Some recent accomplishments include the highly successful "low-e" (low-emissivity) coatings on vision glass and exterior envelope air/vapor-barriers. Each of these product categories is important to the two cornerstones of green building envelope design, energy conservation, and indoor air quality. Low-e coatings for glass, as well as improved forms of all types of building insulation, offer some of the best payback-to-expenditure values in current building practice. Energy savings not only provide a direct return on investment in terms of lower operating costs, but also increase occupant comfort through fewer drafts and cold spots.

Air barriers in the exterior wall system allow moisture vapor to flow outwards through a building's skin, while preventing non-tempered air from infiltrating. By encouraging the same sort of breathing process as human skin, the building envelope can keep occupants warm and dry, while allowing contaminants to escape. *(See Figure 2.3.)*

A key element in the building envelope is the roof, and many options exist for the design of a green roofing system. One is to minimize the heat absorption of the roof by using white or light-colored reflective roofing materials. With the advent of more types of membrane roofing products in recent years, this is not a difficult objective to achieve, with minimal (or no) added costs. A further step might be to consider a "living roof," where the roof structure is increased to support earth and plant materials

Figure 2.3
Air Barrier on Exterior Wall System
New classroom wing at Newton South High School, Newton, MA.
Photo Credit: Drummey Rosane Anderson, Inc.

above the waterproof roofing system. In a living roof, rain is absorbed by the plant material on the roof, and transpired directly back into the environment, eliminating or reducing run-off. The added insulation provided by a living roof can also contribute to minimizing temperature swings inside a building, particularly in sunnier climates. This can reduce or eliminate the need for an active air-cooling system.

Building Interior

Natural daylighting has been established as a priority for school design by the CHPS standard, which states: "Quality daylighting designs have been proven to improve student productivity. When integrated properly with the electric lighting system, daylighting saves significant amounts of energy."[5]

Although it might be more appropriate to discuss daylighting for schools in terms of learning enhancement as opposed to productivity (a more suitable measure for the corporate environment), the point made in the CHPS manual is significant; people prefer natural light to electric light, and natural light saves energy. Effective design for superior daylighting involves consideration of building orientation, placement of windows, and various techniques to introduce light further back into the interior spaces. An important point in the LEED standards is awarded for a "direct line of sight" to the exterior from 90% of interior spaces. *(See Figures 2.4 and 2.5.)*

Although air quality has been mentioned previously, it bears repeating as a consideration in the context of green school interior design. Good air quality is achieved by careful control of air movement, moisture content, and temperature. Today's building-control systems allow the sophisticated operator to monitor conditions throughout the building from one central location, and to effect responses to demands at specific locations. This information can even be monitored remotely, via a Web connection, so that the building is never "left alone." Carbon dioxide monitoring devices can be used to automatically increase the flow of fresh air into a space as the number of occupants increases. Sampling equipment is now available, which can be permanently installed in a building to provide constant feedback on the quality of air in a building space, by giving actual particulate counts of CO_2 and other substances.

Another important technology to consider for the green school, and a prerequisite of LEED certification, is the separation of the ventilation of chemical storage areas from the general building ventilation, so that fumes do not leak into the learning environment. Cleaning chemicals and similar products should be stored in separate spaces that are directly ventilated to the exterior. In addition, environmentally safe cleaning products should be a part of the facilities maintenance plan.

Figure 2.4

Daylighting of Classroom Space
Science lab in new classroom wing, Newton South High School, Newton, MA. Interior shades are used to control glare on extremely bright days, while still admitting daylight at these south-facing windows. Forested area outside also diffuses light.

Photo Credit: Drummey Rosane Anderson, Inc.

Figure 2.5

Daylighting of Stairwell
South facing wall at central stair lobby, Newton South High School, Newton, MA admits full sun, contributing light and warmth. Interior masonry helps balance temperature swings via thermal mass storage.

Photo Credit: Drummey Rosane Anderson, Inc.

Materials Selection

Increasing varieties of building materials are being manufactured from recycled materials. Recycling of tires into entrance mats, and plastic milk jugs into toilet stall partitions, are two examples. In some cases, materials have been made from recycled stock for years, and manufacturers are just now learning to explain this in their literature. The steel industry is learning that it is an advantage, not a disadvantage, to let people know that their products are made from melted automobiles and other recycled steel items. With renewed interest in natural resources, linoleum (essentially a mixture of linseed oil and sawdust) has made a huge comeback in recent years with new colors and patterns. Rapidly renewable products are also important for consideration in the green school. A popular example is bamboo hardwood floors, which are not only elegant, but are made from a material that can replenish itself quickly, while helping to support third-world economies. *(See Figure 2.6.)*

Figure 2.6

Bamboo Harvesting[6]

Increased use of bamboo has helped to stimulate economies in underdeveloped regions.

Photo Credit: Teragren/Timbergrass Company

Additional examples of recycled content in building materials include:

- Fly ash used in concrete mixtures
- Auto glass converted into decorative wall tiles
- Newspapers ground up and converted into building sheathing panels

Examples of rapidly renewable materials include:

- Wheatboard, similar to products made from wood chips and sawdust, a construction board product that is made from wheat byproducts
- Grasses used in wall treatments and other decorative finishes
- Structural baled-hay adobe construction

There are other important considerations in materials selection, beyond just recycled content and rapid renewability. Green products should also have a low Volatile Organic Content (VOC) rating. These products, such as low-VOC paints and adhesives, are designed so that they do not give off harmful fumes during the curing process. Formaldehyde has been used in the past in the manufacturing of various building products, including fiberboard cores for cabinetry and doors, and various insulation products. Similar to the VOC issue, it is important to select building products with low or no formaldehyde content, as this compound "off-gasses" into the building interior over time, and can cause (or aggravate) chemical sensitivity in occupants.

The considerations for materials selection are almost endless when designing a green school. Is it more "green" to select a bamboo flooring or linoleum for a cafeteria floor? Does it make a difference if the bamboo product has to be trucked in from a long distance, while the linoleum is made locally? Or, is it even more "green" to simply apply a colored finish to a concrete surface, and forgo a traditional finished floor entirely? Or would the concrete contribute to leg discomfort among staff? All of these considerations, and more, need to be evaluated and balanced in the process of materials selection for the green building.

Use of local, low-tech, indigenous materials and methods is recommended to avoid high energy and resource consumption associated with transportation and to support the local economy and tradition.

Building Mechanical and Electrical Systems

Just as there are many choices for the selection of green building materials, there are several options available for green mechanical and electrical systems. Some of these, such as fuel cells and photovoltaic systems, are more "high-technology" choices, while others, such as light shelves, involve lower technology. (*Light shelves* are reflective horizontal surfaces adjacent to windows positioned to "bounce" daylight deep into buildings.) Many of the low-technology features blur the line between architecture and engineering, and underscore the integrated team approach to green design. For example, the combination of a large overhang on the south side of a building, along with energy-efficient lighting and appliances, may significantly reduce the air-conditioning loads of a space.

The following are a few of many high-technology ideas for mechanical and electrical systems.

Photovoltaic (PV) Systems

These systems, which produce electrical energy directly from the sun, have been traditionally expensive, though their costs are coming down. Earlier installations often called for on-site battery storage of PV-generated electricity. Current installations have evolved into a preference for a tieback into the common electrical grid, eliminating the need for expensive batteries and space to house them. In this newer scenario, maximum energy production (hot summer days) directly offsets maximum energy demand on the typical grid (air-conditioning), so utility companies are motivated to provide a payback to PV producers as a means of helping shave the top off of peak-demand periods.

PV arrays are available in a variety of types, in two general classifications: conventional (single and polycrystalline silicon PV cells) and thin-film photovoltaic modules. Each type has advantages and disadvantages in terms of cost and productive output. In general, the conventional "pure" silicone-based wafer cells are more efficient in the conversion of sunlight to energy, but cost more than the newer, thin-film modules.
(See Figure 2.7.)

Figure 2.7
Photovoltaic Array on a College Building[7]
This large array contributes a significant portion of the electrical needs of the building it serves.
Photo Credit: Humboldt State University

According to a popular Web site on the "Basics of Photovoltaic Technology":

> *"On a sunny day a one square meter surface perpendicular to the sunlight receives approximately 1,000 watts input power. Modern crystalline solar modules are about 12%-13% efficient, and hence will produce about 120-130 watts per square meter. Amorphous (non-crystalline) cells are about half as efficient, but have a potential in the marketplace due to their lower manufacturing cost."[8]*

Wind Energy

This technology has tremendous potential, but it can be difficult to implement successfully. Careful site selection for wind power is critical. Local geologic features and weather patterns at a potential site can result in a markedly different performance than what might be inferred from consulting large-scale wind-speed maps. Also, it should be noted that local popular opinion is often strongly opposed to wind generation towers in urban and suburban environments. This opposition is a result of concerns about safety and noise, as well as a growing awareness of possible threats to avian wildlife from rapidly spinning turbine blades. If a suitable site can be found, however, wind energy is relatively inexpensive and efficient.

Low-Water-Use Fixtures

Water is a valuable resource to be conserved. Many cities and towns have started to restrict and control water use by residents, and in some areas, these restrictions are severe. Building codes often require low-water-use fixtures and automatic use-limiting controls on public restroom fixtures. As water use charges continue to rise, the economies of water re-use technology will encourage other remedies. Graywater recycling is an example and can be implemented in a school environment. In this type of recycling, water from sinks and athletic showers is captured, stored in tanks, and then used to irrigate athletic fields. Some facilities have gone so far as to recycle wastewater through clarifying processes using man-made marshes and are re-using the cleaned byproduct in the facility.

Fuel Cells and Co-Generation

Fuel cell systems may prove to be a long-term solution to the nation's energy needs. Current traditional power plants have a 24% heat rate or efficiency; which means the BTUs of energy in, relative to the net power out, averages 25%. Co-generation systems revert to an approach used in the old mills of the late 1800s where the waste heat was recovered and used as a process. Co-generation also uses waste heat energy to increase the net plant heat rate to approximately 75%.

Fuel cells use hydrogen as a fuel source through a catalytic type of process, producing electricity and giving off heat and small amounts of hot water as byproducts. The heat is captured for space heating needs, and the electricity generated provides for power needs—thus, the term "co" generation, which stands for "combined" generation. Co-generation can also be achieved with other more conventional devices, such as diesel engine-driven generators. Fuel cell technology is particularly attractive as the driver of a co-generation system because the basic fuel, hydrogen, can be derived from water.

In the traditional approach to fuel cell design, machines called *electrolyzers* convert distilled water into hydrogen, releasing some heat and trace amounts of nitrogen and oxygen. The hydrogen is then passed through a fuel cell to create electricity, heat, and water. Although the efficiency of each step of the process is relatively low, the efficiency of the overall process is higher, as all of the byproducts are used. In this scenario, buildings produce their own hydrogen gas, generate their own electricity, and are heated in the process. This technology can be used in homes, commercial buildings, and institutional buildings, including schools. In home environments, the hydrogen gas can be used to fuel the family automobile, which would also require a fuel cell.

Fuel cell technology is currently available, although expensive. Research and development are ongoing, leading to more efficient technology than the traditional approach noted above. For example, the FCS 1200™ model, by IdaTech, LLC, operates on a methanol/water fuel mixture, and produces hydrogen "on demand" through a process known as "steam reforming." *(See Figure 2.8.)* As evidence that this technology is "real," and readily available, consider the following advertisement:

The FCS 1200™ is a portable fuel cell system that incorporates the FPM 20™ fuel processing module, Ballard's Nexa™ power module, a fuel tank, complete balance of plant and an optional pure sine wave inverter, all in a very compact package. IdaTech has incorporated a variety of options into the system to simplify use. With one-touch start capability, the FCS 1200™ sets a new industry standard for ease of operation. Additionally, power output is automatically responsive to changing demands. Optional features allow users to monitor and control a broad range of product functions from remote locations.[9]

Figure 2.8
Example of a Small Fuel Cell: FCS 1200™ Fuel Cell, by IdaTech Corporation, Bend, Oregon[10]
Just add water and methanol, push button, generate heat and electricity!

Photo Credit: IdaTech Corporation

Case Study

Newton South High School, Newton, Massachusetts

Overview:

This project involved the renovation of an existing high school where enrollment was planned to increase from 1,600 to approximately 2,000 students. The community is relatively affluent and is committed to green design. A large new classroom area addition, cafeteria, and athletic facility are features. The project was awarded a grant from the Massachusetts Technology Collaborative,[11] to substantially support the high performance and renewable energy aspects of the design. A computer monitor will be featured in the lobby of the new athletic facility to display the activity of the roof-mounted, solar PV array, which will be tied directly into the local utility company grid.

Features:

- Energy-efficient building envelope design
- High-performance glazing systems with passive solar design strategies
- Roof water capture; flushes building toilets
- Waterless urinals
- 60 kW photovoltaic system
- High-efficiency lighting and HVAC system design

Challenges:

A plumbing variance was required by the local code officials to allow the use of rainwater for flushing of the toilets. The variance required all graywater piping to be painted purple, and called for additional, frequent piping identification signage.

Anchorage of the rooftop solar array was still under consideration as of the time of publication. The solar array system selected sits directly on the low-slope membrane roof. No supporting steel is required, but a tie-down system to protect against wind uplift was still being refined.

Status:

Project in progress at time of publication. Anticipated completion 2005.

Design Team:

Architect: Drummey Rosane Anderson, Inc.,[12] Newton Centre, MA

Mechanical Engineer: Griffith & Vary, Inc., Wareham, MA

Photovoltaic Engineer: Zapotec,[13] Cambridge, MA

Constructed by: Mello Construction Company, Inc., Taunton, MA, General Contractors

Newton South High School, Newton, MA
Classroom wing addition, northwest corner of building. (Entrance is at left.)
Photo Credit: Drummey Rosane Anderson, Inc.

Case Study

Goodwillie Environmental School
Ada, Michigan

Overview:

Goodwillie Environmental School is a unique educational facility where children in the fifth and sixth grades study environmental issues in coordination with their core studies. The students, teachers, and administration treat the building and its site as active participants in the curriculum. This public project was funded through a generous private donation, which required an innovative, environmentally sensitive building and resulted in a commitment from the school district to pursue a LEED rating for this, and for all future building projects.

A passive solar technique was utilized to collect heat through south-facing windows during the cooler months. Large overhangs and trellises shade the windows, keeping the building cool during the warmer months. Thermal mass was integrated into the building design so that walls and floors are used to capture, store, and distribute thermal energy. In addition, windows were placed to make full use of natural lighting and cross ventilation for summer cooling. Cool air is drawn from the north side and shaded parts of the building. To save energy and reduce maintenance, the school is equipped with a closed loop, geothermal, earth-coupled heat pump and a permanent performance monitoring system. This system relies on the natural heat sink of the earth itself to help heat and cool the building. The monitoring system allows remote analysis of the building's energy and air quality performance to ensure peak efficiency and comfort.[14]

Features:

- Energy-efficient building envelope design
- High-performance glazing systems
- Geothermal heat pump
- Natural ventilation strategies
- High-efficiency lighting and HVAC system design
- Exceptional use of recycled and local materials

Challenges:

Extensive research was required to find innovative, environmentally sensitive products, while still using time-tested materials for a demanding learning environment. This required a careful review with the owner regarding standard specifications.

High-voltage power lines crossed the site near the building location and were relocated away from the building.

The remote location of the site relative to public utilities made selection and design of the mechanical systems complex, and resulted in the decision to use a geothermal heat pump.

An existing, diseased apple orchard on-site was removed and the site restored to native prairie.

Status:

Completed 2001; LEED Certified

Owner & Design Team:

Forest Hills Public Schools, Grand Rapids, MI

Architects and Engineers: Progressive AE, Grand Rapids, MI

Goodwillie Environmental School, Ada, MI

Photo Credit: Chuck Heiney, Heiney Photography

Case Study

Third Creek Elementary School
Statesville, North Carolina

Overview:

Third Creek Elementary School is a new, 800-student elementary school designed with the goal of creating an energy-efficient, healthy learning environment.

The building was oriented on the site to allow natural daylight in all classrooms. Building systems were designed for energy-efficient performance. Specific building materials contribute to healthy indoor air quality. Many materials had recycled or rapidly renewable material content. The contractors performed their work in accordance with an indoor air quality management plan and recycled over 50% of their construction waste.

Third Creek Elementary School was the first K-12 school to earn a LEED v2.0 Gold Certification from the U.S. Green Building Council. In addition to meeting the seven prerequisites, the project earned a total of 39 points, including several innovation points.

Features:

- A natural wetland helps slow and filter storm water run-off before it reaches a nearby stream. This wetland will also be used as an outdoor classroom and living wildlife laboratory.
- Additional landscaping and specific roofing materials to keep the building and parking lots cooler, lessening "urban heat island" effect.
- Building site oriented to maximize natural daylighting in classrooms.
- Waterless urinals and low-flow automatic spigots.
- Wall paint with low gas toxicity.
- Energy recovery ventilation to dehumidify and constantly freshen the air.
- Highly energy-efficient water-source heat pumps for heating and cooling.
- Wood doors from certified, environmentally responsible forests.
- High level of recycled content in the building's concrete.
- Mulch in the landscaping from trees that had to be cut down to build on the site.[15]

Status:

Project completed fall 2002; LEED Gold Certified – 39 points.

Owner & Design Team:

IREDELL – Statesville Schools, Statesville, NC

Architect: Moseley Architects, Morrisville, NC

Civil Engineers: Timmons, Richmond, VA

Mechanical Engineer: Consulting Engineering Services, Inc., Winston-Salem, NC

Electrical Engineer: Design Engineering, Inc., Lexington, NC

Third Creek Elementary School, Statesville, NC

Photo Credit: Spark Productions, Raleigh, NC

Conclusion

The tremendous groundswell of interest in green design is due to the promise it offers to enrich our lives. By using resources more efficiently, we will have healthier air quality and more plentiful resources for future generations. By protecting our health, we reward ourselves with more energy and vitality in the pursuit of life's activities. By encouraging innovation, we reinforce our faith in our ability to improve and learn as we continue to build and renovate.

The following principles should be a focus of the design, planning, and construction of a green school:

- Understand the project goals, and be sure to achieve consensus and "buy-in" from the project team.
- Select the design and construction teams based on qualifications and experience, not the lowest cost.
- Involve the contractor early in the process.
- Consider a qualifications-based selection process instead of the traditional "design-bid-build" approach to project delivery.
- Re-evaluate the project goals frequently as the design progresses, and understand the specific design features and technologies that will be used to achieve those goals.
- Involve the entire team in the process, including those who will be asked to operate and maintain the facility after it is completed.
- Hire a skilled and enthusiastic commissioning agent, and get him or her involved early in the process.
- Involve the teaching staff during the design process, and brainstorm ideas for educational curricula related to the building design and operation.
- Utilize the resources and standards of the USGBC (LEED) and CHPS organizations as guidelines for achieving project goals.
- Understand any specific needs regarding maintenance and operations of the green school.

If recent history is any indication of what the future holds, then we are truly at the very beginning of an exciting period in the development of improved building techniques and educational opportunities, as we continue to expand our understanding of green school design.

1   Greg L. Roberts, AIA, CSI, CCS, ACHA, LEED. "Top 10 Green Building Myths."
    Healthcare Design Magazine, March 2003.

2   Roberts.

3   Leopold, Luna B., and Kenneth S. Davis. *Water.* Des Moines, IA: Time Books, 1966.

4   Roberts.

5   Collaboration for High Performance Schools (CHPS), *Best Practices Manual*, Volume
    III – Criteria, page 3.

6   Teragren/Timbergrass Company, Seattle, WA: http://www.teragren.com

7   Humboldt State University; reprinted with permission.

8   EE Solar Electric Solutions: http://users.oc-net.com/eesolar/pv101.htm

9   IdaTech, LLC, Bend, OR: http://www.idatech.com/solutions/system_integration/
    fcs_1200.html

10 IdaTech.

11 http://www.masstech.org

12 http://www.draws.com/index.htm

13 http://www.zapotecenergy.com

14 https://www.usgbc.org/LEED/Project/project_detail_step_1.asp?PROJECT_ID=44

15 http://www.iss.k12.nc.us/greenschool.htm

Chapter 3

Integration of Technology

Drummey Rosane Anderson, Inc.

Although the scope and scale of school buildings have grown enormously over the past hundred years, basic classroom layout has changed little until recently. Most classrooms were designed primarily as a venue for lecture in which the teacher conveyed information orally, aided by chalkboard notes, printed textbooks, and hand-outs. When audiovisual equipment and computers began to appear in classrooms, they were considered powerful new tools, but they were used primarily to enhance the lecture-style presentation.

Federal, state, and local initiatives, together with the advancement and lower prices of computer technology, have brought about a dramatic transformation in school environments. Today's classroom is likely to include not only networked multimedia computers with peripherals, such as printers, scanners, TVs, VCRs, and projectors, but distance learning opportunities through the Internet, and possibly even interactive whiteboards and video teleconferencing. The pace of change is not expected to slow down anytime soon.

The influx of technological applications in schools, particularly in classrooms, is causing serious re-examination of educational philosophy in many school systems. Technology is combining with a fundamental paradigm shift in educational thinking from passive, teacher-centered lecturing to more active learner-centered project participation. Strongly promoting the concept of "*learning by doing and failure*," more radical educational thinkers, such as Professor Roger Schank of the Institute for Learning Sciences, have already begun to dismiss the idea of a conventional classroom.[1] This shift will have as significant an effect on school facility design as the movement from the one-room schoolhouse of the 1800s to the educational "factories" of the last half of the 1900s. *(See Figures 3.1 and 3.2.)*

In a rush to invest in technology, many people involved in public or private K-12 education—from administrators, teachers, and parents to the general public—must learn quickly about this powerful new venue. When planning a school construction project, there is a need to know:

- What technology exists in schools.
- How it is being integrated.
- How it impacts the school design.
- Who has the expertise.
- How much it will cost.

Figure 3.1
Redstone Schoolhouse,
Longfellow's Wayside Inn
Historic Site, Sudbury, MA
One-room schoolhouse, exterior.

Photo Credit: Pao-Chung Chi, AIA

Figure 3.2
Redstone Schoolhouse,
Longfellow's Wayside Inn
Historic Site, Sudbury, MA
One-room schoolhouse, interior.

Photo Credit: Pao-Chung Chi, AIA

Technology Integration Defined

The term "technology integration" can mean different things in different contexts. In school design, it should cover these two distinct, but complementary areas:

- Assimilation of technology resources and technology-based practices into the daily teaching, learning, and administration of schools.
- Incorporation of technology assets and technological applications into the routine school facility operation and management systems.

Technology resources and assets include both equipment and infrastructure. Equipment includes: multimedia desktop and laptop computers; tablet PCs; PDAs; pocket or hand-held PCs; and other computing devices and peripherals, such as printers, scanners, digital cameras, fax, speakers, projectors, TVs, interactive whiteboards, standard and custom software. Infrastructure includes wired or wireless voice/data/video telecommunication networks, servers, associated routing and switching gear, and software.

Technology-based practices and applications include, but are not limited to, technology-integrated teaching and learning environments and curriculum, school business administration, collaborative work and communication, Internet-based research, remote access to instrumentation, network-based transmission, data storage and retrieval, security, and other means and methods.

The ultimate goal of technology integration is to make technology a part of the school culture—routine, seamless, proficient, and effective in supporting a school's mission. The National Center for Education Statistics further suggests:

> "It is a goal-in-process, not an end state. The goal of perfect technology integration is inherently unreachable: technologies change and develop, students and teachers come and go—things change. It is the process by which people and their institutional setting adapt to the technology that matters most. The process of technology integration is one of continuous change, learning, and (hopefully) improvement."[2]

Because the role and impact of technology in education are extremely broad and the need to know correspondingly pervasive, this chapter will focus on the integration of technology related to a school's planning and design—that is, specific questions related to the physical transformation of the school design as influenced by the integration of technology. Technology integration-related curriculum development, school business administration, staff training, professional development, and IT maintenance and support are all important topics, and much has been written about them. However, their proper discussion exceeds both the scope and the purpose of this book. Readers interested in learning more about technology integration in instructional and administrative applications should examine the National Center for Education Statistics, publication 2003-313 *Technology in Schools: Suggestions, Tools, and Guidelines for Assessing Technology in Elementary and Secondary Education*. Related publications and Web links are listed in the Resources section at the end of this book.

Integration of Technology into a School Design

Influenced by technology integration, changes in the school's role and operations demand serious re-thinking of facility design. While we recognize the value of past investment in the existing school facilities, we must also acknowledge what is new, possible, and essential. Both the learning process and the design of school facilities are transformed, differing sharply from traditional schools. Both educators and school designers will have to re-evaluate their design decisions in the course of renovation, addition, or building of a new school.

Technology Infrastructure as a Building Utility

No matter how technology is integrated into a school design, it generally involves an investment in the following categories:

- Network infrastructure and operating systems.
- Technology furniture, furnishings, and equipment.
- Educational, business, and facility management application software.
- Staff training and professional development.
- IT maintenance, technical support, upgrades, and supplies.

Among these categories, the network infrastructure is probably the most complex and is normally integrated, or "built-in," to a school building. Similar to its corresponding mechanical and electrical counterparts, technology infrastructure has become an indispensable "utility" in today's school facility. A building's network infrastructure may assume a critical role in facility control and automation.

No one would think of building or improving a school facility without employing the skills of an experienced architect. The same principle applies when building or improving the technology infrastructure. Its design should be assigned to a trained professional engineer and integrated as a part of the school facility design process—beginning with the initial planning and programming, schematic design, design development, construction documents, and bidding and negotiations, and continuing through construction administration and post-construction evaluation.

Selecting a Technology Consultant

Analogous to school building design, technology design is a decision-making process: LAN or WAN typology, cabling or wireless, Intranet, Extranet, Virtual Private Network (VPN), firewalls, scalability, interoperability, and so forth. A labyrinth of techno-jargon must be deciphered by a knowledgeable person. A skillful technology consultant can steer decision-makers through the maze by offering an array of advisory services, including: needs analysis, technology planning, network engineering and design, hardware/and software evaluation and procurement support, installation oversight, performance testing, arrangement of staff training and development, and continued trouble-shooting and support.

Whether a school district is constructing a new building or retrofitting existing classrooms, many schools have found that an effective technology consultant can help maximize limited resources. Even for schools with experienced in-house IT staff, a professional technology designer can provide a valuable due-diligence audit. On the one hand, through their daily practice, most technology consultants are current with the market conditions and industry development. They can challenge a school's present or intended technology practices with evolving and emerging ideas. An added benefit is that working as an "outsider," a technology consultant might be in a better position to facilitate amicable goals, mitigate disagreements, and assist in navigating concerns of the school administration, teachers, parents, local government, and taxpayers. These concerns often include such issues as "digital divide," the amount of spending on technology within the district, teacher retraining, impact of distance learning on the size of the teaching staff, and other changes in the methods of teaching.

Architectural firms specializing in school design are generally familiar with specific educational technological applications and can provide a technology consultant as part of their design service. The school district may also engage the services of a technology design firm directly. This decision will be largely based on the timing of the project, the complexity of the district's technological needs, and available resources. Keep in mind that not all technology consultants are equal. Even though such design services can be obtained in several different ways, a school should be wary of vendors who offer "free design service." Vendor-provided design services might sometimes be partial to the proprietary design or products they represent.

In the selection process, preferences should be given to a product-neutral, BICSI-(Building Industry Consulting Service International, Inc.) Registered Communications Distribution Designer (RCDD) with extensive school design, construction, and technology FF&E (Furniture, Furnishing, and Equipment) experience. RCDD is a designation for individuals who have qualified knowledge in the design, integration, and implementation of telecommunication systems and have successfully passed a certificate examination. RCDD certification also requires continuing education to keep current in the ever-changing telecommunications field. RCDD is an added assurance that the designer's skill set is not inhibited by specific product criteria. Through innovation and knowledge of advancing technology and techniques, as well as long-term planning vision, a school district can benefit from a significant level of professionalism in an RCDD's services.

Developing a Technology Plan

In Chapter 1, it was noted the project plan is the key component of the base information, since it sets the overall direction of a project. A technology plan documents strategies that direct acquisition, use, maintenance, and expansion of technology in a school district. These strategies are expressed in policies. In technology planning, the following major areas should be addressed.

- **Vision:** What is expected from the technology, in other words, what the students, staff, administrators, parents, and community hope to achieve with it. The vision defines the goals and objectives of the appropriate level of technology integration into an educational environment needed to advance a school's performance. For example, this may mean full immersion with a computer for every student, with the ultimate goal of providing virtual-reality applications for such subjects as music, painting, and biology. A lesser immersion might include minimal computer usage with more reliance on traditional learning techniques for specialized classes.

- **Needs Assessment:** An evaluation of the current status and future needs, including infrastructure, equipment, skills, and use, as well as the district's grade level, preparedness, and other political/socio-economic factors.

- **Programming:** Development of a detailed technology program in accordance with the established vision and identified needs for the type and amount of technology needed. This program is needed for the acquisition and deployment of the technology required by the target audience.

- **Funding:** Allocation resources as determined by the school district—how much money is available for technology. Funding for technology may be part of the overall construction budget, or it may come from other sources. Grants may be available from state or other agencies for specific applications. *(See the Resources section at the back of the book.)*

- **Implementation:** Development of a timetable and execution of strategies that make technology both useful and capable of accomplishing the vision.

Balancing the many factors necessary to prepare a technology plan that is acceptable to all stakeholders is an intricate maneuver. Federal, state, local, and funding agencies' technology guidelines, regulations, and mandates must also be considered. The technology plan should always be incorporated as an important part of a school's long-range plan and included in the educational specifications.

Integrating a Technology Engineer into the School Design Team

The technology design of a school construction project should always be a collaborative effort among school representatives, technology consultants, architects, and the mechanical and electrical engineers. Many schools select several representatives to serve on the design team. Representatives may include the school principal, district IT coordinator, teachers, parents, school committee, building committee, or community members. Regardless of who serves on the team, it is essential that all participants take ownership of the project, work collaboratively, and keep an open channel of communication throughout the project.

The technology design and construction process usually parallels the building design and construction process. Ideally, the technology design concepts and requirements should be introduced into the building design process from the very beginning. For example, issues to be considered include type and quantity of electronic equipment to be used in a space, locations of the equipment relative to other activities, room layout and sightlines for intended multimedia presentations, power and air conditioning requirements, and lighting/shading controls. Many schools have found that it is advantageous to have the architect provide the technology consultant as part of the design service, and bid technology infrastructure as a part of the building construction. Some of the benefits:

- From previous collaborative experience, the architect generally has a wealth of qualified technology consultants readily available for the school's review.

- The architect can perform the necessary reference checks, make selection recommendations, and be responsible for the technology consultant's work.

- The infrastructure can be better coordinated and more easily integrated into the building design, along with all other basic engineering disciplines, before the building plans solidify. Once the design is set, it is recommended that the technology infrastructure be bid as a part of the building construction project in order to minimize potential costly moves, additions, changes (known in the industry as MACs), or any other compromise that may be required, resulting in a less than optimal cabling infrastructure.

- Most importantly, cost savings could result from a streamlined consultant selection process, better design and engineering coordination, combined bidding, and the convenience of installing the technology infrastructure during the building construction.

Acknowledging the needs and the potential benefits, the Construction Specifications Institute (CSI), the authority in construction specifications, has expanded its MasterFormat Division 16 – Electrical to cover technology-related sections. This change will hopefully further increase the architectural design community's awareness that today's technology design, consisting of an engineered system of spaces, cabling, pathways, and hardware, is an integral part of the building design and construction process. Its proper design, coordination, and installation will not only affect the building user's performance, but also the building performance itself.

Technology Design Process
Site and Existing Conditions Analysis
Understanding the existing conditions will form a critical basis for making design decisions. For example, issues to be reviewed include: community and school district-wide technology and support; available

local telecommunication, cable TV, and Internet services; available power and HVAC; direction of satellite; and available physical spaces. A new school can usually be designed to accommodate technological applications more efficiently. An existing facility, on the other hand, may have spatial and structural limitations that may preclude adaptation to certain new services. For instance, a classroom may be too small or poorly configured to use full-size desktop computers. In this case, space-saving all-in-one laptop computers may be considered as an alternative. Existing facilities may also consider the use of wireless devices where hard wiring is too costly or structurally impractical.

The proximity of educational resources available to a school may necessitate certain technologies. For example, a rural or small school district with limited access to specialized programs, resources, or instructors may need to rely more on distance education using satellite communications. Communities, libraries, and other municipal functions may also want to share resources via a Wide Area Network.

Schematic Design (SD)

This phase sets the tone for the project by defining system components, locations, quantities, schedule, and costs that meet the goals stipulated in a school's technology plan. The technology consultant will review the technology plan and continue to solicit input from all stakeholders, including teachers and administrators, to verify the project objectives and discuss options to achieve the intended operations within the established budget and timetable. This information will be incorporated into a set of schematic design plans outlining the technology systems and associated preliminary cost.

Design Development (DD)

In this phase, the technology consultant further elaborates on the schematic design by providing a greater level of detail and incorporating feedback from the project stakeholders. The design development documents will provide more detailed product specifications (including specific manufacturers, models, and quantities) and more detailed cost estimates. Infrastructure plans depict locations of electrical outlets, network, audio-visual (AV), and other connections, or wireless access points throughout the building, as well as space requirements for various cabling and devices. This is a critical phase for technology coordination, since all of the other engineering disciplines will be affected before the plans solidify. Alternative solutions might have to be evaluated due to physical, technical, or financial conflicts or limitations. At the end of this phase, a set of the design development documents will be provided to the school for review and sign-off.

Construction Documents (CD)

This phase continues to build on the design development plans, product specifications, and cost estimates for each technology component, as well as its coordination with affected architectural, mechanical, and electrical designs. Preparation of a comprehensive and well-coordinated set of documents will go a long way to ensure better bid responses and more competitive bid pricing. In essence, construction documents are a part of the legal contract that illustrates exactly what the school will be paying for when the project is bid and awarded to a contractor. To that end, it is important to verify one last time that the stakeholders, including teachers and administrators, are aware of what they are getting, that priorities have been established for how the systems will be used, and that the funds have been appropriated for the project.

Bidding and Negotiations

When a final consensus has been reached, the project is advertised either separately or as part of a building construction project, and bidding documents are published and distributed to contractors/vendors. After soliciting proposed bids, the technology consultant will assist the school district in analyzing each bid and reviewing any deviations from bidding requirements. Furthermore, subject to federal, state, or local laws, a school may also evaluate contractors on such criteria as qualifications, experience on similar projects, financial history, bonding capacity, and proximity to the project location. At the end of this phase, the school district will select a contractor, negotiate fees (where permitted by law), and award the contract.

Construction Administration (CA)

During this phase, the technology consultant will act on behalf of the school to administer the technology system's procurement and installation. As such, the technology consultant will perform the following tasks:

- Review the contractor's or installer's qualifications.
- Provide answers and interpretations to any contractor's questions related to the construction documents.
- Review product specifications and samples submitted by the contractor.
- Review and recommend legitimate substitutions.
- Coordinate any changes resulting from design modifications due to unanticipated alterations in use, contractor's means or methods, available products and equipment, or differing field conditions.
- Analyze the impact of the recommended change and its associated cost.

After complete installation of the technology systems, the technology consultant will oversee system performance testing to ensure successful operation. After system integration testing has been completed, the contractor will provide the school with a package of "as-built" documentation to record the actual installation.

Post-Construction Evaluation

Post-construction evaluation is an additional phase, particularly appropriate for technology systems. Many compromises will undoubtedly have been made during the design and construction phases due to scheduling and financial, technical, or physical constraints. A school should establish a procedure to evaluate the actual technology integration and compare it with the goals stated in the technology plan to measure its success. It is important to determine if the goals need to be modified for future implementation as more funding may become available, and as systems and equipment may require upgrades or improvements. New technology will continue to emerge, and a school's needs will continue to expand and change. While it is difficult to predict where technology will be in the future, a school can and should be vigilant of the status of its own technology integration, the developments in other schools, and, in particular, what resources may become available. It is important to plan for and take advantage of new opportunities as they arise.

The Technology Infrastructure: The Network

An understanding of some of the basic technology terminology and concepts will be useful in communicating with a technology consultant. Following are simple explanations of some frequently used terms in the technology planning and design process.

Network

A *network* consists of two or more computers that are linked in order to share resources, exchange files, or allow electronic communications. The computers on a network may be linked by cables, wires, radio waves, infrared light beams, or satellites. Defined largely by its coverage area, there are three basic types of networks, described below.

Local Area Network (LAN)

A *LAN* is a computer network that spans a relatively small geographic area, such as a school or group of adjacent buildings on a campus. LAN computers are rarely more than a mile apart. They reside on private premises and do not use public common carrier transmission facilities.

Each individual computer in a LAN has its own central processing unit (CPU) to execute programs, but is also able to access data and devices anywhere on the LAN. This allows all network users to share data, as well as expensive devices, such as laser printers. Users can also use the LAN to communicate with each other by sending e-mail or by using instant messaging.

In a typical school LAN configuration, one computer is designated as the file server, which stores all of the software that controls the network, as well as software that can be shared by the computers attached to the network. Individual computers connected to the file server can be less powerful than the file server and may have additional software of their own. On most existing LANs, metal wires are used to connect the network interface card installed in each computer.

Metropolitan Area Network (MAN)

A popular network choice for a town or a city, a *MAN* spans a geographic area larger than LAN. By interconnecting smaller LAN networks within a defined boundary, information is easily disseminated throughout the network. School districts, local libraries, and municipalities often use a MAN to connect to citizens and local business enterprises. MAN is characterized as follows:

- Interconnects multiple networks via public or private communication facilities usually within 50 miles or less.
- Most often supports academic or commercial campus environments.
- Because it is designed primarily to provide high-speed connectivity rather than resource sharing, it favors high-speed connections, such as fiber optical cable or other digital media.
- Most often used as a "backbone" technology to interconnect groups of devices within or between buildings.

Wide Area Network (WAN)

Typically, a *WAN* consists of two or more LANs or MANs. It is interesting to note that the largest WAN in existence is the Internet. A WAN is complicated, because it uses common-carrier-provided transmission facilities and/or services to connect LAN and MAN to global communications networks. The interconnected sites can be across the street or on the other side of the globe. To users, a WAN will not appear much different than a LAN or a MAN. However, in comparison, WAN connections typically operate at lower rates, have longer transit delays, and are more expensive.

A wide range of service options (such as telephone dial-up, leased T1, ISDN, Broadband, or satellite) are available from common-carrier providers. For example, T1 operates at 1.544 Mbps and is a common high-speed digital transmission system used by many schools. A school district can lease an entire T1 line to carry its telephone service, provide Internet access, and connect several schools' LANs. Ultimately, the choice of service is based on a number of factors, including locally available common-carrier offering, site location, traffic load, connect time, and cost.

Network Topology

Network wiring can be laid out in several different ways. Topology describes either physical or logical configuration of a network. There are three principal topologies used in network design, detailed below. *(Also, see Figure 3.3.)*

- **Bus/Linear Bus:** All devices are connected to a linear central cable, called the bus, or backbone. Bus networks are relatively inexpensive and easy to install for small networks. Ethernet systems use a bus topology.
- **Ring:** All devices are connected to one another in the shape of a closed loop, so that each device is connected directly to two other devices, one on either side of it. Ring topologies are relatively

expensive and difficult to install, but they offer high bandwidth and can span large distances.

- **Star:** All devices are connected to a central hub. Star networks are relatively easy to install and manage, but bottlenecks can occur because all data must pass through the hub.

Four factors should be considered in choosing a typology:

- Cost
- Expandability
- Location of devices
- Speed

In theory, networks work better in their simple and pure forms. However, when necessary, different topologies can be mixed to create a hybrid typology. In fact, most networks installed are hybrids for one reason or another. For example, a "tree" topology consists of groups of star-configured work stations connected to a linear bus backbone cable. A "mesh" typology connects every device with many redundant interconnections to every other device in the network.

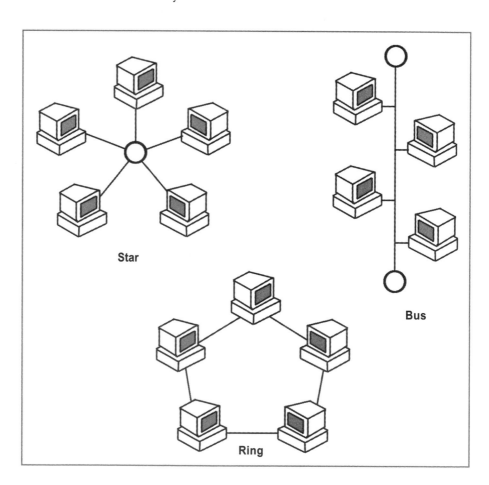

Figure 3.3
Basic Network Typologies[3]
Credit: Webopedia

Network Protocol

Network protocol is a set of rules that governs the communications between computers on a network. These rules regulate the characteristics of a network, such as: access method, physical topologies, types of cabling, and speed of data transfer. Several common protocols are: Ethernet, Local Talk, Token Ring, FDDI, and ATM. Among them, *Ethernet*, although not the fastest, remains by far the most widely used protocol in LANs because of its affordability, support of all cabling types, longevity and readily available services and gears, and continuing innovation. Ethernet allows for linear bus, star, or tree topologies. Data can be transmitted over twisted pair, coaxial, or fiber optic cable at a speed of 10 Mbps.

To meet the ever-increasing demand for higher speed of transmission, the Ethernet has developed a *Fast Ethernet* standard that supports 100 Mbps. Fast Ethernet requires the use of different and more expensive network concentrators, hubs and network interface cards, and Category 5 twisted pair or fiber optic cable. Fast Ethernet has become the preferred choice in K-12 schools in recent years.

With a transmission speed of 1 Gbps, *Gigabit Ethernet* is the latest development in the Ethernet standard. It is used primarily for backbones on a network at this time. In the foreseeable future, it will be more popular for work station and server connections as well. It can be used with both copper and fiber optic cabling. The table below summarizes the Ethernet associated cabling types, designations, and their respective length limitations.

Ethernet Cable Specifications

Cable Type	IEEE Designation[4]	Maximum Length
Unshielded Twisted Pair	10BaseT	100 meters
Thin Coaxial	10Base2	185 meters
Thick Coaxial	10Base5	500 meters
Fiber Optic	10BaseF	2000 meters
Unshielded Twisted Pair	100BaseT	100 meters

Network Cabling

A network may utilize only one or a combination of various cable types. The type of cable chosen is related to the network's topology, protocol, and size. The popular choices are described in the following sections.

Unshielded Twisted Pair (UTP) Cable

Unshielded twisted pair (UTP) is by far the most prevalent network cabling in use today. While there are other available media, UTP is the first choice of most school networks due to its low cost and large market share.

The quality of UTP may vary from telephone-grade wire to extremely high-speed cable. The cable consists of pairs of wires inside a jacket. Each pair is twisted with a different number of twists per inch to help eliminate interference from adjacent pairs and other electrical devices. The tighter the twisting, the higher the supported transmission rate and the greater the cost per foot. The Electronic Industry Association/ Telecommunication Industry Association (EIA/TIA) has rated UTP in the incremental categories shown in the table below.

Categories of Unshielded Twisted Pair

Type	Use
Category 1 (or CAT 1)	Voice Only (Telephone Wire)
Category 2 (or CAT 2)	Data to 4 Mbps (LocalTalk)
Category 3 (or CAT 3)	Data to 10 Mbps (Ethernet)
Category 4 (or CAT 4)	Data to 20 Mbps (16 Mbps Token Ring)
Category 5 (or CAT 5)	Data to 100 Mbps (Fast Ethernet)
Category 5E (or CAT 5E)	Data to 1 Gbps (Gigabit Ethernet)
Category 6 (or CAT 6)	Data to 10 Gbps

A school should purchase the best affordable cable. CAT 3 was a popular choice for most schools just a few years ago, but is quickly being replaced by CAT 5 or its enhanced version, 5E. As technology continues to advance, the latest Gigabit Ethernet (1000BaseT) standard (capable of 1 Gbps data transfer over distances of up to 100 meters using CAT 5E cabling) is gaining recognition in the marketplace. As transmission technologies improve, higher capacity cable means expandability and flexibility—important factors to consider in a technology investment. In addition, many technology grants require a minimum of Category 5 cable installation.

A disadvantage of UTP is that it may be susceptible to radio and electrical frequency interference. Shielded twisted pair (STP) is suitable for environments with electrical interference. However, the extra shielding can make the cables quite bulky. Shielded twisted pair is often selected for networks using Token Ring topology.

Coaxial Cable

Coaxial cabling has a single copper conductor at its center. A plastic layer insulates the center conductor from a braided metal shield. The metal shield helps to block any outside interference from fluorescent lights, motors, and other computers.

Although coaxial cabling is difficult to install, it is highly resistant to signal interference. In addition, it can support greater cable lengths between network devices than twisted pair cable. There are two types of coaxial cabling:

Thin coaxial cable is also referred to as *thinnet*. 10Base2 refers to the specifications for thin coaxial cable carrying Ethernet signals. The "2" refers to the approximate maximum segment length of 200 meters. In actuality, the maximum segment length is 185 meters. Thin coaxial cable is popular in schools using linear bus networks.

Thick coaxial cable is also referred to as *thicknet*. 10Base5 refers to the specifications for thick coaxial cable carrying Ethernet signals. The 5 refers to the maximum segment length of 500 meters. Thick coaxial cable has an extra protective plastic cover that helps keep moisture away from the center conductor. This makes thick coaxial a great choice when running longer lengths in a linear bus network. One disadvantage of thick coaxial is that it does not bend easily and is difficult to install.

Fiber Optic Cable

Fiber optic cabling consists of a bundle of glass or plastic fiber threads surrounded by Kevlar® fiber that helps strengthen the cable and prevent breakage and is further protected by several layers of outer Teflon® or PVC insulating jackets. Each thread is capable of transmitting modulated messages onto light waves rather than electronic signals. This makes it ideal for certain environments that contain a large amount of electrical interference. Fiber optic has become the standard choice for connecting networks between buildings due to its immunity to the effects of moisture and lightning.

Fiber optic cable is thinner and lighter than metal cable, but has the ability to transmit digital signals over much longer distances and at a much higher bandwidth. This capacity broadens telecommunication possibilities to include services such as video conferencing and interactive services. The material cost of fiber optic cable is comparable to metal cable. However, it is fragile and more difficult to install, modify, split, and interface, and is therefore more expensive. 10BaseF refers to the specifications for fiber optic cable carrying Ethernet signals.

Design Standards

Construction in virtually all states is regulated by building codes and life safety standards. Enforced by local agencies having jurisdiction, these codes and standards govern the installation practices and materials used in the construction of telecommunication networks. Although the codes and standards establish the minimum quality of construction with a primary intent to protect occupants and property, they do not protect telecommunication systems from potentially disruptive external hazards. Furthermore, they do not necessarily provide an adequate electrical environment for reliable and error-free operation of the installed system.

Therefore, when designing the technology infrastructure there are a number of telecommunication standards, known in the technology industry as ANSI/EIA/TIA standards, that should be reviewed and followed to the greatest extent feasible. For example:

ANSI/TIA/EIA 568A: Commercial Building Telecommunications Cabling Standards

ANSI/TIA/EIA 569A: Commercial Building Standard for Telecommunications Pathways and Spaces

ANSI/TIA/EIA 606: Administration Standard for the Telecommunications Infrastructure of Commercial Buildings

ANSI/TIA/EIA 607: Commercial Building Grounding and Bonding Requirements for Telecommunications

ANSI/TIA/EIA TSB 67: Transmission Performance Specifications for Field Testing of Unshielded Twisted-Pair Cabling Systems

ANSI/TIA/EIA 72: Centralized Optical Fiber Cabling Guidelines

Although copies of these standards may be purchased from Global Engineering Documents, they are expensive and often written in a technical language and style that is most useful to those who are familiar with the industry and its associated nomenclature. *(See the Resources at the end of this book.)* Schools will probably find all the needed information from a technology consultant or from a vendor's specifications and catalogs. Be aware that these standards are only recommended design and installation guidelines. As such, they provide reference design criteria that may not always reflect the optimal design for a given condition or particular environment.

Developing Technology Trends in Education: Moving from Pilot Programs to Mainstream

Fundamental changes in technology as it applies to school facilities will continue at an even faster pace in the coming years as technology becomes integrated with other building systems, becomes more wireless, and as online learning programs expand. Various types of technology will be treated as more of an appliance, and less of a specialty. The following developing trends are expected to move quickly from small-scale experimental pilot programs in many public and private K-12 schools, to full-scale, mainstream implementation throughout educational systems in the near future.

Mobile Computing

As performance rises and costs fall, mobile PCs such as laptops, notebooks, and tablet PCs, are overtaking desktop computers as the learning tools of choice for progressive educators. With more mobile computing choices than ever before—from the highest performing notebooks to the value-oriented PDAs and pocket PCs—there is a viable mobile solution perfectly suited to nearly every educational need. Specifically, the "all-in-one" multimedia laptop designed with miniaturized CPU, LCD screen, stereo speakers, keyboard, pointing device, hard drives, CD-ROM/DVD, network or wireless interface card, and other accessories all contained in one 5-8 lb. box not much bigger than a regular paper notebook can offer desktop-equivalent performance with many advantages, including:

- Eliminates the wiring clutter between various devices.
- Reduces the chance of hardware incompatibilities and configuration confusion.
- Offers flexibility through its light weight, small "footprint," and portable "all-in-one" design, enabling anytime, anywhere learning.
- Acts as an extension of the classroom and school day. Students can work on school assignments seamlessly whether at home or at school.

Mobile computing seems to have promoted a fundamental change in teaching and learning. Studies have shown that students who have mobile PCs appear to collaborate more and can access the Internet easily and respond to individual or group questions quickly. Being able to target the information they need hones their ability to perform research and improves their efficiency.

Mobile computers have also changed the way teachers teach. Rather than delivering lectures, teachers can direct students in project-oriented activities and concentrate on curriculum development. Individualized active learning becomes a real possibility. Teachers also find the immediate access to their students helpful.

We will continue to see an increase in the number of schools that invest in laptops and tablet PCs with Wi-Fi® (Wireless Fidelity) capabilities. Wi-Fi provides short-range, high-speed data connections between mobile data devices and nearby Wi-Fi access points. *(See the Key Terms at the end of this chapter for more information on Wi-Fi.)* As wireless connectivity and mobile devices continue to mature, so will the software. The power of handwriting- and speech-recognition software will further mobilize technology users. Expect to hear plenty of publicity surrounding technologies such as 802.165.4 (low-power, low data-rate wireless), UWB (ultra-wide-band), and mesh network systems during the next few years.[5]

Wireless Connectivity

To a large extent, wireless technology has already emerged. The challenge is that it continues to evolve and improve exponentially. Many technology experts predict that in five years, at least half of the networks will be wireless. Here are some of the most compelling reasons for a school to consider wireless technology:

- **Mobility:** This is the top benefit of wireless computing. Combined with portable computing devices, wireless networking allows users to roam freely on campus while remaining connected to the school's network.

- **Expandability:** This is probably the second most attractive reason for going wireless, given the cost and difficulties involved in pulling wires and upgrading the infrastructure in existing or older buildings. By adding a new wireless network onto an existing wired network—rather than replacing it—cost-conscious schools are able to expand their technology options without losing the initial investment in infrastructure.

- **Flexibility:** With changing needs, schools are often faced with the demand of moving classrooms, adding portable classrooms, retrofitting older buildings, and reconfiguring computer networks. With WLAN (Wireless Local Area Network) technology, it is possible to connect portable classrooms, older buildings that have hard-to-access walls, and to change computer lab locations and classroom setups frequently and easily with little or no hard wiring.

- **Savings:** Eliminating or minimizing the need to wire and rewire can result in a significant cost savings for schools. Space savings are also possible with wireless mobile computer labs frequently taking the place of the older, space-consuming, hard-wired labs.

To understand the wireless options, one should be familiar with the various versions of the wireless standard IEEE 802.11, as established by the Institute of Electrical and Electronics Engineers. *(See the Key Terms at the end of this chapter.)* Standard 802.11 is an open wireless standard that specifies how radio frequency LANs send and receive data wirelessly. It is designed to integrate seamlessly with wired Ethernet networks and carry all the usual Ethernet protocols. Most WLAN products today are based on 802.11. Standards 802.11b and 802.11a, established versions of the standard, and the latest 802.11g version, with fewer compatibility issues, will soon become more prevalent. The three main choices for schools are:

802.11b: The first widely implemented standard and the most common wireless LAN option today. Because of its current popularity, it is likely to remain a standard for some time. 802.11b devices generally work within a range of 300-500 feet indoors, and up to 1,500 feet outdoors. The biggest drawback is speed—at 11 million bits per second (Mbps), it is considerably slower than CAT 5 wired networks. Also, because it operates at the popular 2.4 GHz frequency band (similar to cordless phones), 802.11b is quite vulnerable to interference. Therefore, its reliability is sometimes questionable for mission-critical applications.

802.11a: A newer version of the 802.11 that offers faster speeds of 54 Mbps, making it possible to access multimedia files such as streaming video. Because it operates at the 5.2 GHz range, which is limited to wireless LANs, it is less prone to interference than 802.11b. The trade-off is that it seems to have more difficulty penetrating walls and other obstacles. Other negatives include: more expensive devices, reduced range (they work best within 100 feet), and backward-incompatibility with most 802.11b systems. This last issue is being addressed by a number of companies with the creation of "dual-mode" wireless access points that are compatible with both 802.11b and 802.11a adapters, allowing individual computers to be upgraded gradually. For these reasons, 802.11a is mostly used for point-to-point wireless access, connecting nearby buildings to one another.

802.11g: The newest standard, receiving lots of attention. It is compatible with and operates in the same frequency band as 802.11b, but has improved security features and speeds comparable to 802.11a. Most observers expect costs for 802.11g to fall as it gains widespread acceptance as the wireless solution for applications that require higher bandwidth.

Although a number of security measures were built into the 802.11 standard, wireless security concerns remain on top of most technology planners' lists. It is universally acknowledged that a wireless network is considerably less secure than a wired network. A number of vulnerabilities can allow hackers to gain access to a school's wireless network. While such "whacking" (wireless hacking) is often used as a way to gain free Internet access, the same security loopholes can also potentially be used to access restricted information, alter school records, or compromise school LANs.

A new security standard (to be called IEEE 802.11i) is now being formulated, as of the printing of this book. In the meantime, schools should consider and utilize a variety of interim security options, including improving encryption schemes, restricting access to sensitive data to wired users only, installing firewalls, and using Virtual Private Networks (VPN). At the same time, it is important to recognize that increased security generally involves many trade-offs—in terms of convenience, cost, speed, and time required to make judicious upgrades, change passwords, and administer the security protocols needed to maintain acceptable user friendliness and work efficiency.

As with any technology in education, the key to successful implementation of wireless computing involves planning, staff training, partnerships, community-wide support, and a focus on what is really important: empowering students to learn and grow.

While wireless technology offers many obvious benefits, the concerns about speed, interference, range limitation, incompatibility, and even the alleged health risk of radio frequency radiation[6] should be carefully evaluated. Even more serious are security risks. With the IEEE working to improve the wireless security measures, we can expect more changes to come in the near future. However, in the meantime, a school should consider the following recommendations:

- Until the wireless technology is more fully developed, it generally serves better as an add-on rather than a replacement for wired networks.
- For high-bandwidth tasks, a wired Ethernet network connected with a fiber backbone is still the best option at this point. The wireless portion of the network should be designed only for lower-bandwidth applications.
- Access points (APS) should be carefully planned and located to minimize interference and improve reliability. It is also important to limit the number of users per access point.
- Firewalls and other security protocols should be used to separate wired and wireless networks from one another. It is important to understand the performance trade-offs. Always take advantage of the viable built-in security features in the wireless system. Additionally, schools should look toward user authentication, SSL (Secure Socket Layer), and VPN technologies to secure remote mobile access.

Online Learning: Schooling Without Walls

Online schools mark the progressive movement of today's educational technology. As demands for choice and flexibility in education increase, online programs are ever more in demand. While most of the contemporary online classes focus primarily on high school (or higher education) students, it is conceivable that once practical course development and delivery systems become viable, there will soon be more courses offered to children of all ages.

Online schools are being developed in both the public and private sectors in different formats and sizes. They serve students from a wide variety of backgrounds, but all share the same concept in terms of school design—a virtual learning environment without walls. The idea that a good education can only be delivered within a brick-and-mortar school building is being seriously questioned. Online schools eradicate the barriers of distance and bring opportunities to students anywhere, anytime.

Just like a traditional brick-and-mortar school, an online program has its unique qualities. Properly designed and developed, it can deliver courses just as robust and challenging as a traditional school. Its scalable class sizes, scheduling flexibility, wider range of elective offerings, and unlimited access to courses are among the advantages over a traditional classroom. A student located anywhere in the world, with a computer and Internet access, can take advantage of online programs.

Online schools not only supplement the lessons at the district level, they also provide an alternative method of delivering education. These programs often work collaboratively with school districts around the country to afford students with courses otherwise unavailable at their local school district. Online programs focus not just on students who need to advance or accelerate, but also look at ways to support students who are at risk, home-schooled, homebound, hospitalized, or otherwise not participating in the traditional classroom. These programs can level the playing field for students in high-need or overcrowded communities that do not have the same resources as more affluent schools.

The virtual classroom can be operated either *asynchronously* (students can take a course at anytime, anywhere), or *synchronously* (students and teachers are required to log in at the same time). Many asynchronous courses allow students to complete their assignments at their own pace, but require periodic progress report submissions. Final exams are usually proctored at a specific location or test center and administered by school staff.

Technology support is crucial to the success of an online school. It is no longer a 9:00 AM to 3:00 PM model of education, and operations must be maintained 24/7. Web sites, servers, and data storage must have redundancy in their design. The technology service and maintenance is usually better if outsourced to professional IT firms with uninterrupted support capacity. Once the online classroom is set up, it should be secured by firewalls against hackers. Until now, schools that offer Internet access have been concerned primarily with filtering content to protect students from accessing harmful sites. With online learning, schools also need to be vigilant in safeguarding and preventing unauthorized strangers from entering the virtual classroom. A thorough and detailed security protocol must be established to scrutinize all visitors—to protect both the integrity of systems and the safety of the legitimate users.

Equitable access to technology is another consideration. Portable computers can be made available to online students through community partnerships, which may also offer discounted Internet connection to their families. Other programs require students to complete their course work at school computer labs, public libraries, or community centers. In this case, computer labs may need to be open after school and on weekends.

Still in their formative years, online classrooms are quickly being developed around the world with much interest. However, even the most passionate online classroom proponents should acknowledge that online schooling is not yet able to substitute for all the functions or courses offered by a conventional brick-and-mortar school. It is certainly not a universal remedy to cure all the problems in the K-12 schools. However, with sufficient support and careful planning, online education can be a powerful tool, one that provides a viable alternative to school administrators confronted with overwhelming challenges, such as the need to accommodate individual learning styles, a shifting student population, decreasing operating budgets, aging facilities, and diminishing capital improvement funding.

Case Study

Following are examples of two schools that are providing online courses to students throughout the world.

The Virtual High School
Maynard, MA

(http://www.govhs.org/website.nsf)

Overview:

The Virtual High School (VHS) operates as a non-profit organization that provides an online education service to participating schools. The service provides accredited online courses that students can take as a supplement to their traditional classroom courses. In the 2003 school year, 1,500-2,000 students in 21 states in the U.S., as well as students in several other countries, were involved in the VHS program. VHS currently offers 127 different student level courses, with 162 schools participating.

The program includes an online teacher trained in the VHS program and software and responsible for developing and teaching the class. The teacher is able to post messages and assignments to the class on a day-to-day basis and can communicate to the class as a whole, or to individuals privately. Another important component of the program is a site coordinator, who is also trained in the VHS program and who physically monitors the students at their particular schools. The site coordinator assists the students with trouble-shooting and works closely with the guidance department to monitor student involvement.

Enrolled students use a computer lab to access online courses during a period that has been set aside for the VHS program. During this period, multiple students can take many different courses. The program offers flexibility by being accessible at the school during free time throughout the day and at home after school for those who have access to a computer and the Internet.

Florida Virtual School
Orlando, FL

(http://www.flvs.net)

Overview:

The Florida Virtual School (FLVS) offers a different approach to online schooling. The FLVS is a statewide, Internet-based public school, fully funded by the Florida Education Finance Program (FEFP). It serves the state of Florida, offering virtual education options for grades 7-12, as well as adults seeking GED equivalents. The program is available to public, private, and home-schooled students. It is free to Florida students, and offered to non-Florida students on a tuition basis. The program offered 75 courses during 2003-2004, including honors and advanced placement courses.

FLVS teachers are certified, develop their own courses, and instruct them. Teachers communicate with students and parents on a regular basis via telephone, e-mail, online chats, instant messaging, and discussion forums. The program also provides online help and tutoring through a support staff, 24 hours a day. It does not require a site coordinator. Instead, it encourages the students to be more independent and to trouble-shoot problems themselves.

The main difference between the two programs is their approach to online schooling. The VHS works with school systems as an outside resource. For the program to work properly, an additional component is added to the traditional school to provide monitoring of both the virtual and physical components. Alternatively, the FLVS is actually part of the public school system. Although the program currently functions as a supplement to traditional classes, it is working toward a system that will allow students to earn a diploma entirely online.

One-to-One Computing

Technological equity will not occur if some students are relegated to drill-and-practice programs, while others use technology tools for creative and exploratory applications. To promote meaningful learning, all students must have access to the same kinds of education technology and opportunities. To bridge the digital divide and take full advantage of the emerging trends in school technology integration, one-to-one computing seems to be unavoidable. To make technology a universal educational tool, just like pencil and paper, true one-to-one computing, accessible and available anywhere and anytime, will be essential.

Today's students grow up in a digital environment full of sights and sounds swiftly transmitted by televisions, computers, video games, the Internet, cell phones, PDAs, e-mail, instant messaging, and more. These "digital students" respond to sensory input so differently that some might even argue that constant exposure to multi-sensory signals actually changes how students learn, retain, and use information. They often multitask in ways previous generations could never imagine. It is not unusual to see today's student using a phone, instant messaging, and the Internet to collaborate on homework, all while watching television.

Unfortunately, many classrooms that are based on pencil, paper, lectures, textbooks, review, and tests do not provide multi-sensory stimulation. In fact, research by the National Center for Educational Statistics *(See Resources at the end of this book.)* reveals that decreasing numbers of 12th grade students think that school is interesting or relevant. *(See Figure 3.4.)*

To break through the digital dissimilation between school and students, some schools have begun to make multimedia laptops available to every

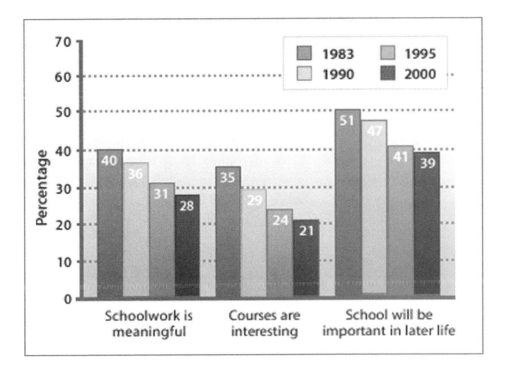

Figure 3.4

Interest in School
Percentage of 12th graders who expressed various opinions about their school experience: 1983, 1990, 1995, and 2000.[7]

Credit: National Center for Educational Statistics (NCES)

student. These laptops are connected via wired or wireless networks and Internet. They are portable and accessible, at school or home, indoors or out. This new digital tool might just provide a new opportunity to engage students and make education relevant again. Here are some of the successful examples:

> Felton Laboratory School in Orangeburg, South Carolina, claims they have seen both students' and teachers' research skills improve since one-to-one computing was introduced, with 100% of both groups showing improvement on pre- and post-assessments of technology skills, plus an increase in student motivation, with parental involvement at an all-time high.

> Carmen Arace, an inner-city middle school in Bloomfield, Connecticut, reports that student suspensions dropped from 432 to 85, with tardiness levels dropping almost to zero.

> Hancock High School, in a rural area of Southern Mississippi on the Gulf Coast, reports that their school attendance improved by 40% in one year, with educators reporting much higher levels of student motivation.

> Crossroads Middle School, an alternative school in Meridian, Idaho, uses laptops for students who had dropped out of school. Jim Core, a Crossroads teacher, noted, "Our at-risk students are motivated to attend class again, and they have overcome most of the fears about their basic educational skills that put them at risk. The improvement has been quick, significant, and lasting."[8]

K-12 schools, public or private, will soon realize the benefits of one-to-one computing, and more importantly, its cause for the true transformation of the technology integration in schools and beyond. Achieving this goal, however, can be costly and require a forward-thinking vision and an enormous amount of effort in planning, implementation, training, and support.

Integrated Network

To support various building functions, today's school building is likely to have several other separate networks (in addition to the data network) that are less glamorous but equally important, such as: telephone (voice), cable or closed circuit TV (video), master clock, paging and intercom, fire alarm, security alarm, access control, temperature control, and energy management system. Each of these systems is typically independent of the others, with dedicated wiring and controls designed for a specific application. The design, installation, operation, monitoring, and maintenance of these systems are seldom combined or interoperable.

As technology advances, the idea of "integrated networking"—where traffic from dissimilar applications and networks converges onto one single, unified, telecommunication network infrastructure—seems to be sensible. Technically, the convergence has already begun. The merging of voice, data, and video onto one secure IP (Internet Protocol) based network is one important, pioneering stride. Through convergence, it is possible to eliminate redundant networks and achieve enhanced communications. For example, migrating to an IP-based telephony system makes it possible to bring video-conferencing, e-learning, and real-time collaboration to the convenience of every computer station. Simplified networks will be easier to maintain and the quality of service, availability, and security easier to manage.

Network convergence has been a technology industry ambition for many years. It brings the promise of significant cost savings through:

- Reduced cabling/pathway costs
- Reduced space requirements
- Simplified documentation
- Simplified management

However, the benefits of a functional converged network go well beyond simple cost reduction. With all of the support and interest in this technology, it goes to the heart of sustainable improvement for today's education. The proliferation of the Internet, IP-based education applications and school business administration, security, and high-performance building design has actually propelled the need for a "smart" school facility.

A quality, sustainable IP network, combined with robust call handling features, can combine with IP-based education applications in remarkable ways to achieve major improvements in schools. This is one critically important step in moving towards designing an intelligent school building.

The concept of *intelligent building* appeared in the early 1980s. Although no one, formal definition exists, intelligent buildings are generally electronically-enhanced and technology-empowered. They are often new buildings equipped with a special structured network infrastructure to enable occupants to control or program (remotely or on-site) an array of automated building electronic devices by entering a simple command. For example, a principal away from school can use a wireless phone or pocket PC to arm the school security system, program thermostats in each classroom, or change lighting schemes, as well as check voicemail and e-mail, and perform many other tasks.

In recognition of the electronic aspects of an intelligent building, the technological applications in a school can be divided roughly into the following four categories:

- High performance (energy efficiency)
- Life safety and security systems
- Telecommunications
- Building automation

The ultimate dream in the design of an intelligent school building is to integrate the four operating areas into one single computerized system. All the hardware and software would share compatible equipment and structured wiring and/or a wireless network that could be managed on-site or remotely. Today, such full integration is still far from reality. However, many aspects of this concept are being implemented in high-end homes and private office buildings.

The concept of the intelligent building is well advanced in the U.S. compared to the rest of the world. Acknowledging the trend and benefits of an integrated network infrastructure system, ANSI/EIA/TIA has established a new standard, *862: Building Automation Cabling Standard for Commercial Buildings,* which specifically extends the benefits of structure cabling to building automation, building controls, building management, and security systems. This will be the beginning of a "Smart School Building" movement. At the least, with progressive vision, careful planning, and coordinated implementation, many building technology integration practices will certainly provide further reinforcement in creating a high performance school building as discussed in Chapter 2.

The Transformation of a School

The integration of technology into the educational experience has placed an unusual demand on school building design. Both the structural "brick and mortar" building elements and the individual spaces must be designed to accommodate the specific needs of technology integration. These considerations must be fully evaluated early in the planning process.

With technology integration, more schools will be designed with the understanding that learning does not begin or end within a classroom. Student commons, atriums, and learning "streets" (instead of corridors) become informal places that stimulate social interaction. Largely underutilized spaces, such as the library/media center, cafeteria, gymnasium, and even outdoor areas, can become additional learning spaces. Technology can readily deliver the resources that help maximize the utilization of these new-found learning spaces on a more flexible schedule.

Reinforced by technology integration, innovative school design ideas can be implemented easily and will continue to gain strength in the coming years. Schools need to transform themselves out of the "factory" mode and into learning environments that offer spaces of various sizes and functions, including:

- Project areas for cooperative learning by groups of varying sizes.
- Work stations where students can work independently.
- Conference rooms for private one-on-one sessions with a coach, mentor, or fellow student.
- Central gathering places and presentation areas for large group instruction and community meetings.
- Community resources and outdoor learning areas.
- Office space with computers, printers, telephones, and e-mail access to parents and colleagues where teachers can perform individual testing and counseling, organize individualized study programs, and perform their own research.

- A full range of social services in or near a school, such as pre-school, day care, parent education, health, and family counseling.
- Spaces that can function as a community center and are available for continuing education, after-school and extracurricular programs, community meetings, and sports and recreational activities.

All of the above seems to be leading to a "multipurpose learning studios" concept, where students can engage in different tasks in various activity zones or areas within a school. Interestingly, the concept bears striking resemblance to architectural school design studio environments where most architects receive their professional education.

The Changing Role of Spaces

Whether access to the school network is available (online or on campus), the function or existence of certain spaces in a school will be challenged or redefined. For example, because of the wide availability of computers, many have questioned the need for a separate computer lab. Also, because of the audio-visual and recording/replaying capability of today's multimedia computers, the survival of a separate, dedicated, expensive language lab is also doubtful. Some schools have already begun to combine the functions of a computer lab and other spaces to create a Project Lab. This technology-rich, multi-purpose lab can be set up for specific projects and can also be used as an open lab, Internet access portal, virtual school, and even for community education. (*See Chapter 5 for more on specialty space requirements.*)

Figure 3.5
Computer Training Room, Tantasqua Regional High School, Sturbridge, MA
This training room is used to integrate technology into vocational programs.

Photo Credit: Greg Premru Photography

Another example is the library. Electronic catalogs, book checking, and security systems are not new to a library. However, the demand for increasing multi-media-rich teaching and learning materials has transformed the library into a multi-media center. It is no longer just a depository for books and other printed materials, as it is often the school's gateway to the Internet and cable TV, as well as the nerve center of the audio-visual and data network. It is not uncommon to find a school's IT or head-end room for computer systems located in the library/media center. With the inclusion of various technologies, today's library/media center functions more like another form of classroom—it is a place for individual study and research, small group projects, and large group lecture. Therefore, many of classroom design considerations should be included here as well. *(See Figure 3.6 and Chapter 5 for more on libraries/media centers.)*

A major issue facing most schools is the administration and operation of the library/media center. Who will be responsible for this part of the facility? There have been two recent trends: the librarian as media specialist, and the science teacher as IT specialist. Neither situation consistently works well. Ideally, a media director with knowledge of both worlds would operate the integrated facility.

Increased Space Requirements
More than the traditional utility space will be needed to accommodate the technology infrastructure equipment. For example, a Main Distribution Frame (MDF) room is needed to house head-end equipment, which connects incoming private or public telecommunication lines with the internal network. Due to the limitation of the network cable run, Intermediate Distribution Frame (IDF) closets (which house cable

Figure 3.6

Library/Media Center, Athol Middle School, Athol, MA
The media center reading room is designed to function as a classroom as well. There are enough seats for an entire class, and computers are available around the periphery.

Photo Credit: Greg Premru Photography

racks that interconnect and manage the telecommunication cabling between the MDF and work stations) are also needed throughout the building. The server room, equipment storage, and repair room are also essential. Many secondary schools also have a radio or TV studio with associated control and editing rooms. In addition, space above ceilings and/or below floors (usually crowded with HVAC ducts, sprinkler and plumbing piping, and electrical conduits) must also be allocated for network cabling and cable trays.

Engineering system design must also respond to the specific demands of technology systems, particularly with regard to electrical power and removal of excess heat. Early in the design process, specific information is needed about the number and type of technology devices that will be installed in particular spaces. MDF and IDF spaces must be designed with adequate power, at the proper locations, and circuited to support the needs of the equipment. These spaces must also be adequately ventilated and/or cooled, to prevent overheating. Ductwork and conduit need to be laid out to avoid interference with one another. All of these items require careful attention to detail and active coordination among the technology consultant, architect, engineers, and school administrator.

Flexibility has been one of the priorities in many schools' technology planning. Although these technology systems and applications will undoubtedly continue to grow and change over the life of a school building, infrastructure that supports the technology is often difficult to change or reconfigure once installed. When feasible, it is important to plan for redundant power and telecommunication infrastructure at the outset in order to avoid costly moves, additions, and changes in the future as system demands change.

Transformation of Classrooms

Looking for maximum flexibility and taking a cue from the theater trade, some college campuses have recently developed a "black box" type of classroom. This classroom has a simple overhead structural grid fitted with adjustable theater-type lighting and moveable robotic cameras. Self-contained displays and classroom furnishings are portable and can be reconfigured easily. Access to the wired or wireless network and power are readily available throughout—above the grid, in the floor, and around the walls.[9]

Technology systems impose unique requirements on classroom design. New construction offers the most opportunities for incorporating technology. Existing school facilities generally lack standardization and provide less opportunity for changing the physical size or structure of the classrooms. These limitations may significantly restrict the technology services and products that can be utilized. Once dominated by "chalk, talk, and book," classrooms are fast becoming highly collaborative environments of technological devices, projects, and multimedia content. To house all the added electronic equipment and the associated activities, the average class size should either be reduced, or the classroom area should be increased by at least 10%-20%.

The furnishing and layout of the classroom must also be flexible and easily rearranged to accommodate the various learning styles: individual independent study, small group activity, lecture, and presentation for the whole class. The wireless network within a classroom certainly will have a distinct advantage, limited only by the available electrical power—either provided by extended batteries or conveniently located outlets.

Sightline requirements to accommodate digital projection and appropriate image display type, size, and limits for nearest and farthest viewers are essential design issues to consider. General-purpose classrooms should, in most cases, be designed so that the length is approximately 1-1/2 times the width of the room. The instructor should be located on the narrow wall of the room. Rooms that are more wide than deep normally present unacceptable viewing angles for projected materials and for information written on the marker board.

Increased Power Requirements

An increased number of electronic devices will impose additional power consumption and loads. New construction and major renovation should make provisions for a minimum of a 20% future increase in the electrical services in the classroom. The increase in heat generated by this equipment will also have an impact on the HVAC loads.

Electrical power should be readily available where technology equipment is located, without the use of extension cords. Each room should have one or more dedicated circuits on a breaker, not shared by any other room. The breaker panel should be on the same floor as the room, and each breaker in the panel should be clearly labeled as to its function. Power must also be conditioned for stable and reliable operation and fortified with surge and lightning protection. An uninterruptible power supply (UPS) back-up battery, and in certain cases, an emergency generator, are added requirements to ensure continued support of all mission-critical operations.

Better Light Control

To minimize reflections on the computer monitor, TV, or other display devices and to better control the artificial and natural light, indirect lighting, light fixtures with parabolic lenses, and window treatments can be added to the classroom design. Preferably, all window surfaces should be located at the side of the room, and not in the front or rear.

While correct lighting can be achieved through a variety of lighting fixture types, layouts, and control design, it is essential that all classrooms have a full range of lighting possibilities—from comfortable reading levels to sufficient darkening, to accommodate all types of presentation systems while still providing an adequate light level at the desktop for note taking. Light control switches should be standardized and clearly labeled as to lighting scenarios. Select a dimmable lighting instrument with fluorescent lamps for lower heat gain, lower energy usage, and an appropriate color temperature for video recording or broadcasting. As the classroom functions evolve into project-oriented activity zones, task lighting and more flexible lighting layout/level controls should also be considered.

Acoustics Design Considerations

A multi-media classroom environment intended for increased audiovisual presentation and communications also requires higher levels of acoustic design. Three basic acoustical components should be considered:

- **Acoustical quality**: Carefully designed acoustical ceiling and wall panels can balance the sound reverberation to support multi-media presentations and communications, but do not reduce speech intelligibility nor impede the instructor's voice projection over an extended period of time.
- **Sound isolation** between adjacent spaces: Increased multimedia sound levels often mean an increased noise level next-door. The classroom wall assembly must be able to attenuate the sound transmission between adjacent spaces. This is particularly important for school buildings that use gypsum wallboard and metal stud classroom walls.
- **Noise impact** of the mechanical and electrical system: Often cited as the single greatest impediment to teaching and learning in a classroom, mechanical noise (such as HVAC rooftop equipment, fans, air movement, etc.) and electrical systems noise (such as light ballasts) are extremely difficult to remediate once installed. Consider noise criteria in the performance requirements for mechanical and electrical equipment. Locate any noise-generating equipment as far away from the instructional spaces as possible. Wherever feasible, added sound isolation barriers and sound insulation can be useful as well. Regular maintenance and repair helps equipment to maintain good acoustic performance.

Convergence of FF&E and Building Projects

Technology integration begins to blur the line that used to separate building construction and FF&E (Fixtures, Furniture, and Equipment) procurement. For example, the built-in, multi-media-ready, multi-functional interactive whiteboard will replace not only the chalkboard and marker board, but also the projector, projection screen, large display device, and all the associated wiring,[10] This implies the promising convergence of AV and IT operations for easier management. It also suggests the shifting of a portion of resources from FF&E procurement to building construction.

Temporal Transformation of School Design

Transformation is not limited to physical form, but can be achieved through temporal design as well. For example, established in 1996, New Tech High in Napa, California, is a small 240-student, grade 11-12 high school. This school has an unambiguous mission of preparing graduates to contribute in the high tech economy. New Tech High was designated as a state and national Department of Education Demonstration Site and California's Model Digital High School.

At New Tech High, lessons are converted into content that is delivered over the Web or posted to a school server available anywhere, anytime. Every student has access to a computer, an e-mail account, and a Web site address for posting work. Beyond technology integration, this high school differs from any other schools by adopting a unique approach in its class schedule. The schedule simulates a modern workplace without bells or class changes.[11] This new approach in education has generated an opportunity to allow the temporal design of a school to have a significant impact on its physical form.

In another example, the Gary and Jerri-Ann Jacobs High Tech High School in San Diego, California provides state-of-the-art technical facilities for project-based learning, real-world (business) connections, and close links to the high tech workplace. The school was founded in September 2000 by an industry and educator coalition with a major goal of integrating technical and academic education. The school's program emphasizes team teaching, integrated curriculum, project-based learning, community-based internships, and assessment through presentation and exhibition.

There are a number of spaces within the facility to support this mission that are not normally found in a traditional school. These include project rooms (used for direct instruction and for project work), which are designed for maximum flexibility in terms of arrangement and use. Other spaces include work station suites that feature individual student work and computer stations and a "gallery" (a widened corridor) that links studio spaces to the rest of the school and is used to exhibit student work and for student presentations. *(See Figures 3.7 and 3.8.)* Glass partitions provide visibility between the project room, work stations, gallery, and other support spaces such as seminar rooms and labs. *(See the "Project Room" section of Chapter 5 for further discussion on this school.)*

Figure 3.7
Gary and Jerri-Ann Jacobs High Tech High School, San Diego, CA
A high-tech school may look very different from a traditional school. This gallery features work station suites and project rooms on lower level.

Photo Credit: High Tech High

Figure 3.8
Gary and Jerri-Ann Jacobs High Tech High School, San Diego, CA, Work Station Suite.
In project-based learning, each student has a work station in an open plan space, allowing project collaboration to happen naturally.

Photo Credit: High Tech High

Conclusion

School and classroom design needs to respond to changes in education methods sparked by the integration of new technology in the schools. The information included in this chapter does not reflect all the technology integration needs in all aspects of a school, especially in the areas of teacher training, curriculum development, business administration, maintenance, and support. It provides ideas to promote further discussion and better understanding of technology integration and what it implies for school planning and design.

Although technology in a school can offer many fresh and viable ways to deliver high quality education, it has not altered the basic goals of a school. The focus of technology integration in a school should never be the technology itself. Technology cannot, at least in the foreseeable future, substitute for good teaching—but it is a revolutionary tool that educators can employ to explore new ways of delivering education.

K-12 education started integrating technology with a focus on acquiring computers and building networks years ago. These efforts by themselves had little relevance to the actual activities occurring in the classrooms. Experience has demonstrated that technology integration did not happen simply by placing computers in classrooms. The problem, as stated by Robert Stolz, was *"Technology – Training = Junk"*.[12] Any program that fails to support teachers in making technology a regular part of classroom activities will fail to connect with the students. Teachers, in real life or in a virtual classroom, are still the key to a successful education. Technology can be a powerful tool only in the skillful hands of an educated teacher. Adequate hands-on courses, ongoing training, and technical support ensure teachers' success in technology integration.

Teaching at its best means making meaningful connections between students and teachers. Technology integration in a school not only enhances those connections, but also broadens them to places and people beyond the classroom walls. Technology revitalizes the learning experience by bringing stimulating new ideas to schooling. It redefines what a classroom should be and makes school a more engaging place. Schools are competing for the attention of a generation growing up with the clamor of the digital age all around them. Educational technology will continue to evolve. As educators and students learn to take advantage of it in new ways, both the systems and facilities will continue to change.

Key Terms

The terminology used in this chapter is further explained in the following list of terms. *(Another good online resource to look up for the technological terms definition is: http://www.webopedia.com, a user-friendly Web site that provides definitions to almost all the technology terms.)*

802.11
An IEEE specification for wireless networking in the 2.4GHz frequency range with a maximum 2Mbps data transfer rate.

802.11a
An IEEE specification for wireless networking in the 5GHz frequency range with a maximum 54Mbps data transfer rate. The 802.11a specification also includes QoS (Quality of Service) technology to protect voice and multimedia data.

802.11b
International standard networking technology for LAN wireless implementations that revised 802.11 to increase transmission speeds to 11Mbps.

AP (Access Point)
Wireless LAN transmitter/receiver that acts as a connection between wireless clients and wired networks.

Bandwidth
The amount of transmission capacity that is available on a network at any point in time. Available bandwidth is dependent on factors such as the rate of data transmission speed between networked devices and the type of device used to connect PCs to a network.

Bit
A Bit is the fundamental unit of digital communications. It takes a value of 0 or 1, and can be represented by an electrical signal. Communications between computers consist of strings of Bits. A small string of Bits can form a byte or a character. A longer string can make up a data Packet and its header.

Bits Per Second
Measurement of the speed of transmission of digital communications on a network. Most computer networks function at some multiple of a Million Bits Per Second (Mega Bits Per Second or Mb/s). Network communications are also grouped into bursts, or strings of Bits, called Packets.

Byte
A set of bits, usually eight, as a single character.

Key Terms (cont.)

Client
Wireless device that accesses the WLAN. Can be a computer, PDA, or other hand-held device with a wireless connection.

Digital Divide
The inequity that arises when some students have access to home computers, and others do not.

Ethernet
The predominant wired LAN technology standardized in the IEEE 802.3 specification.

IEEE (Institute of Electrical and Electronics Engineers)
A professional society serving electrical engineers through its publications, conferences, and standards development activities.

Instant Messaging (IM)
A type of communications service that enables users to create a kind of private chat room with other individuals in order to communicate in real time over the Internet, analogous to a telephone conversation but using text-based, not voice-based, communication. Typically, the instant messaging system alerts users when someone on their private list is online. Users can then initiate a chat session with that particular individual.

IP (Internet Protocol)
The Internet standard protocol that defines the Internet datagram as the unit of information passed across the Internet. It provides the basis of a best-effort packet delivery service. The Internet protocol suite is often referred to as TCP/IP because IP is one of the two fundamental protocols.

Local Area Network (LAN)
A Local Area Network (LAN) is a network that connects computers, printers, and perhaps other devices within a department, building, or house. LANs are generally fairly simple networks, although they can grow fairly large.

Mbps
Millions of Bits Per Second, or Megabits Per Second (Mbps), is the measurement of bandwidth on a telecommunication medium. Bandwidth is also sometimes measured in Kbps (kilobits per second), or Gbps (billions of bits per second).

Mesh
Mesh is a network topology in which devices are connected with many redundant interconnections between network nodes. In a true mesh topology, every node has a connection to every other node in the network. There are two types of mesh topologies: full mesh and partial mesh. *Full mesh topology* occurs when every

node has a circuit connecting it to every other node in a network. Full mesh is very expensive to implement, but yields the greatest amount of redundancy, so in the event that one of those nodes fails, network traffic can be directed to any of the other nodes. Full mesh is usually reserved for backbone networks. *Partial mesh topology* is less expensive to implement and yields less

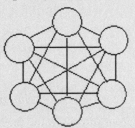

redundancy than full mesh topology. With partial mesh, some nodes are organized in a full mesh scheme, but others are only connected to one or two in the network. Partial mesh topology is commonly found in peripheral networks connected to a full-meshed backbone.

Mesh Diagram

MHz
The MHz, or Megahertz, is a unit of either electromagnetic or alternating current wave frequency equal to one thousand million hertz. The GHz is most commonly used to determine the frequency of ultra-high-frequency (UHF) and microwave electromagnetic signals. GHz is also used in some computers to reflect microprocessor clock speed. Other units of frequency are the kHz, equal to .001 MHz, and the GHz, or gigahertz, which is equal to 1,000 MHz.

Multiplexer
A device that allows multiple logical signals to be transmitted simultaneously across a single physical channel.

Packet
Data is transmitted over a network in groups or bursts called packets, similar to a single sentence or phrase in a conversation. A packet will have a header that indicates where it is from and where it is going. This header is used along the way for routing and is used by other computers to identify packets addressed to them.

RF (Radio Frequency)
Radio Frequency (RF) refers to alternating current that, if put into an antenna, would produce an electromagnetic field suitable for wireless broadcasting and/or communications. The frequencies cover a large portion of the electromagnetic radiation spectrum, varying from 9 kHz, the lowest allocated wireless frequency, to several thousand GHz. When an RF current is placed into an antenna, it creates an electromagnetic field that broadcasts

through space. All RF fields have wavelengths inversely proportional to their frequency. Standard wireless LAN networks use RF technology.

SSL (Secure Sockets Layer)

A protocol developed for transmitting private documents via the Internet. SSL works by using a private key to encrypt data that is transferred over the SSL connection. Many Web sites use the protocol to obtain confidential user information, such as credit card numbers. By convention, URLs that require an SSL connection start with *https:* instead of *http:*

Another protocol for transmitting data securely over the World Wide Web is *Secure HTTP (S-HTTP)*. Whereas SSL creates a secure connection between a client and a server, over which any amount of data can be sent securely, S-HTTP is designed to transmit individual messages securely. SSL and S-HTTP, therefore, can be seen as complementary rather than competing technologies. Both protocols have been approved by the Internet Engineering Task Force (IETF) as a standard.

TCP/IP (Transmission Control Protocol/Internet Protocol)

The basic communication language or protocol of the Internet. It can also be used as a communications protocol in a private network (either an intranet or an extranet). When users are set up with direct access to the Internet, their computers are provided with a copy of the TCP/IP program, just as every other computer that sends or receives messages also has a copy of TCP/IP. TCP/IP is a two-layer program. The higher layer, Transmission Control Protocol, manages the assembling of a message or file into smaller packets (see packet) that are transmitted over the Internet and received by a TCP layer that reassembles the packets into the original message. The lower layer, Internet Protocol, handles the address part of each packet so that it gets to the right destination.

UWB (Ultra Wide Band)

A wireless communications technology that can currently transmit data at speeds between 40 to 60 megabits per second, and eventually up to 1 gigabit per second.

UWB transmits ultra-low power radio signals with very short electrical pulses, often in the picosecond (1/1000th of a nanosecond) range, across all frequencies at once. UWB receivers must translate these short bursts of noise into data by listening for a familiar pulse sequence sent by the transmitter.

Key Terms (cont.)

Because of its low power requirements, UWB is very difficult to detect and therefore difficult to regulate. Because it spans the entire frequency spectrum (licensed and unlicensed), it can be used indoors and underground, unlike GPS.

VPN (Virtual Private Network)
A private data network that uses public telecommunications infrastructure while preserving privacy by using a tunneling protocol and other security measures. Using a VPN consists of encrypting information before sending it through the public network and then decrypting it at the other end. Organizations have recently begun to consider using VPNs to fulfill both their Intranet and Extranet needs.

WEP (Wired Equivalent Privacy)
A security protocol, specified in the IEEE Wireless Fidelity (Wi-Fi) standard, 802.11b, that is designed to provide a wireless local area network (WLAN) with a level of security and privacy comparable to what is usually expected of a wired LAN.
(See http://nct-services.ufl.edu/provided_services/wireless/glossary.html)

Wi-Fi® (Wireless Fidelity)
Wi-Fi® provides short-range, high-speed wireless data connections between mobile data devices (such as laptops) and nearby Wi-Fi access points (special hardware connected to a wired network). Wi-Fi is a trademark of the Wi-Fi Alliance, a nonprofit industry association. The IEEE technical specification for Wi-Fi is 802.11.

There are several variants of 802.11. The most common is 802.11b, which provides speeds up to 11 mbs. 802.11g and 802.a are faster versions. Many 802.11g and 802.11a products are backward-compatible with the original 802.11b. Range for Wi-Fi is typically around 100 to 300 feet indoors and 2000 feet outdoors.

References

Specifying Voice/Data/Video System Installation, National Electrical Contractors Association (NECA), 2000.

[1] Fielding, Randall. *The Death of Classroom, Learning Cycles, and Roger Schank.* http://www.designshare.com/research/schank/schank1.html.

[2] "Technology Integration." *Technology in Schools: Suggestions, Tools, and Guidelines for Assessing Technology in Elementary and Secondary Education.* National Center for Education Statistics, publication 2003, *p.75.*

[3] http://www.webopedia.com, Fig. 3-3 diagram.

[4] This designation is an Institute of Electrical and Electronics Engineers (IEEE) shorthand identifier. "10" refers to the transmission speed of 10 Mbps. "BASE" refers to base band signaling, which means that only Ethernet signals are carried on the medium. "T" represents twisted-pair; "F" represents fiber optic cable; and "2" and "5" refer to the coaxial cable segment length. (The 185 meter length has been rounded up to "2" for 200.)

[5] "The Remote and Mobile Sourcebook." IBM Leadership Development. ftp://ftp.pc.ibm.com/pub/special/haze/remote_mobile.pdf

[6] "Parents Sue School Over Wireless Network." *US National – Reuters.* Fri. Oct 10, 2003.

[7] *The Condition of Education.*, 2002, Source: University of Michigan, Institute for Social Research. Monitoring the Future 12th Grade Study: 1983, 1990, 1995, and 2000. (http://nces.ed.gov/programs/coe/2002/pdf/18_2002.pdf)

[8] http://www.thejournal.com/magazine/vault/A2852A.cfm

[9] Valenti, Mark S. "The Black Box and AV/IT Convergence: Creating the Classroom of the Future." *Educause Review.* September/October, 2002.

[10] http://www.smarttech.com

[11] http://www.newtechhigh.com

[12] Massachusetts Software Council, 1994

Chapter 4

Integration of Security

Drummey Rosane Anderson, Inc.

Although statistically there are relatively few violent incidents in American schools, those that have occurred in recent years seem to have been escalating in severity. As a result, safety and security issues have become increasingly important, not only to community members and school leaders, but to everyone involved in planning and designing a school project. Whether considering a new building, an addition, or renovation, security measures will play a significant role in the planning process. Planning for security systems should begin early, since it will be a large budget consideration.

Over time, security concerns have been more apparent in urban schools, where concerns range from theft, vandalism, and abduction to gang violence. However, recent incidents at Columbine High School and other suburban and rural schools have made it clear that a major security event can occur anywhere—in urban or rural, rich or poor, public or private schools. Schools are no longer facing simple issues of property damage through vandalism and burglary. It is necessary for all schools to consider security measures in order to prevent crime or violence from both outsiders and insiders. The safety and security of faculty and students has become a top priority, second only to schools' primary mission—education. The safety and security of a school has also become one of the biggest challenges for the school planners and designers.

Impelled by the Columbine High School incident, a tremendous amount of political pressure is forcing most schools to "do something." In a rush to find a quick fix, security technology has suddenly become a primary focus as schools strive to address security issues. While security technology may be justifiable where it is structurally impractical or infeasible to modify the existing school facility, it is by no means a universal solution to all security problems at all schools. Furthermore, many shortsighted decisions have failed to take a systematic approach to examining a school's security status and analyzing its real problems before installing technology. Security devices, such as metal detectors, video surveillance, and access control, can be effective, but also controversial. In addition, many schools have found the need to employ security personnel or train staff to operate sophisticated security systems, adding to the overall operating costs of the school. Even with the best intentions, certain hastily installed security devices could be inconvenient, intrusive, and give negative impressions to occupants as well as visitors.

Crime and violence in schools is, to a large extent, a reflection of crime and violence in the surrounding community. A safe school environment requires a commitment from both the community and the school. An optimal security program must consider and adopt varying degrees of policies, procedures, environmental designs, security technologies, and intervention initiatives. No single tool can address all security issues, and no security program can be a panacea that works in every school. Specific issues that may influence the security needs of a particular school vary depending on many factors, such as the school location, building size, layout, community, demographics, security policies and procedures, and local law enforcement. The design team for any new or renovation school project should be well-versed in these issues in order to determine the optimal overall security approach. The design team should work in conjunction with school administrators, law enforcement agencies, and possibly a security consultant to develop a plan that incorporates appropriate environmental solutions and integrated security technology into the project.

Social Background of School Security Issues

The primary purpose of an education in Colonial America was moral and social training. During these times, the expectations for behavior in a school were extensive, well-defined, and generally respected. Teachers were authority figures and had complete control over their classrooms. Even certain forms of physical punishment were generally accepted. Discipline problems in the 1800s were mostly attributed to the poor conditions of early schoolhouses and to teaching methods.

School safety plans first appeared in the 1960s, when it was evident that the highest rates of school vandalism occurred in schools with aging facilities, obsolete equipment, low staff morale, high student dissatisfaction, and heavy financial burdens placed on the school.[1] From the 1960s to the 1970s, fueled by societal changes such as substance abuse, dysfunctional families, and changing values, many students found the school atmosphere to be distrustful, limiting, and frustrating. The erosion of *in loco parentis*[2] power of schools imposed a lasting negative impact on both teachers and students. Increasingly disruptive behavior became tolerated in schools. This led to a clear shift from simple disruptions to actual crimes. Increasing divorce rates, single-parent families, and mothers entering the workforce in unprecedented numbers during the 1980s and 1990s further reduced parental supervision.

Potentially insurmountable social issues are not the topic of this chapter. However, there are some essential steps that can be taken to understand a school's security needs regardless of societal problems. Perhaps the most crucial step is a clear audit of security capabilities and vulnerabilities. Most audits are likely to demonstrate that the depth of a school's vulnerability can be traced to policies, procedures, and user habits, rather than environmental design and technology deficiencies. The policies, procedures, and human behaviors that create gaping holes in security are not the focus of this chapter, which will focus on environmental design and security technology-related issues.

Effectiveness, affordability, and acceptability are difficult trade-offs in establishing appropriate security measures for a school. Occasionally, a seemingly ineffective solution to a security problem is chosen because of lack of funding. Most major changes to security policies, including the introduction of technologies, are often brought on not by careful analysis and foresight, but as a hasty response to an undesirable incident. Relying on technology as a "quick fix" to a security problem without appropriate preparation and communication can sometimes generate a climate of fear and distrust. It could actually undermine the social ecology of a school instead of having a positive impact on the identified problem. So how does a school meld security and education?

Risk Analysis

In the past, schools have rarely understood the need, nor have they had the time or resources to consider security plans from a systems perspective — looking at the big picture of what the school is trying to achieve in order to arrive at the optimal security strategy. Today, schools must understand what they are trying to protect (assets), whom or what they are trying to protect against (threats), and the general environment and constraints they must work within (buildings and grounds, community, and funding). This understanding will allow a school to define and prioritize the potential risks, and to consciously formulate a security strategy that addresses those defined risks. This strategy will likely include some combination of building and site designs, technologies, personnel, policies, and procedures that complement each other in solving a school's security problems within its economic, logistical, and political constraints.

Webster's Collegiate Dictionary defines risk as, "possibility of loss or injury." This definition reflects the most common way we view risk's potential materialization in a given situation as a threat. Risk analysis is essentially problem identification. It involves identifying the sources of risks applicable to the assets, assessing the probable impact of those risks, and creating a priority list of the more problematic sources of risk for specific and timely response. To perform risk analysis, a school should take the following steps.

Understand and Prioritize Assets

Assets include both people and property. *People* include students, faculty, visitors, and others directly or indirectly connected or involved with a school. *Property* includes tangible properties, such as buildings and grounds; furniture, furnishings, and equipment; books, supplies, and software; and built-in mechanical, electrical, and telecommunication systems. Intangible property includes educational resources, intellectual property, student records, and other pertinent school business administration information.

The protection of people is always a top priority under any circumstances. The measures taken to protect the property will usually be driven by the value of particular articles and by the defined threats. Though desirable, few schools can afford to provide a security program that protects all assets against all possible incidents to the same level of confidence. From year to year, a school's security strategy must be re-evaluated and revised to correspond to the changing assets, surrounding environment, perceived threats, and policies.

Identify and Evaluate Vulnerabilities

Risks or threats are those incidents likely to occur at a site, due to a history of such events or circumstances in the local environment. They include accidents, crime, and natural disasters. They also can be based on the intrinsic value of assets housed or present at a particular facility or event. A loss risk event can be determined through a vulnerability analysis. The vulnerability analysis should consider anything that could be taken advantage of to carry out a threat. This process should highlight points of weakness and assist in the construction of a framework for subsequent analysis and countermeasures.

A school must determine who or what the threats are to school personnel and property. Threats may include issues such as:

- Theft
- Weapons on campus
- Alcohol, drugs, or other prohibited substances
- Gang rivalries
- Fights
- Vandalism or break-ins
- Fire hazards
- Harassment and/or assault
- Accidents

It is important to determine how sophisticated (knowledgeable of their task of malevolence) or motivated (willing to risk being caught or injured) the perpetrators seem to be. Measures taken to protect against these threats are often driven by the characterization of the facility and its surroundings.

Establish the Risk Probability

Risk probability is a concept based on the consideration of factors such as incident history, trends, warnings, or threats, and similar events occurring at other comparable schools. It is critically important to distinguish what is truly "probable" from what is merely "possible."

Trying to imagine and address all possible sources of risk can be a paralyzing process. Moreover, a focus on the probable instead of the possible will help schools and communities concentrate on establishing realistic goals for achieving a security program. From a risk management perspective, this approach is much more effective and often better received by all stakeholders.

Determine the Impact of the Risk

Once the probable sources of risk have been identified, a rational assessment will consider both the probability and potential severity of a given risk event. For example, some problems may occur infrequently, but when they do, the results can be catastrophic. Other problems may occur frequently, but their occurrence is more of an inconvenience or relatively minor consequence. Instinctively, different situations warrant different responses. Under a given set of circumstances, the magnitude of risk is a function of the probability of an unfavorable outcome and the severity of the consequences of that outcome. Finally, in assessing a given source of risk, a school should also consider how much power or authority they have to control that risk.

Careful identification of risk is an essential and critical first step in formulating an optimal security strategy because, as mentioned earlier, few facilities, especially schools, can afford a security program that protects against all possible incidents. No two schools are alike, and, therefore, there is no single approach to security that will work flawlessly for all schools. From time to time, a school's security strategy will need re-evaluation and revision because the world around a school and the people inside will always be changing. In an effort to assist schools in assessing risk and identifying threats, the U.S. Secret Service and U.S. Department of Education have jointly published an excellent reference tool, entitled *Threat Assessment in Schools—A Guide to Managing Threatening Situations and to Creating Safe School Climates.*"[3]

Components of a Security Incident

A security incident is a security-related occurrence or action likely to lead to injury, death, property damage, monetary loss, or other undesirable results. The occurrence of a security incident requires three basic components: target, motivation, and opportunity. Removal of one or more of the components will prevent a security incident from occurring—and this is the primary goal of a security program.

1. **Target:** This component describes tangible or intangible objects of desirable value (real or symbolic) to certain people. While it may be possible in some instances to remove certain objects from a school in order to prevent a security risk, this approach is generally impractical or unrealistic.

2. **Motivation:** This component describes the desire or impetus of an individual to commit an undesirable act. Because motivation mainly involves a person's mental condition and process, it is the most difficult component to remove from a school management standpoint. Motivation exists in the realm of psychology, sociology,

and criminology. Although education and applicable social service programs can have a certain influence on a school's students, there are few actions (such as security deterrence) that a school can take to alter an outsider's mental state in order to remove the motivation.

3. **Opportunity:** This component describes the circumstances and conditions that permit a security incident to occur. Every security incident has its own unique set of opportunities, but two conditions are usually present: access to the target, and the perpetrator's perceived success rate outweighs the risk.

Opportunity is probably the one security incident component that is most likely influenced by any security measure. When developing a school security program, the first priority should be recognizing security breach opportunities, followed by the initiating appropriate actions to eliminate or minimize those opportunities.

Security Design Strategies

Once probable risks are clearly identified, a methodical approach to the security plan should examine possible solutions to each area of vulnerability, from the perspective of limiting the opportunity of occurrence by deterrence, delay, detection, and response.

Deterrence

The goal of deterrence is to create an environment that has a negative motivational influence and is perceived as unattractive to a prospective perpetrator. Deterrence should cause uncertainty or intimidation, therefore preventing or discouraging the occurrence of an undesirable action. This is the most appealing step in any school security system. Effective deterrents place psychological and/or physical barriers in a perpetrator's path and imply that there is little or no opportunity to commit the act without being detected or apprehended. The perpetrator's action is perceived as too difficult, risky, or the consequences too severe. Most security measures employed in a school are intended for deterrence. Sometimes, cleverly designed and strategically placed "make believe" warning signs or "look-alike" security devices (such as dummy cameras) can achieve effective deterrence as well.

Delay

In spite of best efforts, some determined perpetrators may not be put off by security measures and other deterrent efforts. In these instances, the next line of defense is to *delay* completion of the action. The longer it takes a perpetrator to complete the action, the greater the probability of detection. Additionally, the perpetrator must be delayed as long as possible to allow the response force to arrive. Barriers, such as solid doors, tamper-proof locks, fencing, and other physical security obstacles, are all devices that could hinder or disrupt a perpetrator's activities.

Detection

Even the best program cannot guarantee total security. To prevent or interrupt a security incident, it is necessary to be able to *detect* an incident or problem while it is occurring. When a security incident does occur, early detection conveys the information to the security response force. It greatly increases the chances to interrupt the ongoing malevolent act and to apprehend the perpetrator.

Early detection can be accomplished by a variety of means and methods. During school hours, the best detection devices are alert, vigilant, and well-educated staff and students. After hours and in areas of the school not normally occupied, various electronic devices can be employed to detect malicious activities. These devices include motion detectors, intrusion alarms, or video surveillance.

Response

Once a security incident has been detected, the *response* force, whether administrative, police, or security personnel, must arrive at the scene and respond to the event promptly. Most schools do not normally have the capability for detection and real-time response to security incidents. After-the-fact investigation is usually the best a school system can hope for. There are three common approaches to achieve the response:

1. **Local police force:** This is still the popular approach used in most schools. Although there is little or no control over the monitoring or the response time, there is also little or no extra cost.

2. **Outsourced security firm:** Full-time, remote monitoring capability with somewhat improved response time, but with additional cost.

3. **Full-time on-site security force:** Physical presence of security personnel, monitoring capability, and immediate response. However, this comes with relatively high cost.

A combination of the above approaches is possible to balance the cost and the acceptable response time. For example, a school can hire a full-time security guard only for specific periods of time or for special events, outsource nighttime security to a private firm for monitoring, and rely on local police for most off-hours response.

It is important to keep in mind that varying levels of consequences for any undesirable actions must be clearly illustrated, explained, and communicated to students and staff and throughout the community. Otherwise, there is little or no deterrence to be gained from any security measures designed to detect, delay, and respond to a security incident. It is imperative, however, that schools do not assume authority that they do not have. Issues governed by law must be reported to the appropriate law enforcement agencies.

Physical and IT Security

In a typical public or private K-12 school, major security issues generally fall into two categories: physical security and information technology (IT) security. An effective security program must address both.

1. *Physical security* focuses not only on the protection of people and properties against potential assessed risks, but also on managing the flow of people and moveable properties into, out of, or within a school. Managing areas, perimeter intrusion, occupancy, access methods, internal and external facility monitoring, and containment are all issues that must be addressed.

2. *IT security* focuses on authorization for users to access network and associated IT services to which they are entitled and helps ensure operation continuity. These resources can include: roles on a network, permissions to access a database, drive space allocations, e-mail access, Internet/extranet and intranet access, and remote access privileges. This enormous task of managing resources can vary from person to person, and can encompass literally hundreds of thousands of items that comprise a network user's tools, allowing them to conduct business on a daily basis.

Except for the protection of the IT infrastructure and resources, most IT security resides in a "virtual world" and must be dealt with electronically. It is therefore not the focus of this chapter. The following discussion will center on the physical security measures provided by environmental design and security technology.

Auditing a School Facility

Routine security assessment can provide an objective review that would not be possible following a serious incident, when people may tend to react more emotionally. Checklist surveys are helpful assessment tools. Model checklists[4] should cover areas ranging from:

1. **Incidence history:** To help direct security efforts where they are most needed, an analysis of the school's incidence history can identify patterns and trends in the types and locations of occurences and perpetrators. Surveys of staff, students, and parents can sometimes yield additional information on unreported crimes and other problematic behaviors.

2. **Existing environmental conditions:** Any security strategy must incorporate the facility's inherent constraints. Answers to questions regarding the physical plant will determine the optimal security measures.

3. **Available security measures:** A school might already have invested in certain physical security measures that are still valid and can be incorporated into the security plan with little or no modifications. This section of the survey assesses the degree and effectiveness of the security measures employed.

Involve school staff, students, parents, community leaders, local police, and fire and emergency medical service teams in creating or adapting checklist surveys to the specific needs of a particular school. It is recommended that a school facility be audited on an annual basis.

Security Consultants

Employing an independent consultant to conduct a security assessment has several advantages, including objectivity, credibility, and expertise. He or she can give professional validation to existing security measures as well as recommending necessary improvements. Politically, seeking an outside opinion demonstrates a school's openness and commitment to safety and may also reduce its liability. It is important to check the credentials and references of prospective consultants and make sure that they are not associated with any particular security product vendors. Currently, organizations such as the International Crime Prevention through Environmental Design Association (ICA) offers recommendations for environmental design consultants. In addition, ASIS International offers a Physical Security Professional (PSP) certification. The PSP designation is a certification for those whose primary responsibility is to conduct threat surveys; design integrated security systems that include equipment, procedures and people; or install, operate and maintain those systems.[5]

For a nominal charge, an architect can survey the existing building and help a school quickly prepare a set of electronic as-built plans. Almost all of today's practicing architects and engineers use computer-aided design or drafting (CAD) software to produce design and construction documents for bidding and construction. These plans are the foundation for analyzing existing conditions and establishing a sound security plan. In many instances, the graphic illustration can clearly identify the weaknesses of a physical plant better than any other means. These plans are also extremely valuable to orient the response team in a crisis situation. The detailed plan data should be considered restricted information and stored on a secured server accessible only to authorized school administrators, local law enforcement agencies, building and fire departments, medical emergency services, and security personnel. CAD data should include at least the following:

- Overall site plans showing perimeter fencing, barriers, vehicular access routes, parking lot layout, neighboring conditions, and adjacent streets.
- Floor plans of every floor, including basement and roof, showing the interior/exterior accesses, and horizontal and vertical circulation paths.
- Building elevations showing window and louver sizes and locations.
- Mechanical and electrical plans showing ductwork layout and outside air intake vents, alarm systems, surveillance systems, and lighting controls.
- IT plans showing telecommunication cable runs, and server room layout and location.

A wide array of security measures involving procedures, personnel, campus modifications, and/or technologies can be considered for most concerns, always keeping in mind the unique characteristics of each school. Once the school's threats, assets, and environmental constraints are understood, security needs can be prioritized so that the school's security goals are understood by all those involved. However, identifying security needs and securing the funding to pay for them are usually two very different tasks. Depending on the available funding, a school must be prepared to have a "Plan B" for security program design that may have all the components as the perfect "Plan A," but with implementation spread out over time. If the desirable strategies (e.g., metal detectors, video surveillance, or locker searches) involve unaffordable installations or personnel, or are not supported by the community, a school may need to modify its options (e.g., fencing, restricting access, or bolting down all computer equipment).

Security Through Environmental Design

Schools are designed to achieve an inviting and open feeling, and to encourage community interaction. Schools should also be capable of resisting vandalism and closely monitoring access. Particularly in light of recent tragic events and public demands for increased security for school children, the question must be asked, "What is the appropriate architectural response to security in school construction?" More specifically, how should a school respond to apparently conflicting desires for more operable windows, multiple entrances, and the need for fortress-like security?

In recent years, a growing understanding of the relationship between the design and management of the physical environment and human behavior has been theorized in a knowledge base known as Crime Prevention Through Environmental Design (CPTED). Inspired by the ideas from Jane Jacobs' book, *The Life and Death of Great American Cities* (1961), and research followed by architect Oscar Newman in his book, *Defensible Space* (1972), CPTED is based on the premise that people's behavior within the environment and perceptions about safety are influenced by the design of that environment. CPTED, therefore, involves the application of a range of design initiatives and principles to an area or site that minimizes the potential for that site to facilitate and support criminal behavior. It aims to improve safety and prevent crime by designing a physical environment that positively influences human behavior.

CPTED principles have been applied in many community settings successfully. Unfortunately, most existing school facilities were not designed with this knowledge in mind. Now that safety has become a high priority in schools, CPTED can be considered when designing a school site or structure, when redeveloping a school site, or when responding to actual crime incidents. It is best incorporated at the planning and design stage of a site development. Examples of CPTED design strategies are described in the following sections.

Clearly Defined Territory that Projects Ownership

Physical design can create or extend a sphere of influence. Users develop a sense of territorial control while potential offenders, perceiving this control, are discouraged. This sense of control is promoted by features that define property lines and distinguish private spaces from public spaces. Examples are landscape plantings, pavement designs, gateway treatments, and fences.

Physical design can create or extend a sphere of influence. Clearly defined territory and boundaries project a sense of control and ownership. They deter intruders by forcing them to consciously trespass, rather than allowing casual entry. Defining a school territory and boundary is the critical first step in protecting its assets. Clear definition does not have to be intrusive or utilitarian in appearance. A good landscaping design will be able to provide visually pleasing and yet distinctively unmistakable boundaries by using elements such as gateway treatments, ornamental fencing, flower beds, groundcover, paving patterns, signage, and other landscaping components that fit the context of a school and the character of the neighborhood. *(See Figure 4.1.)*

Encouraging Natural Surveillance

Clear visibility is a design concept directed primarily at keeping intruders easily observable. Features that can maximize visibility of people, parking areas, and building entrances, include doors and windows that look out onto streets and parking areas; pedestrian-friendly sidewalks and streets; front porches; and adequate nighttime lighting.

School security is not unlike security in any public place where groups of people have an inherently positive effect on each other by providing accountability and supervision. Proper site and landscape design should ensure visibility from all points of access. Clear lines of sight should be maintained to secluded areas adjacent to the campus and student gathering areas, such as the main entry doors, playgrounds, and fields.

Figure 4.1
Greenhalge Elementary School, Lowell, MA
Decorative fencing and plantings are used to protect and define the school play yard.
Photo Credit: Greg Premru Photography

The design must also consider the benefits gained from the natural, desirable surveillance by neighbors, passers-by, and patrolling officers.

Inside a school, faculty and administrators strive to have students move around amicably. Straight lines of sight are useful for navigating, keeping the peace, and maintaining safe areas of passage. Straight corridors with clear lines of sight make everyone—students, faculty, and visitors—visible at all times. *(See Figure 4.2.)* Unarticulated straight corridors can often make a school feel institutional and unwelcoming, however. The sterile, institutional feel of a straight corridor can be mitigated by the richness of the spatial composition and the use of warm colors, pleasing materials, innovative forms, and appropriate lighting.

Figure 4.2
Lynn Vocational Technical Institute, Lynn, MA
Good visibility is achieved while providing an exciting spatial experience.
Photo Credit: Greg Premru Photography

Controlling Access by Building and Site Design

This is a design concept that helps prevent crime opportunity by denying access to crime targets and creating a perception of risk in offenders. Access is controlled by designing streets, sidewalks, building entrances, and neighborhood gateways to clearly indicate public routes and by discouraging access to private areas with structural elements.

Where possible, limit the number of freestanding buildings. In a school building, where permissible by applicable building codes, minimize the number of building entrances and exits. Ideally, having a single main entrance will support efforts to keep outsiders out of the building. Staff, students, and visitors should pass through an area near and closely monitored by the main administration office. In addition, the administration office should be strategically located to maximize supervision of key circulation areas. Satellite administration offices can also be tactically located near other secondary entrances or vulnerable areas, such as the cafeteria, delivery loading dock, or designated publicly accessible spaces. Adequate space should be allowed at the main entry in case a temporary or permanent screening operation is required. Other entrances and exits should be alarmed for emergency use only. Separate and controlled entrances should be provided for the publicly accessible areas.

A lesson learned from school shootings in recent years is that teachers should be able to control access to their classrooms from within the space. It is understandable that most existing classrooms were designed to be locked only from the outside, presumably so that teachers cannot be locked out by their students. However, this inconvenience should be weighed carefully against the potential benefits of delaying an outside intruder's action by controlling classroom access from within.

Protective Night Lighting

When designed properly, lighting can be an effective deterrent. It also enhances natural surveillance and reduces the fear and vulnerability of legitimate users. The type and quantity of lighting fixtures may vary from one school to another, but the goal remains the same in all cases. Where feasible, a constant level of light, providing reasonably good visibility, should be maintained during dark hours. Bright spots and shadows should be avoided. High-risk areas and areas that could conceal a potential intruder should be illuminated. Lighting also plays a part in creating a feeling of territoriality. A bright, cheerful environment is much more pleasing than dark and suspicious places. *(See Figure 4.3 for an example of adequate night lighting.)*

Target Hardening

Target hardening makes a target more resistnat to attack or more difficult to remove or damage. Target hardening is accomplished by features that prohibit or limit entry or access: security hardware such as keyed or tamper-proof window locks, dead bolts for doors, interior door hinges,

Figure 4.3
Night Lighting, Remington Jefferson Elementary School, Franklin, MA
Photo Credit: Greg Premru Photography

rock-guard shields for windows, use of fencing, and surveillance and alarm systems.

Zoned Building Design

An effective way to enhance school security is to use a series of clearly discernible zones to progressively control access by the public and, to a lesser extent, by school personnel. Four zones can be considered by a typical K-12 school for this purpose:

- A *public zone* generally surrounds or forms part of a school facility. Examples include streets or sidewalks, and even the grounds and fields surrounding school buildings.
- A *transitional zone* is located at the entry to a school building where initial contact between the public and the school occurs and access to more restricted areas is controlled. To varying degrees, activity in a transitional zone is monitored by the administrative staff or applicable security personnel. Entry beyond the transitional zone should be indicated by a recognizable physical perimeter, such

as a doorway or an arrangement of furniture and dividers in a more open environment.

- A *private zone* is an area where access is limited to faculty and students and to properly identified and registered visitors. This zone includes almost all classrooms and related spaces not specifically designed for the general public use.

- A *restricted zone*-is an area to which access is limited to authorized personnel and properly identified and escorted visitors. Examples are IT server rooms, mechanical and electrical rooms, and vaults for student records.

The public and transitional zones establish access conditions for the other more restrictive zones. To varying degrees, the line between zones can be blurred by the demand of more community use. A school can be designed to have a certain amount of building space available and accessible to the general public. However, carefully synchronized scheduling, unquestionably clear demarcation, and vigilant physical control are essential to maintain the integrity of school security.

Many school facilities, especially at the high school level, are being designed to provide community access and use. School function areas that will be accessible to the public, such as the gymnasium, fitness center, cafeteria, auditorium, and library/media center, should be located so that their visitor access and circulation can be controlled. Ideally, the links between the publicly accessible and classroom areas of the school would be compartmentalized for separate or after-hours use. *(See Figures 4.4 through 4.6.)*

Building Access Control through Master Keying

One of the most popular and cost-effective ways of access control is by master keying cylinders of a mechanical cylinder locking system. The master keying fulfills many facilities' requirements of user-friendly access, ease of service, and specified access limitations. It allows a school to determine various levels of access that can be granted to staff, students, service personnel, and the general public by issuing keys that can operate only designated cylinders.

The challenge is maintaining key control—the accurate accounting of all keys. This is recognized as one of the most important elements within a secured locking system. Unless the ownership of each key is carefully and continuously tracked, the access control could be compromised by stolen or illegally duplicated keys.

Building Smaller Schools

Statistically, smaller schools appear to have fewer security issues per student than larger schools. Students do not feel "lost" within a large population, and student movement within the school is reduced. Supervision is better since teachers know more students personally, and

Figure 4.4
*Tantasqua High School,
Sturbridge, MA*
Transition zone corridor linking
the school's public and private
zones with security gate open.
Photo Credit: Drummey Rosane Anderson, Inc.

suspicious behavior becomes more readily apparent. However, the trend over the last several years has been to build fewer, larger school facilities at all grade levels. Many school districts have been consolidating their neighborhood elementary schools into regional facilities. There is an economy in larger schools, since they typically result in fewer personnel, a smaller total building envelope, and reduced total energy costs. Middle and high schools tend to be large, centralized facilities concentrating many specialized functions. Some school districts are trying to return to the concept of neighborhood schools, especially for elementary grade levels. However, this approach can be expensive, and not affordable in many school districts.

One method for achieving smaller schools is to consider a "school within a school" (also called a "house" or "cluster") approach. This is essentially a larger facility, subdivided into a number of smaller clusters. Students and teachers spend most of their time in their individual "house," which is equivalent to the size of a small school. The library/media center, cafeteria, and other shared functions can be centrally located between the houses. This approach has the advantage of providing students with the feel of a small school, while still having an economy of scale. The one

Figure 4.5
*Tantasqua High School,
Sturbridge, MA*
Transition zone corridor linking the
school's public and private zones
with security gate closed.
Photo Credit: Drummey Rosane Anderson, Inc.

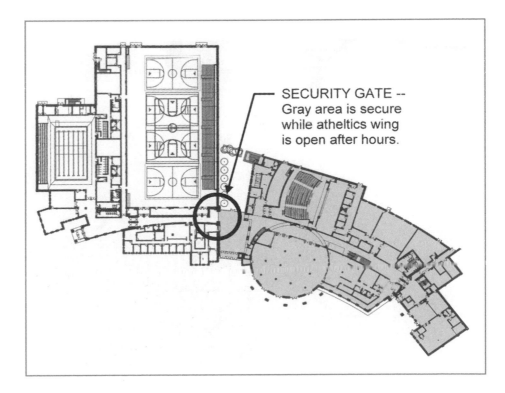

SECURITY GATE --
Gray area is secure
while atheltics wing
is open after hours.

Figure 4.6
*Tantasqua High School,
Sturbridge, MA*
Location of a security gate
separating the athletic wing on
the left from the private zone on
the right.
Credit: Drummey Rosane Anderson, Inc.

disadvantage is that this school would not be readily accessible at the neighborhood level, and would most likely require busing, as would any regional school. (*See the Case Study of a Cluster School in Chapter 1.*)

Humanizing the Environment

Many design approaches can be taken to make a large school facility seem warmer and more inviting to students, while still enhancing security. Some or all of the following methods should be considered:

- Human-scaled dimensions and proportions throughout the building, particularly in elements such as windows, doors, stairways, roofs, columns, canopies, and ceiling heights.

- A sense of continuity between the building façade, approaches, and entrance.

- Use of plants and vegetation to soften building lines and edges.

- "Warm" materials, such as brick, wood, and canvas.

- Daylight entering the building through windows and skylights; and views out of the building.

(*See Figure 4.7.*)

Figure 4.7
John T. Nicols Middle School, Middleborough, MA
A village design helps humanize the large-scale building.
Photo Credit: Peter Vanderwarker

Maintaining Environmental Orderliness

Too often schools underestimate the ultimate importance of environmental orderliness. Deterioration and disorder indicate a system breakdown and suggest that a school is incapable or indifferent about maintaining order. Based on the "broken window" theory (one window left unrepaired will encourage more windows to be broken), if a school shows clear "signs of incivility,"[6] it will become an inviting environment for the "undesirables," will eventually lose community confidence, and will become unsafe. Unattended grounds, buildings in disrepair, accumulation of litter, and widespread graffiti will make the faculty, students, and nearby residents feel increasingly vulnerable and will consequently empower the potential offenders.

The contributions of reliable, conscientious custodial staff to the order of a school environment can be significant. Because custodial staff members have access to and knowledge of a school facility, as well as exposure to students, they need to be screened and selected with great care. They often work on the frontline in combating vandalism and are a valuable resource in identifying the vulnerabilities of an existing school facility.

Physical Security Through Technology

Most existing suburban and rural schools were built at a time when security was not a significant issue. Consequently, little or no effort was made to incorporate security precautions into their design. This makes these school facilities extremely vulnerable to modern malicious acts. After several recent high-profile school tragedies with multiple homicides, many communities have urged school administrators to incorporate security technology into their safety programs. The use of security technology in a school facility should be considered as one of many components in a security strategy. Although technology devices alone are seldom effective and can be costly, they can be valuable tools when integrated into the overall security program. A complete, multi-faceted security program will have a longer and greater impact than technology alone. Its results can be measured, and it can be updated as conditions change.

The following section is designed to help schools, in concert with law enforcement partners, to analyze and suggest possible security technologies and physical designs to address security problems effectively. The overview of commercially available technologies in this section is intended to encourage thoughtful consideration of not only the potential safety benefits, but also the costs schools may incur for capital investments, site modifications, additional staffing, training, and equipment maintenance.

School administrators, planners, designers, and engineers should begin a meaningful conversation and collaboration with security professionals and law enforcement agencies to enable them to make better, more informed decisions on security technology.

School security, like security for other applications, is a complex issue. At any particular school, security is the product of funding, facilities, people, and policies. No two schools will have identical security requirements or circumstances. Therefore, a functional security solution for one school may not just be replicated at another school successfully.

Why Security Technologies?

Security technologies are not the panacea to all school security problems, but technology, such as cameras and sensors, can be an excellent tool if applied appropriately. These devices can provide school administrators or security officials with information that would not otherwise be available, decrease the need for security personnel on-site, and free up manpower and financial resources for more appropriate work. This approach can, in some cases, save money, when compared to the long-term cost of personnel or the cost impact of not preventing a particular incident. Too often though, these technologies are not applied appropriately in schools, are expected to do more than they are capable of, or are not well maintained after initial installation. In these cases, security technology is certainly not cost-effective. Following are several sound reasons for investing in security technology.

Inability of Long-Term Educational Programs to Address Immediate Security Issues

Today, schools are working harder to reach out to students to identify potentially dangerous personalities and develop appropriate intervention strategies. There are many excellent programs that address the policy, procedure, and behavior issues. *(See the Resources section at the end of the book.)* Even though these programs are being pursued expeditiously, unfortunately, they cannot all be successful instantaneously. Indeed, many programs must be initiated early in a student's life in order to be most effective. Not all schools have these programs or offer them to younger students. Meanwhile, security incidents must be dealt with immediately, perpetrators must be apprehended, and consequences enforced. School administrators need to discourage security infractions by means of available deterrents, and security technologies are an important tool being sought more than ever today.

Limitations of Environmental Design Strategies

Limited by existing site and building conditions, some of the environmental design solutions may not be feasible or practical to implement. This is especially true in the renovation of existing schools. Appropriate security technology may need to play a more significant role to supplement the deficiencies of the existing physical environment, such as multiple entrances or poor visibility windows.

Security Personnel Challenges

Simply increasing the presence of adults in a school will reduce the opportunities for a security breach. However, even this has its limitations since it can be difficult to locate and, as necessary, fund qualified faculty, parents, and/or security staff to assume security responsibilities. Training is costly, and the cost is usually not included as a part of the school's operating budget. Labor costs will certainly continue to escalate over time. Turnover of trained personnel can be detrimental to an established security program, and the mundane and repetitious nature of some security tasks can make it difficult to attract and retain qualified security personnel. Security technologies can address some of these issues. Through technology, a school can introduce ways to collect information or enforce procedures and rules that it would not be able to afford if it had to rely strictly on security personnel.

K-12 Security Technologies

Schools may decide to consider technological solutions to security problems when environmental design and/or the addition of security personnel and some programs proves to be inadequate, too costly, or infeasible. Before resorting to security technology solutions, a school should carefully consider the possible and unintended consequences. The presence of security technology equipment may reinforce fear, distrust, or even undermine the school culture. In some cases, it could also be mismatch for a particular security problem. The expenses of staff (to operate the equipment and to be trained), maintenance, repair, and upgrades all impose additional cost on a school's budget.

Following are some of the most popular security technological designs used by K-12 schools.

Video Surveillance

Strategically located closed-circuit television (CCTV) cameras can provide surveillance of entry points and other vulnerable areas and assist in the assessment of events, alarms, or access violations. CCTV can also support access control by providing a psychological deterrent. Video records may serve as an aid for investigating incidents of unauthorized access. Moreover, CCTV can be used for evaluating and improving access control methods and procedures by providing recorded information on critical events. Alternative measures, such as guards or patrolling officers, should be planned when the CCTV is out of service. *(See Figure 4.8.)*

Figures 4.8

Examples of Unobtrusive and Attractive Interior Cameras

Photo Credit: 123CCTV Security Cameras Surveillance Equipment

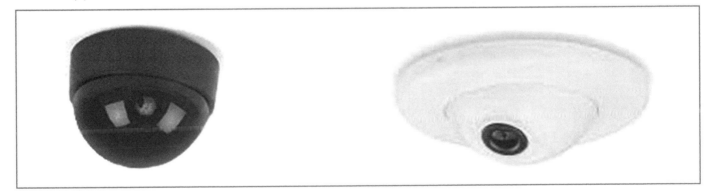

Companies have increasingly turned to CCTV systems as a tool to control costs while maintaining or increasing levels of security and life safety. In response to this demand, the CCTV manufacturing industry has developed a complex array of sophisticated, yet generally cost-effective and aesthetically unobstrusive systems. CCTV has three important functions:

- To deter criminal activity by the conspicuous location of cameras in high-risk or public areas.
- To provide an accurate means of detecting criminal activity or emergency situations, and to provide reliable information.
- To provide admissible evidence to aid in criminal prosecution or in defense of a premises liability case.

Videotaped recording is rapidly being replaced by digital video recording (DVR) technology. DVR can retain voluminous records for long periods of time only limited by the digital storage device. Digital recorders are replacing VCRs in providing schools with more options and lower cost, saving time and storage space. Internet-based systems allow off-site security or emergency personnel to tap into the cameras immediately and remotely. Declining costs of video electronics may allow schools to cover more territory more effectively.

While cameras are generally acceptable in parking lots, the main entrance, the front office, and hallways, they may not be used in areas such as locker and toilet rooms, where there is a reasonable expectation of privacy. Cameras in a classroom are somewhat controversial and often debated. Teachers' opinions should be solicited before placing any cameras in a classroom.

Warning signs that inform faculty, students, and the visiting public that certain surveillance devices may be in force can provide a frontline deterrence. Covert approaches to security can be effective and can also sometimes be open to contention, especially by someone who is caught in this way. Privacy and civil rights issues vary widely from state to state. Before employing any electronic surveillance program, be sure to review all legal issues with the school's legal counsel.

Electronic Access Control

Electronic access controls can pose both physical and psychological barriers and should be capable of recording details of access for audit (for example, time and date of arrival and departure). Unlike mechanical locks, electronic keys can be deactivated when lost or stolen. Electronic access systems can also alert security personnel of potential breaches. As these controls may be expensive, such options as personal recognition, use of I.D. cards, and mechanical locks should be considered first.

Once the number of entrances to a school is limited by its design layout, the process of allowing or denying access can generally be accomplished through the following four approaches:

- A security guard controls the entry, and ID cards or other means of identification may be checked.
- A special ID card or badge with automatic reader (credential-based design).
- A PIN number for entering on a keypad (knowledge-based design).
- A biometric device for feature recognition.

It is possible to combine several functions onto a single student's ID card: controlled access, library card, meal plans, debit accounts for vending machines or school store, and other services.

Card reader or personal identification number (PIN) keypads identify the code on the card or validate the PIN, but cannot identify the bearer. If it is necessary to validate an identity electronically, only credentials that call up information from a reliable data source are to be used. Biometrics, such as fingerprints, voiceprints, or hand-geometry, are features of electronic access controls that counter the threat of sophisticated perpetrators.

Access control technology eliminates the need to replace mechanical locks and keys in response to every event that might compromise building security. A school can simply cancel the authorization of the access-control card in question and issue new cards when necessary. Still, access control technology carries a capital expense that may be difficult to build into a K-12 budget.

Metal Detection

Metal detectors are an expensive and sometimes controversial option. Their potential usefulness for a given school depends on many factors: the severity of weapons problems, the availability of funding for staff and training, the physical design of the buildings, and possible effects on school culture.

Schools that have serious problems with weapons frequently use metal detectors to search students and visitors. A metal detector can accurately detect the presence of most firearms and knives, but only if the metal detecting equipment is used correctly by trained and experienced security personnel. A metal detector alone cannot distinguish between a gun and a large metal belt buckle. This weakness is what makes weapon detection programs somewhat impractical for many schools.

The walk-through type detector must be monitored and set up deliberately in a location to require all students, staff, and visitors to pass through. There should be no space for anyone to walk around the system and evade detection.

Hand-held detectors are more flexible and less expensive and intrusive than walk-through models. Their portability permits random checks at various locations. They are particularly effective in keeping weapons out of events that take place in a confined space.

The effectiveness of metal detection has received mixed reviews for at least three reasons:

- There are usually many weapon infiltration points other than where the metal detection is installed. These include open windows or exit doors that are ajar.
- Metal detection requires a significant amount of processing time and necessitates the staggering of students' arrival at school.
- Current metal detection technology cannot be automated. It is a two-person operation: scanning and monitoring; and responding to detection signals or found weapons. Between the equipment and the staffing, this can be an expensive proposition.

Electronic Intrusion Detection

Intrusion alarms are sensors that detect break-ins or forced entries into a facility. Intrusion alarms have two principal functions: to detect intruders after-hours or in controlled areas, and to signal monitoring personnel when a security event is occurring. These alarms are available in many different types. *Door contacts* monitor doors; *glass break detectors* assure an alarm is sounded if a window is broken; and *passive infrared sensors* respond by sensing body heat. Sensitive microphones incorporated into the system allow a monitoring station to hear the movement and conversation inside the school and relay that information to a security force. Well-designed security systems are engineered in such a manner that they employ the sensors that best fit the requirements of a particular installation. A good security system design focuses on high functional reliability and immunity to false alarms, and should incorporate modular components and simple operating elements.

Every alarm system has three main components:

- **Detectors:** Used to detect an intrusion into the protected area. Passive infrared (which detects radiated heat of an object) and/or microwave (which detects motion) detectors are most appropriate for most schools.
- **Control panel:** Monitors the status of the detectors and processes any alarm condition in order to activate the signaling.
- **Signaling:** Indicates an alarm condition. The most common signaling device is a sounder and strobe, and/or digital communicators. The alarm information is sent to a monitoring station for verification prior to notifying the relevant authorities.

Duress Alarm

A school may need to notify the security force that a crisis is occurring or is imminent when the regular means of communication are either not viable or restricted. There are three general overlapping categories of duress alarms that can send one or more levels of distress signals to a designated location.

- A *panic button* alarm: a push-button mounted in a fixed location.
- An *identification* alarm: a portable device that identifies the owner of the device.

- An *identification/location* alarm: a portable device that identifies, locates, and tracks the person who activated the duress alarm.

The panic button is by far the most common type of duress alarm presently found in schools. The simplest application would be that a strategically located button, when pressed, would send out a prerecorded message identifying the school, the location, and the urgency through a dedicated phone line—to designated locations (such as a security company monitoring center, or the police station if directly connected to it). The panic button has several disadvantages. It may not be readily accessible during a duress situation, or mischievous students may trigger it.

Proximity Alarm

Valuable equipment, such as computers, software, library books, or A/V equipment, can be tagged with infrared and radio frequency devices. Once removed, these devices will activate readers throughout a building, setting off an alarm.

An electronic security system provides important information, but requires a trained response force to address detected events. Depending on the funding and response time required, the response can be addressed by on-site security personnel (quick response, more cost), off-site security firm (less cost, proportionate increase in response time), or local law enforcement agency (least cost and control over response time).

A cost-benefit analysis should be employed to compare the investment in security technology with other school needs. Technology can be attractive, but it is not always the right tool for a particular security need. In some instances, technology can turn out to be unwieldy or impractical. The ease with which a system can be expanded, integrated, and upgraded is also a factor to be considered in response to changing school security needs and technology.

Why Security Technologies Have Not Been Used in More Schools

Although there are many advantages in security technology, many schools have experienced some of the following negatives:

- Initial cost for a comprehensive and sophisticated security programs is too high for most K-12 schools.
- Schools generally lack the expertise and are unable to procure effective security technology products and services.
- School staff rarely have training or experience in using security technologies, nor can many schools afford to hire well trained professional security personnel.
- Security technology requires repair, routine maintenance, and frequent upgrades for which most schools have no infrastructure or funding.

- Issues of privacy (and potential civil rights complaints) may prohibit or complicate the use of certain technologies at some locations and/or times.

As more schools adopt electronic security apparatus, the need for a workable console and a secured enclosure becomes an essential design element and an important consideration. With substantial and diverse monitoring and recording tasks, sensitive monitors and digital recorders have to be operational at all times. The control room's HVAC is important, as is quiet, cleanliness, and user-friendliness. The console must be ergonomically designed to allow a single operator access to all control parameters. A console that accommodates a computer/Internet-based system will have better flexibility to grow and to adjust to changing technology. The enclosure should be located within the school administrative area, have fully welded construction, and be rated to meet local building code and seismic requirements.

IT Security

While computer technology has transformed and greatly improved many aspects of school operations, the Internet and associated network technologies have also opened the door to an increasing number of security threats. Unfortunately, all school IT operations can be affected by computer security breaches of one form or another. The consequences of attacks can range from mildly inconvenient to completely debilitating. Important data could be deleted, privacy violated, and a school computer can even be used by an outside hacker to attack other computers on the network or on the Internet. Innumerable types of IT security threats have been documented, and are common in various forms of viruses, Trojan Horse programs, vandals, attacks, data interception, scams, or spam. The security tools to protect IT systems include anti-virus software, security policies, passwords, firewalls, and encryptions. Except for the protection of the IT system itself, most of the IT security protocols have little to do with the physical environment of a school.

Although IT security breaches can often be prevented by implementing appropriate security policies and procedures, and installing updated protection software and properly configured hardware, it is easy to overlook the physical aspect of IT security. Hackers need to be kept away not only from the secured virtual environment, but also from the secured real world. There are three simple principles to follow:

- Lock sensitive servers behind locked doors. Access should be limited to selected and authorized IT administrators.
- Activate computers' built-in security features to restrict access, as well as using external locks on the computer itself, and security cables to prevent theft.
- Keep network devices, such as hubs and switches, in locked closets and cabinets. Run cables through walls or above ceilings, and follow wireless vendors' security requirements to make the network more difficult to tap or intercept.

Additionally, the physical security for the server room in a school should consider using the following:

- Full-height fire-rated walls around the complete perimeter.
- Penetration-resistant wall construction.
- Windowless perimeter, with interior barrier for external windows.
- Door hinges located inside the room to prevent their access and removal.
- Motion, intrusion, smoke, and fire alarms.

Technology Integration | Integrating Physical and IT Security

In almost every school, a certain amount of physical and IT security is present, but rarely coordinated. In most cases, these two disciplines are completely independent and unaware of the strengths and weaknesses of the other's operation. Similar to the network convergence trend discussed in Chapter 3, several leading security hardware and software companies have recognized the potential advantage of physical and IT security integration and have established a collaboration called *Open Security Exchange*[8] (OSE) with a single mission: to create a vendor-neutral, open specification in hopes of paving the way for integrating physical and IT security management.

The collaboration's first step was to create an interoperability specification designed to illustrate how different products within a security environment might communicate and interoperate. To this end, the group developed a preliminary framework called, "Physical Security Bridge to IT Security" (or PHYSBITS). This data model is intended to help bridge gaps between these two areas. Interoperability allows different products to acknowledge each other and to make an association between different security objects, whether IT or physical.

Integrated security management has the potential to give users a consolidated way to monitor security events rather than tracking from several different independent systems. It allows a more flexible approach to track events linked to both physical and logical security. For example, if events are not linked, it could mean that a student may "badge out" of the school at 3 p.m., but anyone with his/her password can still log onto the network internally after 3 p.m. With integration, if someone badges out at 3 p.m., his/her internal network privileges will be revoked automatically and immediately. Anyone attempting to log onto the network with a stolen password will activate the alarm, alerting the security staff.

Integrated security management can have a number of potential benefits:

- Reduced administrative overhead through automation of manual processes.
- Enhanced security through a coordinated view of both physical and IT environments.
- More effective reporting and investigations through a centralized audit trail.

- Support for a forensic process through consistent audit logs of evidentiary quality.
- Cost savings through combining secure access authentication for both physical and IT systems.

Additionally, to be successful, security management practices must also be integrated within well-defined school business processes for administering people, facilities, and IT systems. Security technology, whether integrated or not, can support each of these processes, but does not define them.

Integrating Security and Building Automation

"Smart Buildings," in which security and building controls, such as lights and HVAC, interoperate, have been touted for years. Unless building controls serve life-safety functions, most experts advise their clients to integrate only intrusion detections, surveillance, access control, emergency response, and life safety systems. However, more and more manufacturers are seeking ways to link HVAC, life safety, fire, digital video, intrusion detection, access control, and asset locator pieces, and to track everything in real time.

Shifting departmental responsibilities should be anticipated, carefully coordinated, and defined among security, facility management, and IT staff. This will certainly slow down the integration process in some cases. Such integration of controls is probably more likely when security functions fall under the facility department's auspices. As security moves into Information Technology's purview, there may be less interest.

As integrated technology becomes more affordable, the time should not be far off when a teacher who needs access to a locked school on a weekend can simply swipe a valid ID card at the access-controlled front door. This action would provide security, log in the entry time, and at the same time, activate the building systems to a predetermined temperature and lighting condition and provide network access. When the teacher leaves, another card swipe will tell the building control system to deactivate the HVAC and lighting systems. In this case, the automated building systems need not be turned on or off by maintenance staff working overtime.

Conclusion

During the planning for a new school or renovation project, it is imperative that the key personnel who will be responsible for day-to-day security operations in the facility be involved in every step of the design process. Local responders (police and fire departments) should also be actively involved in this planning.

A well-designed building can minimize vulnerabilities, while still providing an attractive environment for teaching and learning. A security-conscious design can even help compensate for slower response times when local police and fire departments' performances are impeded by declining budgets. Developing a security plan early in the design process that is unique to the needs of the specific school community, should be one of the top priorities for any school project design team. Through good planning and an architectural design with integrated security technology, it is possible to not only enhance building security, but to also prevent or reduce the likelihood of the kind of violence that has been making headlines.

Given that most schools are unique, each of their needs should be looked at individually. Security measures that may be appropriate for large urban schools are likely to be unsuitable for small, isolated, rural schools. Some older schools may be housed in facilities originally designed for a different purpose. Some schools operate on split sites or on campuses consisting of a number of satellite buildings. Many schools also have dual use, accommodating functions, either in an adjoining community building on the same or adjacent site, or by offering after-school classes within the school buildings. A blanket approach to the installation of security measures in schools would usually result in unnecessary or inappropriate expenditures. A cost-benefit analysis should be employed to compare security investment with other school needs.

In considering the practical methods of security within a school, it is necessary to consider the effect that major security measures may have on faculty and students. A school should be seen by its primary users as a welcoming place, and the security measures installed at a school, while giving comfort to the occupants of the school, should not be of such a nature as to cause alarm. A balance needs to be attained between making a school safe and turning it into a fortress.

Important principles for security go beyond the environmental and technological design. This chapter focuses on physical and technological design concepts and does not address the equally important and corresponding security administrative, policy, and procedural issues. Along those lines, every school should prepare and publish a crisis management plan that prescribes procedures for responding to a wide range of probable crises. The plan should designate individuals to handle specific tasks if a crisis occurs, and establish procedures for communicating among school staff and with parents, community agencies, and the media. When preparing the plan, schools should coordinate with police, fire, medical, and other agencies and determine what local, state, and federal resources exist for crisis and post-crisis assistance. The plan should be clearly explained and distributed to all members of the school community, and all school staff should receive crisis training. Students and staff should practice evacuation and other crisis procedures as routinely as fire drills.

Effective school security planning and design is a complex process requiring the knowledge and skills of an experienced architect and a trained security professional in collaboration with school administrators, community leaders, and local fire, police, and emergency response teams. By understanding and applying the basic concepts outlined in this chapter, a school can at least perform an effective security evaluation of its facility and begin to take necessary steps to eliminate high-risk areas. It must be acknowledged that even the most vigilant efforts cannot make a school completely secure. However, a school can minimize the likelihood of crime and violence and alleviate their impact by taking preventive steps and preparing effective responses.

References

Defensible Space – Crime Prevention through Urban Design. Oscar Newman Collier Books, 1972.

General Security Risk Assessment. ASIS International Guideline Commission, 2003.

Physical Environment and Crime. National Institute of Justice Research Report NCJ157311, January 1996.

Threat Assessment in Schools – A Guide to Managing Threatening Situations and to Creating Safe School Climates. The U.S. Secret Service and U.S. Department of Education. Available at: http://www.ed.gov/admins/lead/safety/threatassessmentguide.pdf

[1] Gordon Crews & M. Reid Counts. *The Evolution of School Disturbance in America,* 1997.

[2] Latin for "in the position or place of a parent."

[3] http://www.secretservice.gov/ntac/ssi_guide.pdf

[4] For example, see POWYS LEA H&S Policy, November 2000 rev2.

[5] http://www.asisonline.org

[6] National Institute of Justice, *Physical Environment and Crime,* Jan. 1996, page 16.

[7] "Camera Watching Students, Especially in Biloxi." The New York Times, September 24, 2003.

[8] http://www.opensecurityexchange.com

Chapter 5

Specialty Spaces

Drummey Rosane Anderson, Inc.

Many specialty spaces, such as libraries, athletic facilities, auditoriums, and science classrooms, are components of most schools, while others are specific to a type of school or to special programs. Specialty spaces have unique features, and their design must be approached carefully. Specialized consultants, as well as the project architect, are often included in the planning and design. A design specialist will become increasingly important as the needs of the spaces are expanded or become complex. Before embarking on the design of any of these spaces, it is critical to listen to and work with the school's department members and program users to understand their requirements. This information gathering will help ensure that the space properly provides for the planned function, within the budget.

The most common specialty spaces include athletic facilities, performing arts centers (auditoriums and music and band programs), libraries/media centers, vocational facilities, computer labs, language labs, science classrooms, and art classrooms. These will be reviewed in this chapter, which offers guidelines for design. The chapter will also include a description of a *project room*, which is a fairly new and still evolving type of space. Very specialized, less common spaces, including health services, student stores, culinary arts, daycare facilities, television studios, and greenhouses, are beyond the scope of this chapter.

Specialty spaces within a school will add to the cost of a renovation or new construction project because of items such as enhanced finishes and specialized utilities and equipment. At the same time, however, these spaces can help the school facility evolve from one that meets minimum standards, to one that provides broad-reaching educational experiences and resources for the entire community.

Schools as Community Resources

When a city or town considers a school to be a truly civic building, the facility may be designed as a community resource. Often music rooms, athletic facilities (including pools and fitness centers), library/media centers, performing arts areas, and cafeterias serve the community during non-school hours. In addition, the school grounds may offer baseball and softball fields, tennis courts, or other playing fields for community use. It is important that faculty, staff, administration, and community members participate in the planning so that each space will offer the most effective, flexible, and comfortable environment possible, within budget constraints.

Private schools have a different point of view, since they do not depend on public taxpayers for funding. Some private schools restrict the use of facilities to their own students and faculty. Other private schools seek to improve public relations by making some parts of their facilities available to the surrounding community, as long as the safety and privacy of the students are not compromised.

By considering community use during the planning process, architects can design schools that welcome the community at large and enhance the educational functions of the building. Parents who feel comfortable in the building are more likely to take an active role in their child's education. At the same time, students can learn from the community around them, rather than just within classroom walls.

Providing for community use of school facilities requires certain design considerations. If the schedule of activities overlaps school hours, considerations for security, such as building access and circulation, must be addressed. If the public's access is after-hours, the building can be designed to allow certain zones to be sealed off from the other areas and to function independently. Separate entrances may be required, as well as careful siting of adequate toilet and other support facilities within the public zone. Large group use of the school by the community during the summer may require air conditioning in climates that might not otherwise require it during the school year. The site layout must ensure that there is adequate parking for athletic events and performances within a reasonable distance.

One example of community participation is the new high school in Belchertown, Massachusetts, a town with a large population of senior citizens. When designing the school, planners involved seniors in the design process, and thus addressed their needs. This resulted in an indoor, raised walking track around the perimeter of the gymnasium, allowing seniors and others to exercise during the day without disturbing physical education classes. *(See Figure 5.1.)*

Some schools also contain or are co-located with community centers or senior centers. For example, at the Mildred Avenue Middle School in Boston, Massachusetts, the school and community center share the same building. The community center includes resources such as a pool, radio studio, and teen center, which also enhance the middle school.

School auditoriums are used by many communities. Outfitted with acoustical panels, theater lighting, and a sound booth, an auditorium can provide the school and community with space for both amateur and professional musical and theatrical groups. Lobbies adjacent to an auditorium or gymnasium can also serve the community when events are held after-hours or on weekends.

In addition to the qualitative benefits that community use of a school may bring, partnerships with community groups can also bring financial benefits to the school or the construction budget. In many towns, community theater groups use high school auditoriums for their performances. These groups will often work with the planning committee to raise additional funds to construct enhanced facilities.

As schools increasingly look outside their doors to understand education in the context of the greater community, and as towns and cities look to expand their resources within limited budgets, community use of school facilities appears to be a growing trend. Organizations such as the Coalition for Community Schools are growing and are lobbying towns and cities to understand the benefits of seeing schools in a broader context. Considering these options early in the planning process may

Figure 5.1
Indoor Walking Track, Belchertown High School, Belchertown, MA
This walking track was designed for school and community use.

Photo Credit: Greg Premru Photography

bring additional rewards to both the school environment and the community. *(See the Resources section at the end of this book for more on these organizations.)*

Sports Facilities

Background

Sports facilities may be used not only by students, teachers, administrators, and staff members, but also by the local community. Sporting events may include basketball, volleyball, track and field, baseball and softball, football, soccer, lacrosse, field hockey, wrestling, dance, swimming, tennis, squash and racquetball, and fitness-related activities. If tournaments and other public events are a consideration, large spaces must be provided, including competition courts, practice courts, spectator bleachers, a running track, long jump and pole vault areas, a swimming pool, and an area for fitness equipment. In addition, large indoor athletic spaces, such as a gymnasium, are typically the only location that can fully accommodate the entire school population for school-wide meetings and events.

Programming and Pre-Design

Sports facilities require a significant effort in developing a space program. Numerous factors are involved, and it is important that the school building committee or representative, design team, and faculty and student representatives be involved throughout the programming and design process. School facility representatives should use the programming exercise to evaluate their needs for various activities and ultimately lead to the question, "How much space is required?" Issues that need to be addressed initially include:

- What activities are going to take place within the sports facility?
- What major event spaces and support spaces are needed/wanted?
- What will be the operating hours of the facility?
- Are there outside sources of funding available?
- How many students are expected to use the facility?
- How will the community utilize the facility?
- What facilities does the community currently have?
- Is there a need for spectator seating and support?

Once a list of activities, operating conditions, and budget requirements is established, appropriate spaces can be determined. If the anticipated budget and/or space available are not sufficient to support all of the desired activities, the school facility representatives, in collaboration with the design team, will need to prioritize the activities to be included.

A school facility may need some combination of a large gym or field house, a natatorium, and a fitness center for strength training and cardiovascular equipment. In addition to the major event spaces, support spaces must also be considered, which may include restrooms, storage rooms, locker rooms, mechanical rooms, and offices for athletic directors, gym teachers, coaches, and trainers.

The major event spaces will have specific requirements, such as minimum dimensions, mandatory safety clearances, and height restrictions. These requirements are established by various sports governing authorities. The National Federation of State High School Association's *Court and Field Diagram Guide* (NFHS Publications, 2000) provides a comprehensive contact list for all sports governing bodies, as well as a summary of specific dimensional and layout requirements for most athletic and sporting events.

It is important to resolve the space issues during the planning and programming phase. During the next (schematic) design phase, the client's requests become architectural elements. Making changes to the original program after schematic design can have a significant impact on the project cost and schedule.

Special Considerations

Each of the major event spaces will have unique characteristics, including the following.

Acoustics

Within a field house, natatorium, or fitness center, acoustic treatments will be needed to contain crowd and mechanical equipment noises. These materials should be durable, low-maintenance, sound-absorbing, and non-corrosive.

Lighting

The quantity and sizes of windows, along with the orientation of the building, should be carefully studied to maximize natural light while controlling glare and heat gain within the space. Typically, the number of windows in an athletic facility is kept to a minimum to reduce glare, which can be dangerous for athletes during competition. In addition, heat gain or loss from large windows can cause fluctuations in temperature, putting stress on the mechanical systems. Low-e glass, translucent panels, and glass block can be effective solutions to this problem. Clerestory windows, shading devices, and indirect lighting techniques are other ways of allowing natural light into the space without the harmful effects of glare, thereby allowing the use of more windows.

Environmental Control

Environmental control is extremely important in sports facilities. Humidity and temperature should be maintained at comfortable levels for athletes and spectators at all levels of occupancy and use. The diversity of users, attendance of many spectators, types of activities, and times of year that the spaces are used should all be taken into consideration.

Material Selection

Materials for natatoriums and locker rooms need to be carefully selected so as to withstand rust, mold, and corrosion. These areas can be expected to have higher than normal humidity, and natatoriums will also have high levels of chlorine in the atmosphere.

Flooring

There are many types of competition-level wood and synthetic flooring systems. Ample time should be spent researching and selecting the appropriate systems for each situation. Field houses, gymnasiums, and fitness centers can all use similar flooring types, making maintenance more efficient. Natatoriums require non-slip surfaces that are safe for use in a wet environment.

If carpet is used in fitness centers or locker rooms, careful attention should be given to non-microbe-enabling carpets—usually 100% nylon. This will reduce the potential for fungus and bacteria growing and spreading. If wood is used, consideration should be given to layout and adjacencies in order to minimize the potential for moisture exposure. Wood flooring expands as it gathers moisture, and can warp if exposed to excess moisture. The floor must also be allowed to expand and contract, so expansion joints at walls and entrance ways are a must.

Bleachers/Seating

Telescoping bleachers along gym walls usually provide spectator seating for athletic events. During physical education classes, the bleachers can be kept folded to allow more floor space. In the swimming pool area, spectator seating is usually fixed, and is sometimes located on a balcony overlooking the pool. Handicapped-accessible seating must be planned into the bleachers in every case. The Americans with Disabilities Act regulations specify that handicapped-accessible seating must be dispersed throughout the seating area, and offer lines of sight comparable to those for members of the general public. Refer to local regulations for the required number of accessible seats.

Handicapped accessibility to outside playing fields is also an issue for press boxes. For example, in the regulations of the Massachusetts Architectural Barriers Board, accessibility to the support spaces of places of public assembly is required, which includes press boxes at high school football fields. Typically, such boxes have been perched above the top seats of the bleachers. Schools planning to renovate their facilities are faced with the choice of installing a lift to the press box, relocating it, or eliminating it altogether.

Management

Some school districts may plan to justify building a major athletic facility by generating revenue for the school and the community—hosting tournaments, running sports camps, organizing other events, and charging admission fees. However, managing these activities takes time, personnel, and experience. A management team should be considered to help run and maintain such a facility.

Examples

The natatorium at Tantasqua Regional High School in Sturbridge, Massachusetts, designed to be a community resource, is located at one end of the school with a separate entrance in close proximity to public parking areas. The natatorium is fully accessible and includes a special lift into the pool for disabled users. Clerestories are used to provide natural lighting with minimal glare. In addition, the school's fire sprinkler system is interconnected with the pool. Pool water can be plumbed to the sprinkler system when required, making it an integral part of that system. *(See Figure 5.2.)*

Performing Arts Centers

Background

Performing arts centers provide significant opportunities for students with varied interests. Stage productions, such as music, theater, and dance, give students experience collaborating with many other participants and require a high level of complex thinking and interaction. Multiple support spaces within a performing arts center allow students to work individually or in small groups in a professional-level atmosphere, as well as in the team-oriented environment required to bring productions together.

Performing arts centers in schools have many of the same features found in independent theatres. As part of a school, they have the advantage of sharing spaces, such as a lobby, dining area, kitchen, and restrooms, allowing for efficient use of facilities without the expense of significant periods of underutilization.

Figure 5.2
Natatorium, Tantasqua Regional High School, Sturbridge, MA
This pool is designed to serve the needs of both the high school and the community.

Photo Credit: Greg Premru Photography

Programming and Pre-Design

As with all specialty spaces, initial planning must include open discussions with potential users and operators of the space. Outcome expectations must be fully covered so that the performing arts center reflects the needs of the school and community in terms of the types of events and performances.

Main "house" spaces may include a stage, lighting catwalk, an orchestra pit, and audience seating. A fly is an additional space built over the stage in the performing arts centers of some public high schools, some well-funded private schools, and in most high schools that specialize in the performing arts. The fly is an open area above the stage that is sufficiently high to enable scenery, curtains, and lighting to be hoisted above the performance area.

Providing adequate and varied support spaces allows for the main performance area to be reserved for its intended function. Rehearsals and readings are often better accommodated in attendant practice rooms, rather than the large stage area. Support spaces may include:

- A workshop for scenery building with high ceilings and ample electrical power
- Storage areas for scenery, costumes, and props
- Costume workshop area
- Loading docks (with access doors to the stage area)
- Changing/dressing rooms (with lockers and restrooms)
- Makeup room with special lighting
- Rehearsal and music practice areas
- Technical support areas (sound and lighting control panels, stage rigging)
- Restroom facilities and drinking fountains separate from both the ones attached to the changing/dressing rooms and others for spectator use

Optional spaces may include a general office, technical director's office, and box office. Special consideration will be needed for sound and lighting systems, projection room, and TV/video production space, as well as main and back curtains.

A performing arts center may have its own formal public entrance and, at the same time, be knit into the everyday fabric of a campus environment. The daily activity of student use will keep the building vibrant throughout the day, and a quality space will enhance the excitement of, and public enthusiasm for, a formal opening-night gala.

Designing and constructing a performing arts center is complex and technically demanding. A strong team of experienced design consultants is required to determine and plan for the needs of the users, and to help identify potential strengths and weaknesses of a proposed approach.

Special Considerations

Resolving the technical issues of stage layout, acoustics, lighting, audience movement, and operations is part of the design equation. In addition, a successful theater experience relies on the design team's ability to attract a large number of people to a venue and lead them through an entry sequence that is logical, comfortable, and anticipatory of guests' needs, and that places the audience in a positive and receptive mindset for the performance.

Acoustics

Whether it is for chorus, band, dance, theater, or another type of presentation, acoustics will play an important role in the design. Each space will have unique acoustical properties depending on its size, shape, adjacency to other uses, and total volume. A few general guidelines include:

- Use hard-surfaced, reflective, acoustical panels at the front of the house, near the stage, and at the ceiling level. This technique pushes the sound out toward the audience so that people in the back of the house can hear the performance.
- Use a combination of reflective and absorptive acoustical panels along the walls from the midpoint toward the back of the house. This allows sound to move through the entire space, but slowly be absorbed as it reaches the back. Absorptive panels also minimize the bouncing of sound.
- Use fabric-finished seating to aid in sound absorption.

The desired result—an even-toned sound—will be achieved by using the appropriate type of acoustical treatment, briefly outlined above. For performing arts centers, it is recommended that an acoustical consultant be involved early in the design process.

Lighting

Properly designed lighting can enhance the atmosphere for performances. If done poorly, the results can be disastrous. It is important to separate stage lighting from house lighting. Providing dimmer switches with preset controls is an effective way to accomplish this task. Lighting control panels and switches should be conveniently located so that adjustments can be made without interrupting the performance. For safety reasons, low-level lighting should be incorporated into the audience area, either in the aisle floor or built into the seats. Wall sconces are frequently used to provide a dim light that allows people to see during the performance without overpowering what is taking place on the stage. Given the number and complexity of lighting types and control systems, a lighting designer should be consulted early in the project.

Environmental Control

Environmental control is also extremely important in performing arts centers. The types of activities (including type and amount of stage lighting), audience size, and times of year that the spaces are used should all be taken into consideration. Humidity and temperature should be maintained at comfortable levels for performers and spectators at all levels of occupancy and use.

Stage

A traditional stage, or *proscenium*, is the most common feature in school performing arts centers. Depending on the desired atmosphere and types of performances, other varieties of stages can be considered. The *end stage*, also called the *open stage*, is a raised platform facing the audience, but not separated from it by the proscenium wall. An *arena stage* consists of a central stage with seating on all four sides. A *thrust stage* projects out into the audience and has seating on three sides. A *black box* is a flexible theater that can be arranged in different configurations for each performance. With the black box configuration, the audience can be seated in movable chairs around the performance area, and there is no separation from the stage. Each type of stage brings unique character to the performance and should be carefully chosen to fit within the school's performing arts program. Rigging and structural concerns must be addressed once the stage type is determined. Depending on the types and sizes of scenery that need to be moved or "flown," the height and structure of the fly space above the stage must be designed accordingly. Figure 5.3 shows some examples of different stage types.

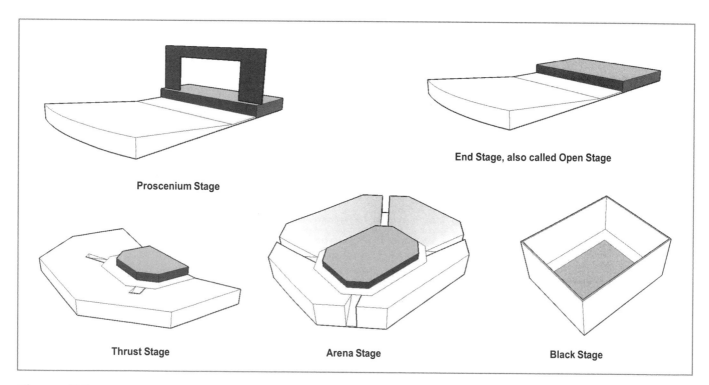

Proscenium Stage

End Stage, also called Open Stage

Thrust Stage

Arena Stage

Black Stage

Figure 5.3
Stage Types
Credit: Drummey Rosane Anderson, Inc.

Technical Operations

It is preferable to locate lighting, sound, and audiovisual equipment controls in the back of the house. Lighting and sound should be controlled from separate, soundproof booths that allow visual access to the entire performing arts space. Each booth should have separate controls and the capability to communicate with other spaces within the theater. A catwalk allows users to move across the house to access lighting and other equipment located at the ceiling level without being seen.

Figures 5.4 and 5.5 show examples of performing arts centers.

Figure 5.4
Performing Arts Center, Tantasqua Regional High School (View from Proscenium Stage), Sturbridge, MA
Photo Credit: Greg Premru Photography

Figure 5.5
Performing Arts Center, Stafford Intermediate School and Elementary School Campus, Stafford Township, NJ
An example of a proscenium stage in a school auditorium.

Credit: NJ Harry Harper Architect and Drummey Rosane Anderson, Inc.; Rendering by Terry Cracknell

Libraries/Media Centers

Background

The traditional school library has evolved into an "Instructional Media Center," or IMC. In addition to the usual printed resources of books, magazines, and newspapers, a successful IMC offers access to electronic media such as DVDs, videos, compact disks, and the Internet. IMCs may include a video production and distribution area and will normally house the central technology equipment ("head end") space for school instructional computer systems. Students benefit from an assortment of settings within the IMC, including independent study and research areas, study carrels, small group settings, and areas for group instruction.

School systems combine the functions of a library and media center into one space at all grade levels. However, high schools generally have greater requirements for computer media needs. Students at the high school level can be expected to rely more heavily on advanced computer systems that are required for independent research. Students in lower grades will rely more on face-to-face instruction.

Programming and Pre-Design

The planning and design of a school library can be a complex assignment. It is extremely important that the librarian or media director responsible for the space be included as early as possible in the process. It is a good idea for the librarian and members of the design committee to visit various recently completed library spaces. Advance research, even before planning starts, can be useful to determine what other librarians and school facility representatives have experienced in the design of their new spaces.

The functionality of the library is its most critical feature. School libraries should be designed as multi-functional spaces with many activities taking place simultaneously. Library activities may include:

- Research
- Group projects
- Individual projects
- Quiet study
- Story telling (elementary schools)
- Conferences
- Administrative work
- Computer access
- Browsing bookshelves
- Display of art

Providing spaces to accommodate these simultaneous activities without undermining their individual functional needs (space, access, acoustics, and lighting levels) requires a significant amount of planning and coordination. There should be a continuous line of communication between the architect and librarian so that needs are addressed.

School library/media center programs differ from school to school. Each facility will entail certain square footage requirements. Several states offer specific space guidelines, and standards, often based on the school population. For example, Massachusetts uses a formula to determine square footage: 40 square feet times 15% of enrollment for high school library/media centers. Each state's Department of Education should be able to provide this type of information if it is available. BiblioTECH, a library consulting firm in Sudbury, Massachusetts, suggests the following minimum space requirements for school libraries:

- High school: 7,000-10,000 square feet
- Middle school: 4,000-6,000 square feet
- Elementary school: 4,000 square feet

These requirements reflect space for book stacks and publicly used library space only, and do not include support spaces, such as circulation desks, staff workrooms, and offices. A rectangular, open floor plan has been found to be the most efficient layout. Other shapes have some advantages, but may require more space.

The location of the library within the school facility is critical to its proper functioning. It should be situated away from loud spaces, such as cafeterias, gymnasiums, and music rooms. It is most efficient if the library is centrally located on the ground floor. This will provide convenient public access for after-hours use, as well as efficient service access, including book delivery. If a ground-floor location is not possible, the library should be in close proximity to an elevator. In order for the library to be used after regular school hours, access through an outside entrance and separate public restrooms should be considered. It is also helpful to choose a location that will allow for future change and expansion.

Special Considerations

The interior layout of a school library should promote a dynamic and stimulating learning and working environment. Careful selection of furniture, flooring materials, colors, and lighting all contribute to the success of the atmosphere within the space.

Technology

Technology has a significant impact on school library/media center design. Innovations have allowed many libraries to replace some printed materials with electronic data, which may decrease shelving and space requirements. Elementary school libraries, however, will most likely continue to maintain larger collections of books for instruction and reading to children. Middle school and high school libraries may rely more on electronic data for advanced research and other types of resource-based learning, resulting in a need for more computers. Technology will also affect the layout of library spaces. Space must be allotted to house equipment for maintaining a library network system. Future technology needs should also be addressed during the planning process.

Lighting

Insufficient lighting can ruin an otherwise well-designed school library, while well-planned lighting can enhance the quality of learning. Effective lighting requires well-balanced illumination, which can be achieved through a combination of direct and indirect lighting techniques. This can be achieved in different ways, such as the use of pendants that can direct more lighting to the ceiling and less lighting downward. Darker colors can be used in the lower portions of the room to reduce glare, while lighter colors can be used above to reflect light downward. The goal will be to create light that closely resembles that of midday natural sunlight. Lighting controls should be zoned so that lighting levels in one part of the room can be adjusted without affecting other areas. User-controlled lamps may be considered in study carrels/rooms and office/meeting spaces. In addition, occupancy sensors should be provided to turn off lighting in vacated spaces.

Furniture

Library furniture should be functional, safe, durable, and conducive to learning. It should also create an inviting atmosphere. The furniture selected will have a major effect on how the library is used, how traffic flows through it, and the space's overall appearance. Furniture can also be used to define specific areas within the library, including shelving sections for fiction, non-fiction, and reference, for example. Special consideration should be made with respect to furniture sizes and locations so as to not obstruct supervision from the circulation desk. Appropriately sized furniture will be needed for lower grade and kindergarten students.

Healthy indoor air quality, in the library and throughout the school facility, depends on an appropriate selection of low-emitting interior products. The Environmental Protection Agency (EPA) has been working on certification programs to establish standards for Environmentally Preferable Products (EPP), which have a lesser or reduced effect on human health and the environment when compared to other products or services that serve the same purpose.

Flooring

Carpet is usually the flooring material of choice for school libraries, as it provides a quiet and safe covering that can accommodate many design features. The soft texture of carpet also improves acoustics within the space by absorbing sound. However, using carpet for visual and acoustic reasons may need to be balanced against its increasing health concerns. If carpet is used, careful attention should be given to non-microbe-enabling material—usually 100% nylon. This will reduce the potential for fungal and bacteria spreading and growth. New carpeting is one of the lowest VOC (volatile organic compounds)-emitting products used in the indoor environment. In addition, carpet can be specified that will have a better long-term appearance than hard surface flooring, with lower maintenance costs. The use of carpet is a decision that needs to be made by the project team early in the design process.

Color

The benefits of color within a library/media center are often overlooked. Often, the woodwork associated with the furniture and moldings represents the entire color palette. Color can be used to tie the space together, add character, and stimulate the minds of students, teachers, librarians, and other users. Color has been proven to affect behavior, mood, and emotion. Generally, a cooler color palette is preferred, particularly for larger study and reading areas. Brighter colors may be considered for specialized spaces, such as meeting rooms. Certain color combinations can help create a dynamic learning environment.

Examples

The library at Bennett Hemenway Elementary School in Natick, Massachusetts, features small gathering spaces for reading, and furniture is appropriately sized for smaller children. Direct access is provided to a private outdoor courtyard space (Figure 5.6). In addition, a storytelling area is located so that it is visible from the main public lobby of the school.

Athol-Royalston Middle School's library, in Athol, Massachusetts, was specifically designed for both school and after-hours use and features large meeting spaces for community gatherings. In addition to the interior student entrance, it has a separate accessible exterior entrance in

Figure 5.6
Bennett Hemenway Elementary School, Natick, MA

Photo Credit: Greg Premru Photography

151

close proximity to public parking. A large group area is adjacent to a computer area, allowing for flexibility in seating. In addition, small group rooms are provided for both student and public use. *(See Figure 5.7.)*

Vocational-
Technical
Education

Background

Vocational-technical programs within high schools are expanding, and the atmosphere in which they are taking place is rapidly changing. A vocational-technical education allows students to learn a trade or develop a hands-on skill in addition to academics, as opposed to learning in an academics-only environment. In years past, vocational programs sometimes attracted students who did not perform well academically. Vocational programs are now designed to attract a diverse group of students who are interested in learning a hands-on skill as well as traditional academic subjects.

A diverse vocational-technical education provides students with several skill sets to bring into the "real world" after graduation. Developing as many skills as possible during the high school years helps students make mature decisions about future education and career opportunities. Working with local industries exposes students to the power of networking.

Vocational-technical programs can be housed in stand-alone facilities (such as vocational schools, technical institutes, and skills centers), or might serve as one component of a comprehensive high school. These programs can also be a smaller part of an academic high school (featuring a few "shops" to provide for electives, along with academic programs). Traditional programs include such areas as carpentry/woodworking, auto

Figure 5.7
Athol-Royalston Middle School, Athol, MA

Photo Credit: Greg Premru Photography

mechanics, and culinary arts. Newer subjects include CAD, graphic arts, photonics, and biotechnical studies. Growth in computer system support programs can be expected. As vocational programs expand from traditional "blue collar" trades into more "white collar" programs, the line between academic and vocational-technical programs will continue to diminish.

Vocational programs are governed by state standards rather than national standards. State educational authorities should be contacted for standards that apply to vocational programs not covered here. One exception is the national standard for automotive programs offered by the National Automotive Technicians Education Foundation (NATEF). These have been adopted at the local level as an extension to state standards.

Programming and Pre-Design

Programming for a vocational-technical facility is a very involved process. After establishing the types of programs that will be offered, it is important to consider the technology and equipment that will be required, which often account for 25% of the budget. A great deal of time must be spent up-front evaluating the school's needs and coordinating with local industries.

Administrators who oversee vocational-technical programs often create advisory councils or alliances with local industries. This type of partnership allows the school to be well informed about current trends—which can help with design decisions about equipment and technology, the types of spaces the school needs to provide, and how to develop the necessary skills that employers are seeking. These alliances help create a more efficient educational system, as well as bring in additional funding to the school.

In Massachusetts, for example, advisory committees are mandated by state law (Chapter 74). They include representatives from business and industry, labor, parents, and students. The committees contribute to the quality of vocational technical programs in six key areas:

- **General Program Planning:** Advisory committees keep up with trends in the local labor market, identify needed new programs and changes to existing programs, and help set priorities for the best use of available resources.
- **Curriculum and Instruction Advice:** Committees help identify new fields in certain occupations, visit workplaces for demonstrations, review student projects and portfolios, and help students become more competitive.
- **Equipment and Facilities Advice:** Knowing the needs of the workplace, advisors help equip the vocational technical program to produce skilled and experienced workers. Sometimes advisors make generous donations of equipment and expertise to the schools, to the benefit of everyone involved.

- **Student Recruitment, Career Guidance, and Placement Services:** Advisors employ students in co-op programs and internships, employ graduates, and direct students to other employers.
- **Professional Development:** Advisors help teachers stay current with developments in technology. Some offer summer jobs to teachers.
- **Community Public Relations:** Advisors work with administrators to help determine when vocational-technical programs should be merged or eliminated. They also suggest modifications to exploratory programs that help attract students.

Vocational-technical schools are also experiencing the same design trends evident in academic high schools. They, too, are moving toward the concepts of cluster spaces, "schools within a school" to provide more interaction between teachers and students, and more technology-based learning.

Although technology design decisions are made early in the project to facilitate infrastructure planning, the final purchase of electronic equipment (such as computers and digital projectors) should be delayed as long as possible in order to acquire the most up-to-date models.

Special Considerations

When planning vocational spaces, it is important to consider special acoustics, lighting, MEP (mechanical, electrical, and plumbing), access, safety, and equipment requirements. Electrical demands should be expected to be greater than for regular lab space. The need for fume hoods, compressed air, and special high-velocity ventilation/exhaust in certain spaces may increase heating requirements. Each of these items has significant design implications and should be investigated thoroughly.

Activities within vocational spaces tend to be loud, and, in many cases, it is best to isolate them from sound-sensitive spaces. Whether the noise is from machinery, electronics, power tools, or a hammer against a nail, acoustical treatment needs to be evaluated.

Proper lighting within vocational spaces helps maintain a safe environment. Many tasks require a combination of balanced general illumination and direct (task) lighting. Computer and graphic labs may require lighting design that reduces glare on computer screens. An experienced lighting designer should be consulted in order to ensure proper lighting techniques.

Vocational spaces may also be exposed to certain chemicals or exhaust fumes (such as woodworking and automotive shops and biotechnical labs) that must be ventilated appropriately. Large spaces with electrical and mechanical equipment require special attention in terms of circulating fresh air. HVAC design should be left in the hands of a professional engineer, experienced in this type of specialized space.

Accessibility should be considered for large deliveries of materials and equipment to and from vocational spaces. Conveniently located, large overhead doors should be used to accommodate the movement of such items.

Power drops (electric power outlets planned to serve specific pieces of equipment) and data drops (connection points to the computer network) should be adequately designed and carefully coordinated by a professional engineer and the architect. It is important in certain vocational spaces, such as machine shops and computer labs, that power drops be provided to accommodate particular types of equipment and work areas. Power requirements for specialized shop equipment, as well as auxiliary systems such as dust collection and special ventilation, must be determined. Careful consideration and preplanning is needed to understand the required uses, such as those for an auto shop (special ventilation for paint fumes), a wood shop (many heavy-duty power drops

Figure 5.8
Lynn Vocational Technical Institute, Lynn, MA
The first floor of the main mall provides access to retail programs. Classrooms on the second floor feature a view into the mall.

Photo Credit: Greg Premru Photography

for equipment), or a computer lab (many standard power and data drops for computer equipment). All of the required equipment must be fully understood prior to laying out the space.

Example

Lynn Vocational Technical Institute (LVTI) in Lynn, Massachusetts, which opened in September 1999, is an example of recent changes in vocational education facilities, and how they enhance the educational experience. One of the school's design goals was to create an atmosphere that would be inviting to the public and non-industrial students, while incorporating "academies," or clusters of vocational programs.

The central corridor of LVTI, known as "the mall," was designed to provide public access to retail programs, such as cosmetology, culinary arts, banking, and general merchandising. Each program has a front entrance on the central corridor and functions as a small business. In addition to classrooms, the building also houses a satellite library, cafeteria, and additional administrative offices. The public can use each facility during school hours, and some programs operate after school hours as well. These programs offer students the opportunity to learn and develop skills, while earning income for themselves and the school.

Computer Labs and Training Rooms

Background

Although future trends may reduce or eliminate the need for dedicated computer labs *(see Chapter 3)*, at present, they are often still being included in school projects. The use of computers has become a necessity rather than an option for students to get through school and enter the job market. Technology is being used more and more in schools as a means to enhance the educational experience. Computer labs and training rooms allow students and teachers to explore new areas of technology, expand their computer skills, and refine the skills they have already developed.

Programming and Pre-Design

Computer labs and training rooms are important focus items during the programming and planning stage of a school building project. These spaces must be flexible so that they can accommodate varying numbers of students, different types of layout configurations, and changes in technology. Planning computer labs and training rooms will require the expertise of a technology consultant.

Considerations during planning include infrastructure, equipment, and assigning responsibility to a specific school staff member for managing and maintaining the facility. Infrastructure and equipment will affect the allowable sizes of spaces, achievable layouts, and intended activities. The individual responsible for running the activities and maintaining the equipment should be thoroughly involved in the planning process since they have the greatest knowledge of the system requirements.

Special Considerations

Redundancy

Computer consultant Michael DiBari, from Systems, Software, Support, Inc., of Northfield, Massachusetts, recommends using a combination of hard-wired and wireless workstations to create a "flexible with full tolerance" environment. For example, a classroom would have hard-wired outlets for fixed computers plus a wireless hub to have the option of using additional wireless laptops. This approach provides flexibility through an alternate, or redundant system. The increased initial cost of redundant systems is offset by the resulting overall efficiency.

Power and Data

The computer lab equipment will have specific power and data requirements. Although technology design decisions are made early in the project, the final purchase of electronic equipment should be delayed as long as possible in order to acquire the most up-to-date models. However, the school will need to make an early decision about equipment types to enable the designer to contact vendors for the needed design parameters. Without this early decision, the designer will be forced to make reasonable assumptions regarding power and data needs. This could potentially lead to adjustments when the equipment and furniture are delivered, causing implementation delays and additional expense.

Consideration should be given to reduced glare lighting, power conditioning, surge protection, backup power, shielding, and computer-integrated projection displays.

Lighting

Indirect lighting is recommended for a computer lab. Light that bounces off of the ceiling produces a more even level of general illumination and helps prevent glare on computer screens. Window placement must be considered relative to work station locations, and artificial lighting carefully designed to reduce glare.

Computer Lab Layouts

DiBari divides computer labs into two categories: *instructional-based* and *activity-based. (See Figures 5.9 and 5.10.)*

Instructional-Based Layout: The instructional-based layout is considered the standard for middle and high school facilities. It features a horseshoe configuration that locates each individual work station along three of the peripheral walls, with the teacher stationed along the fourth wall. This layout provides an open central space for gathering around work tables and/or using wireless equipment. Locating the work stations along the walls allows the teacher to view each monitor and easily work one-on-one with students, and conceals all associated wiring.

Activity-Based Layout: The activity-based layout is similar to the horseshoe in that it utilizes the peripheral walls, but it also incorporates large and small presentation areas, work tables, and project/research areas. Many activities can take place simultaneously in this type of

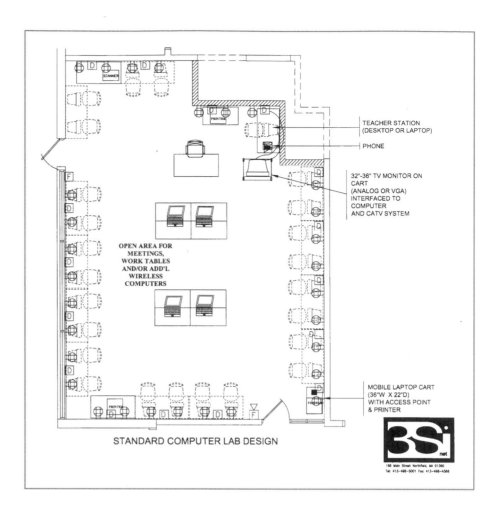

STANDARD COMPUTER LAB DESIGN

Figure 5.9

Computer Lab, Instructional-Based Layout

Credit: Systems, Software,
Support, Inc., Northfield, MA

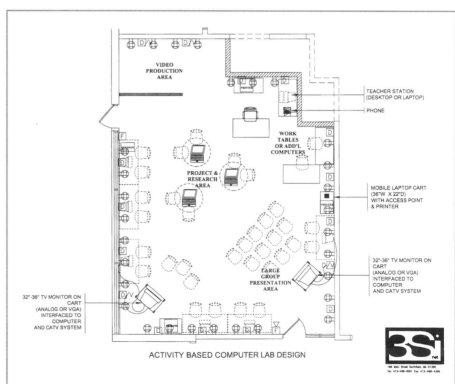

ACTIVITY BASED COMPUTER LAB DESIGN

Figure 5.10

Computer Lab, Activity-Based Layout

Credit: Systems, Software,
Support, Inc., Northfield, MA

arrangement, both independently and in small groups. This layout works well in elementary schools, because it helps instill a sense of teamwork and encourages sharing.

Example

The John Joseph Moakley Center for Technological Applications at Bridgewater State College in Bridgewater, Massachusetts is designed to train teachers in new technology and help them integrate new applications into their teaching methods. The facility houses lecture halls, computer labs, a professional level television studio, exhibition spaces, and state of the art research and development labs—all wired with the latest technology. *(See Figure 5.11.)*

Language Labs

Background

Although future trends may reduce or eliminate the need for dedicated language labs *(see Chapter 3)*, at present, they are often still being included in school projects. Language labs in today's schools are being used for more than just traditional class instruction. For example, adult and community education courses often make use of these spaces. A well-designed lab may also become a centralized testing center for advanced placement students and similar activities. When tied into the school's data network, the language lab can become an instructional resource for automated learning needs in any department.

Figure 5.11
John Joseph Moakley Center for Technological Applications, Bridgewater State College, Bridgewater, MA
A high-tech lecture hall with a computerized demonstration work station connected to a large rear-screen projection display.

Photo Credit: Peter Vanderwarker

Programming and Pre-Design

The size and shape of the language lab is important, as is its relationship to other facilities within the school. One critical design consideration is that language instructors be able to clearly see the faces of students. To teach proper pronunciation effectively, instructors need to be able to observe students' mouths as they respond to prompts from equipment, and listen to students' responses. For this reason, most teachers prefer a wider space, with the students arranged in long rows that wrap the teaching station in a semi-circle, as opposed to a narrower space requiring more rows. In classrooms that are too deep, students at the back may be too far away for the teacher to be able to pick up the visual cues needed to assess their performance.

Special Considerations

Acoustics

The design of the language lab should function to absorb sounds students make, and to limit interference with neighbors. Much of this sound absorption may be accomplished within the furniture system, with acoustic side panels between individual learning stations. The room must be acoustically responsive as well. A highly absorptive ceiling panel, coupled with absorptive acoustical panels on the walls, will usually achieve the auditory "softness" that is needed. Many teachers also prefer to have a carpeted floor to further enhance acoustics, as it helps reduce reflected sound and eliminates the scraping of chair legs.

Flooring

The desire for carpet for acoustic reasons may need to be balanced against increasing concern over the health issues of carpet materials. As noted in the Library section earlier in this chapter, carpet selection should involve attention to prevention of spreading fungus and bacteria. Non-microbe-enabling carpets—usually 100% nylon are recommended. It should also be noted that today's carpeting offers fewer concerns about off-gassing, as it has become one of the lowest VOC (volatile organic compounds)—emitting products used in the indoor environment. The decision to use carpet needs to be made by the project team early in the design process.

Power and Data

As with computer labs, the language lab's equipment should be identified early so that the designer can contact vendors for the needed design parameters. The designer will otherwise be forced to make reasonable assumptions regarding power and data needs. If adjustments have to be made when the equipment and furniture are delivered, there may be delays and additional expense.

Lighting

Indirect lighting is best for the language lab. Light that bounces off of the ceiling produces a more even level of general illumination and helps prevent glare on computer screens. Language lab windows and artificial lighting placement must be planned carefully to reduce glare.

The Server

The computer room equipment for the language lab is powered by its own server, which is basically a larger and more powerful computer, with advanced switching components. The important question to ask early in the design process is where the server will be located. The advantage of locating it in the main data network room (the "MDF" or "head end" room) is that this is a secure environment. The head end room is likely to be monitored by the school's network administration staff, who are capable of recognizing basic equipment problems and performing routine maintenance. The alternative is to locate the server within the language lab itself, or in an immediately adjacent space. This has the advantage of "ownership" of the system, particularly for systems that are not tied into the overall school network. For these "stand-alone" language lab systems, locating the server nearby results in shorter cable runs, and allows service personnel to monitor the behavior of the server interactions with the work stations. IT (information technology) staff normally prefer all the school's servers to be centrally located, to facilitate professional supervision and maintenance.

Technical Support Space

Many schools, particularly those with more than one language or computer lab, employ a support technician in addition to the teaching staff. This person takes primary responsibility for preparing the facility for individual classes, including loading the proper files into the computer, maintaining file organization, and similar tasks. Regardless of whether this work is done by a technician or a faculty member, a support space with needed equipment and storage will be required. Many schools prefer to locate this space toward the rear of the language lab, preferably in a separate room between adjacent labs and with glass vision panels into each lab.

Example

The World Language Division—International Communication Center (ICC) is a new language lab at the Oak Park and River Forest High School in Illinois. It was built in a renovated study hall space and had the advantage of recycling an existing raised platform in the front of the room, now used for the teacher station. The lab has 32 student stations, all within direct view of the instructor.

The room layout consists of a central aisle with rows of work stations between the aisle and the two sidewalls. This arrangement allows for convenient power and data connections at the sidewalls. Small panels mounted between work stations visually separate students from one another. *(See Figure 5.12.)*

Figure 5.12

International Communication Center, World Languages Department, Oak Park and River Forest High School, Oak Park, IL.

A computer-based language lab. Each station is equipped with headphones and is positioned to face the raised teacher station at the front.

Photo Credit: International Communication Center

Science Classrooms

Background

A good science classroom promotes student curiosity and meaningful understanding. Students need to gain knowledge of the disciplines, methods, and philosophy of science, and how science operates in the world. The classroom design can encourage this by maximizing display space and by providing sufficient storage to encourage teachers to maintain a collection of successful student projects for class observation.

Programming and Pre-Design

Progress in technology and science is a driving force behind changes in teaching methods, curriculum, and, ultimately, classroom design. When planning a science classroom, future needs must be considered to ensure that the facility can accommodate technological and scientific advances. Proactive science classrooms should:

- Allow secure storage for hand held electronic equipment
- Provide electrical outlets and network connections throughout for laptop computers
- Plan for digital projection at the front of the room, visible to the entire class

Handicapped-accessible student stations must be provided at lab benches, sinks, and fume hoods. Facilities and equipment should provide a wide selection of experiences and opportunities for varied interests, capabilities, and learning styles.

The primary issues to be considered relate to curriculum, teaching styles, technology, flexibility, and safety. Teachers and administrators should be active in the planning process. Their input will answer such questions as:

- What teaching methods are used? (e.g., departmental, such as the math or language arts department, or a cross-department team approach?)
- Will the space be shared?
- What curriculum will be taught?
- How many students will the classroom serve?
- What teaching support facilities will be required?

The integration of "real world" scientific investigation has become more common in schools and must be included in the planning. For example, some schools have greenhouses and aquariums as part of the science area. Science teachers will need adequate space for their specialized curriculum. There should be ample space to allow students to work safely in groups at various tasks, maintain their work in progress, and display results. There are specific differences in the design requirements of science classrooms for different grade levels.

Elementary Schools

The elementary school level has basic needs for science education beyond those of the regular classroom. Because the science program will typically focus on activities and hands-on learning, the space should allow for individual study, small and large group work areas, and lecture-style instruction. Typical spaces for the elementary science classroom include a sink, project area for observation and storage, learning stations with computers and other equipment, prep area, and storage room.

Secondary Schools

Middle and high school science programs differ from those of elementary schools because of the greater reliance on independent student work. Secondary school science facilities must accommodate students performing experiments with potentially greater hazards. Student safety must be a priority. The teacher must be able to supervise the entire space while moving among the students working in small groups or independently. The layout must provide space for discussions/lectures, as well as laboratory work, and students will move between the areas. The teacher must have easy access to prep areas and storage.

According to a planning study conducted by the National Science Foundation, the typical secondary school science classroom should be a combined discussion space and laboratory. The total area for 24 students should be approximately 1,200 to 1,600 net assignable square feet, and the width of the room should be at least 32 feet. Larger rooms will allow for more flexibility and provide a variety of layouts that respond to changes in curriculum, teaching methods, and technology.

A prep room should be adjacent to the laboratory area of a secondary school science classroom and may have a window into the classroom for teacher supervision. Prep rooms usually feature a fume hood, sink and refrigerator, in addition to work counters and storage cabinets. The size of the room may range from 200-500 square feet. Storage rooms will sometimes be combined with the prep room, and are used to store chemicals, specimens, and materials.

Figure 5.13
Science Classroom, Westford Academy, Westford, MA
Freestanding lab benches and a separate discussion area.

Photo Credit: Greg Premru Photography

In addition, science classroom design must take into account factors such as lighting, acoustics, air quality, mechanical and electrical systems, and energy conservation. Special requirements, such as plumbing for lab sinks, compressed air lines, acid-resistant pipes, acid neutralization systems, special exhaust, and special fire protection systems, must be determined. It should be noted that Bunsen burners are seldom used in new school facilities due to their potential hazardous nature. Today most schools utilize electric hot plates or alcohol burners.

Special Considerations

Information Technology

Interactive programs and Internet access can expose students to an array of scientific topics and provide opportunities for investigation beyond the classroom. Planning for the delivery of technology plays a lead role in design. Science classrooms must, according to the National Science Education Standards (NSES), make the available science tools, materials, media, and technological resources accessible to students. From laptop computers to interactive white boards, the science classroom should have Internet, voice, and video connectivity throughout.

Flexibility

Flexibility is a critical issue within science classrooms. The layout, furniture, and equipment should support a variety of teaching methods and science curricula, as well as accommodate future changes in these areas. Built-in flexibility can be achieved with the appropriate selection of furniture, equipment, cabinetry, storage, power systems, lighting, and sinks.

Safety

Science curriculum is varied and constantly changing. Living labs (for plants and animals) and instrumentation monitoring (for sustainable building systems, such as photovoltaic power cells and graywater recycling) are just small parts of the larger, ever changing science curriculum. No matter what is being taught, student and teacher safety is of primary importance in the planning, design, specification, operation, and maintenance of lab and support spaces. Some lab safety standards include:

- Smoke, carbon monoxide, and heat detectors are recommended in every lab area, including storerooms, prep rooms, closets, and offices.
- Gas, electricity, and water should each have a single shut-off installed in the science lab near the exit.
- Labs should contain safety equipment appropriate to their use, such as emergency showers with floor drain, eyewash stations (15 minutes of potable water that operates hands free), fume hoods, protective aprons, fire blankets, fire extinguisher, and safety goggles for all students and teachers.
- Appropriate ventilation is necessary. The OSHA Laboratory Standard requires protection of students and teachers from overexposure to

hazardous laboratory chemicals. Some high school labs, such as Westford Academy in Westford, MA, are now equipped with local vents at each bench.

- Prep rooms should be maintained in a net negative pressure when compared to adjacent spaces to prevent infiltration of air contaminants into the lab areas.

Regulations

Whether the project calls for a new or renovated science facility, it is important to know that the space and equipment requirements are subject to a variety of federal, state, and local regulations. Most of the regulations address safety issues, such as those listed above. Handicapped accessibility regulations apply to science labs just like the rest of the school, and will require specific heights and clearances for lab equipment and furnishings. An experienced architect will ensure that all the codes and regulations are met.

Examples

The following examples of science classrooms demonstrate how design can provide an opportunity for hands-on, scientific investigation.

Fitchburg High School, Fitchburg, MA
The high school design makes use of the "fingers" of existing wetlands on the site. Each wing of the school building wraps around a wetlands area. These wetland spaces serve as living labs for students. Figure 5.14 shows how the school was designed in a wing formation to work around the fingers of wetlands.

Newton South High School, Newton, MA
In this renovation/addition project, planned for 2005, new "green" elements will be integrated as part of the science classroom. For example, a gray water system will be used as an educational tool. One section of drainpipe from a rooftop collection system will be made of glass, with lighting and a viewing

Figure 5.14
Fitchburg High School, Fitchburg, MA
The high school was designed to fit the site by locating facility wings between fingers of wetlands to be preserved.

Photo Credit: Greg Premru Photography

panel located in a lobby area. Signage with text and graphics will explain that the water collected from the roof will be used to flush the school's toilets. A creative teacher can tie this into the environmental sciences, allowing young people to learn from the experience of being inside a green building. For example, the amount of water collected can be compared to the demand, and cost savings to the school may be calculated.

In addition, a computer monitor will be featured in one area of the school displaying the current activity of an array of photovoltaic cells that serves the school and is also tied into the local electrical grid. Exposed and labeled mechanical systems will allow students to see how the building is operated, enabling them to learn from the building itself.

Cunningham-Collicott Elementary School, Milton, MA
To emphasize the importance of renewable energy technologies, this elementary school will install a 42 kW solar array on the school roof. Recognizing an opportunity to use the school as a teaching tool, the town of Milton intends to implement an environmental and renewable energy curriculum component centered on instrumentation and monitoring of the school complex.

Athol-Royalston Middle School, Athol, MA
The middle school building site will be used as part of the extended science classroom. Nature trails have been built behind the school, and there will be space available for science teachers to conduct classes outdoors.

Art Classrooms

Background

When planning for art education, it is important to note that teaching philosophies and student abilities vary significantly between elementary, middle, and high school grades. Elementary teaching and learning generally involve self expression and play, creating shapes and forms, developing hand dexterity, and understanding more about color. Higher level teaching and learning may involve more independent study; the effects of light on form; color, shade, and shadow; understanding the scale of figures; depth of field; complex shapes and forms; anatomy; photography; ceramics; and sculpture. Exposure to a variety of artistic techniques, in addition to interaction with peers and teachers, is important at all levels. Learning both independently and through group work is critical to the development of young artists.

Programming and Pre-Design

Most schools have an individual appointed to manage the art program, possibly the head art teacher. It is essential that this person be significantly involved in the programming and pre-design process for the layout of the art classroom and support areas.

At the outset of planning, it is important to consider accommodations for project setup, layout of materials, lecture, instructional space with a demonstration area, student production, storage of project materials, and ample space for cleanup. Activities within an art room are diverse in scale and depth. Spaces should be designed to handle a wide range of projects and should be open and flexible. Activities may require work tables, easels, sinks, closets, computer equipment, and areas to display student work. Each school's art curriculum is different and will require different provisions. The need for a darkroom should be carefully evaluated, since digital photography is rapidly replacing film photography. In addition, consideration should be given to both public indoor and outdoor display areas.

Some time should be spent in evaluating where the art classrooms should be located within the school building. It is important to consider the pros and cons of locating art rooms next to or near particular types of spaces. It may be helpful to develop an adjacency diagram (showing the ideal proximities of one space to another) to help with determining the new home for the art program. When assessing art classroom adjacencies, keep in mind the following considerations:

- Various art programs receive large quantities of heavy or bulky materials, such as paper on pallets or clay. Art classrooms should be located to provide access to a loading elevator or receiving area.
- Indirect, natural lighting is preferred. Natural light from north windows or clerestories is preferred, but not required. Glare from direct sunlight can be disruptive to an art classroom.
- Some art projects may require large layout spaces and adequate ventilation for fumes. Providing access to a courtyard or exterior space extends the classroom into the outdoor environment and fresh air. Outdoor access also allows students to study, draw, paint, and photograph objects in natural sunlight.
- Self-expression can manifest itself in noise, from the pounding of clay to the voices of group critiques. Consider acoustical treatment within the space and avoid sound transmission to sensitive spaces.

Space requirements will vary based on specific needs. Some general guidelines:

- **General art classroom** (25 students): 1,200-1,600 square feet
- **Storage**: 400 square feet minimum
- **Art office**: 200 square feet (It is recommended that the office be isolated from the classroom space to keep computers and other electronics safe from dust and fumes.)
- **Kiln room**: 150 square feet (The kiln must be located at least 18" from any combustible materials, but the room does not require fireproof construction.)
- **Ceiling heights**: at least ten feet is recommended to accommodate large pieces of work and to create a more spacious feel to the studio classroom space.

Special Considerations
Acoustics
It is recommended that walls and ceilings be acoustically treated with batt insulation, acoustical ceiling tiles, and acoustical sealants. Tack

board, used as a place to display student artwork, is also sound absorptive.

Lighting/Natural Light

As mentioned previously, art classroom space benefits from a northern exposure, which allows for diffused light without stark shadows—the type of lighting ideal for two-dimensional sketching and painting. General fluorescent lighting can be similar to natural sunlight. Care should be made in selecting fluorescent lighting, in consideration of color rendition, closeness to natural light, and energy-efficiency. Direct task lighting is ideal for still-life displays. If a darkroom is to be included in the program, special lighting is required due to light-sensitive film and paper. Darkrooms must also be sealed off from all white light during photographic production. Special darkroom doors or light locks should be considered. For cleaning purposes and after-hours access, white light can be integrated.

Color

Color can be used to create a stimulating environment. However, contrasting color values should be avoided on work surfaces to help keep the student's attention focused on their projects. Busy work surfaces can

Figure 5.15
Art Classroom, Davis Elementary School, Bedford, MA
This flexible elementary classroom contains several activity areas, as well as student tables that can be rearranged into different layouts as needed.

Photo Credit: Greg Premru Photography

be distracting. Work surface edges should be highly visible with rounded edges on corners for safety reasons.

Storage

Storage requirements will vary greatly depending on the scope of the art program. Art classrooms usually rotate multiple classes of students, sometimes all in one day. It is essential to create enough storage to accommodate each class. Storage should include spaces for:

- Drying developed film, prints, ceramics, silkscreens, and paintings
- Securely housing general supplies
- Flat storage for large-format paper
- Finished and unfinished student work
- Flammable materials (lockable metal storage recommended)

Plumbing

If a darkroom is included in the program, special sinks will be required. In addition, a sink should be provided in the art room for clean up. Special fire protection will be needed in spaces storing or using flammable materials.

Ventilation

Art rooms may contain chemicals that will need to be safely exhausted from the space. Among the products that require proper ventilation are photographic chemicals, fixatives, thinners, and paints. Fume hoods should be installed for soldering, airbrushing, and other types of activities that include potentially dangerous chemicals. Kilns should be isolated from other activities and be directly exhausted. Cabinets containing flammable material may also need to be ventilated and labeled.

Project Rooms

Background

The concept of a *project room*, sometimes called a *project lab* or *multi-purpose classroom*, is a fairly recent development. It is an outgrowth of the emerging project-based learning approach, in which students investigate interesting topics about the real world, often working collaboratively. Students create products as a team, using multiple media and hands-on techniques to explore the subject. Products may take many forms, including demonstration-type presentations, scale models, graphs, charts, slides, and videos. Students use technology to conduct online research and contact appropriate outside experts, with guidance from teachers across many disciplines. Projects are not limited to one subject, discipline, or teacher. An integrated subjects program provides both formal and informal lessons in the various subject areas. Lessons are not scheduled for the same time slot each day or week, but are presented at a time when they are relevant to learning. For example, a plant (or botany) theme may integrate language arts, science, social studies, mathematics, art, and music.

To support this type of learning, many schools are building flexible spaces, called project rooms. Project rooms are designed for both direct instruction and project-related work. The project room looks more like a workshop than a traditional classroom and is comparable, in many ways, to "incubator" space found in higher education programs and industries. In some recent prototypes, project rooms have been clustered around shared student work spaces, where students from several classrooms can work together or present work to a larger group.

Programming and Pre-Design

Flexibility is the key concept for the project room, which is typically rectangular, larger than a typical classroom, contains multiple utilities (power, data, lighting, water, and exhaust), and is equipped with movable worktables, as well as plenty of storage. Equipment items and tools, such as computers, hammers, and saws, are brought into the project room as needed. Movable partitions may allow for two or more project rooms to be combined for larger projects. The room should be lockable, so that in-process products are protected from vandalism. The room should be adjacent to a central studio space (common work area), as well as to teacher work stations and small group spaces, such as conference rooms or seminar rooms. Often individual, but adjacent, spaces are needed to separate "dirty" activities from "clean" areas.

Special Considerations

Storage

Providing adequate storage is critical to allow for flexible use of any educational space. Particularly for project rooms, large storage closets allow for the safe storage of student projects, use of a variety of equipment and furniture, and the convenient location of supplies such as wood, paper, cardboard, electronic components, and construction materials.

Power and Data

Plug molding should provide a generous number of electrical outlets on every wall in order to maximize flexibility of the project room. Certain equipment may have voltage requirements that differ from the general building service. At least one data drop (connection point to the computer network) and an extra outlet should be provided on each wall for a printer. In addition, a power and a data drop should be provided in the ceiling for a digital projector.

Finishes

Walls should be simple painted surfaces, easily repairable if they become damaged. The ceiling can be an open grid, providing opportunities for hanging materials. A combination of white boards and bulletin boards should be provided on parts of at least two walls. No one area needs to be the "front" of the room, as in a typical classroom, as project rooms should be designed for flexibility. Storage cabinets and shelving should be mobile, and a large utility-type sink should be considered.

Visibility

Interior windows into adjacent spaces, such as the shared studio or computer work areas, will allow faculty to monitor students from any location. Doors should also be glazed to increase the feeling of openness within enclosed spaces.

Security

It is important that the classroom door and storage units be lockable in order to limit unauthorized access and to protect the equipment, as well as ongoing student projects and materials.

Example

The Gary and Jerri-Ann Jacobs High Tech High School, a charter school in San Diego, California serving approximately 400 students, is designed to support project-based learning, team teaching, and community-based internships. Specialty labs, flexible classroom space, multi-purpose seminar rooms, and project rooms are connected to an advanced electronic infrastructure. Glass partitions are used to separate different work and study areas, creating a quiet atmosphere while maintaining an open feel in the space.

One portion of the school was designed as a learning community with six project rooms, accommodating 25 students each, clustered around student work stations. The project rooms are used for direct instruction and project work, and include movable worktables, computer stations, and storage. The project rooms are designed for maximum flexibility in terms of arrangement and use and have multiple power and data connections. One computer or laptop is provided for every two students within the work station area. Glass partitions provide visibility between the project rooms and studio.

The work station areas are linked to one another and to the rest of the school by a widened corridor called the "gallery." The gallery is used to exhibit student work and for student presentations to parents and outside professionals. Community members are invited into the school as mentors, tutors, portfolio panelists, competition judges, project advisors, and visiting professionals. Visitors have access a variety of public meeting and conference areas, as well as work stations with computer and telephone access.

High Tech High uses a team teaching approach. One or two teachers may be assigned to each project room, and no teacher instructs more than seventy-five students. The teaching teams have a core curriculum of science/math, humanities, and foreign languages. Teachers provide direct instruction and supervision of projects in the project rooms, as well as supervision of students working independently at workstations in the studio. Teacher work stations are located in close proximity to the instructional areas.

Figures 5.16 through 5.18 show the project rooms, with computer stations, flexible furnishings, and glass partitions to teacher offices and student work station area.

Figure 5.16
Seminar Room, Gary and Jerri-Ann Jacobs High Tech High School, San Diego, CA
Computer stations with flexible furnishings and glass partition between teacher offices and student work station area.
Photo Credit: High Tech High

Figure 5.17
Work Station Area and Project Room, Behind. Gary and Jerri-Ann Jacobs High Tech High School, San Diego, CA
Computer work stations along the wall and moveable tables in the center.
Photo Credit: High Tech High

Figure 5.18
Project Room and Robotics Workshop, Gary and Jerri-Ann Jacobs High Tech High School, San Diego, CA
Photo Credit: High Tech High

Conclusion

Each specialty space described in this chapter has its own individual components, and has the added challenge of fitting appropriately into the overall school facility. Time must be spent organizing and designing these spaces, and selecting the right location for them. The process requires a concerted planning effort that involves the expertise of planners, architects, engineers, teachers, and other specialists. Planning will require the eye of an artist, the precise mind of an engineer, the creatively technical nature of an architect, and a collaborative effort from everyone involved in the project. As described in the discussion of each specialty section, the adjacency relationships, acoustical properties, lighting techniques, HVAC, electrical and plumbing requirements, finish selections, and specialized equipment and furnishings must all be carefully considered and evaluated thoroughly by a knowledgeable professional.

Successfully weaving together specialty spaces with the core classrooms, administrative areas, support spaces, circulation spaces, and gathering areas is what creates the character of a school. Specialty spaces are intended to enhance the educational experience of students at all levels. In addition, each specialty space will have a unique function that will have the possibility of stimulating students to pursue an interest that may lead to a rewarding career. Future professional athletes, actors, musicians, artists, scientists, architects, engineers, librarians, and many more professionals can establish their career goals by learning in one of these special environments.

An additional goal of many of these spaces is to invite members of the local community to participate in school-related activities and after-hours community education programs. Although some of these spaces may add significant cost to a school building project, they may also have the potential of generating revenue for the school and will add extraordinary educational value to any school's program.

Part II

The Construction Process

When the initial planning is complete, and a final design approved, the school building team and their representatives proceed to the construction phase. This means working their way through the contractor selection process, refining the project's budget and schedule, and then overseeing its progress.

This part of the book examines all of the major aspects of the construction phase: cost estimating, scheduling, types of construction contracts, and the bidding process. In Chapter 9, a professional project manager identifies the services typically provided by consultants who fulfill this role, as well as value-added assistance that schools who engage project managers may request. The last chapter describes the importance of a unified project team — owner, architect/engineer, and contractor — and offers practical guidelines for establishing solid, effective working relationships at the start, and maintaining them throughout the project. The chapter also identifies important actions that should be taken to help ensure safety, quality, and on-time delivery.

Chapter 6

Cost Estimating

Joseph Macaluso, CCC

What will a new or remodeled school facility cost? Being able to answer that question with confidence at any given time is of critical importance in a well-run project. If costs are to be managed, they need to be known. Cost estimating is required to set, adjust, and manage the budget. It must be an integral part of the project effort, from early program development through to the ribbon-cutting ceremony and beyond.

Different techniques are used to create estimates at various stages of the project. As a school construction project or program evolves, the method of estimating should progress, from conceptual and approximate, to specific and detailed. The process begins with the Order of Magnitude estimate, followed by the Occupant Unit, then the Square Foot and Assembly estimates, and finally the Unit Price, or detailed, estimate. Estimate accuracy should increase as details about the project are defined. A general rule is to be as precise as the details will allow, and to spend the time required as the details warrant. *(See Figure 6.1.)*

Organizing the Estimate: Work Breakdown Structures

The budget's line items should be appropriately categorized as the level of detail increases. (The term *line item* in budgeting and estimating refers to the description and costs associated with a particular item. The word *line* is used because these costs are usually represented on a single row or line in a budget or estimate.) The line item can be as broad as the foundation, walls, or roof in preliminary estimates, or it can be as specific as rebar ties, drywall taping, or snow guards in detailed estimates. One useful tool to manage these line items, or details, is called a *work breakdown structure*, or WBS. This is a hierarchical breakdown of a project that contains successive levels of detail. Each level is a finer breakdown of the preceding level. The estimator can use either an existing WBS or a unique number- or letter-coding system. The WBS provides a way to incorporate project details as they become available without having to prepare an entirely

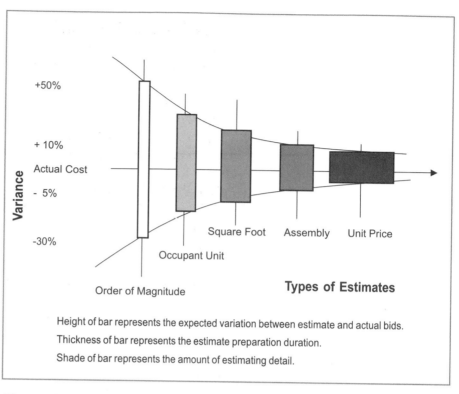

Height of bar represents the expected variation between estimate and actual bids.

Thickness of bar represents the estimate preparation duration.

Shade of bar represents the amount of estimating detail.

Figure 6.1
Types of Estimates and Their Accuracy

new estimate or budget at each new level. The first level, 1, can further be defined in a second level of detail that will begin with 1.1, 1.2, and 1.3, etc. The next would be 1.1.1, 1.1.2, and 1.1.3, and so forth.

The two most popular WBS formats used for construction are the Construction Specifications Institute's (CSI) MasterFormat and the UNIFORMAT II system, adopted by American Society of Testing and Materials (ASTM). MasterFormat is based on materials for the related installation tasks, such as wood, concrete, and masonry, whereas UNIFORMAT II is based on installation of complete building systems, such as substructure (a basement foundation or slab), building shell (a roof, exterior wall, or window), and so forth. In addition to these popular formats, some architectural, engineering, and construction firms use their own form of WBS. For school projects, custom WBS formats are likely to be based on MasterFormat or UNIFORMAT II systems, with only slight variations. Most top-level divisions in any WBS will follow the order in which a building is constructed. For example, in MasterFormat, excavation (Site Construction – Division 2) will precede foundation work (Concrete – Division 3).

CSI MasterFormat

In the MasterFormat system, typically used for detailed estimates, basement wall costs, for example, would be included in "Concrete–Division 3." *(See Figure 6.2.)* The concrete forms part of the cost would be included in the "Structural Cast-in-Place Forms" section of Division 3. The actual cost per unit of basement wall may be defined with a line number, such as 03110-455. The complete MasterFormat WBS is available for purchase on the Internet at www.csinet.org

UNIFORMAT II

In the UNIFORMAT II system, typically used in preliminary estimates, the basement wall costs would be included in the "Substructure–Major Group Element A." The particular system selected would be included in the more specifically defined "Basement Construction (A20)." The actual cost of the foundation wall may be defined with a line item number, such as "A2020." *(See Figure 6.3.)* The complete UNIFORMAT II WBS is available for purchase on the Internet at www.uniformat.com

Contractor Estimates vs. Owner Estimates

Estimating departments or consultants preparing estimates for the owner should estimate the project as closely as possible to the way a contractor would estimate these costs. However, there are some unavoidable differences:

Contractors:

- Estimate projects using their own detailed cost data compiled from actual project costs.
- Have exact pricing knowledge, including available discounts from suppliers.
- Can obtain firm quotes or guaranteed prices on equipment and materials.
- Know which construction methods they will use.
- Know what their overhead is and how much profit they will include.
- Have as their goal to be the lowest bidder (on projects where the lowest bid is the one accepted), while still making a profit. (Some bidding procedures seek the "most qualified" bidder.) *See Chapter 8 for more on contracts and bidding.*

Owners or Their Representatives:

- Must often rely on third-party cost guides, and do not have as much access to actual, detailed job cost data.
- Have less access to exact pricing from suppliers.
- Cannot always obtain firm quotes or guaranteed pricing for equipment and materials.

Division 1—General Requirements
01100 Summary
01200 Price and Payment Procedures
01300 Administrative Requirements
01400 Quality Requirements
01500 Temporary Facilities and Controls
01600 Product Requirements
01700 Execution Requirements
01800 Facility Operation
01900 Facility Decommissioning

Division 2—Site Construction
02050 Basic Site Materials and Methods
02100 Site Remediation
02200 Site Preparation
02300 Earthwork
02400 Tunneling, Boring, and Jacking
02450 Foundation and Load-bearing Elements
02500 Utility Services
02600 Drainage and Containment
02700 Bases, Ballasts, Pavements, and Appurtenances
02800 Site Improvements and Amenities
02900 Planting
02950 Site Restoration and Rehabilitation

Division 3—Concrete
03050 Basic Concrete Materials and Methods
03100 Concrete Forms and Accessories
03200 Concrete Reinforcement
03300 Cast-in-Place Concrete
03400 Precast Concrete
03500 Cementitious Decks and Underlayment
03600 Grouts
03700 Mass Concrete
03900 Concrete Restoration and Cleaning

Division 4—Masonry
04050 Basic Masonry Materials and Methods
04200 Masonry Units
04400 Stone
04500 Refractories
04600 Corrosion-Resistant Masonry
04700 Simulated Masonry
04800 Masonry Assemblies
04900 Masonry Restoration and Cleaning

Division 5—Metals
05050 Basic Metal Materials and Methods
05100 Structural Metal Framing
05200 Metal Joists
05300 Metal Deck
05400 Cold-Formed Metal Framing
05500 Metal Fabrications
05600 Hydraulic Fabrications
05650 Railroad Track and Accessories
05700 Ornamental Metal
05800 Expansion Control
05900 Metal Restoration and Cleaning

Division 6—Wood and Plastics
06050 Basic Wood and Plastic Materials and Methods
06100 Rough Carpentry
06200 Finish Carpentry
06400 Architectural Woodwork
06500 Structural Plastics
06600 Plastic Fabrications
06900 Wood and Plastic Restoration and Cleaning

Division 7—Thermal and Moisture Protection
07050 Basic Thermal and Moisture Protection Materials and Methods
07100 Dampproofing and Waterproofing
07200 Thermal Protection
07300 Shingles, Roof Tiles, and Roof Coverings
07400 Roofing and Siding Panels
07500 Membrane Roofing
07600 Flashing and Sheet Metal
07700 Roof Specialties and Accessories
07800 Fire and Smoke Protection
07900 Joint Sealers

Division 8—Doors and Windows
08050 Basic Door and Window Materials and Methods
08100 Metal Doors and Frames
08200 Wood and Plastic Doors
08300 Specialty Doors
08400 Entrances and Storefronts
08500 Windows
08600 Skylights
08700 Hardware
08800 Glazing
08900 Glazed Curtain Wall

Division 9—Finishes
09050 Basic Finish Materials and Methods
09100 Metal Support Assemblies
09200 Plaster and Gypsum Board
09300 Tile
09400 Terrazzo
09500 Ceilings
09600 Flooring
09700 Wall Finishes
09800 Acoustical Treatment
09900 Paints and Coatings

Division 10—Specialties
10100 Visual Display Boards
10150 Compartments and Cubicles
10200 Louvers and Vents
10240 Grilles and Screens
10250 Service Walls
10260 Wall and Corner Guards
10270 Access Flooring
10290 Pest Control
10300 Fireplaces and Stoves
10340 Manufactured Exterior Specialties
10350 Flagpoles
10400 Identification Devices
10450 Pedestrian Control Devices
10500 Lockers
10520 Fire Protection Specialties
10530 Protective Covers
10550 Postal Specialties
10600 Partitions
10670 Storage Shelving
10700 Exterior Protection
10750 Telephone Specialties
10800 Toilet, Bath, and Laundry Accessories
10880 Scales
10900 Wardrobe and Closet Specialties

Figure 6.2
MasterFormat Classification with Subcategories

Division 11—Equipment

11010 Maintenance Equipment
11020 Security and Vault Equipment
11030 Teller and Service Equipment
11040 Ecclesiastical Equipment
11050 Library Equipment
11060 Theater and Stage Equipment
11070 Instrumental Equipment
11080 Registration Equipment
11090 Checkroom Equipment
11100 Mercantile Equipment
11110 Commercial Laundry and Dry Cleaning Equipment
11120 Vending Equipment
11130 Audio-Visual Equipment
11140 Vehicle Service Equipment
11150 Parking Control Equipment
11160 Loading Dock Equipment
11170 Solid Waste Handling Equipment
11190 Detention Equipment
11200 Water Supply and Treatment Equipment
11280 Hydraulic Gates and Valves
11300 Fluid Waste Treatment and Disposal Equipment
11400 Food Service Equipment
11450 Residential Equipment
11460 Unit Kitchens
11470 Darkroom Equipment
11480 Athletic, Recreational, and Therapeutic Equipment
11500 Industrial and Process Equipment
11600 Laboratory Equipment
11650 Planetarium Equipment
11660 Observatory Equipment
11680 Office Equipment
11700 Medical Equipment
11780 Mortuary Equipment
11850 Navigation Equipment
11870 Agricultural Equipment
11900 Exhibit Equipment

Division 12—Furnishing

12050 Fabrics
12100 Art
12300 Manufactured Casework
12400 Furnishings and Accessories
12500 Furniture
12600 Multiple Seating
12700 Systems Furniture
12800 Interior Plants and Planters
12900 Furnishings Repair and Restoration

Division 13—Special Construction

13010 Air-Supported Structures
13020 Building Modules
13030 Special Purpose Rooms
13080 Sound, Vibration, and Seismic Control
13090 Radiation Protection
13100 Lightning Protection
13110 Cathodic Protection
13120 Pre-Engineered Structures
13150 Swimming Pools
13160 Aquariums
13165 Aquatic Park Facilities
13170 Tubs and Pools
13175 Ice Rinks
13185 Kennels and Animal Shelters
13190 Site-Constructed Incinerators
13200 Storage Tanks
13220 Filter Underdrains and Media
13230 Digester Covers and Appurtenances
13240 Oxygenation Systems
13260 Sludge Conditioning Systems
13280 Hazardous Material Remediation
13400 Measurement and Control Instrumentation
13500 Recording Instrumentation
13550 Transportation Control Instrumentation
13600 Solar and Wind Energy Equipment
13700 Security Access and Surveillance
13800 Building Automation and Control
13850 Detection and Alarm
13900 Fire Suppression

Division 14—Conveying Systems

14100 Dumbwaiters
14200 Elevators
14300 Escalators and Moving Walks
14400 Lifts
14500 Material Handling
14600 Hoists and Cranes
14700 Turntables
14800 Scaffolding
14900 Transportation

Division 15—Mechanical

15050 Basic Mechanical Materials and Methods
15100 Building Services Piping
15200 Process Piping
15300 Fire Protection Piping
15400 Plumbing Fixtures and Equipment
15500 Heat-Generation Equipment
15600 Refrigeration Equipment
15700 Heating, Ventilating, and Air Conditioning Equipment
15800 Air Distribution
15900 HVAC Instrumentation and Controls
15950 Testing, Adjusting, and Balancing

Division 16—Electrical

16050 Basic Electrical Materials and Methods
16100 Wiring Methods
16200 Electrical Power
16300 Transmission and Distribution
16400 Low-Voltage Distribution
16500 Lighting
16700 Communications
16800 Sound and Video

Figure 6.2
MasterFormat Classification with Subcategories (cont.)

Major Group Elements Level 1		Group Elements Level 2	Individual Elements Level 3
A	Substructure	A10 Foundations	A1010 Standard Foundations A1020 Special Foundations A1030 Slab on Grade
		A20 Basement Construction	A2010 Basement Excavation A2020 Basement Walls
B	Shell	B10 Superstructure	B1010 Floor Construction B1020 Roof Construction
		B20 Exterior Enclosure	B2010 Exterior Walls B2020 Exterior Windows B2030 Exterior Doors
		B30 Roofing	B3010 Roof Coverings B3020 Roof Openings
C	Interiors	C10 Interior Construction	C1010 Partitions C1020 Interior Doors C1030 Fitting
		C20 Stairs	C2010 Stair Construction C2020 Stair Finishes
		C30 Interior Finishes	C3010 Wall Finishes C3020 Floor Finishes C3030 Ceiling Finishes
D	Services	D10 Conveying	D1010 Elevators & Lifts D1020 Escalators & Moving Walks D1090 Other Conveying Systems
		D20 Plumbing	D2010 Plumbing Fixtures D2020 Domestic Water Distribution D2030 Sanitary Waste D2040 Rain Water Drainage D2090 Other Plumbing Systems
		D30 HVAC	D3010 Energy Supply D3020 Heat Generating System D3030 Cooling Generating System D3040 Distribution Systems D3050 Terminal & Package Units D3060 Controls & Instrumentation D3070 Systems Testing & Balance D3090 Other HVAC Systems & Equipment
		D40 Fire Protection	D4010 Sprinklers D4020 Standpipes D4030 Fire Protection Specialties D4090 Other Fire Protection Systems
		D50 Electrical	D5010 Electrical Service & Distribution D5020 Lighting and Branch Wiring D5030 Communications & Safety D5090 Other Electrical Systems
E	Equipment & Furnishings	E10 Equipment	E1010 Commercial Equipment E1020 Institutional Equipment E1030 Vehicular Equipment E1090 Other Equipment
		E20 Furnishings	E2010 Fixed Furnishings E2020 Movable Furnishings
F	Special Construction & Demolition	F10 Special Construction	F1010 Special Structures F1020 Integrated Construction F1030 Special Construction Systems F1040 Special Facilities F1050 Special Controls and Instrumentation
		F20 Selective Building Demolition	F2010 Building Elements Demolition F2020 Hazardous Components Abatement

Figure 6.3
UNIFORMAT II Classification and Subcategories

- Must approximate methods that will be used by the contractor.
- May not always have the specialized expertise to be able to identify all of the tasks associated with a work item (e.g., a retaining wall may require waterproofing, French drains, and select backfill material).
- Must approximate the amount of overhead and profit the contractor will include.
- Have as a goal the ability to predict what a reasonable low bid will be.

Order of Magnitude Cost Estimates

Even before a school construction budget is developed, a figure must be established as a starting point to begin discussions of costs for the proposed school. This type of "ballpark" figure is typically referred to as an *Order of Magnitude estimate* and may be somewhat anecdotal in nature. Cost may be estimated per classroom and derived from recent projects, or from published sources, such as RSMeans cost data. Order of Magnitude estimates typically fall in the range between 30% below to 50% above what the actual cost of the project will turn out to be. This estimate may or may not include owner costs, such as legal, architectural, and engineering fees; changes to the original plans and specifications; or other post-bid-award costs.

The costs included in any estimate should be spelled out as clearly as possible, even at this early stage. A cost escalation factor should be added to adjust for increased costs, because the proposed school will be built at some point in the future, and the schools used as a basis for the estimate were built at some point the past. Because there are virtually no details to consider, examine, or analyze, an Order of Magnitude estimate for a typical school building can be derived in a matter of minutes.

It is important to exercise caution when doing early estimates, because such approximations of costs will be used in feasibility studies and initial project budgeting. It is human nature to remember the first (or lowest) cost mentioned. If the estimate is too low, it will cause problems throughout the project.

The following is a statement based on an Order of Magnitude estimate:

> *Based on past experience, construction costs for a 40-classroom high school to be built in an urban area of the Northeast two years from now would be in the area of $60,000,000.*

Occupant Unit Cost Estimates

As a school program develops, the first information to solidify is likely to be the number of students the school will serve. At this stage, costs are likely to be thought of in terms of *per pupil*. Estimates that use a common unit relating to the facility's occupants are called *Occupant Unit, End Product Unit, End Unit,* or *Capacity* estimates. Costs are expressed in terms of costs per the common unit, which can be seats for auditoriums, beds for hospitals, or rental rooms for hotels. For schools, the common element is pupils (alternatively expressed as students, desks, or seats).

The first step is to gather data on as many recently completed schools as possible. Schools used as a basis for estimating the proposed school should be of the same grade level, (elementary, middle school, junior high school, or senior high school), same general geographic area, and roughly the same size. High schools, for example, tend to cost more than elementary schools because of additional labs and physical education facilities, more sophisticated technology (computers, video equipment, etc.), and more sophisticated equipment in auditoriums and theatre facilities. Schools in harsher climates tend to cost more to construct than those in more temperate climates. (Facilities with very warm or cold weather, such as Florida and Alaska, require more air-conditioning or heating equipment and more insulation.) School facilities that are more than 20 years old are not appropriate for comparison, since building materials, design, and technology change over time. For each school, the total cost is divided by the number of pupils that the school is designed to accommodate to arrive at a *cost per student*.

Adjusting Costs for Escalation and Location

The preliminary Occupant Unit estimate will have to be adjusted, or factored, to account for cost escalation between the time the other schools were completed and the proposed project's construction time frame for the new school facility being estimated. This adjustment requires calculating an escalation rate for each of the completed projects, from the midpoint of their construction to the expected midpoint of the proposed new project's construction.

In addition, regional labor and material cost differences must be taken into account—between each of the completed projects and those project locations and the location of the proposed new school project. Cost escalation and location factors can be found in Means Cost Data publications (in the form of "Location Factors," "City Cost Indexes," and "Historical Cost Indexes"). *Engineering News Record* (ENR) magazine also publishes escalation rates for specific cities. *(See Part IV, "School Construction Costs," and the Resources section at the back of this book for additional information.)* These adjustments and the resulting estimate will be more precise than in the Order of Magnitude estimate, as the proposed school's location and construction time frame are likely to be better defined at this stage.

Numbers Used to Express Central Tendency

The cost per student of the proposed school (whether in Order of Magnitude, Occupant Unit Cost, or Square Foot estimates) can be expressed as a range or a single number. A single number can be used for a *central tendency* representing a range of numbers by stating the middle ground. The three most common ways to measure central tendency are the *mode, mean,* and *median*.

- The *mode* is the most frequently occurring value in a distribution of numbers. If one wanted to determine the central tendency in the ages of a group of people, and their ages were 30, 35, 35, 38, 38, 38, 40, 41, the mode would be 38 because it occurs most frequently. This method works fine for small numbers, but in the case of construction costs, it would be very unusual for two or more projects to have the same costs. For example if per-pupil school construction costs for seven different schools were $31,000, $57,800, $58,500, $59,100, $60,300, $61,400, and $63,100, there is no mode, and it is not always useful for estimating construction costs.

- The *mean*, often called the *average*, is the sum of all the values in the distribution, divided by the number of values. Using the same example with per-pupil school construction costs in seven different schools of $31,000, $57,800, $58,500, $59,100, $60,300, $61,400, $63,100, the mean cost per pupil would be $391,200/7 = $55,885.

- The *median* represents the number at the midpoint; in other words, half of the distribution has values less than this amount, and half of the distribution contains values greater than this amount. For example, with the same distribution of per-pupil school construction costs of $31,000, $57,800, $58,500, $59,100, $60,300, $61,400, $63,100, the median would be the fourth number in the list, $59,100.

As is evident from the examples of the mean and median, these two measures will yield different results if the values are not evenly distributed. Use of the median will cancel out values that are atypical, such as the $31,000 figure in this example.

The per-pupil, or Occupant Unit cost, estimate is a useful tool, because the budget can be adjusted easily as a better idea of the number of expected pupils is finalized. The accuracy of this type of estimate falls between that of an Order of Magnitude estimate and a Square Foot estimate. This type of estimate can be produced in one day and has an accuracy range of from about 25% below the actual cost of the project to about 40% above.

The following statement is based on an Occupant Unit estimate:

> The expected construction costs for an 800-pupil high school built in Queens County in New York City with an approximate mid-point of construction in 2006, is $65,000 per pupil or $52,000,000.

Square Foot Cost Estimates

After the educational specifications have been written, and a program has been developed by an architect, the next likely discussion will center on the square footage of the proposed school building. This is the stage where the physical aspects of an actual building are developed, and the size of the building is discussed. At this time, the cost per square foot is an important part of the budget. As in the occupant unit estimate, the first step is to gather cost information on as many recently completed schools of the same type as possible. This information is available for public schools, since they are government-funded. Cost data for private schools may be available through the architect, builder, or owner, though in some cases, they may not be able or willing to release this data. *(See also the "Historical Costs" section of this chapter.)*

For each school, the total cost is divided into the gross square footage of that school to arrive at a cost per square foot. Next, the cost per square foot for each school will have to be adjusted for inflation over time to the expected midpoint of construction of the proposed new school, and for location differences between the completed schools and the proposed new school. These adjustments, and the resulting estimate, should be more precise at this stage, as the location and the time frame will likely be better defined than they were at the Order of Magnitude and Occupant Unit stages.

As in Occupant Unit cost estimates, after the cost per square foot of each school has been adjusted, the result is expressed in terms of a range, mean, or median cost per square foot. In addition to overall construction costs, it is also worthwhile to calculate square foot costs for the major WBS headings (concrete, masonry, metals, etc., for estimates prepared in CSI MasterFormat; and substructure, shell, interiors, etc., for estimates prepared in UNIFORMAT II). Calculating the square foot costs at more detailed levels than these major headings is usually not very helpful. More detailed costs are rarely required and are not very accurate at this stage.

Calculating Area for Square Foot Estimates

Square foot construction costs are based on the gross square footage of building area. Generally, basements, sub-basements, mechanical spaces, stair bulkheads, and other enclosed spaces should be included in the total square footage. Balconies, canopied areas, and open terraces should be counted as one-half of their total square footage. The space above auditoriums and gymnasiums that extends beyond the first floor should not be included in the square footage. If there is an interstitial (between floors) space without any equipment in it, it should also not be included. If, however, the interstitial space houses equipment that would otherwise need dedicated space, the area should be included in the square footage. *(See Figure 6.4.) (For a complete list of guidelines, refer to the American Institute of Architects Document D101, or the Association for the Advancement of Cost Engineering International's recommended practices and standards for square foot calculations.)* When working with square foot costs, remember that due to the decreasing relative contribution of exterior walls and the economies of scale that come with a larger building, square foot costs will tend to be lower for larger buildings. *(See Figure 6.5.)*

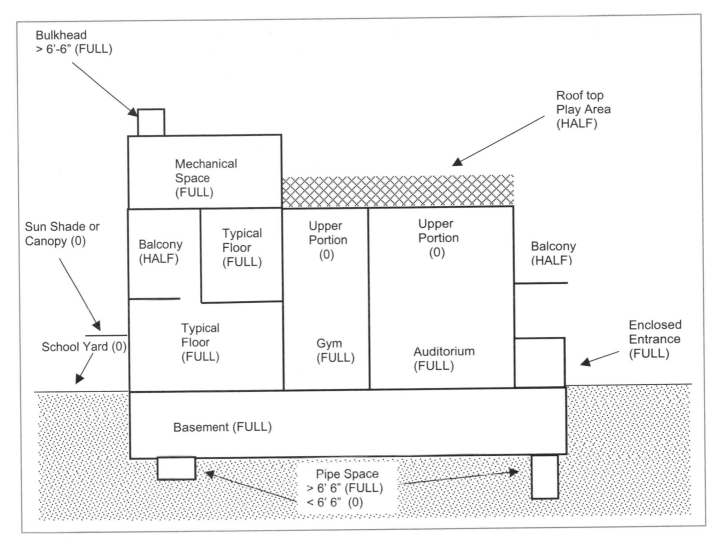

Figure 6.4
Standards for Calculating Gross Square Footage

School administrators may be accustomed to thinking in terms of square feet of program area, or net square footage. Program area can be converted to gross building area and vice versa using a factor called the *gross to net ratio* for each program area. Similarly, there are factors for gross square footage of a school to the number of pupils. *(See Figure 6.6.)*

When working with Square Foot estimates, site construction and site improvements (CSI MasterFormat Division 02, UNIFORMAT II Division G), costs should not be included, but rather added as a separate figure, since there is no direct relationship between the amount of site construction and site improvements required for a specific size school building. As a matter of expedience, however, site work is sometimes included in the square foot cost. Notes accompanying Square Foot

Building size in Square feet	Square Foot Project Size Modifier			
	Elementary	Junior High	Senior High	Vocational
20,000				1.10
25,000	1.10*			↑
30,000	↑			
35,000				1.00*
40,000	1.00*			
45,000				
50,000	↓	1.10	1.10	
55,000	0.95	↑	↑	
60,000				
65,000				
70,000				
75,000				↓
80,000				.95
85,000				
90,000		1.00*		
95,000				
100,000			1.00*	
105,000				
110,000				
115,000		↓		
120,000		.95		
130,000				
135,000				
140,000				
145,000				
150,000				
155,000				
160,000				
165,000				
170,000			↓	
175,000			.95	

Figure 6.5

Square Foot Project Size Modifier Table

This table shows the typical gross square foot ranges for elementary, junior high, senior high, and vocational schools. The figures in the shaded areas represent the range of adjustment factors to convert square foot costs of a typical size school building (see asterisks) to the particular building project based on its size.

estimates should always indicate whether the estimate is based on gross square footage of the building or on program area, and whether or not site work is included in the cost per square foot.

The Square Foot estimating method has an accuracy range of about 20% below to about 30% above the actual cost of the project. Estimate preparation time for a new school building would typically be about one day.

The following statement is based on a Square Foot Estimate:

> *The expected construction cost for a 140,000 square foot high school built in Queens County in New York City, with an approximate mid-point of construction in 2006, is $345 per square foot, or $48,300,000.*

Assemblies Cost Estimates

At the design development stage, after the program and schematic design have been completed by the architect and preliminary plans are starting to be prepared, it is time to consider the major systems to be used in the school facility. Should the school be air-conditioned? What type of heating system should be used? Should the exterior of the building be brick, concrete block, or another material? During this stage of development, cost estimates are necessary to determine not only the overall building cost, but the cost for major building systems. The Assemblies (or Systems) estimating method is often used at this stage to evaluate the relative costs of major systems and their impact on the project budget.

The Assemblies estimate method breaks down a building into individual building systems. Each of these systems, or assemblies, is further broken down into sub-assemblies. For example, a partition assembly is comprised of studs, drywall, and other components. To expedite the estimating process for this partition assembly, these components are all combined and priced out in a common unit. In the case of the partition assembly, the unit is one square foot of wall. The estimate may show a single cost for the whole assembly or include a breakdown of all the components that make up the assembly, depending on how much information is available or the level of detail required. Normally,

Gross Square Footage Per Pupil				
Quality Level	**Elementary**	**Junior High**	**Senior High**	**Vocational**
Higher	90	129	145	195
Median	77	110	130	135
Lower	65	85	102	110

Figure 6.6
Square Footage Per Pupil

Assemblies cost estimates are organized by the UNIFORMAT II WBS, or a variation of it.

The Assemblies estimating method has an accuracy range from about 10% below to about 20% above the actual cost of the project. Preparing an Assemblies estimate for a typical new school building is likely to take about one week.

Unit Price Estimates

The Unit Price estimate is the most detailed of the estimating methods, and should be used when the plans and specifications are more than 65% complete. It is not uncommon to have two or three versions of an estimate prepared as the level of plans and specifications progresses to completion. For example, estimates may be prepared at the 75%, 90%, and 100% levels of completion.

The Unit Price estimate will include costs for each individual item of work. A breakdown of material, labor, and equipment should be provided for each line item. Major headings and subheadings are used to subtotal individual costs. With this type of estimate, the contractor's overhead, profit, owner costs, potential construction change orders (construction contingencies), and potential design changes (design contingencies) are all provided as separate line items. When estimating the cost of a new school using the Unit Price method, the project plans can be separated into general construction, mechanical, and electrical categories, and estimated by estimators specializing in those trades. Computer software allows several users to work on the same project simultaneously.

The accuracy of Unit Price estimates is in the range from about 5% below to about 10% above actual costs. Estimate preparation time for a Unit Price estimate of a typical new school building is approximately a month, but that time can be reduced significantly if several estimators are assigned to the same project.

Unit Price estimating is also used for estimating renovation work because there is such a variation of existing conditions and scope of work from project to project. For preliminary estimates, sizeable allowances and contingencies are required, because of the many unknowns, such as unforeseen existing conditions that will affect the renovation cost. Occupant Unit, Square Foot, or Assemblies estimating methods can be used to arrive at preliminary renovation costs for classrooms, gyms, kitchens, and administrative areas, but this approach requires access to a large database of similar projects.

Accounting for All Unit Costs

It is important to define what cost items are included in any cost estimate. Many terms have different meanings to different people, so it should never be assumed that a particular cost is or is not included in any estimate. The following is a general outline of costs included in school construction budgets:

The contractor's bid amount includes:

- Contractor's direct costs
- Contractor's indirect costs
- Contractor's overhead and profit
- Contractor's contingencies

Construction costs usually include the contractor's bid amount, plus:

- Architectural and engineering fees
- Project management/oversight fees
- Change order costs

Project costs usually include construction costs, plus:

- Furnishings and equipment costs
- Land acquisition costs and fees
- Project administration costs
- Legal fees
- Financing costs
- Environmental studies costs
- Permits

It is important to note that while the contractor's bid amount is usually straightforward (depending on the type of project delivery method used), construction and project budgets vary considerably in terms of what is or is not included. Therefore, it is critical that every estimate include a basis of the estimate statement with the following information:

- *Purpose:* A clarification of how the estimate is to be used, the standards of accuracy, and the intended purpose of the estimate, e.g., a study, a bid, a budget, and so forth.
- *Scope of Work:* A brief overview of what is included in the estimate and what portion of a larger project the estimate may represent.
- *Assumptions and Exclusions:* A list of assumptions made because of incomplete design information, and a listing of anything excluded from the estimate.
- *Time/Cost Association:* The project schedule and escalation rates that were assumed in the estimate.
- *Contingency Development:* The method and/or rates used to develop contingencies.
- *Significant Findings:* A notice of any items of significant risk, concern, or interest that the estimator is aware of in regard to the estimate.[1]

As the project progresses, and the estimating method changes from Order of Magnitude to Occupant Unit Cost, to Square Foot, to Assemblies, to Unit Price, the basis of the estimate should become more and more detailed.

Contingency

A contingency is the amount added to an estimate and budget to cover costs that are likely to be incurred, but are difficult or impossible to precisely predict. The two major categories are costs *due to design changes*, and *costs due to unforeseen construction conditions*. These contingencies should be included in the total of all estimates. Order of Magnitude, Capacity, and Square Foot estimates will have these costs built into their totals. Assemblies estimates may have contingencies built into the totals of each system or added to the total as separate line items at the end of the estimate. Unit Cost estimates list contingencies as separate line items, and may include two contingencies:

- *Design Contingency* to cover additional costs for possible design changes. The amount of contingency varies with the stages of design. At first, a larger design contingency will be used. As the design is finalized, the contingency should be reduced to near zero for most new school building projects.
- *Construction Contingency* to cover the additional costs of unforeseen factors relating to construction, such the additional costs of dealing with unanticipated conditions such as utility pipes, underground storage tanks, or large rock ledges on the site, which have to be removed in order for the work to continue. This contingency will be reduced somewhat as field conditions are better defined, and typically will end up at about 5%-10% of total construction costs for most new school building projects.

Sometimes an *Owner's Contingency* is also included in the estimate and budget to specifically cover costs directly attributed to the owner. In a *Guaranteed Maximum Price* (GMP) contract agreement *(see Chapter 8)*, budget contingencies may be categorized as *Owner's Contingency* and *Builder's Contingency*. The Owner's Contingency is for costs over and above the base budget for which the owner is responsible, and the Builder's Contingency is for costs over and above the base budget for which the builder is responsible.

Historical Cost Data

If an estimator does not have access to his or her own source of relevant completed school project cost data to use as a basis for an Order of Magnitude, Occupant Unit, or Square Foot estimate, there are other ways to obtain cost information. Since the vast majority of schools are publicly funded, the overall costs, and possibly more detailed costs, may be public record. Case studies will often include the project's basic description, total cost, size, location, and completion date, and may also include a cost breakdown by MasterFormat division, or by the first level of detail in the UNIFORMAT II system. A more detailed description, number of pupils, photographs, and floor plans may also be available from periodicals and Internet Web sites.

Building Design & Construction, School Construction News, and *Design Cost Data* are three magazines that publish case studies of recently completed construction projects, including schools. These are a good source of useful information. Case study information is also available on the Internet, through B*uilding Design & Construction* (www.bdcmag.com), *School Construction News* (www.schoolconstructionnews.com), and the *National Institute of Building Services* (www.edfacilities.org). Featured case studies on these Web sites are available free of charge, though the selection may be limited. *Design Cost Data* (www.dcd.com) offers an extensive selection of case studies for purchase. It is even possible to recalculate the Design Cost Data projects to arrive at theoretical costs based on adjustments to the construction dates, location, and project size, using D4Cost software or the *Design Cost Data* Internet Web site.

In addition to case studies of individual school projects, third-party cost data from RSMeans and other providers can be used for Square Foot, Occupant Unit, Assemblies, and Unit Price estimates. RSMeans cost data is compiled from a large database of current projects, and includes verification through contacts with suppliers, manufacturers, and contractors. The cost data provider should spell out the sources used to compile the data, the methods used to collect and present it, what costs are included, and specifics as to what costs are not included. The cost data source should also provide instructions on how the data should be used. RSMeans cost data is updated annually and available in printed books, and electronically on *CostWorks* CD-ROMs and on the Internet (www.rsmeans.com). RSMeans also supplies electronic cost databases to leading estimating software developers.

For Assemblies and Unit Price estimating, it is helpful to create a customized cost database (using the above-mentioned sources) for a particular school facility early on, so that it is available for future estimating projects. The assemblies in RSMeans' books, *CostWorks*, and other software can be modified easily to reflect variations in design standards, and standard details used by individual school districts and construction agencies. It is even possible to build a database that includes all the assemblies contained in a typical school. This database can be used to create a model that can be used for quickly estimating prototype school buildings. All third-party cost data, whether Occupant Unit, Square Foot, Assemblies, or Unit Price, must be adjusted to account for escalation and regional differences, including productivity differences. These factors are available in Means Cost Data books. (*See Part IV of this book.*) Typically occupant unit and square foot cost data is arranged according to the type of facility, assembly data by UNIFORMAT II, and unit price data by MasterFormat.

Change Order Cost Estimates

Modifications to the project scope—after the project has been awarded, and after the start of construction—are almost a certainty. These changes will affect individual construction contract costs and the overall construction budget. They may also affect the performance times and the overall construction schedule. Changes can occur because of the following conditions:

- Unforeseen field conditions
- Design discrepancies, errors, or omissions in the contract documents
- Changes in building code interpretations or other public authority requirements
- Completion date changes for reasons unrelated to the construction process
- Changes in availability of resources
- Owner-requested changes by design criteria, scope of work, or project objectives

For schools, change orders average about 5% of construction costs, but can easily reach 10% if any of the above factors get out of hand. This is why contingencies are included in the pre-construction cost estimates.

When preparing individual change order estimates, the estimator must take on an entirely different perspective than with pre-construction estimates. In this case, he or she must be prepared to justify a point of view. Unfortunately, human nature being what it is, the owner, architect, construction manager, and general contractor may have vastly different opinions not only as to whether a change order is justified, but also what the change is worth. Bear in mind that change order estimates are used for negotiation, and usually other estimates are prepared to justify other opposing points of view. The estimate must be detailed enough to justify the desired point of view, but it must also be reasonable. An estimate that is inflated and unreasonably one-sided will give cause for an equally inflated and one-sided response from the other camp. All costs in the estimate must be defensible. Specifications for a project should clearly define the format, level of detail, and backup documentation requirements, as well as overhead and profit percentages allowed for change order submissions. Unrealistically low allowances for overhead and profit will only encourage contractors to inflate the costs of the hard cost line items in their estimates.

Several factors must be included in estimating the cost of change order work. Post-installation change orders may need to include modification and or demolition of existing work, re-mobilizing costs, additional instruction time to understand the nature of the change work, reduced productivity due to less than optimum scheduling requirements, and increased labor costs due to work being done during overtime hours. Change orders often have an impact on the schedule, which should be included in schedule updates. *(See Chapter 7.)*

Reviewing Estimates Prepared by Others

The one sure way to verify the accuracy of an estimate prepared by others is to create a separate, independent estimate for the entire project. This is often impractical because of the amount of time that would be required to re-estimate every line item of the estimate being reviewed. Fortunately, experience and the *Pareto Effect*[2] tell us that most of a project's cost variation can be attributed to only a small percentage of the line items in the estimate. Therefore, the major effort in reviewing an estimate should be devoted to the items that have the greatest potential for cost variation. The estimate review can include an independent estimate of select individual line items. Before individual items are reviewed, however, the following tasks should be undertaken:

- Make sure the scope of work is correct and complete.
- Confirm the rationale behind the percentages used for indirect costs and contingencies.
- Make sure major cost items are included and correct.
- Check the overall project square foot or per-pupil costs to ensure they are reasonable.

To make the review process more efficient and allow for direct comparisons and cross-checking, all architects, engineers, consultants, and owner's representatives should use the same format. This holds true for every stage of the estimating process. The estimate type (square foot, unit price, etc.), level of detail, work breakdown structure system (MasterFormat, UNIFORMAT II, or specialized), and line item breakdown required (material, labor hours, hourly wage, and equipment requirements) should all be consistent.

Special Considerations in Estimating School Projects

Estimating school buildings is fairly straightforward, as schools tend to employ traditional designs and construction methods. Often, municipal and county school districts maintain design standards and standard details. Most of the existing school building stock tends to be the generic, post-war, red brick, three-story variety, although there are some truly unique older architectural gems, especially in urban areas. In the past, an estimator may have spent most of his/her time costing new schools. Now the estimating task is often more challenging and interesting when new projects include remodeling, renovation, and historic preservation work.

There are special considerations in school design and construction based on the facility's ultimate clients—children and adolescents. Because of their developing minds and bodies and dependency on others for help, they are at a greater risk to environmental hazards than most other segments of the population, and require special measures to ensure their health and well-being. Compounding the increased sensitivity of students to environmental conditions is the fact that schools have a high concentration of occupants—four times the number of occupants per square foot than the typical office building. Schools are also subjected to greater oversight and public scrutiny than most other types of buildings. Any problems that are perceived as potential threats to the health or safety of students can be emotional and quickly turn into a "media event." Special attention to environmental conditions and associated factors has both direct and indirect cost impacts on school construction.

Asbestos Abatement

It is ironic that asbestos was originally installed in so many schools to protect children from one kind of danger, fire, only to become a source of health concerns later on. Because the damaging health effects of asbestos exposure increase over time, school-aged children are at an even greater health risk than adults. In fact, symptoms of lung cancer may take over 20 years to appear. The removal of any friable (loose) or potentially friable asbestos is a higher priority in schools than in most other buildings.

Because of the justifiable concern for adequate fire-resistance by designers in the past, it should be assumed that unless remediation has been done, there is a very good chance that substantial amounts of asbestos are present in schools built before the 1970s. Asbestos was used extensively from the 1940s to the 1970s and was even used in schools built before the 1940s. When the public first learned about the dangers of asbestos in the early 1980s, there was a huge demand for immediate removal. Guidelines, procedures, and regulations were developed, and implementation was initially quite costly. As the demand for removal or abatement has leveled off, and procedures and regulations have become more practical through the years, the cost has become more reasonable.

The Asbestos Hazard Emergency Response Act (AHERA) of 1986 mandated schools to inspect for asbestos, both friable and non-friable, and to develop a management plan. As part of the inspection process, all areas that contain asbestos must be identified. This process can be a good first step for architects, engineers, and estimators in the preliminary stages of a school renovation project, as it will indicate potential additional costs for abatement work. AHERA regulations provide loans and grants to financially-strapped schools to correct serious asbestos hazards. Still, asbestos is an additional expense that must be considered when estimating school renovation projects, demolishing existing structures on the site, or whenever it is deemed necessary to maintain, repair, enclose, encapsulate, or remove asbestos.

Lead Abatement

Lead is considered the number one environmental health risk for children today, causing developmental problems even in low doses. An amount equal to only three grains of sugar a day can cause irreversible damage. Symptoms may not be noticeable for years, but can cause damage to the liver, kidneys, brain, nerves, and bones. Lead contained in layers of old paint is the primary risk to children. It should be assumed that lead is present in the paint of school buildings built before 1978. A study of California schools conducted between 1995 and 1997 revealed that over 75% of the facilities surveyed were painted with lead-based paint. Of that 75%, over 37% had deteriorating paint surfaces. The study also found that lead levels were likely to exceed the federal action level in the water sampled from drinking fixtures in about 10% of the schools tested.[3]

As with asbestos, the cost of lead paint abatement has been reduced as experience in safe and effective abatement methods has grown, and much of the work has already been performed. Buildings that require lead abatement will incur additional costs to the project, including testing, inspecting, and miscellaneous costs for additional procedures, such as wrapping windows in plastic upon removal. Reductions in the lead content in drinking water may sometimes require replacing water service pipes, but often the source of elevated levels can be isolated to individual fixtures. Procedures such as flushing out the water after long periods of disuse, or shutting off individual fixtures that have elevated lead levels, can also reduce the lead levels in drinking water significantly.

ADA Requirements

The Americans with Disabilities Act (ADA) has made a dramatic difference in the quality of life for millions of individuals—both young and old—by helping to make buildings more accessible to disabled users. Requirements include incorporating ramps, wide doors, special plumbing fixtures, and other features into the design of buildings, especially schools. The additional cost of these features is minimal in new construction, as frequently it is just a matter of location, placement, or selecting a slightly different product. For renovation work, however, implementing ADA guidelines may be more costly. Existing rooms may need to be entirely renovated, fixtures may need replacement, and stairs may need to be replaced by ramps, elevators, or lifts. An excellent source for budgeting and costing modifications necessary to meet ADA requirements is the Means *ADA Compliance Pricing Guide*.

Vandalism and Security

Unfortunately, vandalism is a fact of life in schools today, especially in urban areas. In general, materials specified for school projects must be durable and vandal-resistant, and are therefore more costly than those used for other projects, or what may have been used in the past. Examples include graffiti-resistant coatings, window guards, tall fences, and alarms to ward off intruders. Copper leaders and gutters on historically significant schools may have to be lead-coated to reduce the possibility of theft. (The coating makes it more costly to extract the copper for its scrap value, reducing the incentive for removing these items from the building, and the lead coating does not pose a heath issue in this application.) Similarly, stainless steel may have to be used where aluminum might have been planned, as it is more difficult to cut and has a lower scrap value than aluminum.

Additional security measures may include metal detectors, security mirrors, and other hardware. Some design considerations include the placement of the gymnasium, cafeteria, and auditorium (if these parts of the building will be used after normal school hours) in such a way that these facilities can be closed off to prevent access to the rest of the school building. Maximizing the lines of sight in hallways and other key areas is another design technique. Some security measures, such as employing security guards, will add to the operating budget, but not the construction budget. *(See Chapter 4 for more on security in school facility planning and design.)*

Technology

The electronic revolution has had a dramatic effect on schools. Use of the Internet as a teaching and research tool has added a whole new category of cost that did not exist for schools before the 1990s. Most new school projects include Local Area Networks (LANs) that tie several computers together, allowing them to communicate with one another. Wide Area Networks (WANs) connect several schools, usually by LANs. The cost of these systems includes the equipment itself, as well as wiring using standard copper or fiber optic cable. For new schools, the cost of cable is minimal as a percentage of the equipment, if installed before the interior walls are closed up. For existing schools, retrofitted cable needs to be snaked through existing walls and ceilings, which is quite labor-intensive. Wireless networks are emerging and will eliminate the cost of fishing wires through the existing structure, but will increase the cost of the equipment. *(See Chapters 3 and 5 for more on planning the technology features of a school project.)*

Other costs that go along with adding computers and electronic equipment include additional electrical service requirements, runs to the equipment, power backup systems, power conditioning systems, additional security measures, dry fire protection systems, and special accompanying furniture. The electrical and equipment portions of the budget must reflect these needs.

Cost Impacts on Government-Funded Schools

With government funding comes government regulation. The level of detailed reporting and public disclosure required is much greater than for privately funded projects. The aim of the additional conditions and regulations imposed by the government for publicly funded projects is to protect taxpayers and improve social conditions. As noble as these goals are, there is likely to be a cost impact. Conditions and regulations of government-funded school construction projects may include additional bonding, multiple contracts, prevailing wage, targeted business segment participation, and public art requirements.

Bid, Performance, and Payment Bonds

School contract administrators must be fiscally conservative in order to protect public funds. This includes requiring bid and performance bonds. A *bid bond* is an assurance and guarantee by a surety company that the contractor who takes out the bond will execute the contract if the owner selects that contractor for the project. If the selected contractor does not execute a contract for the work, the owner will be entitled to up to 10% of the bid amount. Sometimes in lieu of a bid bond, a public agency may ask for a cashier's check as a deposit at the time that bids are accepted.

A *performance bond* is the surety company's guarantee to the owner that the contractor will complete the project being bid under the terms of the contract. A *payment bond* is a guarantee by the surety company that the contractor will pay all material, labor, equipment suppliers, and subcontractors. This helps ensure that the project will be lien-free. The combined costs to the contractor for performance and payment bonds range from about 1% to 4% of total project costs. Bid bonds cost the contractor several hundred dollars per year. Though these bonds are often required for other types of construction, it is more likely that they will be included in publicly funded school construction projects.

Multiple Contract Requirements

For a typical private school construction project, the owner executes one contract with a prime contractor. The prime contractor then subcontracts to plumbing, HVAC, and electrical or other specialty contractors with whom he or she has experience and a good working relationship. The prime contractor can also utilize his or her own licensed tradespeople for any of these trades if this is more cost-efficient. The prime contractor takes on the responsibility and bears the financial burden of completing the project on-budget and on-time, and has the leverage to maximize performance from subcontractors. As the prime contractor has a strong financial interest in completing the project on budget, coordination of subcontractors is in his or her best interest to reduce inefficiencies.

In some states, multiple contracting statutes require that state-funded construction projects, including schools, be separated into four separate contracts: general construction, plumbing, HVAC, and electrical. Each must have a separate set of plans, specifications, and bidding documents. This approach is contrasted with the typical private sector construction project with one set of specifications, plans, and bidding documents.

Proponents of the multiple contracting law argue that it helps to protect the quality of construction, making the case that some unscrupulous general contractors, once they are awarded contracts, put pressure on their subcontractors, who have already submitted their low bid to the general contractor, to reduce their bid even further. This pressure can force subcontractors to cut corners in their work.

Opponents of multiple contracting claim that since the coordination of the four independent, and possibly incompatible, contractors with their own agendas is transferred from the prime contractor to the contracting government agency, overall project costs will be increased. The lack of direct coordination often leads to increased costs in the form of change orders and schedule delays. A government agency does not bear as great a financial risk as the prime contractor who needs to complete projects on-budget in order to stay in business. Additional costs are incurred due to the separate set of specifications, plans, and bid documents needed for each trade.[4]

Some states allow single contracting on school projects, while others require multiple contracting. Several states have reversed their requirements, and at least one has changed its position more than once over the past decade. New York, for example, allows certain agencies temporary exemptions from multiple contracting laws. Currently, there are multiple contracting requirements in one form or another in several states.

One 1997 study comparing the costs of New York City government projects concluded that the cost of multiple contract projects added approximately 24% to the total project costs for buildings that were about 3,000 square feet in size, and 8% for buildings about 65,000 square feet, but that the added amount was negligible for buildings more than 147,000 square feet.[5]

Massachusetts uses a variation of multiple contracting laws called the Filed Sub-Bid System. Under this system, the project is broken up into as many as 17 different subcontracts (plumbing, electrical, roofing, etc.). These subcontracts are bid first. Then after the bids for the subcontracts are received, the contracting agency gives the list of bids to general contractors who are interested in bidding the project. General contractors choose which "filed" subcontractor bids they wish to incorporate into their bid for the total project.

Prevailing Wage Rates and Union Work Rules

Another cost consideration is labor. Prevailing wage rate regulations have been written into publicly let contracts in many locations, requiring workers to be paid wages comparable to union rates. The goal of these requirements is to ensure that workers are being paid established wages adequate for the geographic area where the project is located.

Union labor rates, which are frequently the same as prevailing wage rates, tend to range from about 25%-35% higher than non-union labor rates. Labor accounts for about 60% of the costs of a typical school construction project. The overall construction costs can be about 20% higher for a union project, as opposed to a non-union or "open shop" project. However, it can be argued that the increased labor costs attributed to higher paid workers may be offset as union workers are often better trained, more experienced, safer, and therefore more productive and capable of producing a higher-quality building.

Another effect of using union labor is the impact of union work rules. These rules may require adding more workers or the use of higher-paid tradespeople, as opposed to lower paid laborers, to perform a particular task, than may be required on non-union projects. Union work rules may also restrict the use of prefabricated products. As in the case of union wages, the additional cost of these work rules may be offset by a higher-quality and safer installation.

A 2001 study that examined prevailing wage laws in Kentucky, Ohio, and Michigan concluded that there were no statistically significant differences in overall project costs between schools built under prevailing wage rate regulations and those that were not.[6]

Requirements for Targeted Business Segment Participation

Frequently, government-funded school construction projects include regulations that require or strongly encourage participation of minority-, women-, local/small, or disabled veteran-owned enterprises (often referred to as MBE, WBE, LBE, and DVBEs) as prime or subcontractors. In certain cases, a percentage of the work must be set aside for these businesses. Proponents point out that, historically, these groups have been under-represented in the construction industry, and may need additional help in gaining a foothold. Over time as these firms gain experience, they will able to bid competitively with established firms and actually help lower bid costs by increasing competition.

This type of program is much more frequently used on publicly funded school construction projects than on privately funded school projects. Opponents claim that additional costs are borne by the prime contractors, who must prove that they are aggressively seeking bids from MBE/WBE/LBE/DVBE subcontractors. Some states require a staff member to be employed full-time to carry out the program requirements. Costs for subcontracts may be higher if bids are limited to MBE/WBE/LBE/DVBE subcontractors. However, some states allow contractors to reject higher quotes (and hire a non-MBE/WBE/LBE/DVBE subcontractor) if they can prove a significant cost difference; others do not.

Percent for Art Programs

Percent for Art Programs, implemented to improve the aesthetic quality of schools and other public facilities, are another potential cost to consider. These programs mandate that at least 1% of a construction project budget be used for artwork. At the time of this publication, there are Percent for Art programs in approximately 27 states. It can be argued that it is unlikely that 1% will be eliminated from the construction portion of the project budget to fund the 1% amount spent for art; instead, the percent is likely added to the total budget.

Sales Tax Exemptions

When non-profit institutions, including state and local governments, own schools, contractors are not required to pay state and local sales tax on materials purchased for their construction projects. Equipment rentals and labor costs are not included in tax exemptions. Combined state and local sales tax ranges from 0% to about 11%, and materials account for about 40% of the total costs of a typical school construction project. Therefore, total construction costs for a tax-exempt school construction project can be reduced by up to 4% compared to non-exempt projects.

Overhead Costs of Government-Funded School Construction Projects

Increased Reporting Requirements

The public demands that government-funded school boards and contracting agencies must be socially and fiscally responsible in awarding contracts. The contracting agency must go the extra mile to ensure that it has taken all reasonable steps to award contracts to contractors who are free of corruption and operate safely. For these reasons, government-funded projects typically have more contract requirements, including greater demands for reporting and public disclosure, than is the case with privately funded projects.

Some of the overhead costs associated with government regulation requirements may also be included in privately funded projects, and some are minimized because similar data is needed for other purposes. Most contractors use computers for payroll and other functions of their business, which have the ability to collect and organize huge amounts of data. The incremental cost of capturing additional information and government-required data is relatively minor. Still, the additional overhead costs for complying with Prevailing Wage Rate Laws, MBE/WBE/LBE/DVBE, Percent for Art programs, and other public agency-specific requirements may add anywhere from 1%-5% to the project. The responsibility for coordinating the multiple contracts (plumbing, HVAC, and electrical) is, however, shifted from the contractor to the sponsoring public agency, which actually reduces the general contractor's overhead costs.

Owner-Controlled Insurance

Traditionally, contractors have been responsible for obtaining and paying for their own insurance. To protect against risk, Worker's Compensation, general liability, builders' risk insurance, and environmental liability insurance are some of the policies that can be purchased. With "wrap-up" insurance plans, the owner or its contracting agency purchases a large insurance policy that covers the insurance needs of all contractors working on all of the projects in the owner's building program. This type of plan may also be called an *Owner-Controlled Insurance Program* (OCIP). School construction projects are often covered by OCIPs, since public agencies and large non-profit organizations have the financial backing to purchase such a large policy.

This type of insurance arrangement can reduce the cost of the project by reducing insurance costs that would have been included in the contractor's price. The overall project insurance costs can be reduced in two ways. First, insurance carriers may provide better rates due to the large size of the policy, and second, the size of the bidding pool competition may increase, as small contractors often have difficulty in obtaining affordable insurance. One criticism of owner-controlled insurance policies is that they may indirectly subsidize contractors with poor safety records. By absorbing the high insurance cost of these contractors, the owner enables these firms to avoid paying their own insurance costs, including the added premium for their poor records. This plan has a cost impact of reducing the bid cost by 3%-20%, but increasing the owner's cost by about 2%-15%. The net effect is to reduce the total project cost by about 1%-5%.

Urban Schools

Schools in urban areas present unique estimating challenges. Because there are fewer available lots, new schools are often impossible to build from scratch. Existing structures are sometimes bought or leased and extensively renovated to create classroom space. These structures can be as diverse as office buildings, retail spaces, and even factories. Renovation is the most difficult type of work to estimate because of the number of variables and unknowns. Since properties are sometimes leased, the landlord may also have his or her own requirements and restrictions. Sometimes, parts of the renovation may be performed through the landlord's own construction resources, which have an entirely different cost structure.

When a new building lot is available in an urban area, the higher real estate costs often result in facilities situated on smaller footprints with more stories than their suburban or rural equivalents. It is also more likely that an existing structure on the site will have to be demolished, increasing project costs even more. These kinds of design restrictions increase the cost per square foot, as it is more expensive to build a structure several stories tall than one or two stories tall, and because urban settings typically offer little room for setup and material storage. In addition, there is less room for relocating the activities of a working facility to another area so that the construction crew can work unimpeded ("swing space"). Both of these conditions reduce productivity. The higher cost of living in urban areas drives wages up. In a healthy economy, urban areas tend to generate more construction projects than rural areas. This creates an increase demand for labor, which also drives up labor costs.

Alternative Construction Approaches

Many cities throughout the U.S. have experienced sudden increases in the number of school-aged children, often due to unexpected increases in immigrant populations. There has been pressure to add classroom space quickly. At the same time that new capacity is added, more construction dollars are required to address the backlog of deferred maintenance, repairs, and renovation of existing facilities. To keep up with this demand, administrators are employing techniques used routinely in private industry, but previously used only rarely in school construction, including fast tracking, design/build, and temporary and modular construction. Non-academic structures are converted to classroom space more frequently than in the past.

Temporary Buildings

There was a time when temporary buildings were used only in higher education facilities. Because of fiscal constraints and swelling school populations, however, it is common to find temporary buildings in schoolyards and grounds of high schools, intermediate schools, and elementary schools. Because of the quick delivery times, temporary facilities are used to keep up with the capacity of the school population while a new building or addition is being built. The estimator must work with suppliers and the architect to develop cost estimates for these manufactured structures, which are typically modified versions of manufactured homes, or trailers commonly seen at construction sites. Modifications include the addition of stairs, ramps, and other features to make them suitable for use by children and the general public. Temporary buildings offer some cost savings because they often do not need a permanent foundation, which additionally reduces site work costs. Long-term cost reductions are offset due to the fact that the structure will have to be replaced sooner than permanent structures.

Modular Buildings

Modular buildings are built in sections or "boxes" in a factory and offer some enticing benefits. Material costs are reduced because large quantities of materials can be purchased in advance for several projects, taking advantage of quantity discounts. Materials can then be stored directly in the factory where the modules are built, which reduces shipping and storage costs. Productivity is increased, because the module is moved assembly-line style to workers with all tools, materials, and supplies conveniently located within easy reach, instead of workers having to move from one part of a building to another. Because the modules are built under a roof in a controlled environment, there are no weather-related delays during their construction.

Modular buildings offer the potential of faster completion time. With the exception of items such as plumbing connections, electrical connections, and work required when the modules are connected to each other (which must be completed in the field), the majority of the work is performed in the factory. Overall, the possibility that the completion of a modular school will be delayed is greatly reduced. Some of the savings, however, are offset by the extra structural supports required for transportation, actual transportation costs, and equipment costs for the large crane required to lift and place the individual modules. The estimator should have a clear idea of the work to be done in the field versus that to be performed in the factory. In urban areas, special attention must be paid to additional costs of transporting and lifting modules in a congested environment. Delivery may have to be at night due to traffic restrictions, and streets may have to be closed to accommodate the large crane.

Preservation of Older Schools

The National Trust for Historic Preservation placed historic neighborhood schools on its year 2000 list of "America's Eleven Most Endangered Historical Places." Through awareness, a greater number of older schools may be renovated rather than destroyed and replaced, with as many architectural features as possible accurately restored. Restoring historic schools not only preserves the beauty of these buildings, but also offers other benefits, such as helping to keep the downtown area active, economically and socially. It is almost impossible to find new building sites, and if one is found within the downtown area, building a new structure is often difficult and costly. Building outside the downtown area imposes the additional cost and inconvenience of bussing students to a new location. Renovating and restoring old schools also has a "green" benefit of preserving the environment by reducing both construction waste and the consumption of new building materials that may not be sustainable or may require substantial energy to produce. (*See Chapter 2 for more on green building design.*)

Schools designated as historic may be eligible for substantial tax breaks, but are also subject to restrictions and regulations. Historic designation, requirements, and regulations vary considerably between federal, state, and local authorities. The cost of complying with these regulations will increase renovation and restoration costs for designated schools. Professional fees alone will be about 5% higher than those of a new building of comparable size. (*See Figure 6.7.*) Additional costs may be the result of:

- Increased cost to obtain (or fabricate) appropriate materials
- Increased cost for additional time and/or methods required to install special materials
- Increased cost for specialty subcontractors or craftspeople
- Increased likelihood of encountering unforeseen conditions
- Increased cost of restoring items to historical standards vs. repair
- Increased cost of documentation
- Cost of using qualified preservation experts and consultants
- Cost of the required destructive and non-destructive investigation procedures

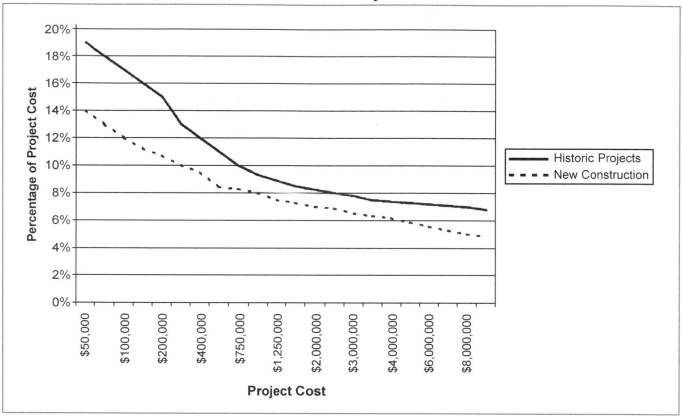

Comparison of Fees for Historic Projects vs. New Construction

Figure 6.7

Comparison of Design Fees for Historic Projects vs. New Construction

Credit: Historic Preservation: Project Planning & Estimating, *Copyright RSMeans*

- Less competition due to fewer subcontractors and manufacturers of individual products
- Cost of providing protection of historic features that remain in place during the restoration

Although only a select number of schools are designated as historic landmarks, others may still be treasured for their historic architectural features, and well worth the effort to achieve harmony between the new or renovation work and the original structure. *Historic Preservation: Project Planning & Estimating*, published by RSMeans, is an excellent resource for determining whether a structure qualifies as historic; where to obtain funding information and other assistance; how to evaluate and repair more than 75 historic building materials; and how to properly research, document, and manage historic projects to meet code, agency, and other special requirements.

Creative Approaches to Controlling Preservation Costs

There are many new products available today that can reduce the costs of replacing original materials while replicating the building feature's original appearance. These products can also offer additional advantages such as reduced delivery time, reduced installation time, and increased durability. Listed below are just two examples of new products that offer potential advantages.

A popular product used to replicate intricate damaged concrete, terra cotta, or stone features at a reasonable cost is *glass fiber reinforced concrete* (GFRC), which has several useful characteristics:

- Easily molded to reproduce shapes, details, and textures
- High strength results in thin sections that are lightweight and easy to handle
- Can be colored with pigments and paints
- Can be used to replace non-structural elements where weight is a problem

For damaged wood features, *fiberglass reinforced plastics* (FRP) are used with success. Features of FRP include:

- Corrosion-resistance
- High strength-to-weight ratio
- Adaptable to complex shapes
- High chemical resistance
- High electrical resistance

The largest cost consideration for these two materials is in making the initial mold. If many different molds are required, the price can be quite high, but if a pattern is repeated many times throughout the building, the cost per unit can be substantially reduced.

Green Building Costs

Green building practices are being incorporated into school facilities because they protect the health of the building users, conserve energy, protect natural resources, and protect the environment. Green buildings work particularly well for schools because they complement environmental science courses. As described in more detail in Chapter 2, some green building features serve as working models of the principles the students may be studying.

Green building and energy conservation systems and materials may be more expensive initially than traditional choices, but they typically save money in the long run. What is the dollar impact? According to the U.S. Department of Energy's Rebuild America K-12 Schools Program estimates, school districts can save 30%-40% on utility costs each year for new school facilities, and 20%-30% on renovated schools by applying sustainable and high-performance design and construction approaches. Life cycle cost analysis, discussed in the next section of this chapter, is a technique for assessing the long-term costs and savings in order to compare and select from different design and construction approaches, such as green building versus traditional systems.

A good source for green building cost data is the RSMeans publication, *Green Building: Project Planning & Cost Estimating*, which provides guidance on green building goals, established standards, and funding opportunities, along with actual costs for green building materials and systems. A useful tool for evaluating both the environmental impact and cost impact of building products and systems is the BEES software program, available at no charge at the Department of Energy Web site (and explained in the publication just mentioned). The BEES software program uses an evaluation technique that helps the user make a rational environmental and economic decision on what products and systems to incorporate into a building.

Value Engineering and Life Cycle Cost Evaluation

Along with the design team, the school construction project estimating staff should have a working knowledge of value engineering (VE) and life cycle cost analysis (LCCA) programs, and should be expected to be called on to participate in them. Though often used to compliment one another, VE and LCCA are really two distinct tools. Both are thorough, logical, structured, and systematic decision-analysis processes that can be used to reduce the overall cost of a facility.

The use of VE and LCCA studies is growing in all types of construction projects. Life cycle cost analysis guidelines are recommended or required by many states (including Massachusetts, New York, California, and Arizona) and municipalities for energy-related components such as HVAC, electrical, window, and insulation systems. In the state of Alaska, all public facilities, including schools, are required to employ LCCA for all the major systems of a building. This trend is likely to continue. (An informative handbook is available at the State of Alaska Department of Education and Early Development Web site at *www.eed.state.ak.us/facilities/publications/LCCAHandbook1999.pdf*.)

Value engineering is used to examine a project's required functions, proposed design elements, and construction costs. The focus of a VE study is to provide for the facility's essential functions, while exploring cost savings through modification or elimination of nonessential design elements. LCCA is used to evaluate alternatives that meet the facility's functional and technical requirements with reduced cost or increased value, including consideration of maintenance and operating costs over the life of the facility.[7] LCCA may be included as part of a VE study.

School facility projects lend themselves well to both VE and LCCA, because they are often government-funded and intended to last longer than many commercial facilities. The focus of these analyses can be on either initial value or long-term value. Unfortunately, because of construction budget pressures, VE and LCCA studies are not always included in the design phase. VE is often misused as a hasty last-minute effort to reduce the low bid to fit within with the budget. This often cuts construction costs at the expense of function and overall value of the building. The aim of VE and LCCA should be attaining the best value, which may in some cases mean finding ways to improve building function within the established budget, not merely cutting costs.

VE and LCCA programs in a large school construction program can typically add about 0.1%-0.5% to the school project costs. These programs can save about 5%-10% in initial costs, and an additional 0.5%-10% of operation and maintenance costs.[8]

Value Engineering

The VE process consists of specific steps, including cost estimating and analysis, with the goal of getting the most value out of the project. In other words, it aims to reduce costs without sacrificing important elements of a facility. The term "value" refers to the ratio of the function of the building to its cost. For a school building, the primary function would be to create an environment where children can learn, but function may also include other attributes, such as meeting spaces for community events.

Although there are minor differences between practitioners, a value engineering study should follow these basic phases:

1. **Goal Definition**: The study's goals are defined, and limits of the study are set. For example, the goal of the study may be to find the best value between two alternatives, but may be limited to economic and immediate community needs.

2. **Information Gathering**: Assembly of information relating to the project, including budget, design standards, applicable building codes and regulations.

3. **Functional Analysis**: Basic and secondary functions of the school and its systems are identified in a generic way (using an action verb and a noun). Specifics are avoided so as not to restrict the possible ways to accomplish the functions to pre-conceived notions. An example of a basic function would be, "illuminate classrooms." A secondary function might be, "beautify the room."

4. **Creative Phase (Brainstorming)**: Gathering ideas for accomplishing the basic and secondary functions. As many as 25 or so ideas are recorded, along with obvious advantages and disadvantages of each. Ideas to illuminate the classroom, for example, might include skylights, incandescent lights, halogen lights, or clerestory windows.

5. **Analytical Phase**: A review of the ideas gathered in the creative phase, selecting 2-5 of the best ideas. A further review is done to evaluate how these options comply with the functional goals individually and as part of a system. Life cycle costing is a part of this analysis. In addition to cost and compliance with the primary goals, other attributes are included and weighted as part of the evaluation.

6. **Proposal**: Recommendations are summarized and presented into a proposal that has answered the following questions: What criteria were satisfied? What solutions are being proposed? What will it cost? What value is anticipated? What other options were seriously considered?

7. **Follow-up**: The performance of the selected options is tracked to see how the actual results compared to the planned results. [9]

Life Cycle Costing

Although life cycle costing is not always included in a VE program, it is recommended that it be a part of school construction projects. Life cycle costing offers a means of arriving at the true cost of an individual component, system, or entire building by taking into account energy, maintenance, and other operations costs over the life of the facility.

LCC expresses costs in a way that can be used for more accurate comparisons, considering all the major costs associated with an item over a long period of time, usually the life span of the item, component, system, or building of which it is a part. Besides the initial costs to acquire and install a building component, there are other, less obvious associated costs that should be recognized and considered in order to arrive at a true picture of the cost. (*See Figure 6.8.*) A component that has a

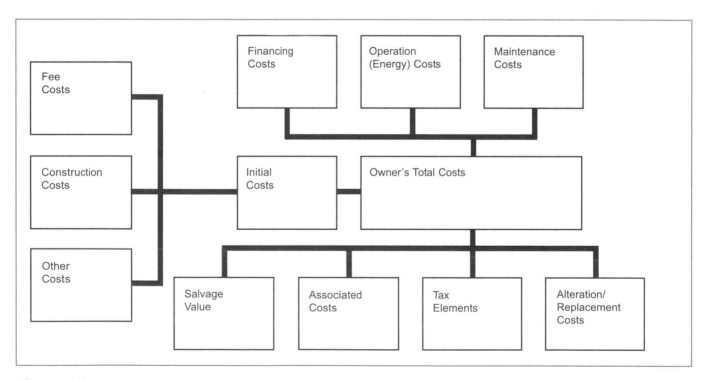

Figure 6.8
Life Cycle Cost Elements
Credit: Life Cycle Costing for Facilities, *Copyright RSMeans*

lower initial cost often winds up costing more over the life of the building, due to increased maintenance costs, more frequent replacement requirements, or other factors.

Before the life cycle cost of a system can be calculated, its function and limitations must be determined. It is also necessary to establish a way to determine its performance, and alternatives to that particular system. Next, all relevant data must be compiled, including, but not limited to, the initial purchase, transportation, installation, maintenance, and operations costs. In addition to costs, there may be some revenue associated with the components over the life of the system. This revenue may include salvage and resale value. Only after this information is assembled should the actual calculations be performed.

The Time Value of Money

Costs associated with a system component occur at different times over the life of the system. Clearly, the initial purchase costs may occur just once at the start of the life cycle for the component. Others occur regularly, such as scheduled maintenance and interest payments on loans. Still others occur at irregular intervals, such as repairs. Simply adding up these costs would not give an accurate representation of them.

In order to study the cost impact of a project over time, a method to equalize the value of money over the life of the facility is required. The time value of money principle states that a dollar is worth more today than it is in the future. The reason for this is if a dollar is invested today, it will earn more money in the future. To account for the time value of money, each cost or income associated with the item of the study must be converted to a value in terms of its present day value (present value) or a value in terms of an annual series of payments (annualized). Figure 6.9 is a life cycle costing worksheet, which may be useful to the project team to organize building system options and analyze which has the lower total cost over time.

Life Cycle Costing - General Purpose Worksheet					Original Design		Option 1	
Study Title:								
Discount Rate :		Date:	18 mar.03		Estimated Costs	Present Worth	Estimated Costs	Present Worth
Life Cycle (Yrs.)								

					Estimated Costs	Present Worth	Estimated Costs	Present Worth
INITIAL / COLLATERAL COSTS	**Initial/Collateral Costs**							
	A. Stucco							
	B. _____							
	C. _____							
	D. _____							
	E. _____							
	F. _____							
	G. _____							
	H. _____							
	I. _____							
	J. _____							
	Total Initial/Collateral Costs							
	Difference							
REPLACEMENT / SALVAGE COSTS	**Replacement/Salvage (Single Expenditures)**	Occurance Year -or- Cycle	Inflation/ Escal. Rate	PW Factor				
	A. _____							
	B. _____							
	C. _____							
	D. _____							
	E. _____							
	F. _____							
	G. _____							
	H. _____							
	I. _____							
	J. _____							
	Total Replacement/Salvage Costs							
ANNUAL COSTS	**Annual Costs**		Inflation/ Escal. Rate	PW Factor				
	A. _____							
	B. _____							
	C. _____							
	D. _____							
	E. _____							
	F. _____							
	G. _____							
	H. _____							
	I. _____							
	J. _____							
	Total Annual Costs							
	Sub-Total Replacement/Salvage + Annual Costs (Present Worth)							
	Difference							
LIFE CYCLE COSTS	**Total Life Cycle Costs (Present Worth)**							
	Life Cycle Cost PW Difference							
	Payback - Simple Discounted (Added Cost / Annualized Savings)							N/A
	Payback - Fully Discounted (Added Cost+Interest / Annualized Savings)							N/A
	Total Life Cycle Costs - Annualized				Per Year:		Per Year:	

Figure 6.9
Life Cycle Costing Worksheet
Credit: Life Cycle Costing for Facilities, Copyright Reed Construction Data

Case Study

High School Trade-Off Analysis of Initial vs. Staffing Costs

Overview:

The VE team isolated the staffing costs as the largest expenditure—representing 31% of the total costs. The initial costs were isolated at 18%. The team developed an alternate involving a slight modification to the student-teacher ratio, to see what impact it would have on initial costs.

The following spreadsheet presents an assessment of how much can be saved in staffing costs in the high school if the student-teacher ratio can be increased from 16 to 17 students per teacher. Assuming all other issues remain constant, the results indicate that nearly $5,000,000 could be invested initially and still achieve a break-even. In other words, if changes in space efficiency, technology, lighting, or other facility aspects could improve teaching efficiency, as much as $5,000,000 could be saved and used for expansion or other investment.

Statistics:

Number of Years for Period	30	
Discount Rate (Interest)	8%	
Escalation Rate(Inflation)	3%	
Gross Area	sf	244,000
Students	Each	1,600
Student per Teacher		17.0 (Modified from 16)
Staff Support per Teacher		2.2
Benefits/Overhead	%	32%

ITEM	Measure	Units	Unit Cost	Current Cost	Factor	Present Value	Percent
Capital Costs							
Construction	$/sf	244,000	$133.00	$ 32,452,000	1	$ 32,452,000	18%
Furnishings/Fitout	$/sf	244,000	$26.50	$ 6,466,000	1	$ 6,466,000	4%
Fees	$/sf	244,000	$7.00	$ 1,708,000	1	$ 1,708,000	1%
Other Project Costs	$/sf	244,000	$7.00	$ 1,708,000	1	$ 1,708,000	1%
Construction Contingency	$/sf	244,000	$6.50	$ 1,586,000	1	$ 1,586,000	1%
Sub-Total - Initial Capital Costs	$/sf	244,000	$180.00	$ 43,920,000	1	$ 43,920,000	24%
Major Capital Replacements	$/sf/yr	244,000	$ 2.50	$ 610,000	15.63	9,534,894	5%
Grand Total Capital Costs						$ 53,454,894	30%
Operations & Maintenance							
Maintenance	$/sf/yr	244,000	$ 1.40	$ 341,600	15.63	$ 5,339,541	3%
Energy	$/sf/yr	244,000	$ 0.80	$ 195,200	15.63	$ 3,051,166	2%
Sub-Total				$ 536,800		$ 8,390,707	5%
Functional Operation							
Educational Staffing	Teachers	94	$ 38,000	$ 3,572,000	15.63	$ 55,833,838	31%
Support Staffing	Staff	43	$ 31,000	$ 1,333,000	15.63	$ 20,836,088	12%
Benefits/Overhead	%	32%		$ 1,569,600	15.63	$ 24,534,376	14%
Textbooks	Student	1,600	$ 90	$ 144,000	15.63	$ 2,250,860	1%
School Allotment	Student	1,600	$ 65	$ 104,000	15.63	$ 1,625,621	1%
Other Support Costs	Student	1,600	$ 135	$ 216,000	15.63	$ 3,376,290	2%
Transportation	Student	1,600	$ 360	$ 576,000	15.63	$ 9,003,441	5%
				$ 7,514,600		$ 117,460,515	66%

Grand Total			
Present Value Cost		$	*179,306,115*
Equivalent Annual Cost	0.0640	$	*11,471,206*
Equivalent Annual Cost per Student	1,600	$	*7,170*
Equivalent Annual Cost per Student (Excluding Capital)	1,600	$	*5,032*

Original Approach =	$	*184,010,413*
Investment Potential =	$	*4,704,298*

Life Cycle Cost Calculations

Case Studies copyright Reed Construction Data, reprinted from: Life Cycle Costing for Facilities by Alphonse J. Dell'Isola and Stephen J. Kirk.

Case Study

Life Cycle Cost Assessment— HVAC System for a High School

Overview:

A local school authority put a high school project out for bid, and the resulting bids exceeded their budget. In an effort to realize their project on-time and within budget, they decided on a VE study, with emphasis on total costs. In fact, the bid documents stated, "the basis of HVAC award would be the lowest Life Cycle Costs."

The following spreadsheet presents the summary of the VE consultant's review of the bidder's HVAC systems as proposed for the school. The analysis indicated that spending $1.7M more initially would yield net savings of $3.2M over the life of the facility and pay back within 5 years. The VE proposal represented a 45% reduction in the school's operations and maintenance costs. The extra initial costs were approved by the school board, and the VE proposal was implemented.

General Purpose Worksheet					Alternative 1 Individual Rooftop Units		Alternative 2 Central Plant with 4 - Pipe Fan Coil Units	
Study Title: HVAC System Analysis					Estimated Costs	Present Worth	Estimated Costs	Present Worth
Discount Rate: 8.0% Date: 12/17/97								
Life Cycle (Yrs.): 30								
Initial/Collateral Costs								
A.	Equipment				1,212,354	1,212,354	2,803,000	2,803,000
B.	Screening				55,501	55,501	40,000	40,000
C.	Plant Space						128,000	128,000
D.								
E.								
F.								
G.								
H.								
I.								
J.								
	Total Initial/Collateral Costs				$1,267,855	$1,267,855	$2,971,000	$2,971,000
	Difference							($1,703,145)
Replacement/Salvage (Single Expenditures)		Year	Inflation/ Escal. Rate	PW Factor				
A.	Rooftop Units (70%)	8		0.540	770,000	416,007		
B.	Rooftop Units (70%)	16		0.292	770,000	224,756		
C.	Rooftop Units (70%)	24		0.158	770,000	121,428		
D.	Fan Coils(100%)	15		0.315			408,888	128,899
E.	Central Plant Equipment	20		0.215			600,000	128,729
F.								
G.								
H.								
I.								
J.								
	Total Replacement/Salvage Costs					$762,191		$257,627
Annual Costs			Inflation/ Escal. Rate	PW Factor				
A.	Maintenance - Rooftops		1%	12.496	75,360	941,693		
B.	Maintenance - Fan Coils		1%	12.496			37,680	470,847
C.	Maintenance - Central Plant & Distrib.		1%	12.496			28,800	359,883
D.	Energy		3%	15.631	468,000	7,315,296	192,000	3,001,147
E.				11.258				
F.								
G.								
H.								
I.								
J.								
	Total Annual Costs				$543,360	$8,256,989	$258,480	$3,831,876
	Sub-Total Replacement/Salvage + Annual Costs (Present Worth)					$9,019,180		$4,089,504
	Difference							$4,929,676
	Total Life Cycle Costs (Present Worth)					$10,287,035		$7,060,504
	Life Cycle Cost PW Difference							$3,226,531
	Payback - Simple Discounted (Added Cost / Annualized Savings)							3.9 Yrs.
	- Fully Discounted (Added Cost+Interest / Annualized Savings)							4.8 Yrs.
	Total Life Cycle Costs - Annualized				Per Year:	$913,771	Per Year:	$627,166

HVAC System Analysis

Case Studies copyright Reed Construction Data, reprinted from: Life Cycle Costing for Facilities *by Alphonse J. Dell'Isola and Stephen J. Kirk.*

214

Conclusion

What will a school renovation or new construction project cost? The answer is never simple, and requires information gathered by and from all the project team members, including:

- What will be built? (A new school, addition, renovation, or restoration?)
- Who will it be built for? (Elementary, middle school, junior high, senior high, or vocational students?) How many students will the facility serve?
- Why will it be built? (Population increase? Demand for community use?)
- Where will it be built?
- When will it be built? (One year from now, two years, or five years?)
- How will it be built? (Traditional construction, modular, or manufactured?)

These basic questions are a starting point for planning the project. As they are answered in more detail and the project design evolves, construction cost estimates become more precise, and an increasingly accurate cost estimate can be created.

[1] Dysert, Larry and Bruce Elliott. "The Estimate Review and Validation Process." *Cost Engineering*. Morgantown, WV, January 2002.

[2] The Pareto principal or effect was named after Vilfredo Pareto, an Italian economist and sociologist who lived in the late 19th century. It is also known as the 80-20 rule. Pareto developed a curve that plotted variations against causes. From this curved he concluded that typically 20% of the causes were responsible for 80% of the variations.

[3] California Department of Health Services. Department of Health Services Childhood Lead Poisoning Prevention Branch. *Report to the Legislator, Lead Hazards in California's Public Elementary School and Child Care Facilities.*

[4] Buono, C. *The Push for Repeal of the Wicks Law, Issues in Focus.* #94-71, Senate Research Service, New York State Senate, Albany, NY 12247, March 22, 1994.

[5] Orley, Ashenfelter, David Ashmore, and Randall Filer. "Contract Form and Procurement Costs: The Impact of Compulsory Multiple Contractor Laws in Construction." *Rand Journal of Economics.* 1997, Vol. 28, No 0 pp. S5-S16.

[6] Peter Phillips, Ph.D. *A Comparison of Public School Construction Costs.* University of Utah, February, 2001

[7] Alphonse J. Dell'Isola and Stephen J. Kirk. *Life Cycle Costing for Facilities.* Reed Construction Data, 2003.

[8] Alphonse J. Dell'Isola. *Value Engineering: Practical Applications.* RSMeans, 1997.

[9] Kenneth Humphreys. *Jelen's Cost and Optimization Engineering.* McGraw-Hill, 1997.

Chapter 7

Scheduling a School Construction Project

Joseph Macaluso, CCC

The question of when the school project will be completed is directly connected to what it will cost, since the duration of the project has many cost ramifications. As the cliché goes, "time is money," but meeting the schedule affects more than just money. It has an impact on the project team's success, reputation, and legal obligations. In the case of public schools, the schedule is tied to the public mandate to provide an appropriate space to educate students—in keeping with the school calendar.

Construction has become both increasingly complex and more time-sensitive. Many school projects are being "fast-tracked," which means that portions of the building, called "bid packages," are constructed while others are still being designed. Although fast-tracking reduces overall project time, it requires more careful scheduling and monitoring, as any delay in construction can drastically reduce the anticipated time savings. Furthermore, a delay in the design of an item that precedes construction of other items can have a devastating impact on the overall schedule and budget.

Along with time sensitivity and construction complexity, there is a growing potential for legal action resulting from delays caused by the owner, the contractor, or the architect. All of these factors make an accurate schedule essential—for all of the project team members.

One thing that can be said about most school projects is that at the very least, everyone knows the deadline. For most large school projects, the "drop dead date" is directly related to the opening day of school. (The actual date is usually earlier than opening day, since two or more weeks are typically needed to furnish the building, and because administrators need access prior to the start of school). How to reach the project deadline is the key. The schedule is the map that shows where the project stands, where it should be, and where it should finish, all in terms of time.

Typically, the construction schedule is prepared by an engineer (scheduler) working for the general contractor or construction manager. In addition, schedulers often work for the architect or owner, or directly for a project management firm specializing in scheduling.

The schedule is an important tool for determining expected project completion, and for tracking, correcting, and reporting progress. However, it is still only a tool. There is no substitution for hard work, diligence, skill, experience, and the cooperation of all project team members in doing what is necessary to make sure dates are met. This chapter will describe:

- The types of schedules:
  — How they can be used to shorten project duration.
  — How they are prepared.
  — How they can be integrated with cost estimates.
- How to manage the schedule.
- Scheduling issues specific to school construction.

Types of Schedules

Bar, or Gantt, Charts

Early schedules were exclusively in the form of bar charts (also known as Gantt charts), which listed construction activities on the left-hand side of a page with a scaled, horizontal bar to the right showing the duration of the corresponding activity; the longer the bar, the longer the activity's duration. *(See Figure 7.1.)* Bar charts have been used since the 1920s, and many large projects, including the Hoover Dam, have been scheduled this way.

Bar charts are useful for summarizing the major elements of projects. They are easy to read and can clearly display the duration of critical activities, once those activities have been determined. Bar charts are not very useful for finding the interrelationships between activities, or determining which activities are critical to completing the project on time. For these functions, the Critical Path Method is the best scheduling tool.

Critical Path Method Schedules

The Critical Path Method (CPM) is a scheduling technique that shows:

- The duration of each activity.
- The relationships between all construction activities.
- The successive activities that require the most time and are therefore critical to the completion of the project.

All the activities of a CPM schedule can be, and often are, listed in a tabular format. This type of schedule becomes more useful when plotted out on a computer in the form of a *chart*, *diagram*, or *network* (terms used interchangeably). The CPM diagram identifies the "critical path," or the order of construction tasks that results in the least amount of time required to complete the project. Knowing which activities are critical and when they occur in the project is vital for determining which ones

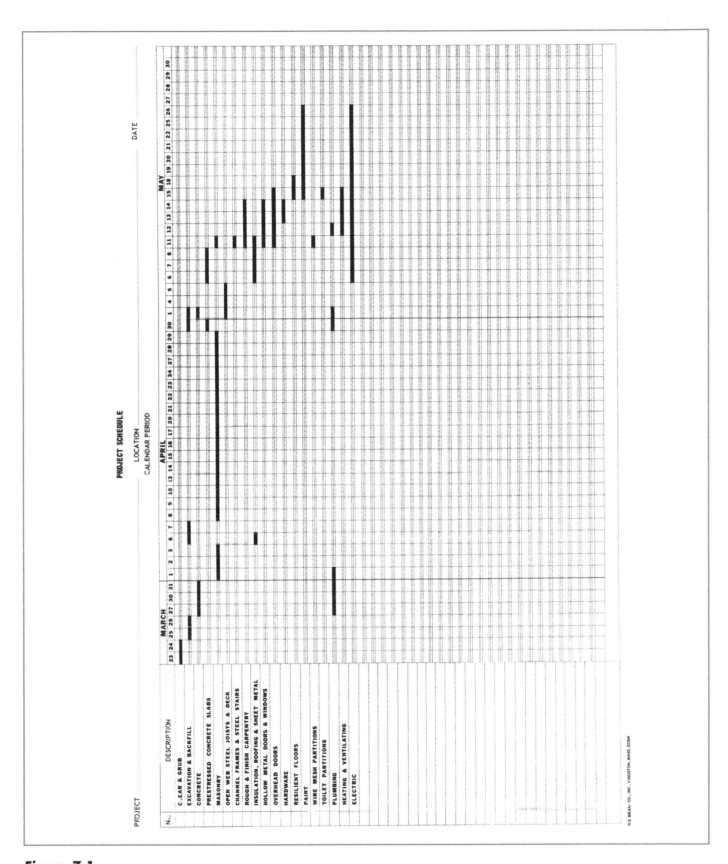

Figure 7.1
Gantt Chart–Project Schedule
Sample Project Timeline

Credit: Means Scheduling Manual, Second Edition, Copyright RSMeans

should receive the most attention. Extending the time to complete crucial tasks will delay the overall project completion date. Reducing the time to complete these activities can reduce the overall project duration. Activities that are not on a critical path can slip behind, up to a point, without necessarily delaying the job. The CPM schedule is required on almost all medium-to-large-sized school projects.

An important part of scheduling is determining the amount of time, or *float*, that each activity (not on the critical path) can fall behind before it starts delaying the rest of the project. The frequently debated issue is who "owns" (gets to use) this float. If, for example, the school system, its project manager, or contracting agency thinks the float is theirs, they may want to use this extra time in the schedule as they see fit, and not allow the contractor to apply this time as he or she chooses. Does the float belong to the school/owner, or does it belong to the contractor? The simple answer should be that it belongs to the project as a whole. Float time should be applied to whatever will benefit the project the most directly. Project meetings are the appropriate venue for discussing and resolving float and other specific project issues.

M.R. Walker of DuPont and J.E. Kelly of Remington Rand developed the CPM Schedule in the late 1950s and first used it in the construction of a new chemical plant. Shortly afterward, it was used to significantly reduce the time required for a maintenance shutdown at a chemical plant. Around the same time that CPM scheduling was being developed for industry use, another type of scheduling technique, called *Program Evaluation Review Technique* (PERT), was being developed by the military for the Polaris missile system. The major difference between CPM and PERT is that CPM is activity-based, while PERT is event-oriented and considers the likelihood of achieving individual events on time as the key to the success of the program.

CPM Schedule Preparation

So how does the CPM schedule work? Before it (or any type of accurate schedule) can be prepared, several tasks must first be completed:

- Identify all activities required to complete the project.
- Determine the relational logic between activities.
- Determine the duration of all activities. (*Duration* is the amount of time estimated to complete an activity based on the scope of work and the resources being used.)

Identify Activities: Identifying the activities in the project is a lengthy and detailed process, usually performed by reviewing the plans and specifications. As the project progresses from the early (conceptual) design stage to the final (detailed) design, the schedule is fully developed in detail. The detailed schedule for a large project may include thousands of activities. This level of detail is required for both the contractor's and the owner's representatives who are working the job every day. Based on the full, detailed schedule, other schedules can be prepared with varying degrees of detail, as required. For example, an executive summary is better suited for use in a presentation to non-technical project team members, such as the school principal or senior school administrator, who may need an overall project time frame with a breakdown of only the major components. The school's architect, or senior manager in the school system may require more detail.

Determine Rational Logic: Like detailed cost estimates, detailed schedules require a hierarchical *work breakdown system* (WBS), such as the CSI MasterFormat, UNIFORMAT II, or other suitable system for organizing the thousands of individual construction tasks. Perhaps even more critical than in cost estimating, the scheduler must mentally build the project, visualizing and accounting for each and every task and the interrelationships between tasks, while considering factors such as inclement weather and seasonal temperatures. This process is important not only to make sure that all work items are covered, but also to determine the proper sequencing of activities. If the sequence is not correct, the schedule will be off. Proper sequencing affects the project's overall duration and critical path. Scheduling requires time and patience to work with the potentially thousands of activities involved in completing the project, with all the possible arrangements of those activities. For example, these are some of the possibilities for just two activities:

- Activity "B" must start after activity "A" finishes.
- Activity "B" must start when activity "A" starts.
- Activity "A" must finish when "B" finishes.
- Activities "A" and "B" must finish and start at the same time.
- Activity "B" must start X days after "A" finishes.
- Activity "B" must start X days after "A" starts.
- Activity "A" must finish X days after "B" finishes.
- Activity "B" must start X days before "A" finishes.
- Activity "B" must start X days before "A" starts.
- Activity "A" must start X days before "B" finishes.

The good news is that many of the thousands of combinations of activities can be ruled out because they would result in an incorrect or illogical sequence. For example, if activity "A" represents "build formwork," and "B" represents "place concrete," we know that "A" must come before "B." The bad news is that the scheduler must be able to determine the correct and logical sequence, which can be difficult and subjective. Typical activity sequences need to be adapted to the circumstances of a particular project. Real scheduling skill comes in knowing how to alter the sequence of activities to maximize or balance particular and often competing goals, such as reducing the overall duration of the project, reducing the cost of the project, or minimizing disruption caused by construction. Often, the scheduler may hand-sketch key relationships of a broad project schedule to get a feel for how the work will flow and to make sure that the logic is correct before assembling a formal schedule.

Determine Duration of Activities: Unit labor hours are used to calculate activity durations. Labor data can come from third-party sources, such as RSMeans cost data publications; from the contracting firm's own database compiled from actual, completed projects; or from the subcontractors who will perform the work. Rates are usually expressed in labor hours per unit associated with the work item. Labor hours are ideal for scheduling purposes because they are relatively independent of crew size.

For example, if the labor rate for placing concrete for footings is 1.6 labor hours per cubic yard of concrete, and there are 200 cubic yards to place, the total duration of that activity is:

1.6 labor hours x 200 cubic yards = 320 labor hours

If there are four members in the crew, the actual duration would be:

320 labor hours ÷ 4 crew members = 80 hours

If the crew is increased to eight members, the duration would be:

320 labor hours ÷ 8 crew members = 40 hours

Typically, the duration of activities for construction projects is thought of and presented in terms of days. To determine the duration in days, simply divide the work, or labor hours, into the number of hours the particular crew works per day. If there are eight hours in the workday, the duration, in days, would be:

80 labor hours ÷ 8 hours/day = 10 work days for the four-member crew

40 labor hours ÷ 8 hours/day = 5 work days for the eight-member crew

Durations should be plotted on a calendar in order for the schedule to be useful. If the normal work week is 5 days, and the calendar week is 7 days, the number of calendar days would be:

10 work days ÷ 7 days/week = 1.4 calendar weeks for the four-member crew

5 work days ÷ 7 days/week = 0.7 calendar weeks for the eight-member crew

All of these conversions are easily handled by today's scheduling software.

Just as unit costs must be adapted to the particular project conditions, so too must durations. The basic calculations are simple, and there is historic scheduling data available. As in cost estimating, however, historic data must be altered to suit the particulars of the project. Factors such as learning curves, weather conditions, number of laborers that can access the work site, and many others all affect productivity and, therefore, activity durations. This is why it is so critical that the scheduler visit the job site often to make sure these factors are taken into account.

Some questions a scheduler may need to answer in order to determine a project's activity durations include:

- Will increasing the number of crew members result in a reduced productivity per member?
- Will increased overtime reduce the productivity of each crew member?

- Will productivity increase as a crew becomes more familiar with a specialized task?

Only after the duration of each individual activity has been determined can the total project duration be determined. Building a proper schedule takes several iterations with input from the project supervision on how work will be sequenced, and from subcontractors to determine the durations and crew sizes. After durations are solicited from subcontractors and integrated into the schedule, relationships between the work items may need to be altered to arrive at the project completion date and the critical path. (Some contractors prefer to build the schedule first and have subcontractors and suppliers bid to the schedule.)

Scheduling for Weather Delays: The number of inclement weather delays to be used in a schedule can be based on historical data for specific geographical regions, supplied by the Associated General Contractors of America (AGC) or other reputable sources. If the actual number of weather days exceeds those planned, the contractor should notify the owner and then add them to the updated schedule. Documenting, tracking, and plotting the agreed-upon weather delays on the schedule is also beneficial as a first step in finding ways to make up for them.

How Does a CPM Schedule Work?

Once all the activities have been identified, durations (abbreviated as *DUR*) have been calculated, and the logical relationships between activities have been set and sketched out, the scheduler goes through the network of activities from the beginning to the end, calculating the earliest time that each activity can start and finish. Although logical constraints can complicate the calculations somewhat, the mechanics of calculating the critical path are fairly simple. A computational diagram based on the PDM technique can be used to make the task easier. (*See Figure 7.2.*) First, the early start times (abbreviated as *ES*), and the early finish times (abbreviated as *EF*) are calculated in a first pass through the network called the *forward pass*. The forward pass starts with the first activity of the network. The ES for this activity is always "0." The EF for

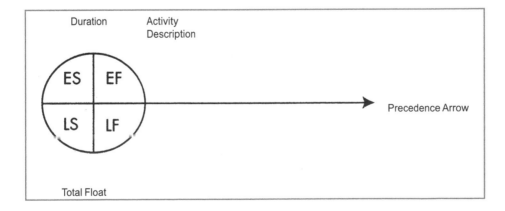

Figure 7.2
CPM Notation: Precedence Diagram Method

Credit: Project Scheduling & Management for Construction, Third Edition, *Copyright RSMeans*

this activity and each succeeding activity is the ES, plus the duration of the activity. The EF becomes the ES for the succeeding activity. When multiple preceding activities merge into an activity, the ES with the highest or longest duration is used. (*See Figure 7.3.*)

The next step is to calculate the latest time that each activity can be started (abbreviated as *LS*) and finished (abbreviated as *LF*), without delaying the project. This is done in a second pass through the network, called the *backward pass*, by starting at the last activity in the network and working back to the beginning of the network. This pass begins with the last activity in the network. The EF that was calculated for the last activity of the project becomes the LF. The LF minus the duration of the activity becomes the LS for the activity. This LS becomes the LF for the preceding activity. When there are multiple succeeding activities merging into an activity, the lowest or shortest duration is used. (*See Figure 7.4.*) After the forward pass and backward pass are complete, the float can be calculated by subtracting the ES from the LS or the EF from the LF for each activity on the network. Activities where the result of this calculation is zero, means that they are on the critical path. (*See Figure 7.5.*)

A simple network diagram can be sketched out quickly with pencil and paper, and calculating the ES, EF, LS, LF, float, and critical path can easily be done with a calculator. However, construction projects of significant size consist of thousands of activities. Fortunately, computer software has made what used to be a laborious task into a manageable one, not only in terms of the time it takes to create the original schedule, but also in that the scheduler can make modifications to items within the schedule. The software will automatically adjust the rest of the schedule to reflect the modifications.

CPM Scheduling Techniques

There are two types of CPM schedules in use today: the Arrow Diagram Method and Precedence Diagram Method. The *Arrow Diagram Method,* or ADM, was the first CPM scheduling method to come into popular use. It utilizes arrows to represent the individual activities of a project. The arrows can be scaled in relationship to the duration of individual activities. Looking at the arrow from left to right, the tail end represents the start of the activity, and the head represents the finish of the activity. To identify activities, circles between each arrow, called *nodes,* are used. The nodes at the tail end of the arrow are referred to as "i," and the nodes at the head of the arrow are referred to as "j" (an arbitrary coding convention, having no relationship to any other construction terminology). If, for example, an arrow was drawn to represent an activity called "place rebar," the node at the tail of the arrow was #1, and the node at the head of the arrow was #3, the "i -j" number would be "1-3."

Arrows drawn with a dashed line are called *dummy arrows*. Dummy arrows are not activities, but represent restraints or logical dependencies.

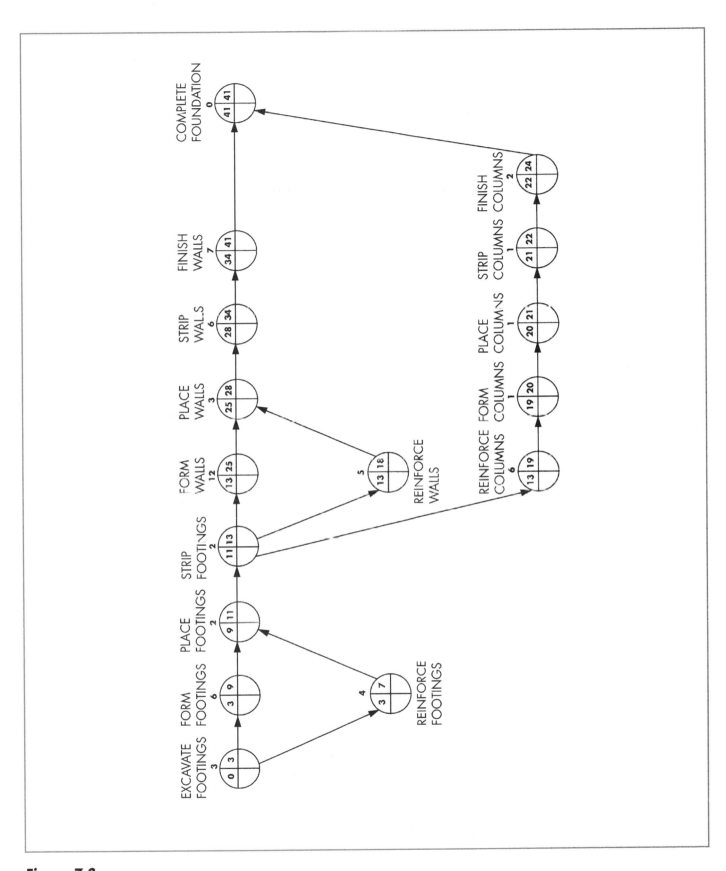

Figure 7.3
Forward Pass

Credit: Project Scheduling & Management for Construction, Third Edition, *Copyright RSMeans*

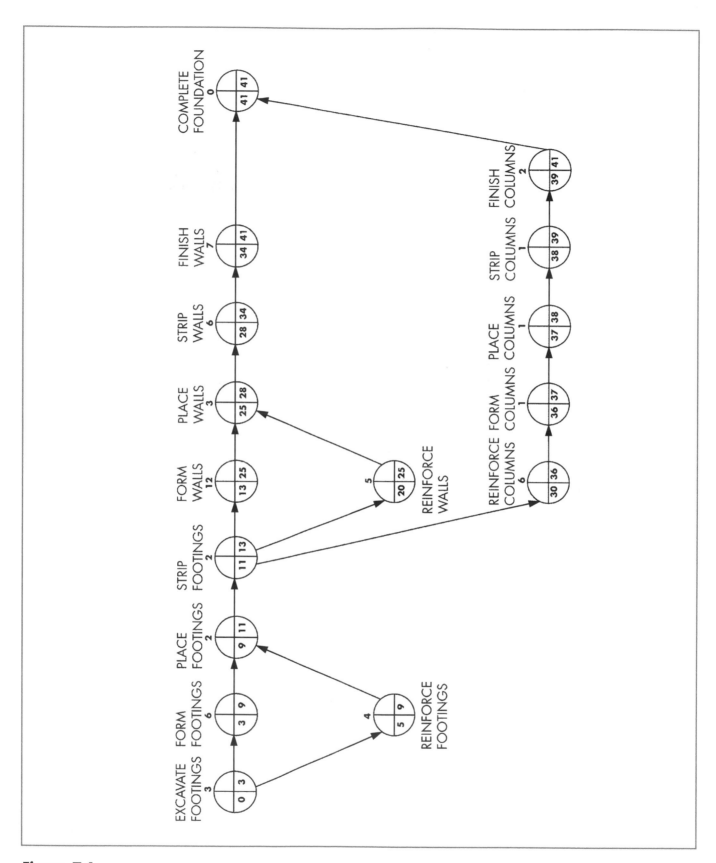

Figure 7.4
Backward Pass

Credit: Project Scheduling & Management for Construction, Third Edition, *Copyright RSMeans*

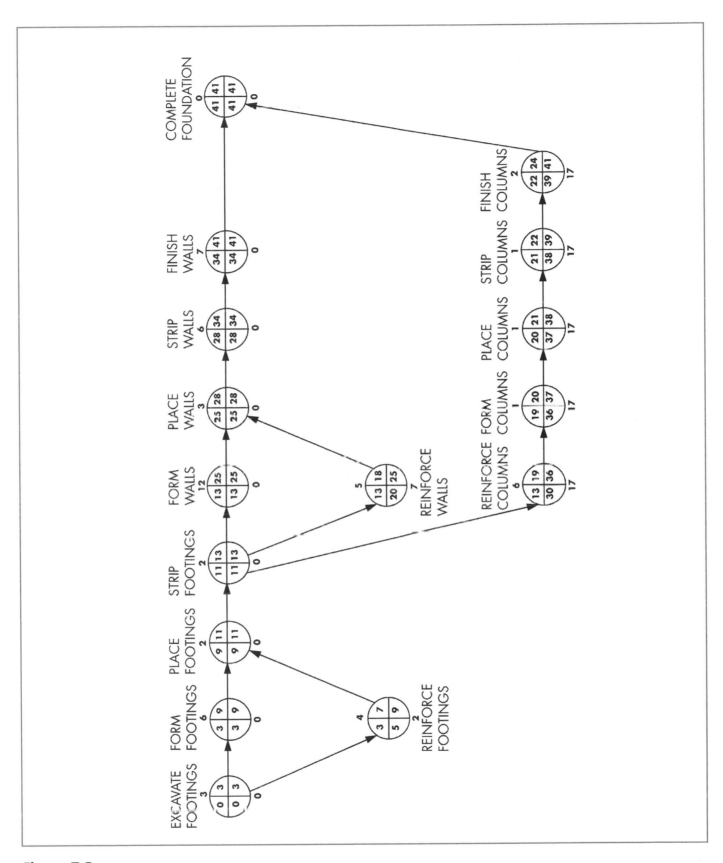

Figure 7.5
Total Float Calculations

Credit: Project Scheduling & Management for Construction, Third Edition, *Copyright RSMeans*

ADM is a practical and effective guide through the logic of a project's schedule in that incorrect logic becomes readily apparent in a graphic way. ADM is great for quick sketches to determine the logic of a group of activities.

The *Precedence Diagram Method,* or PDM schedule, was developed in the 1960s and quickly rose in popularity—so rapidly that currently it far exceeds ADM in usage. In fact, most currently available scheduling software programs support only the PDM method of scheduling. The PDM schedule differs from the ADM schedule in that instead of arrows representing activities, nodes represent the actual activities (circular or rectangular), and the arrows represent only the relationships between the activities. This configuration allows the activity name, duration, activity number, and other information to be included in the node. The nodes can also be time scaled to graphically show the duration of the activity. The PDM schedule is also easier to read than the ADM, since it can show relationships between activities in a simpler fashion.

With the PDM schedule, there is no need for dummy activities. The main reason why PDM schedules are easier to read is because the relationship arrow can be drawn from and point to the front of the activity node, or the back of the activity node. This is a "cleaner" way of representing how activities start and finish in relation to one another.

Schedule/Cost Integration

If time is indeed money, is a schedule a form of estimate? Can an estimator schedule? Can a scheduler estimate? Estimators and schedulers can certainly gain a lot by collaboration, and often do. Estimators often provide a scheduler with quantity takeoffs (how much of an item is to be installed), labor hour durations, and other useful data for their schedules. Likewise, information obtained in the preparation of schedules is often useful to the estimator. Durations from a schedule are used for estimating the project's labor costs. If, for example, the duration of a task is ten days and requires a three-member crew working an eight-hour day at a weighted average wage rate of $35.00 per hour, the labor costs for the task would be:

10 days x 3 workers x 8 hours per day x 35 dollars per hour = $8,400.

The Challenge of Selecting a Common WBS

Some engineering firms locate their estimating and scheduling departments in close proximity, often reporting to the same manager. It is rare, however, that estimators or schedulers are responsible for preparing both the estimate and the schedule on a major project. This separation is a good way to check and balance each other's work, but it also creates duplication of work. Steps have been taken to integrate these two disciplines more closely. An example is software that allows line items to be imported from an estimate as an "activity list," including the associated resources (materials, labor hours, and equipment hours) as a starting point for the preparation of a schedule. There are problems with this approach, however. For one, the WBS for an estimate may not be compatible for use in the schedule. Often, estimates are prepared according to the CSI MasterFormat breakdown, which is a material-based system. It may be acceptable to summarize estimates, but because schedules are activity-oriented, summarizing by materials will not work.

To integrate schedules and estimates, it would be better to use a logical, hierarchical WBS that works for both functions. The scheduler and estimator must work together in developing a WBS that will serve both purposes and provide the level of detail appropriate for both. The schedule activities must match up with the estimate line items. The UNIFORMAT II WBS, or a variation of it, works well for this purpose, since it is systems- and activity-based.[1]

Resource-Loading

What if there was a way to state the various aspects of a project's progress, once and only once, in a form that all the stakeholders to a project could use concurrently, instead of having to present it separately in different formats to the different stakeholders? There is already some blurring of the lines between estimating and scheduling, since schedules can now be more easily *resource-loaded*. The amount of resources expended with each activity can be incorporated into the schedule. Resource-loading of a schedule can be accomplished by determining the amount of resources (material, labor, and equipment) used for each activity in a schedule and entering the data into the software as the schedule is being prepared. The approximate amount of resources used can be estimated at any stage of the project. Keeping track of the resources used is an important budget management tool. The cost of these resources can be calculated, and the schedule can be *cost-loaded* to show the cost of the project as it progresses towards completion.

Earned Value Management

Another method of integrating scheduling and estimating is called *earned value management*, a concept first applied to, and now a requirement for many large and complex federal projects. This method is now beginning to be considered for medium-sized construction projects. According to the Department of Defense,

> *"Earned value is a management technique that relates resource planning to schedules and to technical cost and schedule requirements. All work is planned, budgeted, and scheduled in time-phased 'planned value' increments constituting a cost and schedule measurement baseline. There are two major objectives of an earned value system: to encourage contractors to use effective internal cost and schedule management control systems and to permit the customer to be able to rely on timely data produced by those systems for determining product-oriented contract status."[2]*

Many in the construction industry perceive earned value management, perhaps incorrectly, as too complex and burdensome for use on typical construction projects. What this method really does is break a project down into definable tasks. For each task, it provides a way to measure how much work was planned to be completed by a certain date, how much work was actually completed by that date, and the actual cost of the work completed by that date. By comparing and graphing these three measurements, project stakeholders, including school building committees/agencies and contractors, have an effective early warning system for detecting cost overruns and determining which activities are causing the problems. Earned value has not yet found its way into many construction projects, but it is likely to become a standard feature of medium to large projects in the future.

Interoperability – Core Database

There is a new approach to integrating not only estimating and scheduling, but also other disciplines, such as project management, accounting, design, and engineering. This approach uses a core database that takes into account each discipline's different vocabulary, culture, and way of thinking and presenting information.

Traditionally, project information is not shared among all stakeholders, and when it is, it is frequently in a form that cannot be used by all. Estimators work with spreadsheets, schedulers work with networks, and architects and engineers work with plans. Conversion from one format of information to another can be inefficient, time-consuming, and prone to error. Computer software for each of these disciplines has increased efficiency within the disciplines themselves. Naturally, the software uses a format compatible with what each of the disciplines is used to working with, so that estimators work with databases and electronic spreadsheets, schedulers work with algorithm-based software, and architects and engineers work with CAD software. Currently, these programs are not really compatible, which leads to inefficiencies as each party to the project works to create information that may have already been substantially developed by another.

Interoperability would come out of a central core database for a project. This would not only allow for the sharing of project information, but with controls, would eliminate current inefficiencies. The goal is to provide a more efficient exchange of information between not only estimating and scheduling, but all stakeholders. One of the ways to do this is to define a task or object only once and be able to share that information with all the parties to the project. Interoperability will allow stakeholders to look up all the scheduling, cost, design, and other information associated with a particular item in a project with relative ease. In addition, as changes are made on an item in the project, all associated elements will automatically be updated. If, for example, additional partitions are added, the cost will be increased, the schedule duration will be lengthened, and other affected items in the project database will automatically be adjusted to reflect that change. The major proponent of this approach is the International Alliance of Interoperability (IAI), which encourages advances in software platforms and applications and works with software developers and industry groups to create standards that would facilitate interoperability in the construction industry.

The potential for interoperability to improve the construction process is enormous. There may soon be a time when merely highlighting a particular item of work on a set of CAD plans will yield all relevant information on that item. The cost, duration to complete, progress made, inspections results, and other items will all be found instantly with a click of the mouse. Standards that permit interoperability are being incorporated into the latest software. There is still a lot of work that needs to be done before all project information can be exchanged seamlessly, but the day will come.

Practical Schedule Applications

If the schedule is to be of any use, all members of the project must buy into it. This means that the contractor must have confidence that the schedule is realistic, and the owner must be confident that the schedule will meet the school's needs. To suit the purposes of all stakeholders, different versions of the schedule need to be prepared. A detailed construction schedule can contain thousands of activities and require a whole wall to display. It is appropriate for the contractor to have that level of detail for the entire project. For school administrators or building committees, however, this level of detail is not necessary, and in fact gets in the way of understanding the overall project. Suppliers for such items as classroom furniture need only the portion of the schedule that relates to their delivery and installation. (For classroom furniture, this would be the portion of the schedule that follows completion of the building shell.)

Schedule Variations and Purposes

The Master Schedule

The master schedule is the most thorough schedule for a project. It covers not only the construction portions of the project, but also includes items that are not strictly construction-related, but are part of the project, such as financing deadlines and community board reviews. The master schedule includes all the details of the project, but can be presented in a summary or executive-level format, with the ability to "drill down" into specific parts to get more detailed information, as needed.

The Design Schedule

The design schedule is used mostly to track the design process. It is important even though the design process does not represent the largest portion of the cost or duration of a project. Design is one of the first activities that must occur, and, if significantly delayed, the timing of the entire project can be affected. A delay in the early part of the project can also negatively affect funding and foster perceptions that the project is in trouble. To prevent this situation, the schedule should include clearly defined, ambitious, but reasonable milestones that the designers should meet. A *milestone* is a measurable event that is expected to be accomplished by a certain date. It is usually graphically designated on the schedule by a small diamond shape. An example of a milestone would be completion of "finish final plans."

Pre-Bid Schedule

A *pre-bid schedule* is a summary-level schedule that shows the project designer's general anticipated view of the project schedule. It is not very detailed, because many of the project details will not have been developed at this stage. The pre-bid schedule should indicate any known or anticipated scheduling requirements or potential problem areas, such as staging or building closings.[3]

The Fast-Track Schedule

Fast-tracked projects are projects where the total duration is shortened by starting construction before the design is complete. Schedules prepared for fast-tracked construction projects are particularly challenging, because they include both design and construction activities. In order to coordinate design and construction milestones on fast-tracked projects, the general contractor or construction manager can build a proposed schedule and then use start/finish relationships to show material fabrication, submittal, and bidding times that, when added in front of the work item, will indicate when each of the design packages must be completed. *(See Chapter 8, "Contracts and Bidding," for more on fast-track projects.)*

Construction Schedules

The Baseline Construction Schedule

Before construction starts, a *baseline schedule,* or *target schedule,* is prepared. This schedule outlines the major tasks in the project and the resources required to complete each task. The goal is to order the work in such a way that tasks are completed as efficiently as possible. Attention is given to both the sequences of the work and to the number and nature of tasks occurring on the job site at any given time. This approach helps prevent activities from interfering with each other. If too many workers or trades are scheduled to work in a particular area at the same time, work may be inefficient due to crowding. In addition, care should be given to sequencing the work of each subcontractor so that he or she can maintain a stable crew size over the duration of the work.

The Working Schedule

The working schedule is prepared after the project is awarded, so there should be little guesswork about the project requirements or the capabilities of the contractor and major subcontractors. This schedule should include enough detail to allow tracking of construction, and serves as the realistic basis on which the project will be built. The working schedule can also be *resource-* and/or *cost-loaded. (See the "Resource-Loading" section earlier in this chapter.)* One advantage to cost-loading the construction schedule is that it enables the owner to tie payments more directly to progress, according to schedule expectations. This working schedule is updated as the project progresses.

The Post-Construction Schedule

Modifications to original plans are inevitable. As construction progresses, changes will continuously be made to the schedule. In the same way that final budgets update the planned construction costs and as-built plans update the construction drawings to reflect what was actually built, *post-construction schedules* incorporate all changes to the schedule. The post-construction schedule will show actual work, including the dates when all work was performed and the actual duration of all activities on the project. These schedules provide important documentation for use in any claims that may come about after the project is completed.

The Schedule Review Process

Reviewing the schedule before the start of construction ensures that it is accurate and reflects the understanding of all project team members. The owner's review of the scope for the initial schedule is a time-consuming, but important process. One approach is to put the onus on the contractor to make sure that all the activities are covered in the schedule by stating in the contract that anything missing will be the contractor's responsibility. Another approach is for the school's project manager or other representative to review all the activities in the schedule, cross-checking them with what appears in the project plans and specifications. If the schedule is *resource-loaded*, the process may be easier, since project materials, labor, and equipment that are incorporated into the activities of the schedule can help in matching up what is on the plans and specifications with what is on the schedule. The cost estimate can provide a cross reference in this process. If the estimate was coordinated with the schedule, this task will be easier and significantly faster. In addition to uncovering potential errors before they become major problems, reviewing the schedule scope also provides the owner with an opportunity to become more familiar with the work as it is planned for the project.[4]

Schedule Review Meeting

As part of the initial construction schedule review meeting, the scheduler should explain to the school building team or the school's representatives how the durations for activities were derived, and the scheduling logic—followed by discussion of the schedule itself. Input should be gathered from knowledgeable construction managers and other specialists from both the contractor and the school's representatives, before and during the schedule review meeting. A pinch of cynicism and a good portion of curiosity are assets for the school building team or its representatives in reviewing both schedules and cost estimates. An unfortunate assumption that still exists to some degree is that if the schedule was generated by a computer, it must be correct, especially in the case of large, intricate, neatly plotted, color schedules, which can look impressive.

During construction, the construction schedule is normally reviewed as part of the weekly construction meeting. On larger projects, the schedule may be discussed at a separate schedule review meeting (usually weekly).

Often, the contractor submits a schedule for review, and the owner's project manager marks it up without direct discussion. These review meetings provide an opportunity to discuss why the contractor has chosen a certain approach, or why the owner or architect is placing certain restrictions on the contractor. The flow of information can facilitate compromises that will work for all project team members or foster creative new ways to approach scheduling problems. Meetings should start with an agenda, and with start and finish times. Rambling, inconclusive meetings will accomplish nothing and turn off all parties involved. At the end of the schedule review meetings, a summary of the comments, resolutions, and items that need further development should be prepared and acknowledged by all members. *(See Chapter 10 for more on project team meetings.)*

Reviewing construction schedules can be a source of friction between the school, as owner, and the contractor, but it need not be. To begin with, the owner and the contractor usually share the common goal of completing the project as quickly as possible. When overtime hours are required, or when less cost-efficient use of resources is necessary to meet deadlines, the contractor may not be on-board unless compensated for the additional costs. The owner sometimes perceives these requests as an excuse to inflate the cost of the project. It is helpful in the schedule review process to establish open communication between the contractor and owner—and keep it open.

Monitoring Job Progress: The Three Steps

One advantage of a well-prepared schedule is that it can be used as a tool to monitor the job's progress. There are basically three steps to schedule monitoring:

- Monitoring progress
- Comparing progress to goals
- Taking corrective action

Monitoring Progress

Monitoring is also referred to as *progress measurement*, or *updating the schedule*. It involves collecting field data, such as actual activity durations or actual resources used, and updating the schedule with this information. Basically, the goal of monitoring is to determine if the project is currently on schedule.

Monitoring is a two-step process. The first is to update the individual activities. The second is to measure their impact on the project as a whole. This is accomplished by recalculating the schedule. Depending on the size of the project and the software used, the actual recalculation and reprinting of the schedule can be accomplished in a matter of a few minutes. The data for updating the schedule can come from daily job logs, interviews with field personnel, or other job records. Daily job logs are often kept by project superintendents. The amount of detail can vary considerably from project to project. If detailed enough, logs can supply data, such as the amount of concrete poured by location per day and other useful scheduling information.

Interviewing workers is another method schedulers use to obtain information for updating the schedule. It is sometimes not as accurate, because it depends on the memory of the respondent, but at times it may be the only way to get information. In addition to these sources, there are many other job records that can be consulted, including time cards, purchase orders, and job-meeting minutes.[5]

Comparing Progress to Goals

The next step in monitoring project progress is to compare actual progress to the project goals. These goals are marked on the schedule as milestones (technically, an activity that has no duration—practically speaking, a point in time, such as the end of a phase of the project). This comparison requires a target or baseline schedule, which reflects the original plan. The current, actual schedule is then compared to the target schedule. This is best accomplished by means of a bar chart, which superimposes both schedules so that the variance can be easily seen. To present progress clearly, it is best to reduce extraneous information so that the most important items are not lost among the other details. Only the relevant parts of the schedule (those affected by the change) should be shown.

After updating a schedule, a separate tabular list of the project activities should be generated and sorted by the amount of float each carries. This process will bring the critical activities (shown graphically on the schedule diagram) to the top of the tabulated list of activities.

If time has been lost on the critical path, job site supervisors should be consulted on how to make it up. The project scheduling logic should be revised or activity durations decreased accordingly. Activities that are not going as planned should be highlighted.

Some key items to look for when reviewing project reports include:

- **Status of activities on the critical path.** Any delay in these activities will delay the project as a whole.
- **Status of non-critical activities that start late.** Late-starting activities, in many cases, continue to progress at a slower rate that they should. If they exceed their float, they can become critical and affect the project duration.
- **Activities with low production rates.** Even though an activity starts on time, the progress rate may be slower than planned, to the point that it becomes a critical path item. If undetected until later, the problem is more difficult to correct.
- **Delays in resource delivery.** Material sources frequently move material delivery dates back, which can delay a crucial activity.
- **Activities similar to activities yet-to-occur.** An activity that starts late or has a longer than expected duration should be checked to see if there are other activities of the same type, crew, or contractor further into the project. If there is a delay in one, chances are there will be a similar delay in other similar activities if nothing is done to correct the problem. For example, if floor slab formwork started two

weeks late and took twice as long to complete as predicted, special attention should be paid to the yet-to-be-built floor slab forms on the rest of the building.

- **Changes in outside factors.** The natural tendency is for the scheduler to concentrate on conditions relating directly to construction tasks, but quite often outside factors or events can have a direct effect on the schedule, and may not be taken into account. For example, a ribbon-cutting ceremony could require halting normal construction work in that area of the project and reallocating resources to make the area safe and presentable for the local press and dignitaries.

Taking Corrective Action

The final step in schedule monitoring is taking corrective action, which must be done quickly enough to maximize the benefits of taking the action. Usually, corrective action results in reducing the project schedule duration. The most obvious corrective action is to adjust resources. This can mean adding more members to the crew or increasing the overtime hours of existing crews in order to reduce the duration of that activity. The key is to make sure that reducing the activity's duration will reduce the overall project duration. This should happen if the activity being reduced is on the critical path. If it is not on the critical path, this change may not reduce the overall project duration.

Sometimes applying more resources will not reduce the duration of an activity. If, for example, the activity that needs to be reduced requires operators and equipment (backhoes, dump trucks, etc.), adding more labor alone will not help. The addition of resources must be balanced against increased costs.

Another option is to re-examine the job logic. It may be possible to have some activities run concurrently that were originally scheduled to run sequentially. However, one must be careful to avoid having too many trades working in the same area at once. Experience on the project may yield insight that can lead to scheduling activities in a way that will deliver the desired results. Brainstorming with other stakeholders can also lead to some fresh ideas to solve the problem and improve the schedule to achieve the desired goals.

Monitoring progress must be done on a regular basis to be effective. Depending on the size and duration of the project, schedule meetings, which include key general contractor personnel and the owner's (the school's) representatives, are usually held weekly, with special sessions to address urgent events that have an impact on the schedule. An explanation should be presented and documented as to what has been accomplished since the last meeting. Has the project gone as expected? Which activities have been completed? Which have not? Is the current status a significant departure from what was planned?

All the major project team members need to be brought up to date. Some, such as subcontractors or specialty consultants, may require a separate, detailed sub-schedule illustrating a particular part of the overall schedule, with an analysis of the problem, possible alternatives, and cost studies (cost estimates comparing alternative solutions). Most important, the scheduler must determine if there has been a change in the critical path. If so, are there any major changes in float durations of any of the activities? The scheduler should be cautious of any activities where the float duration has been reduced to the point that it is close to zero. This may put these activities on the critical path. A change can also increase the amount of float in other activities, offering some breathing room and possibly a chance to save money by reducing overtime, crew members, and other expenses, or possibly allow a shift of the crews to more pressing activities.

If there has been a major change in the schedule, the scheduler must determine if it is the result of a one-time situation, or if there is a possible trend developing. If there is a crew consistently ahead of schedule, it is worth investigating what they are doing differently from other crews. They may be using a technique that can be utilized elsewhere, or they may be leaving out a step in the process. Conversely, if there is a crew that is consistently delayed, the cause may be poor productivity, or they may be including additional steps in a procedure that were not accounted for in the original schedule. These additional steps may be necessary (in this and subsequent, similar project activities), or they may be unnecessary. For the schedule to be accurate, all change orders that have an impact on the schedule should also be included.

Follow-up is perhaps the most critical aspect of project monitoring. The effort must continue consistently throughout the project to be effective. Like a long-distance race, it is sometimes easy to stay ahead in the early stages, but it takes discipline to stay with the program for the entire project. It is important not to surrender to events and let them overrun the project. The effort must start when the project starts and finish only when the project is finished.

Using the Schedule for Progress Payments

Resource-loaded schedules (discussed earlier in this chapter) can be a powerful tool to help keep the contractor on schedule. On a typical school construction project, a contractor submits a project payment schedule, which breaks down the project into several components with their associated values. These components are used as a guide for the owner to determine payments due to the contractor based on the percentage of work completed. For example, the excavation work may be listed on the payment schedule as $1,000,000, and foundation work at $3,000,000. The total for all categories must equal the total bid amount that was submitted for the project. If the excavation is 50% complete, the contractor can requisition for $500,000.

There are two problems with this approach. First, the dollar amount associated with a particular category is difficult to verify. The tendency is for the contractor to overstate the value of work items that occur early in the project in the project payment schedule. This is called *front-end loading*. By doing so, the contractor receives more money up-front, and may receive much more cash than will actually be spent on the project at a given point. This is a good position for the contractor, but not for the owner. It can negate the incentive for the contractor to finish work before he or she can expect to get paid. The owner may retaliate by withholding early payments as a defense against front-end loading. If this strategy is overly aggressive, it may backfire on the owner and force the contractor into accepting a payment schedule that does not adequately compensate for costs expended. A reliable cash flow is especially critical early in the project, as the contractor incurs costs even before the first shovel is put into the ground. A restricted cash flow can create a huge burden on the contractor, possibly causing him or her to tap into cash reserves or even borrow large amounts of money. Unjustifiably restricting cash flow to the contractor is not only an unfair burden; the financial strain that this restriction creates on the contractor can jeopardize the firm's solvency and ultimately affect the project.

The second problem is difficulty in determining what percentage of a work item has been completed. The categories used for progress payments are often broad, and measuring them cannot always be precise. Differences of opinion on the amount complete for each category are not uncommon.

The cost-loaded schedule (also covered earlier in this chapter) can help to reduce the impact of progress payment disagreements. By loading resources and costs into the construction schedule, the owner can see both the cost and duration of individual work items. Scheduling software can present this information visually, with resource usage charts. Being able to see the cost, duration, and resource usage of each work item, the owner and owner representatives are better equipped to review, analyze, verify, and understand the validity of each cost item on the payment schedule. Likewise, if the costs are reasonable, the contractor will be able to explain and defend each work item. By tying costs directly to the schedule, the progress of completing those work items will be more accurately tracked, and there will be a systematic way to convert durations into costs. An additional advantage is that the duplicated effort of separately tracking work items for progress payments purposes is eliminated, as it will be tracked concurrently, along with the construction schedule. It should be noted, however, that because of the demands cost-loaded schedules place on the contractor's management resources, they are usually a requirement only on very large projects where they are more cost-effective.

Key Scheduling Issues for Schools

Decision-Making

Although preparing a schedule for a typical school construction project may not be as daunting a task as preparing one for a huge chemical plant, a poorly prepared schedule can just as easily doom the project to failure. It is important to pay attention to key conditions that can affect the schedule. One thing to bear in mind when preparing and working with a school construction schedule is to provide adequate time for decisions that involve official approvals. These are likely to take more time than expected, especially when compared to corporate or commercial projects. Since most schools are publicly financed through the state, municipality, and local government, there are certain regulations that must be followed and often require sign-off by several administrators. These individuals are often bound by procedures, which may cause further delays. Adequate time must be included in the schedule for all major financial, design, and construction decisions and approvals because of regulations and required procedures.

Financing

Financing considerations can have a profound impact on a school construction schedule. In most municipalities, construction contracts cannot be signed unless the actual funding for the project is in place. This can wreak havoc on the schedule. Sometimes there is a delay in obtaining funding, last-minute complications that prevent the sale of bonds, an unexpected loss of funds, insufficient budgets, or technical glitches. Unless funding is in place and contracts are signed, it may be illegal for a contracting agency to authorize work to proceed. Funding may be delayed for so long that a contract will have to be re-bid or re-negotiated, creating an even longer delay to the project.

Working with Consultants

Adequate consideration must be given in the schedule for the process of selecting and approving food service, technology, and other consultants. Public contracting agencies are bound by rules that are designed to reduce the possibility of favoritism and corruption. These requirements may include advertising requests for proposals for a set minimum amount of time, the assembling of review/selection panels, contractor qualification processes, and competitive bidding procedures. These measures tend to add time to the contracting process. With implementation of more sophisticated components into schools, including information technology, audio, video, security, and sports and stage equipment, special suppliers and consultants may be required. In addition to selection and approval of these consultants, coordination of their schedules is critical to the project.

Specialized Equipment

These items can impact the schedule with longer lead-time requirements for material deliveries. In some cases, factory-trained technicians are required to perform installations. Such technicians are more difficult to schedule because the contractor has less control over them and less leverage in getting them to meet the project schedule. This is especially true if the contractor is tied to a specific manufacturer. Often, a specified manufacturer is the only one that can fulfill special requirements or expand an existing system.

Coordinating Construction with School Activities

If construction is performed during a school break or summer vacation, there must be enough time factored into the schedule to allow for unanticipated problems or delays. Security and coordination must also be allowed for in the schedule. An efficient custodial staff is key to keeping a project on schedule and helping coordinate community events. School facility calendars are often filled in the summer and evenings with community group, club, and team events. Failure to take these events into account can result in many days of lost construction time or low productivity. In addition to coordination with community events, it is important to make sure there are no conflicts with other construction projects that may be going on in the school, such as asbestos removal by the school districts' abatement consultants and contractors.

The main coordination issues involve possible:

- Disruption of learning
- Safety
- Phasing of construction

(Chapter 10 also addresses safety and construction phasing, in terms of the general contractor's actions in overseeing school projects.)

Disruption of Learning

Most of us can recall from our own experiences as children how easily the slightest change in the classroom environment can cause a distraction. A faint smell of tar, the distant sound of jackhammers, or sight of a delivery truck can disrupt a classroom. There may be some construction tasks that are so obtrusive that there is no choice but to perform them after school hours. Time must be factored into the schedule for coordinating such after-hours activities.

Complaints from parents and teachers should never be ignored. The project team must be cognizant of the level of commitment teachers have to educating, and the stress they frequently encounter. This awareness will help in understanding why what may seem like a petty complaint may be a significant issue in the classroom. These issues, if not sensitively addressed, can result in serious protest and project delays. Remember, too, that school districts may not allow any construction during state-required annual testing or exams.

Safety

If a school construction project is taking place while school is in session, the schedule is much more challenging. These issues are greater in schools than in office buildings and commercial sites. Swing space trailers may have to be brought in to house students displaced by construction. The main thing to keep in mind is the obvious—that construction is near children, who may be easily distracted, frightened, curious, or injured. As such, precautions must be taken to separate students from the construction activity. Many activities that would normally be quite acceptable in an office or commercial setting are totally out of the question where children are involved, in an educational environment. A door mistakenly left unlocked or a tool carelessly left behind can spell disaster.

Adequate time must be allowed in the schedule for activities such as provision of construction barriers and protective fences. *(See Chapter 10 for more on barriers, signage, and other safety precautions.)* The required protection on a school project may be more than what the contractor is used to, or even what some safety experts may deem necessary or reasonable. After a tragic accident in one school district, the local school board was justifiably so cautious about public safety and media attention that it demanded sidewalk protection on almost every subsequent construction project. In this case, the sudden demand for materials exhausted local supplies. Any contractor unprepared for the possibility for such an event would have fallen behind schedule while waiting for supplies to become available. Contractors should work with the school project manager and administrators to develop notices and hold meetings or class assemblies. Students and school staff must be made aware of potential construction dangers and how to conduct themselves.

Areas for school bus loading and unloading are another matter that must be given special attention. These are particularly critical areas because of the mix of bus traffic and the high concentration of school children. This should be a zero-tolerance area for construction activity during pick-up and drop-off times. If there is construction in such an area, it must be scheduled with enough lead time to ensure that there is no overlap of construction activity with pick-up and drop-off times. *(See Chapter 10 for more on traffic patterns and requirements.)*

Phasing of Construction

Another issue to consider is whether or not the project needs to be phased. Phasing is required when construction activity is not permitted at certain locations, at particular dates during the project. Usually phasing is something that the school administration or its project manager will suggest. In reviewing the project, however, the contractor may be the one to make the suggestion. The phasing of a school project can impact students, staff, and the community by necessitating the relocation of activities and redirecting pedestrian and vehicular traffic patterns at several different times during the course of the project. If the project is phased, a phasing diagram needs to be prepared. The diagram must be detailed enough to accommodate planning of construction activities. An easy-to-read summary version of the plan must be prepared for the school administration's approval. The summary should address the concerns of the school, specifying the affected areas, when work will start in these areas, and when it will finish.

Scheduling Software

Because of the sheer numbers of calculations required for the preparation of construction schedules, it is no surprise that computers are an integral part of scheduling. With the advances in computer graphics, large, intricate schedules can be produced in a matter of minutes once the required data is input into the program. Another great feature of scheduling software is its ability to produce bar, or Gantt, charts (often preferred by field personnel); PDM schedules; and a multitude of variations—to the extent that there is a blending of schedule styles. This allows the scheduler to incorporate the most desired features of each of the different styles. For example, the readability of the bar or Gantt chart can be combined with the PDM schedule's ability to show interrelationships between activities. *(See Figure 7.6.)*

A variety of line styles, such as dotted lines to represent dummy activities, is used in today's schedules. Different colors are available, such as the red used to indicate critical paths, and another color used to show actual progress. A virtually unlimited variety of graphic symbols, in addition to the diamonds used to show milestones, are also offered. In addition, many different reports can be generated from the same data.

Scheduling software is available in a wide range of prices, computing power, and features. Among the most popular suppliers of scheduling software for the construction industry are Primavera® and Microsoft®.

It is recommended that all stakeholders use the same software, so that sharing information is easy and efficient. The scheduling software to be used for a project should be included in the specified, contract requirements for all contractors and consultants on the project.

Both computerized estimating and scheduling share the risk of passively accepting the result of what was input to the computer. As some say, "to err is human, but to really mess things up requires a computer." Since scheduling is so dependent on computers, there is a danger of adding an extra zero, leaving out decimal points, omitting items, and hundreds of other inputting and formatting errors. While these errors can also happen easily on calculations performed manually, when working with computers, there is less involvement with calculations and the process, so inputting has the potential to get sloppy. While the output may reveal obvious errors, other mistakes may not be dramatic enough to show up vividly—especially in the case of a large schedule where an error can easily be buried in the larger network. Again, because the scheduler is detached from the calculations, there is a tendency to make assumptions about the computer defaults, which may be incorrect. There is no substitute for thorough checking and review of the schedule by an experienced scheduler or schedulers before the schedule is submitted. If the scheduler's logic and the durations are correct, the scheduling software should produce a precise schedule.

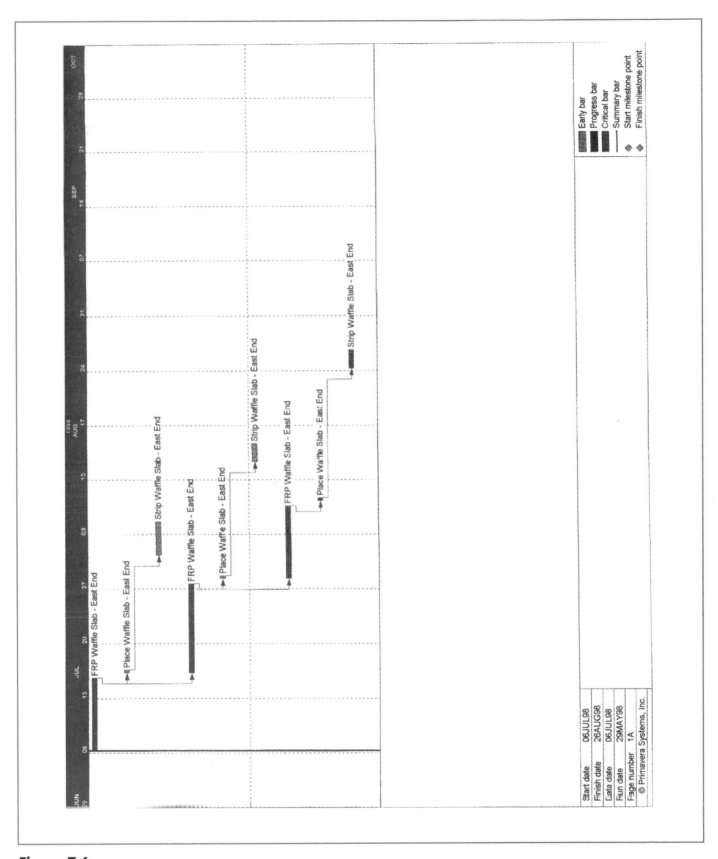

Figure 7.6
Time-Scaled Schedule

Credit: Project Scheduling & Management for Construction, Third Edition, *Copyright RSMeans*

Judgment Calls

There is also the human element involved in the overall scheduling process. Construction does not take place in a controlled environment. The number of variables to be considered is staggering. Judgment calls must be made as to the duration of activities, the sequence, and dependencies. Also, since the schedule is a graphic representation, there is sometimes the need to simplify interrelationships between activities and make other adjustments to make the schedule more readable. At a certain point, the scheduler may want to override the logic of software and "fudge" some of these relationships. At best, this can make the schedule more readable; at worst, it can produce a schedule that is just plain wrong. When checking a schedule, it is best to work from electronic software files and view it through the scheduling software. This will reveal details that are not shown on the printed reports and graphics.

Conclusion

A proper design will provide the plans to ensure that the new or renovated school facility meets the needs of both the students and the community. Accurate estimating will provide the information needed to ensure the project is built at a cost covered by available funds. Precise scheduling will provide a tool to ensure the construction is completed in a reasonable time frame that meets the school's needs. Nevertheless, even the clearest of plans with the most reliable estimates and schedules will not be enough to guarantee a successful project. The proper contractor selection process, and appropriate project delivery methods are other essential components. Capable firms and appropriate project delivery methods are needed to make the design, budget, and schedule a reality. The key procedures and issues in the contractor selection and project delivery methods are outlined in the following chapter.

Key Terms

Activity: The basic element of the schedule. In Critical Path Method (CPM) scheduling, a task or item of work required to complete a project.

ADM: Arrow Diagram Method of scheduling.

Backward Pass: Computations to establish Late Finish Times.

Critical Path: The order of events (each of a particular duration) that results in the least amount of time required to complete a project.

Critical Path Method (CPM): A system of construction management that involves the complete planning and scheduling of a project, and the development of a diagram showing each activity, its appropriate place in the timetable, and its importance relative to other tasks and the overall project.

Early Finish (EF): The earliest finish time of an activity, assuming work started at its early start time.

Early Start (ES): The earliest start time of an activity if all preceding activities are completed as early as possible.

Forward Pass: Computations used to establish Early Start and total project duration.

Late Finish (LF): The latest an activity may finish and not affect the finish of the project.

Late Start (LS): The latest an activity may start and not affect the finish of the project.

Milestone Activity: An activity with a zero duration, which marks the end of a particular phase of work.

Network: A continuous group of activities showing a logical interrelationship between activities.

Node: A junction of arrows containing the "i"-"j" number, Early Start, and Late Finish computations in the ADM or the work activity in the PDM schedule.

PDM: Precedence Diagram Method of scheduling.

Restraint: An addition to the schedule of a non-productive activity that restricts the start or finish of other activities.

Schedule: A chronological itemization, often in chart form, of the sequence of project tasks.

[1] Larson, Phillip D. "Cost Estimating and Scheduling Integration." *Cost Engineer*.

[2] Department of Defense: http://www.acq.osd.mil/pm

[3] Wallwork, Joseph W., and Ian A. Street. *Project Controls in the Pre-Construction Phase.*

[4] Fredlund, Donald J., Jr., and Fred King. *Owner's Reviews of Schedules: How Far Should They Go?* AACE Transactions, 1992.

[5] Pierce, David R., Jr. *Project Scheduling & Management for Construction, Third Edition.* Kingston, MA: Reed Construction Data, 2004.

Chapter 8

Types of Contracts and Contractor Selection

Joseph Macaluso, CCC

Contracts define the working relationships between all parties in a construction project. Before the architect begins drafting the first set of plans or the contractor hammers the first nail, each must be selected and signed to a contract. The contract administration team—whether they are on-staff members of the school system or design professionals and project managers hired by the school system—must first gather input from all involved parties about the particular project being bid. What is the time frame for this project? What contracting methods have been successfully used before in this school district? What experience has the owner had recently with designers and contractors? What special requirements does this project have? Answers to these kinds of questions will help decide not only what type of contractor is needed, but also (in school districts where these options are available) what type of contracting arrangement will be used. If the project must be built in a short time frame, a fast-track contracting arrangement may be required. If design elements are likely to be complex and need to be reviewed thoroughly before construction begins, a traditional contracting method may be best. For publicly funded projects, the funding source and state law may determine the rules for designer and contractor selection and bidding, and may limit the options for the type of contracting arrangement.

Chapter 1 of this book describes processes used to select and contract for professional design services. While the main focus of this chapter is the process of selecting contractors and construction services, guidance is additionally included on documents such as RFIs, RFPs, and RFQs that may also be used in selecting design professionals and specialty consultants.

Contracts

The contract is an essential element in a construction project. A contract is an agreement between two or more parties, for a stated, valid consideration or payment for the performance of an act or provision of services or goods, or forbearance, by the one making the promise, to the one to whom the promise is made. For the contract to be valid, it requires three elements: offer, acceptance, and consideration. In construction, the bids form the offer, the owner's and contractor's signatures form the acceptance, and the contract amount is the consideration. The contract is the basis for the entire construction project. It defines the scope of the project, how it is to be built, the time frame, the specific rights of the parties, and the agreed upon price.

The contract for construction is the keystone in a series of legal instruments described as the contract documents. In order for any agreement to be complete, the following information must be recorded:

- A complete and legal identification of all involved parties
- The mutual responsibilities of those parties to one another
- The rights of each party
- Other anticipated definitions, relationships, conditions, procedures, requirements, and alternatives that will help to avoid disputes when misunderstandings arise

A typical construction project requires the services of parties who are indirectly related to the contract, being employed by one of the parties to the contract. For example, the architect/engineer is employed by the owner, and subcontractors are employed by the contractor. The architect/engineer has no *direct* contractual agreement with the contractor; nor does the subcontractor have a direct agreement with the owner. The identities and roles of parties indirectly related to the contract must be described in no less detail than those of the parties directly related by the contract. Potential misunderstandings and disputes between all parties must be anticipated and remedies described.

The object of the Contract for Construction, or Agreement, is the *Work*, or the project as defined in the Contract. The most convenient method for the architect/engineer to describe the Work is by preparing drawings and technical specifications, which will become part of the Agreement by reference and attachment.

In view of the countless disputes that have taken place over contract arrangements, the language of the contract for construction has become more and more explicit and detailed, as the architect/engineer preparing the contract documents attempts to anticipate and avoid such situations. The most common approach to preventing disputes (in addition to seeking the advice of an attorney) has been the preparation of additional explanatory documents, which, like the drawings and specifications, are complimentary, referenced and attached to the Agreement. One of these explanatory documents is the *Conditions of the Contract for Construction* discussed later in the chapter.

Contractual Relationships

The Contract for Construction is an agreement between the owner and the contractor. However, there are other issues and relationships that complicate this arrangement. There is usually a distinct and separate agreement defining the services of the architect/engineer to meet the owner's objectives. The architect/engineer will often contract with an engineer and other consultants to perform portions of the design. The contractor contracts with various subcontractors. Each subcontractor then has the option of contracting portions of his work to others, sometimes referred to as *sub-subcontractors*. Each of the contractors is also related to various producers (suppliers and manufacturers), either by contract or by purchase order. The purchase order is, in effect, a contract wherein the contractor agrees to purchase materials or services for use in executing the work.

Because the relationships of parties in the construction process can be so complex, disputes are possible when any of the involved parties do not agree on how specific work or materials are to be furnished or the installation sequence. Over the years, common solutions have been found for many problems, and certain language has been developed and accepted among most participants regularly involved in building construction. Much of this information, in written form, is commonly included in *Contract Documents* and the *Conditions of the Contract*.

The Conditions of the Contract are most often contained in a document separate from, but part of, the Contract for Construction. The Conditions of the Contract uses detailed descriptive language, supportive of, and incidental to, the *Agreement between Owner and Contractor*, recognizing the related work of others acting under separate agreements toward a common goal. The Conditions of the Contract are made a part of the Contract for Construction by reference and/or attachment.

Standardized Conditions of the Contract Provisions

Midway into the 20th century, committees comprised of architectural and engineering societies, ownership groups, construction industry organizations, and interested individuals met and discussed their respective problems and objectives related to construction contracts. Each group made compromises and jointly produced language, which was published as a document describing Conditions to the Contract for Construction.

Over the years, improvements have been made periodically, resulting in a number of familiar forms of contract conditions. Some of these documents have become standards in the construction industry and are used to avoid, adjudicate, or provide a mechanism to resolve disputes. The American Institute of Architects publishes *The General Conditions of the Contract for Construction*. The Engineer's Joint Documents Committee (EJDC) publishes the *Standard Conditions of the Construction Contract*. Many ownership agencies of state and federal governments prefer to use their own proprietary forms of Conditions of the Contract that have been specially written to suit particular types of public works projects and political objectives. Among these are the Corps of Engineers of the U.S. Army, the U.S. Navy, and the U.S. Postal Service, to name a few. Whichever "standard" is used, each is intended to achieve the same goal: to facilitate the successful administration of the Contract for Construction.

AIA General Conditions

Since its inception over a century ago, the American Institute of Architects (AIA), in collaboration with other industry organizations such as the Construction Specifications Institute (CSI) and the Associated General Contractors of America (AGC), has dedicated itself to establishing and continually perfecting an interrelated series of published documents. The aim of these documents is to facilitate all contractual relationships in modern building construction.

Over the years, the AIA has produced a number of standard documents and contracts, such as agreements between owner and contractor, owner and architect/engineer, contractor and subcontractor, and others. The *Conditions of the Contract for Construction* (or any one of several variations of the Conditions of the Contract) published by AIA can be used to supplement, interrelate, or otherwise expand on the purposes, agreements, covenants, and responsibilities between and among the parties to the various types of contracts.

EJCDC Standard Conditions

While architects have tended to organize themselves into one or two national organizations, the AIA being the most prominent, engineers organized by engineering discipline. There are many nationally recognized engineering societies and institutes such as the American Society of Civil Engineers (ASCE), the Institute of Electrical and Electronic Engineers (IEEE), and the National Society of Professional Engineers (NSPE). In the mid-20th century, several professional engineering organizations who were engaged in building design and related fields organized the Engineers Joint Contract Documents Committee (EJCDC) and created and published a library of proprietary contract documents that serve the needs of the wider and diverse engineering community.

Owner-Generated Conditions of the Contract

Today, it is not unusual for local governments, taxing districts, school districts, and similar jurisdictions to create and maintain standard contract conditions that they believe better serve the needs of the local community. Washington, D.C. and the Fairfax County, Virginia, School Board are examples of local public owners who make such a practice.

The Selection and Award Process for Construction Contracts

The process used to select contractors and design professionals should match the needs of the school project. The purpose of developing selection and award policies is to enable the school administration to contract with the best qualified firm at the most reasonable overall cost. Such policies should incorporate procedures to protect against the possibility or appearance of favoritism, fraud, and corruption. The bidding process should ensure that bids are selected in a manner that is ethical and legal, while obtaining the best value for the owner, the school system. These procedures are mandated in public agencies and are built into good practices for private entities. Different states have specific laws as to how school project work is procured. Some require the school system to select the bidder with the lowest responsible price. Others allow selection of the most qualified contractor, even if theirs is not the lowest bid.

The selection process should be fair and open. One important way to ensure this is to advertise projects for bid early. Advertising also is the best way to promote competition by increasing the number of bids. Each state has different requirements for advertising bids. For example, some require that a public notice be posted in a local paper for two successive weeks, two weeks before bids are to be accepted. Listed below are some of the acceptable ways to advertise for bids:

- Advertisements in trade papers or industry magazines
- State contracting notices
- Mailings to industry associations
- Direct notification of known, interested parties
- Postings with state and local economic development agencies and departments
- Posting in local newspaper classified section under "Public Notices"

Bidding Documents

A complete set of Bidding Documents consists of:

- Bidding Requirements
- Contract Forms
- Conditions of the Contract (General and Supplementary)
- Technical Specifications
- Contract Drawings

(Refer to Figure 8.1 for a list of documents used in the bidding process and how they relate to one another.)

Bidding Requirements

Bidding requirements include the Invitation to Bid, Instructions to Bidders, Information Available to Bidders, and Bid Forms and Supplements.

Invitation to Bid, or Bid Solicitation: As the name implies, this is a notice of an intent to receive bids. For private firms, it may be issued selectively to whomever the owner desires. For publicly bid work, it usually must be advertised. The Invitation to Bid should include:

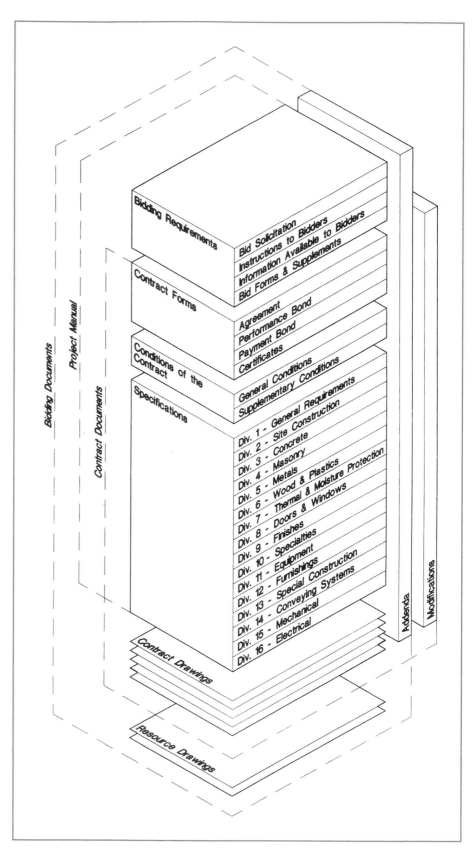

Figure 8.1

Construction Documents

Credit: The Construction Specifications Institute

- Brief description of the purpose of the Invitation to Bid
- Issuing office
- Point of contact for any questions
- Date and time of the bid opening
- Bid opening location
- Location for the completed bids to be returned
- Additional documentation to be submitted by the bidder
- Bidder's qualifications requirements

The bidder qualifications define the minimum acceptable standards for bidders. Some questions to be addressed include:

- Is the contractor:
  - Technically qualified to perform the proposed work?
  - Able to comply with the delivery or performance schedule?
- Does the contractor:
  - Have adequate financial resources to perform the proposed work?
  - Have a satisfactory record of past performance on projects of similar size and complexity?

Alternates: It is usually good practice to include alternates in the Invitation to Bid. This gives the contracting authority a chance to examine the cost of different options to the base scope of work. Alternates can include additional desired work, upgrades, or features *(add alternates)* that the school, as owner, would like to have included in the project if the bids come in under-budget. Alternates can also be deletions of portions of the project *(deduct alternates)* should the bids come in over-budget. Usually add alternates are used so that it is assured that the base project includes, at a minimum, all the work that will meet the needs of the school. The project budget should include an amount of contingency funds sufficient to cover unplanned costs. This "cushion" can be used in case bids come in higher than expected, and to cover change orders during construction. What should be avoided is a budget that is unreasonably low. This may result in a scramble to cut costs, which could bring about an unsatisfactory finished project. The use of alternates in the contract documents helps to provide this much needed flexibility.

Method of Award: The method of award should be specified in the Invitation to Bid. An award can be based on the lowest price or best value from a responsible bidder. "Best value" can be based on life cycle costs in lieu of first price amounts, or an overall score. *(See Life Cycle Cost Analysis in Chapter 6, "Estimating.")* Both the method for determining the responsiveness (e.g., bid submitted on time and complete, with additional bidding requirements fulfilled) and the bidder's responsibility requirements should be stated. Some school districts use a point system to select the contractor based on best value. The system rates contractors based on price, references, MWBE (Minority- or Women-based Business Enterprises) participation, proposed schedule, and the overall strength of the proposed project team.

Instructions to Bidders: The Instruction to Bidders should include the following items:

- List of bid documents.
- Definitions of terms used in the bid requirements.
- Bidder's representation form indicating that the bidder has:
  —Read and understands the full intent of the bid documents, and that the bid is made in accordance with the bid documents.

  —Visited the site and understands the local conditions where the work is to be performed, and has taken these observations into account in preparing the bid.

  —Included all the materials, labor, and equipment required for the job without any exceptions.
- Bid documents article, which describes the access, use, and legal attributes of the bidding documents.
- Notice of pre-bid conference: A pre-bid conference provides an opportunity for the design professionals to describe the project, and for the owner's representatives to express the goals of the project. It offers prospective bidders an opportunity to ask questions about the project.
- Notice of Substitutions: A notice that substitutions in materials, products, or equipment specified in the bidding documents will not be considered unless an addendum has been issued.
- Interpretation of Bidding Documents Statements: A statement that the bidder is responsible for studying the bid documents and is expected to be familiar with all codes and regulations applicable to the project. The bidder should report any errors, inconsistencies, or omissions to the design professional of record for the project.
- Form of Proposal: This is the actual form that the bidder fills in with information such as the bidder's name, the amount of the bid, and the bid expiration date. The Form of Proposal is signed by a designated person from the bidder's firm.

Contract Forms

Contract forms can include the Agreement, Performance Bond, Payment Bond, and the Certificate of Insurance. The Agreement, or Contract for Construction, deals with the direct legal responsibilities of the parties of the contract. The Performance Bond is a form of security purchased by the contractor, which is a guarantee that the contractor will satisfactorily perform all the work and other services related to the project for which he is responsible. The Payment Bond is a form of security purchased by the contractor which provides a guarantee that the contractor will pay all costs of labor, materials, and other services related to the project for which the contractor is responsible in the Agreement. The Certificate of Insurance is a document signed by an authorized representative of an insurance company stating that the coverage is applicable in accordance with the contract documents.

Conditions of the Contract

The Conditions of the Contract document uses detailed descriptive language, supportive of, and incidental to, the *Agreement between Owner and Contractor*, recognizing the related work of others acting under separate agreements toward a common goal. Conditions of the Contract can include General Conditions, Supplemental Conditions, Regulatory Conditions, Wage Rate Requirements, Equal Opportunity Requirements, and an Index of Drawings.

General Conditions: The General Conditions contain general statements of the responsibilities of the parties during the construction process. As noted earlier, the American Institute of Architects (AIA) publishes *The General Conditions of the Contract for Construction, see Figure 8.2,* the Engineer's Joint Contract Documents Committee (EJCDC) publishes the *Standard Conditions of the Construction Contract,* and some ownership agencies of state and federal government use their own proprietary forms of Conditions of the Contract, specially written to suit particular types of public works projects and political objectives.

Supplementary General Conditions: The Supplemental Conditions are used to modify and expand the General Conditions to address the unique requirements of the specific project.

General Conditions (AIA A201)

1. General Provisions
2. Owner
3. Contractor
4. Administration of the Contract
5. Subcontractors
6. Construction by Owner/Separate Contractors
7. Changes in the Work
8. Time
9. Payments and Completion
10. Protection of Persons and Property
11. Insurance and Bonds
12. Uncovering and Correction of Work
13. Miscellaneous Provisions
14. Termination or Suspension of the Contract

Figure 8.2
General Conditions (AIA A201)

Specifications and Contract Drawings

Specifications are the written qualitative requirements for products, materials, and workmanship of the project. Contract drawings are the graphic representations of the project. The specifications and the contract drawings should be correlated with the other contract documents.

Information Available to Bidders

This section includes items such as soils reports, the owner's financial qualifications, and surveys of existing conditions.

Addenda

Addenda provide additional information on corrections issued during the bidding period, before the contract has been awarded, to clarify or modify the contract work. All addenda should be issued to all parties bidding on the project.

Financial Risks Associated with Construction Projects

Owner's Risk

The owner takes certain calculated risks regarding the capability, experience, and integrity of the people who become involved in whichever project delivery method is chosen. This begins with the design team, which will be relied on not only to produce a successful design to meet the school's needs, but to do so within its designated budget.

The opportunity to reduce the cost of the project is greatest during the pre-design phase of project development, when the architect/engineer can apply skill and experience to this goal. The ability to reduce project cost diminishes rapidly as the project design progresses. As the process continues from schematic design through the creation of contract documents, cost savings opportunities diminish from a high of about 15% down to about 5% in possible reductions at the end of design development. Once the contract documents have been completed, there is little further opportunity to reduce probable cost, although it is conceivable that a savings of up to 2% may be realized during bidding and negotiations if market conditions are competitive. After bidding and negotiations, changes in the design intended to save money may actually result in additional cost if change orders are required. As a result, the Savings Opportunity Curve will dip below the 0% line. *(See Figure 8.3.)*

The owner also takes certain calculated risks regarding the credibility and integrity of the constructor chosen for the job. To help offset these risks, the architect/engineer, when acting as the owner's agent and representative thoroughly investigates the experience, financial resources, and capability of the bidding contractors. (Qualification procedures are covered later in this chapter.)

Architect/Engineer's Risks

The primary risk of the architect/engineer in the process of project procurement lies in two definable areas of professional practice: the cost of marketing the time invested in the preparation of work to complete the project. The competition among architect/engineers for desirable commissions is intense and increasingly expensive. Recent statistics revealed by the AIA and a number of engineering societies indicate that the most successful firms have a reasonable expectation of winning only 15%–20% of the projects for which they compete. Marketing expenses are high, often up to 15% of the firm's annual earned income. Considering that profits on earned fees average 10% or less, the financial risks associated with normal business practice are high.

Of the alternative project procurement methods mentioned in this chapter, the design/build method poses the highest financial risk to the architect/engineer. Depending on the owner's selection methods, the financial risk can be prohibitive for proposals that require substantial design work as part of a competitive proposal.

Figure 8.3

The Savings Opportunity Curve During Design

Credit: Waller S. Poage, AIA

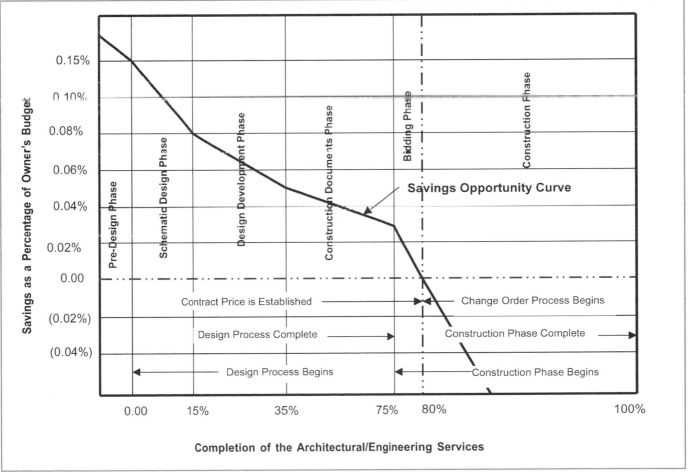

Contractor's Risks

Statistics show the business failure rate of companies engaged in general contracting is high, and that many general contracting companies in the United States declare bankruptcy or are forced into receivership by creditors. In recent history, it has not been unusual for contractors to become insolvent during the process of building some projects, which is the reason why performance bonds are often required.

The process of competitive bidding requires the contractor to study the construction documents, estimate the total cost of building the project, factor in a profit, and be prepared to pay all costs (foreseen and unforeseen) that are included in the Contract Documents. To "win" the award of the Contract for Construction, a bid must usually be lowest among all other bids submitted by competitors. The bidder's work includes computing quantities, discerning exactly what is required by the documents, and anticipating changes in wage rates. Mistakes in any of these areas or the unforeseen failure of a subcontractor or material vendor to deliver as promised can result in losses to the contractor who wins the bid.

Project Delivery Considerations

An owner who expects to obtain a project at the lowest possible cost, with the highest quality of construction, in an absolute, pre-conceived time frame, may be unrealistic and setting up a formula for disappointment, if not failure, in the project results. It is important to fully understand what constitutes the elements of cost, quality, and time.

Project cost is defined in terms of the total "hard" cost and "soft" costs. Hard Cost is the cost of construction including the contractor's overhead and profit and any modifications to the contract for construction. Soft Cost is the cost of land, professional fees, owner's contingencies, and other incidental costs. *Quality* is a combination of attributes, properties, value, and other characteristics of a particular design, material, system, or equipment or other element, according to comparative excellence and degree of perfection in workmanship, manufacture, performance, longevity, or attractiveness. *Time* is the period required to do all that is necessary to bring the project to completion. This includes the time required to establish the program of design plus the work of the Architect/Engineer leading to the preparation of the Contract Documents and, finally, the work of the contractor required to complete the construction process.

It is important to understand that these three primary factors—cost, quality, and time—when identified as of primary importance in the decision process, are not mutually exclusive. When cost is the primary goal in the project delivery process, it usually means the lowest possible cost, with quality and time becoming compromises in the decisions made by the owner to achieve the primary goal of a fixed cost objective.

When time is the primary decision driver, then quality, to some extent, and cost will be the result of decisions made in order to deliver the project in a predetermined time frame. The result of a *time limited* construction period often results in inflated costs as contingencies are included to cover unknowns that cannot be thoroughly evaluated for economy. The time-driven process of construction will be more costly because overtime and extended work weeks may be required, and these drive up the cost of labor. Expedited delivery demands may increase the cost of materials and subcontracts.

When quality is the primary decision driver, then both cost and time required to deliver the project will be determined by decisions that ensure the highest possible quality. The most effective way to control quality, as the primary objective, is to select the architect/engineer on the basis of proven ability to provide unusual or award-winning "signature" design, rather than for cost-related reasons, such as competitive fees. In this case, material selection may also be made on the basis of quality rather than competitive price and availability. It is not possible, in most projects, to achieve lowest possible cost within a foreshortened time frame when highest available quality is the priority for the owner.

Once the owner has made a choice to prioritize cost, time, or quality, then one of the remaining decision drivers affecting project delivery can be selected as the secondary project priority. An owner in the 21st century can choose from a number of well-established alternative project delivery systems—each of which has distinct advantages and disadvantages. From the owner's perspective, the process may begin by deciding on an appropriate priority among cost, quality, and time.

Project Delivery Methods

Traditional Method (Design/Bid/Build)

Design/bid/build may be the methodology of choice when the owner identifies the decision drivers to be (1) cost, (2) quality, and (3) time, in that order. The design/bid/build method is executed and delivered in a two-step process. First, the Architect/Engineer is selected. Under agreement with the owner, the project is designed, and contract documents are produced. Next, the bidding or negotiation process results in the selection of a contractor. The second step begins when the contract for construction is awarded, and then the construction takes place. Owners rely on the education, skill, and experience of the architect/engineer to guide them (and their objectives) through the process of selecting the contractor.

In the traditional design/bid/build delivery system, the design professional and the contractor have no direct contractual relationship with one another. The architect/engineer contracts with, and is responsible for, any sub-consultants he/she may employ to enhance the service provided to the owner. The contractor, in turn, awards subcontracts for portions of the work that may include such specialties as mechanical (HVAC) systems, plumbing systems, and electrical systems. Either the contractor or the subcontractor may purchase materials, systems, or equipment for the project from manufacturers or suppliers. (*See Figure 8.4.*)

Advantages of the design/bid/build form of project delivery to the owner include:

- The owner's initial project investment is limited to architect/engineer's fee if the project is abandoned or postponed because the bid amounts exceed the budget.
- The architect/engineer works directly for the owner and owes no allegiance to, nor derives any benefit from, work of contractors, subcontractors, or manufacturers.

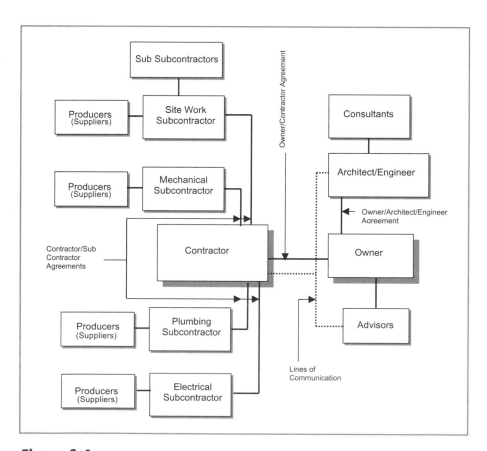

Figure 8.4
Design/Bid/Build Organization
Credit: Waller S. Poage, AIA

- The architect/engineer, as representative of the owner, is also the interpreter of the contract documents.
- Through competitive bidding, the owner, assisted by the architect/engineer, is assured of reasonable project cost by a qualified contractor.
- A single contractor is responsible for the coordination and management of the construction process.

Disadvantages of the design/bid/build project delivery method include:

- Assurance of contract price and date of project delivery is established late in the process.
- The contractor is selected on the basis of price, not managerial ability.
- The relationship between the owner, architect/engineer, and contractor has the potential to become adversarial and may lead to costly claims and disputes.
- More time may be required to complete the process of project delivery than alternative methods of project procurement.

Construction Management (CM) Project Delivery

Early in the 1950s, the Construction Management form of project delivery began to emerge as a viable method. The advent of CM evolved naturally from the owners' need to oversee complex design/multiple-bid/build projects while lacking the skill or desire to manage the process themselves. In the traditional design/bid/build methodology, the contractor was both builder and manager of the construction process. When the concept of multiple contracts was introduced, the problem became identifying who would manage the work of separate contractors.

With CM came the need for the Construction Manager, defined as an individual selected by the owner for the express purpose of managing the construction process. Typically, a CM is employed to manage multiple contracts under the design/multiple-bid/build project delivery system. Since the mid-1900s, several distinctive types of CM methods have appeared. Among the most prominent are the Construction Manager as Advisor (or agent) and the Construction Manager at Risk, that is, as combination constructor (contractor) and construction manager.

The Construction Manager as Advisor or Agent

Under this construction management approach, the CM may serve in an advisory role to the owner, and be compensated in the form of a fee without risk. The CM as advisor or agent (CM/A) acts as an extension of the owner, serving as the owner's agent, managing one or more prime contracts between owner and prime contractor. The CM/A might also be known as the *Agency Construction Manager*. Today, many government agencies, such as large school districts in major metropolitan areas, may employ one or more CMs to oversee their ongoing building construction programs.[1] Sometimes these agencies act as CM/A for another agency or group of agencies.[2]

Advantages of the CM/A arrangement include:

- The architect/engineer works directly for the owner and owes no allegiance to, nor derives any benefit from the work of the construction manager-as-agent, prime contractors, subcontractors or manufacturers.

- The owner/architect/engineer benefits from the CM/A's assistance during the design development process (if he/she is hired early on), providing the owner with an additional "layer" of expertise in efforts to achieve a more reasonable assurance of balance between economy and quality.

- By the CM/A managing competitive bidding among multiple subcontractors, the owner is assured of reasonable project cost by qualified contractors.

- The owner/architect/engineer relationship, in coordination with the work of the CM/A during construction, provides the owner with assurance of the contractor conforming with the quality of materials and workmanship described in the contract documents.

- The owner/architect/engineer relationship, when coordinated with the work of the CM/A during the warranty period, provides the owner with reasonable assurance that construction defects will be identified for contractor remedy under the general first year unconditional warranty period recognized in most jurisdictions.

- The owner has reasonable assurance of adequate coordination of multiple contractors, which helps to minimize delay claims and disputes.

Disadvantages of the CM/A project delivery include:

- The added burden of the CM/A's fee, which means that the cost of the project may be higher than project delivery by traditional design/bid/build methods.

- The services of the CM/A may not be bonded and may not offer protection of errors and omissions liability insurance.

(See Figure 8.5.)

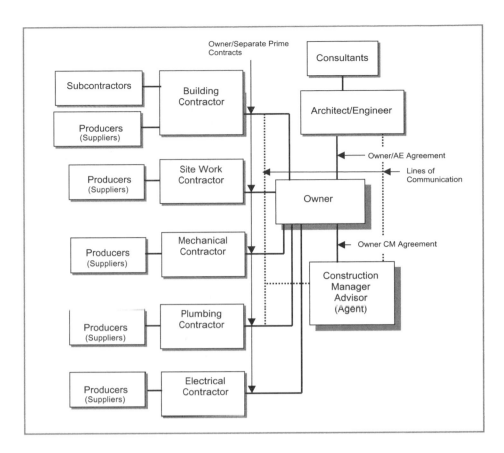

Figure 8.5

Construction Manager-Advisor Contract Organization

Credit: Waller S. Poage, AIA

The Construction Manager at Risk

Under the construction manager at risk approach, the CM may act as contractor (CM/C), awarding and managing one or more prime multiple subcontracts. The CM-at-Risk (CM/R) may accomplish portions of the work with his own forces, but he is responsible for the completion of the project under terms of the contract, including a defined contract price, and is therefore at risk for either profit or loss depending on his ability to manage the work of multiple *prime contracts*.

CM/R is usually compensated out of total contract price under which the CM has agreed to deliver the project. The owner may acquire the services of the CM/R either by competitive bid or in the case of a private owner, by competition or negotiation.

Advantages of the CM/R method include:

- The architect/engineer works directly for the owner and owes no allegiance to, nor derives any benefit from, work of the CM/R, prime contractors, subcontractors, or manufacturers.
- The owner may opt to award the CM/R contract by competitive bid and therefore may be reasonably assured of the lowest reasonable contract price.
- By employing competitive bidding among multiple prime contractors, as with design/bid/build, the owner is assured of reasonable project cost by qualified contractors with the work of all prime contractors coordinated by the CM/R.

- The owner may opt to employ the *fast-track* method of project delivery in order to reduce the time required for construction.

Disadvantages of the CM/R project delivery process include:

- The owner does not have the same assurance of professionalism from the CM/R that he has with the CM/A method.
- If the CM/R is awarded a contract by competitive bid, the CM will not be part of the project design process and therefore does not provide the owner with an added "layer" of expertise to assist in guiding the project's decision process.

(See Figure 8.6.)

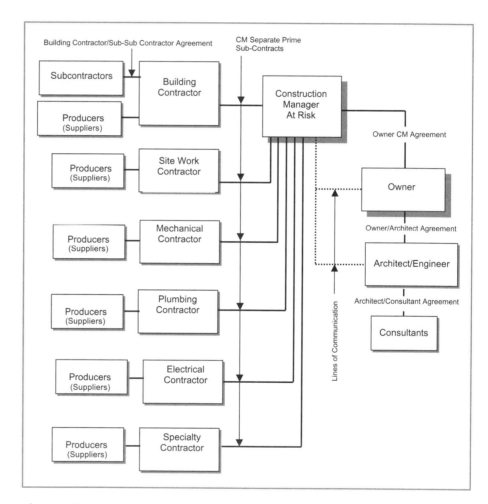

Figure 8.6

Construction Manager at Risk Contract Organization

Credit: Waller S. Poage, AIA

Design/Build Project Delivery

The time required for delivery of the completed project has become increasingly important to owners. In the past 50 years more owners require that their projects be fast-tracked or delivered in unusually short time frames. Some owners have the need for "high-tech" or highly specialized buildings, which require particular expertise on the part of both architect/engineer and constructor. Other owners have limited or fixed budgets and need to employ a delivery strategy that establishes a Guaranteed Maximum Price (GMP) early in the process. This need to mandate the control of cost, quality, or time in the delivery of a project has given rise to a project delivery methodology called Design/Build. *(See Figure 8.7.)*

The design/build process can be defined as "one-stop shopping" for the owner. It requires the owner to award a contract to a single entity who becomes responsible for designing and constructing the project under a single contract. Although design/build has come into favor in recent years in the U.S., it may in fact be the oldest project delivery system known to mankind. Many of the world's oldest monuments, such as the

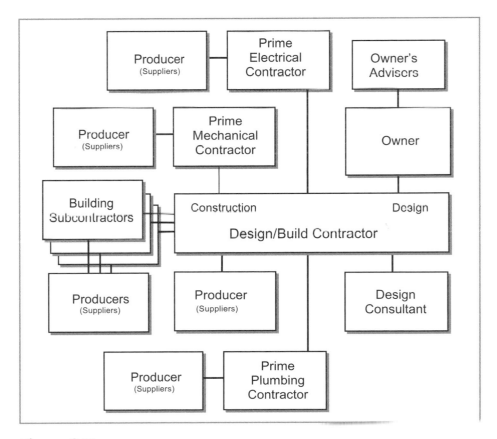

Figure 8.7
Design/Build Contract
Credit: Waller S. Poage, AIA

Great Pyramid of Egypt, were products of a design/build team. While design/build may seem simplified, it holds certain risks to all of the parties, especially the owner.

The traditional design/bid/build method has been used predominantly over two centuries in the United States, offering the owner assurance that his project will be delivered for the lowest possible cost, and that the architect/engineer acting on his behalf (being independent of the contractor or the construction process and its potential rewards,) can assure that the owner will receive a quality project. Neither of these traditional safeguards may be fully available to the owner in the design/build process. Owners considering design/build are advised to conduct a risk analysis. The design/build process, by definition, places both the design process and the construction process under a single contract responsibility.

Organization of the Design/Build (D/B) Team

As the demand has grown for design/build among private and public owners, D/B teams have assembled themselves in a variety of ways. Typical arrangements may include:

- A D/B team assembled to respond to a specific project or series of similar projects. Typical teaming in this circumstance has been between an independent constructor (either a construction management firm or an independent general contractor) who agrees to join an independent architect/engineer (either an architect or an engineer or an architect/engineer) in response to an owner for a specific project. Typically the constructor becomes the *prime entity* of the association, and the architect/engineer becomes a subcontractor to the prime entity.

- A design/build firm assembled to specialize in the design/build process as its primary business. The design/build firm is staffed with both constructors and architect/engineers under one system of management, or it may be a joint venture between a constructor and an architect/engineer.

An owner may select a design/build team through direct selection or competitive selection, depending in large part on the primary objective— be it cost, quality, or time.

Advantages of the Design/Build method include:

- The owner's procurement process is simplified to a "one-stop-shopping" experience. Time that is otherwise expended in the selection of an architect/engineer, negotiating a contract for design, preparing the design through the Contract Documents Phase, and the subsequent competitive bidding or negotiating for selection of a constructor is considerably reduced.

- Project cost and schedule of delivery are identified early in the process. Although some time is required for the design to be produced before a final price and schedule can be expected, the time required to reach a basis for contract is much less than would be expected in more traditional design/bid/build approaches.

- In the typical Design/Build project, design documentation is simplified; less detail may be required in completing the construction documents because of the elimination of the bidding or negotiating process that is part of the traditional design/bid/build approach.

- The total cost of the project as reflected in the agreed contract price may be lower than the total of design fees plus contract price that might be expected of the design/bid/build approach. However, there is no expedient way to provide absolute assurance of that fact.

- The owner may opt to employ the fast-track method of project delivery in order to take maximum advantage of time. In general, the design/build method of project procurement may be an ideal choice for the owner who has identified time as the primary objective in his project decision process for reasons previously discussed.

Disadvantages of the Design/Build process include:

- The owner has a limited opportunity to be assured that the contract price for the project has had the full advantage of a wide range of competition in the marketplace.

- The owner has little or no advanced approval opportunity over the quality of materials, equipment, and methodology employed to produce the project.

- The owner cannot rely on the architect/engineer's independent advice or assurance that the architect/engineer component of the D/B team will act as the owner's advocate in the project delivery process.

- "One-stop-shopping" heavily favors the Design/Build contractor's interests; therefore, the owner's interests rely on both the integrity and professionalism of the selected D/B team.

Fast-Track Project Delivery

The evolving CM and Design/Build techniques have given rise to some creative project delivery methodologies, such as the fast-track method. The basic premise behind the fast-track method is that time (and often money) can be saved if the construction can begin before all of the traditional pre-construction functions, including design, are completed. The fast-track method may be used under CM/A, CM/R, or Design/Build contracts.

The Selection Process

Selecting firms for a school construction project involves collecting information, evaluating a host of criteria, and negotiation. Each step is crucial, as the decisions based on this process will ultimately determine who the school system will contract for architectural, engineering, construction, management, and other services required for the project.

The Quality-Based Selection Philosophy

Quality-Based Selection (QBS) is often used to select architecture, engineering, and other specialty services. QBS addresses the difficulty in quantifying creativity and competency, as well as the dangers of placing too much emphasis on the initial price of services. Using the QBS method, price may be a factor, but it is not the main or only factor in making a decision. QBS has the backing of the American Bar Association, the American Public Works Association, the American Institute of Architects, the American Consulting Engineers Council, and the Association of General Contractors.

The Brooks Act of 1972 recommends the use of QBS for federal projects through a policy that mandates engineer selection based on competence and unique abilities for each project, at a fair price. Since the Brooks Act was passed, over 40 states have enacted variations for their own procurement policies, known as "Mini-Brooks Acts." While the QBS must be used in many state-run school projects, it is optional for most private projects. However, many privately run school contracting departments still use it as a basis for sound contracting procedures.

With the goal of making quality and schedule the priorities, the QBS procedure typically prescribes three basic steps:

- Announce the availability of the contract.
- Evaluate the qualifications of interested firms.
- Negotiate the scope of services and fee.

Announcement

The announcement can be in the form of an RFI, RFQ, or RFP and can include a Statement of Qualifications form. The Statement of Qualifications should require the names of the firm's owners, number of years in business, types of services offered, experience of key personnel, similar past projects, and other important information that the contracting team can use to evaluate the firm's ability to handle the particular project. A recommended form is the AIA Qualification Statement; B431 for Architects, A305 for Contractors.

Evaluation

The first part of the evaluation process is to assemble the evaluation team. Depending on the size and scope of the project, this team should consist of about six individuals with skills and experience relevant to the project. An evaluation sheet (spreadsheet or matrix) should be prepared for the team's use. The rows of the sheet can provide specific criteria desired for the project. The criteria should be the same as listed in the RFQ (Request for Qualifications). After each criterion, there should be a column where the reviewer can assign a rating. Following the rating column, space can be provided to record the relative weight assigned to that criterion. The weight assigned to each criterion should reflect its relative importance to the project as a whole. The assigned weight must be consistent for all firms being rated. The last column can be used to record the scores for each criterion. Scores are determined by multiplying the rating by the weight assigned to a particular criterion. The total score is the total of all the scores for that particular firm. *(See Figure 8.8.)*

The next part of the evaluation process is to rank the firms in order of lowest-to-highest scores. The top scorers, usually about three firms, will be the basis for the "short list." On larger projects, interviews with the three top-scoring firms are recommended as a way to solicit additional information that is not as easily obtained by means of formal correspondence. An assessment based on this interview should be included as part of the firm's overall evaluation. Once the evaluation committee identifies the most qualified firm, it should contact that firm for preparation of the next step, negotiating the contract.

Negotiating the Scope of Services and Fee

At this point, the school system, as owner, begins discussions with the bidder deemed most qualified, and further defines the particulars of the project. From these discussions, the bidder begins preparing a detailed fee proposal. Once the fee proposal is prepared and delivered, the school system begins the review and evaluation process. If it is determined that the fee is excessive, or above what has been budgeted, negotiations begin. At this point, the parties can agree to reduce the scope of work, reduce the fees, or both. If the two parties still cannot reach agreement on the amount of work in the scope or the fees, the next step is to negotiate with the firm ranked second on the list.

Sample Consultant Rating Sheet

Project: _____

Consulting Firm: _____

_____

Criteria	Rating (1 thru 5)	x	Weight (1 thru 10)	=	Score Rating x Weight
Number of years in business					
History of creative design solutions					
Green building experience					
Past performance in building schools					
History of controlling costs					
History of meeting schedules					
History of creative design solutions					
Past performance in building schools					
Total Score					

Figure 8.8
Sample Consultant Rating Sheet

Use of RFIs, RFQs, and RFPs

Requests for Information (RFI), Requests for Qualifications (RFQ), and Requests for Proposals (RFP) may be used for work that includes architectural, engineering, or management services which are difficult to quantify. Use of these forms helps the school system or its representatives evaluate the services by offering an opportunity for the respondents to describe what they will be providing and how they will do it.

RFIs

RFIs are frequently used to request preliminary information for the evaluation of potential bids for design services, construction services, or both. This request does not usually signify a firm commitment by the school system, but it gives them a better feel for the potential bidders and their capabilities. The information gathered by RFIs is sometimes used to develop a list of architects, engineers, or contractors who will eventually receive an RFP.

RFQs

The Request for Qualifications (RFQ) is also used as a vehicle to solicit bids from architects, engineers, project managers, and developers. An RFQ may or may not ask for an actual price for delivering the services. Normally an RFQ is used as a precursor to an RFP. *(Note: Caution should be exercised when using this terminology, as RFQ is also used to designate a Request for Quotation.)*

A Request for Qualifications should include a description of:

- The project (with plans and specifications, if available)
- Services required
- Special expertise that may be required
- Project budget and funding sources
- Anticipated time schedule for the project
- Selection process
- Special criteria used for selection
- Invitation for firms to submit a statement of qualifications
- Deadline for all interested parties to submit their statement of qualifications

RFPs

RFPs are typically issued by the school system or its representative further along in the decision process and are more likely to signify that there will be a commitment to one of the respondents. The respondent's proposal to an RFP may be part of the final contract. For example, RFPs are used in some states to solicit fees and general proposals for CM at Risk work.

Selection Methodologies

The following sections briefly describe the most common methods of selection—direct and competitive, and the variations of each. The selection method chosen should support the owner's priorities and requirements.

Direct Selection

In this method, the owner selects the architect/engineer or program manager or design/build team by judging credentials, experience, and response from candidates. The owner first documents the project's objectives, then prepares a statement of acceptable credentials and experience expected of respondents in the form of an RFQ. Secondly, the owner may prepare a Request for Proposal (RFP). The RFP process may have two or more successive steps in the selection process.

The One-Step Selection Process: The one-step selection process relies solely on a candidate's response to the RFQ for selection, and subsequently a design/build contract. The one-step process is particularly appropriate for the owner who chooses *quality* as the first priority for project delivery. The quality-oriented owner will look for the candidate who presents significant evidence of *tenure*, that is, years of experience in delivery of projects with similar attributes to the proposed project and secondly, evidence of *availability*, that is, that the candidate has the ability to pledge sufficient human resources, management skill, and financial viability to accomplish the design and construction of the project in an acceptable time frame for delivery. Once the tentative choice is made from the slate of candidates, the cost and schedule for delivery of the contract documents by the architect/engineer—or, if Program Manager or Design/Build team, the construction of the project will be negotiated and a contract executed with the successful candidate.

The Two-Step Direct Selection Process: In the one-step process, the owner may negotiate and then award a contract for desired services. An additional step in the selection process is necessary if the owner's primary objective is assurance of competitive cost (with time of secondary importance). The two-step process of selection involves first determining a "short-list" of finalists based on response to a published RFQ (much as is described in the one-step selection process above). The second step is focused on an RFP. The finalists of the first step (usually no more than five candidates) are invited to make a second-step response to the RFP. In the case of selection of an architect/engineer for either a design/bid/build or a CM project, the second step usually involves individual interviews with the short-listed candidates.

The selection can be made on the basis of both written and in-person responses. Because the relationship between owner and architect/ engineer will be close for a considerable time, the face-to-face interview is often the deciding element in the selection process.

In the case of selection of a design/build team, the RFP may ask respondents to make an offer of price for the delivery of the design or design/build construction of the project. The combination of first-step selection by qualification and second-step selection by competitive price is particularly suited to the owner who has decided that *cost* is the primary objective.

There is considerable advantage to the owner in selecting the two-step process of D/B team selection, but there is substantial financial risk for the design/build team, particularly the architect/engineer component of the D/B team. In order for the D/B team to determine a price for the project, the architect/engineer must first produce construction documents to a high degree of completion to describe the Work sufficiently to allow subcontractors and producers to offer competitive bids on which a competitive price will be based. This usually translates to the architect/engineer being required to risk as much as 60%-70% of a potential fee in order to comply with the requirements. For the two-step selection process to be attractive to potential design/build teams and therefore to be of any consequence to the owner's objectives, several alternatives in the development of the owner's RFP may be considered:

- The owner may elect to have a set of *bridge documents* included in the RFP. These offer a program of design and a well-developed set of concept drawings for the proposed building and site, sufficient to provide a basis of competitive bid for price. Bridge documents are prepared by an outside consultant or owner's on-staff architects at the owner's expense. While this option reduces some of the risk for the D/B team, there remains a significant amount of financial risk for the competitors who may be offering too low a price for both design and construction, based on incomplete construction documents.

- The owner may offer a *cash incentive* in lieu of bridge documents for all "short-listed" candidates in order to "share" the risk with the remaining field of candidates. This option, however, because of the risk to the owner in compensating the non-successful candidates, tends to limit the number of D/B candidates to two or three through the second step of the process.

If the two-step process yields a satisfactory design/build team based on final selection by price, a contract between the owner and the successful candidate is negotiated. This process includes negotiating a schedule for delivery and agreeing on an amount for liquidated damages per day should the project be delayed beyond the agreed date for final completion.

The Three-Step Design/Build Direct Selection Process:
The three-step selection process applies to the selection of the design/build team and is seldom useful if the owner is selecting an architect/engineer for a design/bid/build or CM project. In the case of selecting the D/B team, the three-step selection process is similar to the two-step process, except that the second step requires the D/B team to present a well-detailed design proposal. The third step requires subsequent disclosure of a price for the project delivery. The three-step process works to an owner's advantage because he may be able to choose between two or more proposed designs at the end of the second step, with the proposal for price being disclosed in a later step. To decrease the potential financial

risk to the D/B candidates in the three-step process and to make the competition more attractive to more candidates, the owner may include in the RFP portion of the process the following:

- Bridging documents (prepared at the owner's expense), which include:
  - Program of design
  - Concept drawings of site and building
  - Outline specifications that set quality standards for critical portions of the project
- Offer of minimum compensation for candidates who do not survive the second step of the three-step process.

Competitive Selection of the Design/Build Team

The two- and three-step direct selection processes are particularly suited to the owner's project budget when it is sufficient to cover the additional expense of the suggested risk reduction incentives. These will attract viable D/B candidates who are, themselves, willing to assume some risk in order to survive elimination at any step for award of the contract.

The competitive selection process for identifying a satisfactory Design/Build contractor is a little more straightforward in terms of defined risk for the candidates and risk containment for the owner. Before the competition begins, viable potential candidates may be narrowed to a manageable number by invoking the RFQ process described in Step One of the direct selection process. Once a slate of potential candidates has been identified, the candidate D/B teams are invited to respond to a design competition by an RFP that identifies the following:

- A detailed program of design describing the owner's project requirements.
- A description of the site, including a recent boundary and topography survey including:
  - A geotechnical report
  - A Phase One Environmental Report made to federal environmental standards
  - Any site development required by local ordinances
- A monetary prize for the design submission judged by a jury of peers to be most responsive to the owner's program of design and local ordinances

Procedures: The design community has recognized the design competition as a means of project procurement since the mid-1900s in the United States. The American Institute of Architects (AIA) established procedures for design competitions that have been used for many years. According to the rules of competition, the owner does not have an obligation to award the contract for design to the winning submission as judged by an independent jury, as long as a monetary prize is offered and paid to the apparent winner as described in the solicitation. The submissions become the property of the owner, who has the right to select the architect/engineer for execution of the project, regardless of the jury's judgment.

The recommended procedure for competitive selection of a design/build team follows the general guidelines of the design competition process. The owner prepares and advertises an invitation to design/build contractors or firms to submit a proposed design solution. Design competition rules have generally held that the owner should not unnecessarily restrict the competition to a "short-listed" group of candidates. However, if the project, by its character, requires considerable specialized skill, the owner may find an advantage in using the RFQ solicitation as a preliminary step to identify a group of contestants.

The competition solicitation explicitly states how the submission should be presented, and the way in which candidate submissions will be judged, and describes the prize offered to the competition winners. The solicitation should provide a highly developed package of information about the project, including but not limited to, a fully developed description of the site, a detailed program of design, and disclosure of any restrictive conditions that would limit the design approach, including appropriate local ordinances related to zoning or building codes. The competition should allow a sufficient amount of time before the due date for submissions to allow candidates to react to the solicitation and to prepare a well-developed candidate design solution.

The Two-Step Process: In the first step, the competition is held, the submissions judged, the winners announced and otherwise advertised, and the promised prizes awarded. In the second step, the owner may enter negotiations with one or more of the selected candidates. The owner should not be restricted to those companies who were judged winners of the design competition. Candidates should be prepared to offer a price for the project delivery and a schedule for delivery.

The Three-Step Process: The owner may elect to individually negotiate a more thoroughly developed design, price offering, and schedule between two or more candidates as a second step in the process. As a third step, the owner may request that each of the finalists submit a Best and Final Offer (BAFO) for the owner to consider after award of the design/build contract.

Qualifying Firms for Construction and Related Work

The qualification process should be more than simply making sure that competing firms meet a minimal set of standards. The firm selected must also be the most appropriate for the project. While this may not guarantee success, contracting with an inappropriate firm will almost certainly guarantee failure. The qualification process is appropriate for architects, engineers, testing and inspection, services, construction managers, general contractors, or specialty contractors. Qualifying firms work in the best interest of both the firm being considered and the school system. A firm that is not qualified to work on a project may negatively impact not only the school project, but the firm itself, in terms of a loss of finances, time, and reputation.

The qualification process needs to be logical, consistent, systematic, fair, and efficient. The process should balance the use of scores and rules with assessments and judgments. Rules yield "black and white," "yes or no" results. Scores and indexes yield statistical, numerical results. These are easy to defend, but often the big picture is missed without careful analysis. The danger in analysis is that it can easily be abused by subjectivity, prejudice, and even corruption. Another danger is that decision makers are sometimes punished for honest mistakes, and not rewarded for taking the initiative to look beyond the rules, scores, and indexes. All qualification teams need to have rules, scores, and indexes as a basis for decision-making, but they should also encourage the use of independent, objective, thoughtful analysis when appropriate. Should negative information be found on a firm, the firm should always be given a chance to dispute, defend, or explain it.

There are four key areas that a school system's qualification team needs to examine before signing a contract with a firm:

- Experience
- Performance
- Integrity
- Finances

Experience

A successful school project needs experienced management and crews. Throwing inexperienced personnel into the potentially rough waters of a school construction project to "sink or swim" is a mistake for all involved. General construction experience alone is not enough. Each type of construction, including school construction, has its own particular set of challenges. Firms seeking work on a school construction project should have experience working on schools. Commercial, residential, and/or industrial experience is helpful, but it is often not enough to provide the assurances that a contractor will know what to do and when to do it, especially on large projects.

School qualification teams can check a firm's experience by asking for a list of similar projects that a firm has completed. The location, size, and type of construction of the school buildings in the firm's portfolio should be a good fit with the proposed project. To get a better feel for the depth of experience, the contracting team should request the resumes of the firm's key personnel.

Performance

Years of experience are an important measure. However, a contractor can have 20 years of experience doing shoddy work. This is where performance comes in. Performance is the measure of how well a firm performs the work it was hired to do. Did the firm complete all the specified work? Was it performed on time? Was the quality of the work acceptable? Did the firm stay within the budget? The qualification team can try several methods to get an idea of a firm's track record, such as:

- Comments solicited from owner's representatives from the list of recently completed projects supplied by the firm.
- Records and comments from project managers on work that this firm may have performed for the school district.
- Records and comments from other school systems, or other state and city agencies for which the firm is likely to have done work.
- Central information systems (maintained by some large municipalities) on contractors' performance. These systems collect input from several agencies. In New York City, for example, the system is called VENDEX.

Integrity

A firm can have a record of good performance on their last few projects, but do they comply with the applicable environmental laws, safety regulations, labor laws, minority-owned business participation initiatives, and other requirements and standards of conduct? Are the principals of the firm tainted by scandal, or do any of their personnel have a history of illegal business activities? An affirmative answer to any of these or similar questions should raise a red flag for the school qualification team. (Some school systems require contractors to sign a Felony Conviction Notice stating that no convicted felons will be allowed to work on existing school sites.)

The Environmental Protection Agency (EPA) provides a list of firms with outstanding violations relating to environmental laws. To check a firm's safety record, the school building team can search the Occupational Safety and Health Administration (OSHA) records for violations. Some of this information is available on the Internet. If the information cannot be found online, the regional offices for the applicable agencies may be helpful. When evaluating a firm's overall safety track record, remember that some building trades are inherently more dangerous than others. Another way to get an idea of how well the firm is looking out for the safety of workers is to obtain a copy of its Worker's Compensation Experience Modification Rating, which is based on the number of claims that have been filed by the firm. The rating is determined by comparing the rate the subject firm pays with what it would have paid had it been an average employer in the same industry.

Checking references can uncover issues related to a firm's integrity, but interviewees may be unwilling to discuss some of the issues because of fear of potential legal implications or that voicing opinions may damage business relationships. The reference-checker should be pleasant and personable. This task should never be relegated to an uninterested, uninvolved clerk. It is important that the basic, but important questions such as, "Were you satisfied with the overall performance of this firm?" and, "What aspects of the firm's performance was lacking?" should be posed first, in case the interviewee does not have time for a more in-depth conversation. If time permits, it would be worth following up to find out specific ways in which the firm's performance was lacking. Two good questions to ask are, "Would you hire this firm for your next project?" and "Did the contractors provide workers who had adequate experience for the project?"

To be fair, the first group of essential questions should be identical for all references for all firms being considered. Initial questions should require simple yes/no or numerical ranking answers. Others questions should be more probing, some objective, such as, "Did the contractor complete the project in the time promised?" and others subjective, such as, "Did the contractor complete the project in a reasonable time given the circumstances?" If the firm has conducted business with the school system in the past, interviews and reports from the school project managers can also provide insight. Mere innuendo should not be the basis for disqualifying a firm.

Finances

There are many firms that have good experience levels, performance records, and reputations. Unfortunately, it often takes more than those qualities to deliver projects on-time, on-budget, and to expectations, especially large projects. The firm must have adequate financial resources, and be in sound financial condition. Contracting with a firm that has financial problems can jeopardize the project. Often firms take on more work than they can handle, or for one reason or another, risk financial insolvency. This does not mean that every firm looking for school construction work needs to be a Fortune 500 company; in fact smaller firms are often more responsive than large firms and may be perfectly capable of handling smaller projects. The key is to make sure that a firm can handle the specific project, should it be awarded to them. There are several ways in which a qualification team can analyze a firm's financial picture.

Financial Statements

Reviewing a firm's financial statements is a good way for the contracting team to get a feel for the financial condition of a firm. Reviewers should have extensive financial analysis experience. If that experience does not exist on staff, the services of a CPA should be employed. Privately held firms are often reluctant to disclose their financial statements. If this is the case, the qualification team should have procedures in place to ensure that this financial data is held in the strictest confidentiality, and should notify the firms being reviewed of its confidentiality measures. These may include signing a nondisclosure agreement, storing financial information in locked cabinets, and shredding statements or returning them to the firm when finished with them.

The firm being reviewed should supply the most current financial statements available, and should also supply the financial statements from the previous two years. Three years of statements show financial trends within a company, for example, a steady decline in profits, or an increasing amount of liabilities. Financial statements should be "audited," as these carry more weight than those that have been "reviewed," but not audited. Financial statements that have not been reviewed or audited, or are designated "for management purposes only" are of little value. Many ratios and percentages are used to evaluate the financial health of companies, including the current ratio, quick ratio, debt to equity ratio, and the gross sales to anticipated contract.

Since not all ratios are of equal importance, the school system or its financial advisor should weight the ratios to reflect their relative importance. These ratios, when combined with other relevant financial information, and evaluated by a knowledgeable financial advisor, can be used to compare the financial stability of the competing firms.

Bonding Capacity

Single Bonding Capacity is the maximum contract value that the firm's bonding company will extend to a contractor in performance bonds for an individual contract. Aggregate Bonding Capacity is the maximum total contract value that the firm's bonding company will extend for all of a firm's current contracts in performance bonds. These two measures are helpful in determining the maximum value of work that a firm can handle. The firm should be able to supply a letter from their bonding company stating what these two amounts are.

Obtaining Qualification Information

There are two ways for a school system or its representatives to obtain the information needed to qualify or approve a firm. They can investigate, or they can ask the firm directly. Investigating can be a lengthy and expensive process. While much of this information is public, much more is not, especially the type of information that can hurt a firm's chances of winning contracts. Clearly, a firm is not going to advertise bad news. Information obtained by third parties can also be disputed.

Asking for information directly is, of course, easier than investigating, but there is a risk of incorrect or incomplete answers. This is why the most important wording that needs to be included in the pre-qualification form is that which appears right before the space for the firm's signature—language to the effect that the person who completed the application testifies as to the accuracy of the information and acknowledges that the information was provided as an inducement to receive the contract. This language should provide legal grounds for the school system or its representatives to cancel the contract if it was based on deliberately false information, and also protects the school system from having to pay for shoddy work that has already been performed. All contracts and important forms used in contracting should be prepared by an attorney. Qualification forms are no exception. Appropriate language and a means to back it up will afford a reasonable assurance that the information supplied in the qualification statement is accurate. Good qualification procedures call for both supplied information and obtained information. As Ronald Reagan said, "Trust, but verify."

Timing of the Qualification Process

Traditionally the school system, or its representatives (architect or project manager), must wait until bids are in, select the low bid or proposal, and then begin the task of approving a firm. A diligent approval process takes time, a precious commodity at this stage, because a bid is valid for only a limited period. For a construction contractor, a delay in awarding of a project means the firm will have an open bond. This will reduce the firm's bonding capacity and may prevent a firm from bidding other projects. Quotes from suppliers and subcontractors included in the bidder's proposal all have expiration dates. A substantial delay in awarding the project may result in price increases as those dates expire, forcing the bidder to pass on those price increases to the school system. Increasing the amount of time for which a firm will hold its bid price will only build escalation costs into the bid, and discourage bidders from bidding the project. The New York City School Construction Authority, the New Jersey School Construction Corporation, and other school contracting agencies pre-qualify potential bidders, not only for construction contractors, but also for architects, engineers, consultants, construction managers and testing/inspection firms, to avoid having to qualify these firms within the short time available once the bids or proposals have been presented.

Pre-Qualification

Pre-qualification buys the contracting agency time to thoroughly research the background of firms before the expiration of the contract award period. When a pre-qualified firm is being considered for a project, their qualification folder is simply updated, since most of the preliminary information has already been gathered. For example, the Gross Sales to Anticipated Contract ratio can be updated to include the contracts under consideration for award by the school system.

Using the pre-qualification approach, firms must first be pre-qualified in order for their bids to be accepted. For a firm to become pre-qualified, they must fill out an application that contains questions aimed at determining the type of work the firm is qualified to perform, the size and financial status of the firm, and their level of experience, performance, and integrity.

The pre-qualification form should be thorough enough so that the qualification team can obtain the desired information, yet simple enough so that it will not dissuade smaller businesses from completing it. It should be consistent within similar categories of firms (prime contracting, subcontracting, engineering, architectural, construction management, etc.) in order to simplify the data gathering, analysis, and comparison. The form should be prepared with the input of the construction management, design, and legal teams.

The firm name, tax identification number, bonding capacity, type of work they perform, and any other important information should be entered into an electronic database to facilitate locating, sorting, and filtering key information. Firms can be categorized by the primary work in which they specialize, using a well known hierarchical work breakdown system that allows a "drill down" search, such as the North American Industry Classification System (NAICS), UNIFORMAT II, or CSI MasterFormat. *(See Chapter 6 for more on the UNIFORMAT II and CSI MasterFormat work breakdown systems.)* Under NAICS, for example, a masonry contractor can be found by looking under Section 23 for Construction—then under Section 238 for Specialty Trade Contractors. Code # 23814 would represent masonry contractors. Prime contractors specializing in school buildings would use Code # 236220. Roofing contractors would be found under Code # 238160. Architectural services would be found under Code # 541310.

Many more firms will apply for pre-qualification than will actually be awarded contracts, and files need to be updated periodically to stay current if this method is to be used on an ongoing basis. For these reasons, creating and maintaining a pre-qualification process entails a greater investment of time overall than the traditional method of qualification after the bids are submitted.

Select Bidders List

The Select Bidders List is a powerful tool used on projects in which the school system's contracting representatives require firms with a specific expertise, a certain level of financial capacity, or other special requirements. However, as with pre-qualification, some public contracting agencies may not be permitted to use this bidding method.

The main advantage of the select bidders list is that it is fast. This is especially true if there is an ongoing pre-qualification process in place, which will supply a pool of qualified contractors from which to draw. An electronic database of qualified contractors can be sorted and filtered easily to search for contractors that fit the desired set of requirements. With the select bidders list contracting method, the school system's contracting representatives first define specific criteria. Then, instead of advertising a bid, waiting for firms to respond, and wading through a potentially vast number of bidders to qualify and approve, a limited number of short-listed firms are contacted directly. Selection is made from this small group of bidders. To ensure that the process is fair, great care must be taken to base the process on specific requirements, not subjective or personal preferences.

Conclusion

The contract is the mortar that holds the project team members together. It defines their rights and responsibilities and establishes the project cost. Before the entire project team is in place and committed to contracts, two critical decisions need to be finalized: the *method of project delivery*, and the *selection of construction and design professional firms*. The method of project delivery establishes the contractual relationships between the owner, contractors, and design professionals, such as the Construction Manager at Risk or Construction Manager as Agent arrangement. The method of delivery also helps to determine the type of payment, such as lump sum, unit price, or guaranteed maximum price. In short, the project delivery method is the "plan of action." The selection process is used to determine which firms will be part of the project team that executes the plan of action. The goal of this process is to find the best match between talents and resources of construction and design firms and their respective tasks in the project.

With a contract that ties together the most appropriate plan of action with the project team members best qualified to execute it, the project is off to a good start.

[1] Fairfax County in Northern Virginia maintains the 12th largest school district in the United States. The Fairfax County School District employs an entire staff of Construction Managers who manage up to $200 million in new construction projects.

[2] The Department of Public Works for the City of Washington, D.C. manages construction programs for public school projects in the District of Columbia.

Chapter 9

The Importance of Project Management

David J. Lewek

As school building projects become more complex, and as time, money, and quality become more important for school districts, the need for an experienced project manager becomes ever more pronounced. In this chapter, a *project manager* can be defined as an individual or firm working directly for the school district and responsible for the overall planning, organizing, direction, and control of a school building project. The project manager serves the school district as the main point of contact and facilitator of communication and direction among the architect, general contractor, and Clerk of the Works (the school building committee's on-site representative). Figure 9.1 illustrates the relationship between the project manager and the other primary players in the project.

Why Project Management?

A study by the National Center for Educational Statistics indicated that the average age of the public school buildings in the U.S. in 1999 was 40 years. The growing age of many school buildings, coupled with changes in population and, in some cases, curriculum, often leads school districts to consider additions, renovations, or an entirely new facility.

The training of school administrators is focused on providing the best possible educational experience to students, not on managing construction projects. Given that most school districts undertake major building projects once every 20-40 years, it is not realistic to expect school board members, school building committees, or administrators to possess the expertise necessary to manage multi-million dollar construction projects. Having a project manager who is experienced in the construction of school facilities can make a critical difference in the success of the project and the experience of the school administrators.

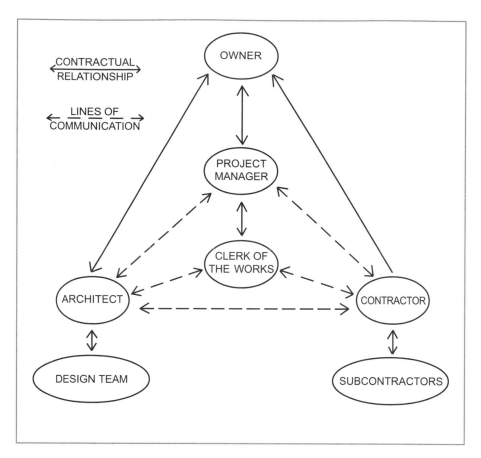

Figure 9.1
Relationships in the Project Team

A project manager should be brought on board early in the project, before the architect is chosen. In this way, he or she can assist in setting up preliminary budgets and in advising on selection of the architect to get the project underway.

A school building team may hire an individual project manager as an employee or a consultant of the school district, or may hire a project management firm. Depending on the size of the project, a full-time on-site representative, often referred to as a *Clerk of the Works*, may also be involved, reporting to the project manager. When there are multiple projects to be managed for one school, the term *program manager* is frequently used for the project manager. The term *construction manager* refers to an "at risk" firm hired to directly manage subcontractors and the construction process. At minimum, a project manager is recommended. A good project manager can provide the planning, organization, direction, and control necessary to bring school construction projects to timely, successful conclusions.

A professional project manager is:

- Well-organized
- Enthusiastic
- Capable of solving problems
- An effective delegator
- A good communicator
- Capable of motivating the project team
- Capable of handling multiple tasks concurrently
- Knowledgeable in current construction methods

Selecting a Project Manager

There are various ways to select the right project manager for a school construction project. In some cases, the individual may already be part of the school or district organization. However, many school building committees will have to search outside their organizations and districts. A job description should be established based on the scope of responsibilities outlined in this chapter. If a project management firm is sought, than a Request for Proposal can be developed. In either case, whether an individual or a firm, the project manager should have experience in school construction projects, a strong track record for bringing in projects on-time and within budget, and outstanding communications skills.

The following information should be requested from potential candidates:

- Namc and location of individual or firm
- Experience managing new and renovation school projects
- List of references from school projects
- Resume(s) of key individuals in the firm
- Project management plan (how they would approach the particular project)
- Financial statement (for project management firms)

The selecting authority should have a detailed plan in place for evaluation of proposals (or resumes, if individuals are sought).

Duties of a Project Manager (PM)

Basic Responsibilities

The project manager should act as the building committee's representative in all negotiations with the design team and contractor, and should keep the building committee informed on all matters. The PM should establish procedures for coordination between the building committee, the design team, and the contractor, regarding all aspects of the project. The PM should schedule and conduct regular site meetings with the design team and the contractor to monitor progress of the work, identifying any difficulties and initiating actions to resolve problems, and ensure compliance with drawings and specifications. The PM is also responsible for putting proper control procedures in place for production and approval of shop drawings by the design team and for monitoring fabrication and delivery of materials. Effective control must be maintained over changes, and compliance must be verified.

The project manager will work with local utility companies to prevent problems that even well-planned and managed projects can suffer if dates are not met involving local gas, electric, water, or cable service. Early involvement by the project manager can define exactly what each utility company needs to do, and when the work needs to be accomplished so that the schedule is not compromised. The project manager may also need to negotiate with utility companies if the utility wants large sums of money to build additional infrastructure. It may be possible to work out a payment plan. The project manager should also research possible rebates for energy-efficient design offered by some utilities. *(See Chapter 10 for more on regular project meetings and advanced planning for utilities.)*

Additional Value-Added Tasks
Minimizing Disruption
A project manager might also be asked to develop a project mitigation plan to minimize disruption caused by construction activities. Working closely with the superintendent, school administration and teachers, the PM can lessen the disruption to school functions if a project must be carried out during school operating hours. Work hours need to be established, phasing plans developed, and security measures undertaken so that all parties are confident that they are working in a safe, secure environment.

Rights of adjacent property-owners (abutters) and other neighbors must also be considered, including issues regarding work hours, water run-off, dust control, and utility use and potential interruption. (Many school districts hold informational meetings for abutters before construction begins, so their concerns can be aired and addressed.) Traffic plans must be developed, and areas laid out for contractor use.

Coordinating Volunteer Services
Local talent can sometimes assist in school projects by reviewing plans and approaches to the work. Often, there are talented professionals who are able and willing to donate time to a project they know will benefit children and the community. This resource may provide a fresh perspective on a proposed project or aspect of the project.

Interacting with School and Neighborhood Groups
Tours of the project site can be arranged for school and community officials, teachers, staff, and parent-teacher organizations. Taxpayers and end users benefit from keeping abreast of project developments, and tours of the site or video presentations showing progress can generate interest and pride in the project. The project manager and architect can work together to provide these services to clients.

Assisting Teachers with Project-Related Curriculum

The school building project can also be incorporated into the curriculum for students. This is an excellent way of showing students how the material they are learning, particularly math and computer skills, is used by architects, engineers, and tradespeople on their construction project. The project manager might make classroom visits and conduct tours so that students can learn about the project.

Managing Risk for the School District

Any construction project faces risk on several fronts. A good project manager will help position the school district to avoid or minimize it. Among the risks an owner, or in this case the school building committee, faces are those associated with the current economic climate, regulatory environment, soils, and neighbors.

Owner Responsibilities, Risks, and Insurance

The project manager should assist the school building committee in minimizing the risks associated with tasks that fall within its domain. Failure to obtain a title, easements, or rights of way, for example, can become a basis of a delay claim from a contractor. The school building committee may also be responsible for relocating students and administrative functions, moving or demolishing existing structures, and abatement of asbestos and lead paint. Last-minute changes made by the school administration can be a source of costly delays to the project. The school building committee is in control of the school project, but in order to remain in control (usually through their project manager), they must make timely decisions and communicate them effectively. *(See Figure 9.2.)*

Risks against outside forces, such as fire, flood, severe weather, and vandalism, can be protected against through Builder's Risk and other appropriate insurance policies. Acting on behalf of the building committee, the project manager should be in contact with the school's insurance professional and make sure that proper coverage is in place.

Figure 9.3, a Priority Analysis/Problems Status Report, provides a mechanism for recording risk problems, along with a Progress of Risk Resolution recording area.

Project Site Risks

In analyzing the site, it may become apparent that there are significant issues associated with the congested area, local politics, or difficult soils conditions. All of these factors increase the risk to the school building committee. Additional funds may have to be spent on soils investigations well before bid time. These may include testing for hazardous materials, such as lead or oil leaks from tanks. Discussions about the site, prior to design and construction, can save hundreds of thousands of dollars once the project is underway.

Work in or near an existing school can be risky for a school's occupants in terms of physical safety. Noise and possible relocation of students can also cause disruption to learning routines. Proactive effort is needed by all

Topic Outline of a Project Risk Management Plan

A. Construction Services (means, methods, and techniques of construction)
B. Design Services (schematic design, design development, working drawings, bid/award, contract administration)
C. Organization Structure and Operating Procedures of the Company. (Adequate authority, responsibility, and duties described for each company position)
D. Contracts
E. Communications
F. Time, Budget, and Quality
G. Compatible Architectural Program and Budget
H. Work Load
I. Ability to Work Well with Others
J. Suitable professional attitudes and ethics
K. Suitable project for one's services
L. Choosing team members well
    1. Owner
    2. Architect
    3. Contractor
    4. Consultants
    5. Subcontractors
    6. Suppliers
M. Maintaining excellent management information and control systems
N. Leadership and ability to expedite work
O. Problem identification and solving methods
P. Safety program
Q. Self-protection mechanisms
    1. Record-keeping procedures
    2. Adequate notice and correspondence
    3. Use of management information and control systems
    4. Documentation of existing conditions
    5. Others
R. Review of project regulations and legal parameters
S. Appropriate and available resources
    1. Manpower
    2. Materials
    3. Equipment
    4. Money
        a. Fixed
        b. Liquid
T. Adequate contract documents
    1. Plans
    2. Specifications
    3. Agreements
    4. Addenda
    5. Change Orders

Figure 9.2
Topic Outline of a Project Risk Management Plan

Credit: Risk Management for Building Professionals, *Copyright RSMeans*

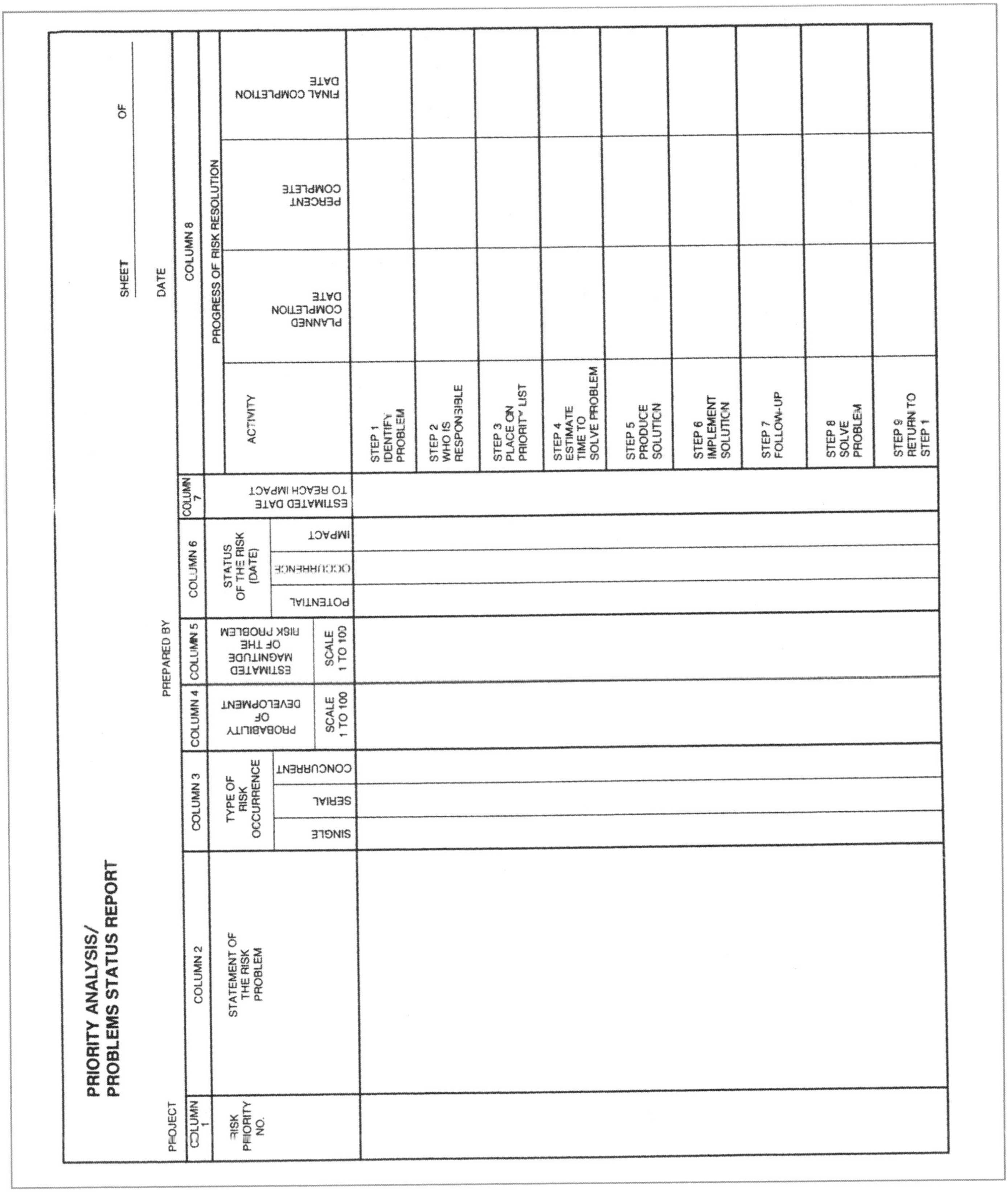

PRIORITY ANALYSIS/
PROBLEMS STATUS REPORT

PROJECT

PREPARED BY

SHEET ______ OF ______

DATE

COLUMN 1	COLUMN 2	COLUMN 3			COLUMN 4	COLUMN 5	COLUMN 6			COLUMN 7	COLUMN 8			
RISK PRIORITY NO.	STATEMENT OF THE RISK PROBLEM	TYPE OF RISK OCCURRENCE			PROBABILITY OF DEVELOPMENT	ESTIMATED MAGNITUDE OF THE RISK PROBLEM	STATUS OF THE RISK (DATE)			ESTIMATED DATE TO REACH IMPACT	PROGRESS OF RISK RESOLUTION			
		SINGLE	SERIAL	CONCURRENT	SCALE 1 TO 100	SCALE 1 TO 100	POTENTIAL	OCCURRENCE	IMPACT		ACTIVITY	PLANNED COMPLETION DATE	PERCENT COMPLETE	FINAL COMPLETION DATE
											STEP 1 IDENTIFY PROBLEM			
											STEP 2 WHO IS RESPONSIBLE			
											STEP 3 PLACE ON PRIORITY LIST			
											STEP 4 ESTIMATE TIME TO SOLVE PROBLEM			
											STEP 5 PRODUCE SOLUTION			
											STEP 6 IMPLEMENT SOLUTION			
											STEP 7 FOLLOW-UP			
											STEP 8 SOLVE PROBLEM			
											STEP 9 RETURN TO STEP 1			

Figure 9.3

Priority Analysis/Problems Status Report

Credit: Risk Management for Building Professionals, *Copyright RSMeans*

members of the project team to mitigate these risks. Projects in inner-city locations are more difficult because of traffic, congestion, and limited work site space, and are typically more costly. *(See Chapter 10 for more on safety issues.)*

Contract Document-Related Risk

Another area of risk is in the contract documents. Potential problems include ambiguous or conflicting terms; unclear instructions; late responses to submittals, RFIs (Requests for Information), and sketches; and omissions. Delays in completing contract documents can also ripple through the entire project. The design team should be given the proper amount of time to complete the contract documents for the project. They must be aware of all applicable building codes, must make a strong effort to coordinate the work of all their members, including mechanical and electrical engineers, and should allow sufficient time for a thorough review of the contract documents. *(See Chapter 8 for more on contracts.)*

Contractor Risks

Risk related to contractor-generated problems can include:

- Bid errors
- Proper pre-bid site visit
- Scope of work mistakes
- Inexperienced field management
- Inadequate scheduling
- Poor workmanship
- Inadequate labor force
- Inadequate contractor capital/cash flow
- Subcontractor default
- Procurement delays
- Poor labor relations

A project manager who establishes a good working relationship with the general contractor may be able to help to avoid or work through many of these issues. At a minimum, an experienced project manager should be able to warn a contractor about potential pitfalls associated with the contractor's methods.

The PM's Role During the Design Phase

Although projects vary in size, complexity, and impact to the school population, the PM should always provide the services outlined in this section to the school building committee. Communication is crucial to the success of the project, and should be emphasized at several key points, including during the definition of the project scope, budgeting and scheduling, and in the definition of performance and quality criteria. Excellent communication is also critical when reviewing construction document language, when assessing economic or scheduling impacts of changes in scope, and when the project is ready for its intended use (substantial completion).

Budgeting and Cost Review

During the design phase, the project manager assists in the budgeting and review process, in conjunction with the building committee and the design team. Specific tasks include:

- Reviewing the established project and construction budget in relation to program and design performance criteria.
- Advising on adjustments to be made, if necessary.
- Reviewing cost estimates to confirm cost targets for each of the major design packages (e.g., structural steel, mechanical, electrical, and finish work, etc.) within the program.
- Assisting the design team in updating and refining cost estimates for the building committee's approval as development of the drawings and specifications proceeds.
- Advising the building committee and design team if it appears that the project budget will not be met, and making recommendations for corrective action. *(See Figure 9.4, Typical Middle School Budget Analysis.)*
- Anticipating all areas of potential cost, including A/E fees, project manager fees, and cost of the construction, furniture, technology, moving, security, and other items.

Schedule Development and Management

During the design phase, the project manager (in conjunction with the building committee and design team) prepares a detailed overall master schedule of activities, which coordinates and integrates the design team's efforts with construction and the building committee's objectives, including moving out of areas to be renovated; delivery and installation of furniture, fixtures, and equipment (FF&E); and moving into completed areas. Later on, during the construction phase, the PM will be making detailed reports at regular intervals to show both completed and delayed activities, adjusting the schedule appropriately, and recommending activities to be expedited to meet predetermined completion and delivery dates. If the contract allows, site work and structural proposal packages can be released early to help the project start early.

Provision of Input to the Design Team

It is important for the project manager to schedule and attend regular meetings with the design team during the development of conceptual and preliminary design to advise on site use and improvements, and the selection of materials, building systems, and equipment. This includes identifying long-lead items, and coordinating their procurement with the school administration and design team to ensure delivery by the required dates.

Typical Middle School Budget Analysis

Description of Work	Scheduled Value	Previous Invoices	Current Invoice	Complete to Date	% Complete	Balance to Finish
ARCHITECT	$751,350	$597,323	$13,149	$610,472	83%	$140,878
SEPTIC ENGINEERING	$14,300	$11,000	$0	$11,000	77%	$3,300
ARCHEOLOGICAL	$18,760	$18,760	$0	$18,760	100%	$0
PROJECT MANAGER	$118,650	$58,716	$5,733	$64,449	54%	$54,201
SURVEY	$25,000	$24,420	$0	$24,420	99%	$580
GEOTECH	$23,600	$23,595		$23,595	100%	$5
TECHNOLOGY	$20,000	$15,574	$0	$15,574	77%	$4,426
PERMITTING	$40,000	$38,099	$0	$38,099	96%	$1,901
FF&E	$75,000	$45,000	$0	$45,000	60%	$30,000
ACCOUSTICAL/LIGHTING	$5,000	$538		$538	11%	$4,462
OTHER CONSULTANTS	$7,000	$6,995	$0	$6,995	99%	$5
BONDING/LEGAL FEES	$85,000	$3,207	$3,000	$6,207	7%	$78,793
CLERK OF WORKS	$55,000	0	$4,584	$4,584	8%	$50,416
PRINTING/ADVERTISING	$35,000	$26,989	$0	$26,989	70%	$8,011
CONSTRUCTION TESTING	$40,000	$15,190	$1,777	$16,967	43%	$23,033
MISCELLANEOUS FEES	$3,000	$1,995	$34	$2,029	67%	$971
CONSTRUCTION	$10,891,210	$1,706,395	$1,062,476	$2,768,871	25%	$8,122,339
FF&E	$1,100,000					$1,100,000
MOVING EXPENSES	$20,000					$20,000
OWNER CONSTRUCTION	$40,000					$40,000
OTHER EXPENSES	$10,000	$0	$0	$0		$10,000
PROJECT CONTINGENCY	$622,130					$622,130
TOTALS	$14,000,000	$2,593,796	$1,090,753	$3,684,549	26%	$10,315,451

Figure 9.4
Typical Middle School Budget Analysis

The project manager also provides recommendations on:

- Functional compatibility and fulfillment of the school administration's requirements
- Construction feasibility
- Consistency with project budget/affordability
- Availability of materials and labor
- Time requirements for installation and construction
- Factors related to cost, including costs of alternative designs or materials, preliminary budgets, and possible savings *(See the "Value Engineering" section to follow.)*

Cost Control

Another key responsibility of the project manager is the development of a logical cost control and accounting framework, within which the various design packages, if applicable, can be monitored and controlled to the budget amounts already established. Each design package is to be separately controlled to its own budget.

At regular intervals during the design phase, the project manager reviews the design team's estimates (usually prepared by their cost consultant) for the project. If necessary, the PM makes recommendations for remedial action to bring any package that is out of line back on budget. See Figure 9.5, "Project Influence vs. Project Cost," which emphasizes the importance of the project manager's early involvement. The PM should prepare regular reports showing the total project status relative to the overall budget and schedule.

Value Engineering

As the design moves into the selection of the basic building systems and components, the project manager can provide valuable recommendations on selection. He or she can compare alternatives utilizing a value engineering process, when appropriate, and make recommendations as to the systems that offer the lowest life cycle cost and best value. Alternatives should be considered at each stage of the design phase, and the anticipated life cycle costs of each should be presented and compared for the lowest life cycle cost or best value. *(See Chapter 6 for more on value engineering and life cycle costing.)*

Contract Documents

The project manager is, in some cases, responsible for the coordination of contract documents for each design package, and for creating bid packages. Part of this responsibility is ensuring that all information is available by the bid due date. The PM should review the drawings and specifications with the design team to eliminate areas of conflict, omission, and overlap.

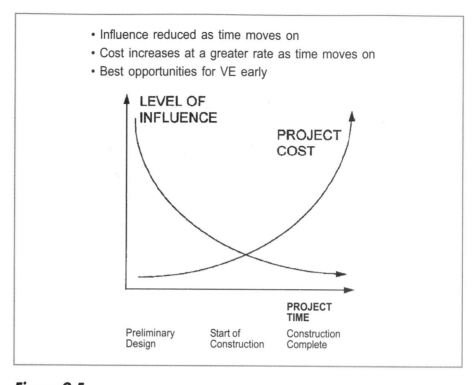

- Influence reduced as time moves on
- Cost increases at a greater rate as time moves on
- Best opportunities for VE early

LEVEL OF INFLUENCE

PROJECT COST

PROJECT TIME

Preliminary Design | Start of Construction | Construction Complete

Figure 9.5
Project Influence vs. Project Cost
Credit: Advanced Project Management Seminar Workbook, Copyright RSMeans

Scheduling and Phasing

The project manager makes recommendations to the school administration and the design team regarding the timing and extent of work in the drawings and specifications. Frequently, the PM must work closely with the school building committee to ensure that sufficient educational space is available during each phase of construction; that the appropriate number of athletic facilities remains in use; and that adequate parking for teachers, staff, students, visitors, and construction personnel is available. This process should allow for phased construction, if applicable. The project manager must take into consideration such factors as time of performance, availability of labor, overlapping trade jurisdictions, and provision of temporary facilities.

Bidding Responsibilities

Prior to bid calls, the project manager should review a final cost estimate for each design package prepared by the design team, if applicable. The PM should make recommendations for final changes and arrange for cost estimates to be prepared in a format suitable for direct comparison with the contractors' bids.

A master construction schedule should be included with the bid documents, showing major milestones and reinforcing that time is of the essence for bidders. Bidders should be made aware of the required schedule and its relationship to other contracts.

The project manager assists the architect in identifying state-mandated requirements for equal employment opportunity programs (e.g., minority- and women-owned businesses, prevailing wages, etc.) for inclusion in the bidding documents and should discuss the implications with the school administration. *(See Chapter 6, "Estimating School Construction Costs," for more on these requirements.)*

The next step is to set a date for the bid opening. As far as possible, the goal is to avoid conflict with other major bid openings, so as many potential bidders as possible can focus on bidding this project.

The project manager also represents the building committee at a pre-bid conference, an informational meeting with contractors who might be interested in bidding the project. Typically, the PM will conduct such conferences, along with the design team, school administrators and building committee members, detailing the building project objectives and the proposed timeline, and answering questions.

The project manager assists in analyzing the bids received for compliance with bidding instructions. The PM can be instrumental in evaluating the impact of alternatives on the total financial implications in the bids submitted, as well as in assisting the building committee and the design team with any pre-contract negotiations. The PM should help the building committee develop a grading system to evaluate the proposals and companies—if the state in which the public school project will be built allows contracts to be let based on the most qualified, versus the low bid.

In summary, the project manager provides guidance to the school building committee on the contract documents (working drawings and specifications) and, with their consent, plays a leading role in obtaining competitive bids and the award of contracts. The drawings and specifications should be consistent with the school's objectives, the physical conditions of the site, and the project budget. *(See Chapter 8 for more on the contract and bidding process.)*

The Project Manager's Duties in the Construction Phase

Communications are a central feature of the project manager's role in the construction phase of a school project. During this time, the PM initiates, reviews, and suggests improvements to reporting procedures between all parties, consistent with the building committee's policies. There are several critical points at which project communications should be emphasized:

- When evaluating the contractor's suggestions for alternative methods, materials, or equipment
- When dealing with significant problems of design or construction
- When receiving and reviewing applications from the architect and general contractor for payment by the school district
- At *substantial completion* of construction

The project manager acts as a liaison between the building committee, the school superintendent, the design team, and the contractor. The PM should observe the work of contractors on a periodic basis and coordinate with the activities and responsibilities of both the school building committee and the design team. The goal is to complete the project in accordance with the school's objectives of cost, time, and quality.

The project manager should solicit proposals on behalf of the building committee for a full-time, qualified, and experienced Clerk of the Works to coordinate and provide general on-site direction and observation of the contractor's progress on the project. On-site organization and lines of authority will also have to be established in order to carry out the building committee's objectives. (*The Clerk of the Work's responsibilities are described in depth later in this chapter in the "On-Site Observation of Construction" section.*)

The project manager provides the school building committee with brief weekly reports outlining the likely cost, time, and logistical implications of potential changes before instruction is given to the contractor. The PM also identifies potential modifications to the contract documents that may involve the issuance of a change order.

Permits and Inspections

The project manager should assist the building committee and design team in obtaining building permits that will be obtained by the contractor. Early involvement by the PM and design team to prepare local officials for the upcoming projects can speed up the review process and allow for timely issuance of building, conservation, and environmental permits. The PM should meet with the local building officials, fire department, health department, and other concerned agencies so that questions are asked, and responded to, early in the project.

Furniture, Fixtures, and Equipment

The project manager is responsible for monitoring budget expenditures and providing a liaison with consultants for furniture, fixtures, and equipment (FF&E). If directed by the building committee, the PM may also solicit bids for an FF&E consultant to work with them. In addition, the project manager should oversee the delivery process to ensure coordination with activities of the contractor and to meet the needs of the superintendent of schools or school contracting agency. This includes assistance in resolving "short" deliveries and replacing damaged materials, as well as anticipating disputes and taking action to prevent or abate them.

Pre-Construction Meeting

Prior to construction, the project manager should convene a pre-construction meeting to coordinate and communicate the duties and responsibilities of Clerk of the Works and contractors. Among the topics to be discussed at this important meeting are:

- Site rules and regulations
- Lines of communication and submittals
- Constructor's designated areas and coordinating procedures
- Procedures for issuing and revising design information and authorizing changes
- Procedures for overtime and shift work
- Methods and schedules of payment
- Project schedule program
- Project cost program
- Quality control
- Claims and disputes procedures
- Survey information
- Specific state and local laws or regulations
- Certificates of insurance
- Environmental procedures
- Community relations
- Safety and first aid
- Security
- Temporary facilities and services
- Site cleanup

On-Site Observation of Construction

To ensure that all elements of the project function properly, the project manager often hires a representative, often referred to as Clerk of the Works, for on-site observation and documentation. Much like a project manager, a Clerk of the Works is an integral member of the school project team. Typically, the clerk plays a distinct and well-defined role as the key quality control field person for the project manager or building committee.

The clerk must be experienced, a good communicator, and be able to observe the daily activities of not only the contractor, but also numerous subcontractors. The clerk should be visible on the project site throughout the workday. The clerk should also work with the school district administration and operations personnel to advise them of a possible disruption to normal school activity resulting from construction operations.

The Clerk of the Works' primary duties include:

- Working with the contractor and architect to clarify the intent of the contract documents.
- Checking work in progress for conformity with the contract documents and approved shop drawings. Deviations should be reported immediately to the project manager, architect, and contractor.
- Verifying that all materials are as specified or approved.
- Being familiar with all reference standards mentioned in the contract documents.
- Evaluating the contractor's suggestions and recommendations to the project manager and architect when there are different views of how something should be done.
- Verifying that the contractor updates the as-built drawings on a monthly basis.

The Clerk of the Works plays an essential role in ensuring successful overall project management. Careful monitoring of conditions and timely communication are crucial. For example, the clerk should review the construction schedule for conditions likely to cause delays and report such conditions immediately to the project manager and architect. Daily weather reports, for example, are a necessity. The clerk should also keep an updated project directory of contact information for everyone involved, available on the construction site. He or she should also record all visitors, their affiliation, and reason for visiting the site. It is good practice for the clerk to accompany visitors, such as representatives of the school district or committee and federal agencies, on tours of the site. The Clerk of the Works should coordinate and be present at all testing required by the contract documents.

One of the keys to a smooth school construction project is thorough documentation. The Clerk of the Works should maintain orderly files of approved shop drawings and samples, correspondence, contract documents, change orders, reports of site meetings, product data, supplementary drawings, color schedules, and requests for payment. It is also important to document with photographs any unauthorized problems that may arise during construction, such as unsuitable soils, utility line breaks, or damaged materials. All materials should be stored as required by the contract documents and reviewed for conformity with approved shop drawings.

The clerk should keep a detailed daily report in a format mutually agreed upon by the project manager and the architect. *(See Figure 9.6 for a typical Clerk's Daily Observation Report.)* This report should list all the trades that were active that day, the work performed, the weather (including temperatures and fluctuations), deliveries received, visitors to the site, and remarks for any activity out of the ordinary. The project manager and architect should be notified if materials are delivered without shop drawing or submittal approval, and when the contractor's samples are ready for inspection. (The clerk calls the architect.) The Clerk of the

Typical Middle School
123 Main Street
Anytown, U.S.A.

DAILY OBSERVATION REPORT

Day of the Week	Monday
Date	8-15-03
Temperature	58°F. 7:00 a.m. 72°F. 2:00 p.m.
Weather	Sunny
ABC Contracting	1 Superintendent—Monitor site activities, schedule work
Al's Site Contracting	2 Operators, 3 laborers—Trench for & install 200' of 12" PVC water line
B&B Concrete Forms	1 Foreman, 2 carpenters, 3 laborers—Form for 100' of footings & foundations north wall of "A" building
Alpha Steel Erectors	1 Foreman, 8 ironworkers—Erect columns & joists "D" building, detail "C" building
Bituminous Industries	14 Workers—Binder course upper parking lot
Fred's Masonry	1 Foreman, 10 masons, 12 laborers—Ground face block upper level "B" building
Solid Steel Co.	4 Ironworkers—Seismic clips, handrails "A" building
Dave's Drywall	6 Carpenters—LGMF & exterior sheathing "B" building
HMC Corp.	7 Carpenters—Soffits "B" building
Walter's Waterproofing	5 Installers—Air barrier "C" building
Sta-Dry Roofing	1 Foreman, 7 installers-Rubber roof gym
Vigilant Sprinkler	3 Pipefitters—Rough In "B" building
Viking Sheet Metal	1 Foreman, 4 tin knockers—Ductwork "B" building
R.F. Meany CP	7 Pipefitters—4" mains for heating loop "A" building
Sparky Electric	1 Foreman, 6 electricians—Rough in boxes & conduits "B" building
Hydro Plumbing	1 Foreman, 5 plumbers—Rough in boy's locker room
Visitors	Zag testing—Compaction at main entrance
Deliveries	12 Pallets of split face block that complies with that specified
Remarks	

Figure 9.6
Clerk's Daily Observation Report

Works should notify the contractor or its agent, the project manager, and the architect of unacceptable work, including work that should be corrected, rejected, uncovered for observation, or that requires special inspection or testing. Complete records of all such work should be kept, including inspections.

The clerk should also review requests for payment and change orders with the architect and project manager. The clerk is responsible for collecting guarantees, certificates, maintenance operations manuals, and the keying schedule. At the acceptance of the project, this documentation should be turned over to the project manager for delivery to the school building committee.

Schedule Responsibilities

As the project progresses, the project manager may find it necessary to arrange for the contractor to update the schedule to reflect variances and to indicate revised targets. (A monthly schedule update is recommended with the pay application to show the original schedule dates in addition to the new proposed dates.) All concerned parties must be advised of the changes. Variances between actual and budgeted or estimated costs must be identified and communicated to the building committee.

The project manager should review the contractor's cash flow schedules in order to ensure cash flow confirms to the baseline budget. This is the time to provide recommendations to the school building committee and the design team regarding the validity and accuracy of such schedules. The PM should also regularly monitor expenditures against the schedule and revise projections as necessary. This should be done to prevent the contractor or subcontractors from getting ahead of the work on payments. The PM should also identify potential variances between the scheduled and probable completion dates. This includes reviewing the schedule for work not started or incomplete, and recommending adjustments to meet the probable completion dates. Summary reports of each schedule review should be provided to the building committee, and all changes documented in the schedule.

Cost Accounting and Payments

The project manager should develop a cost accounting system that integrates with and flows directly from the pre-bid cost control system. The PM should regularly report to the building committee on each individual design package, showing budget, bid figure, change orders, funds expended, estimate of cost to complete, anticipated final cost, and variance from budget. At monthly intervals, a consolidated financial report should be produced showing total project status.

In conjunction with the design team, the project manager is responsible for analyzing requests for payment, processing claims, and making recommendations to the school building committee for payment. Part of this responsibility is ensuring that the contractor has supplied all necessary documentation and performed all the work claimed on the requisition before recommending release of funds.

The project manager is responsible for verifying the flow of payments to subcontractors and suppliers throughout the payment chain. The PM can also be helpful in advising the school building committee on the adequacy of bonds and sureties, taking into account change orders, delays, and other circumstances.

Managing Change Orders

A standard system should be developed for review, initiation, documentation, costing, and negotiation of change orders. The project manager should coordinate the agreement of all change orders with the contractor, include financial reports, and make written recommendations for approval. A change order log should capture:

- An accurate description of the changes
- The general contractor's proposed change order number
- The origin of the change [architect's drawing issue, RFI, or owner (school building committee)-requested change]
- The date of origination
- The architect's or project manager's estimated cost of the change and estimated change in time/schedule
- The contractor's submitted cost, along with the date, forwarded to the architect. (The architect typically has a 21-day review period.)
- The school building committee-approved amount and date of approval (or non-approval)
- The final disposition of the change order

The PM should monitor and record quantities of work for unit price portions of the project. *(See Figure 9.7, Change Order Log.)* Electronic spreadsheet templates and commercial software packages can facilitate this process, but a simple spreadsheet can also be used.

Documentation

Continuously updated records must be kept of all contracts, shop drawings, as-built drawings, samples, purchases, materials, equipment, applicable handbooks and manuals, technical specifications and standards, and all other related documents. The project manager should coordinate hand-over of as-built drawings, maintenance manuals, and other documentation to the school building committee upon completion of the project. The PM should maintain the following documents, making sure the building committee can access them for review (through the Clerk of the Works at the site) on a current basis:

- Contract documents – working drawings and specifications
- Drawings – shop drawings, revisions, and sketches
- Samples
- Approved shop drawings
- List of school-owned equipment

Junior High School

QuickBase

Change Request No	Description	PCO No	PCO Rev No	Origin	Origin No	Rev No	Cat	Date Issued	Architect Est Value	Date Sent to Architect	Contractor Submitted Value	Disputed Value	Approval Date	Owner Approval Value	Disapproval Date	Disposition	CO No	Days Delay
1	Specification and Addenda Clarifications			ASI	1		C	10-19-1999	$0									
2	Kitchen Disposals Deletion	4		CCD	1		C	10-25-1999		1-25-2000			6-30-2000	-$5,200				5
3	Civil Eng'g Rev'ns	5	R	CCD	2		C	11-22-1999		3-16-2000			3-30-2000	$59,440				1
4	Small Car Stall/USGS Disk Protection			ASI	2		C	11-29-1999	$0									
5	DMH Elevation			ASI	3		C	11-29-1999	$0									
6	Ceiling & Elec Panel Revisions	6		CCD	3		C	11-30-1999		4-14-2000			6-16-2000	$705				2
7	Vehicular Concrete Paving Clarifications			ASI	4		C	11-30-1999	$0							VOID		
8	Addenda Dwg Clarification	16		ASI	5		C	11-30-1999	$0	5-1-2000			7-3-2001	$0	5-8-2000			19
9	Foundation Wall Dims.			ASI	6	R	A	12-1-1999	$0									
10	Ledge Removal	71		GC	1		C	12-7-1999		9-15-2000		$60,209	9-29-2000	$49,392				10
11	Casework Shop Paint	139	R	PR	1		B	12-16-1999		7-13-2001			7-16-2001	$10,000				18
12	Gym Column Bay Dims.			ASI	7		C	12-16-1999	$0									
13	Addendum 5-S-24 Bent Plate Clarification			ASI	8		C	12-16-1999	$0									
14	Roof Framing RTU-9 & CU-4	7		CCD	4		C	12-20-1999	$0	1-28-2000			1-27-2000	$0				1
15	Add Fire Hydrant	2	R	PR	2		C	12-20-1999		3-16-2000			3-30-2000	$19,747				1
16	Locker Rm Dimensions			ASI	9		C	12-28-1999	$0									
17	Aluminum Roof @ Gyms & Media Center	3	R	PR	3		C	12-28-1999	$0	2-18-2000						VOID		
18	Lower New Gym Floor Slab			ASI	10	R	C	1-12-2000	$0									
19	Beam: U line, 4 - 5			ASI	11		C	1-18-2000	-$3,000	1-24-2001	$3,000	-$3,000		$0				
20	Tunnels Structure	8		CCD	5		B	1-18-2000	$0					$0		F&B		
21	Corridor F100 Floor Elevation Transition	9		PR	4		C	1-19-2000	$2,248	6-5-2000	$2,248					@ JTC		
22	Project Sign			ASI	12	R	C	2-4-2000	$0									
23	Skylight Curb	87	R	ASI	13		C	2-11-2000					9-6-2001	$1,583	5-8-2000			20
24	Area D/E Expansion Joint Coordination			ASI	14		C	2-11-2000	$0									
25	Vestibule A100A Foundation Revisions			ASI	15		C	2-11-2000	$0									
26	Wind Girt Connection			ASI	16		C	2-11-2000	$0									
27	Partition Type Rev's @ Area E Corridors	5		PR	5		C	2-11-2000	$2,000									
28	Misc. Door Frame	20		ASI	17		C	2-11-2000	$0	5-1-2000		$0						
29	Eye Wash Relocation			ASI	18		C	2-18-2000	$0					$0	5-8-2000	REJECTED		
30	Intelli/key Door Security	38		PR	6		B	2-18-2000		6-19-2000			8-7-2000	$18,964				8

Figure 9.7
Change Order Log

- Testing reports
- Maintenance and operating manuals and instructions
- Other construction-related documents, including all revisions

The PM should obtain data from the contractor needed to maintain a current set of record drawings, specifications, and operating manuals. *(See Figure 9.8, Checklist of Project Records.)*

Dispute Resolution

It is essential that the project manager provide independent interpretation of contract documents to the school building committee on issues where a dispute occurs. The PM should provide claims analysis, including preparing opinions independent to that of the design team, suggesting a course of action, and providing a liaison with the school building committee's attorney.

Substantial Completion

The project manager should determine, with concurrence of the design team, the substantial completion of the work. He or she should organize and assist the design team in the final delivery of the building to the school building committee and ensure that all defects are identified. Items identified in the walk-through and recorded on the punch list must be rectified by the contractor to the satisfaction of the architect before final monies are released. When all punch list items have been completed, the general contractor provides a notice to the architect that the work is ready for final inspection. All guarantees, affidavits, releases, bonds, and waivers must be delivered to the building committee, along with any specific written warranties given by others. The project manager coordinates the collection of all paperwork. When all paperwork is complete, the PM notifies the building committee, and final payment is authorized.

Conclusion

The project manager functions as the key project coordinator within the rigid schedule limitations imposed by the school year. Many schools rely on a PM to guide them through projects that are increasingly complex in terms of technology and other specialty systems. The PM is often responsible for the overall success of the school project in the role he or she plays in meeting quality, budget, and schedule targets. The PM serves as a leader in accomplishing goals, directing and supervising the flow of the project, and coordinating communication between all involved parties.

Checklist of Project Records

SECTION I—BID DOCUMENTS
A. Information for Bidders
B. Bid Documents
C. Pre-Bid Agreements & Quotes
D. Bonds: Performance, Payment, Bid
E. Insurance Certificates
F. Certificate of Need
G. Specifications—Bid Set
    1. General Conditions
    2. Supplementary Conditions
    3. General Provisions
    4. Special Provisions
    5. Bid Calculations & Back-up
H. Contract Drawings—Bid Set
I. Other Pre-Bid Information
    1. Clarifications
    2. As-Builts (if rehab)
    3. Meeting Minutes
    4. Schedule
    5. Bid Calculations & Back-up
    6. Addenda

SECTION II—CONTRACTS
A. Prime Contract
B. Subcontracts
C. Addenda, Exhibits, Amendments
D. Revisions, Change Orders, Field Changes, Extra Work, Additional Work, Resequenced Work, Suspensions, Acceleration, Intentions to Claim
E. Notice to Proceed
F. Design Contract

SECTION III—CORRESPONDENCE
A. External: Letters, Memos, Field Orders, Transmittals, Mailgrams, Telegrams
B. Internal: Interoffice Memos, Memo to File, Phone Call Records
C. Daily Report: Contractor, Subcontractor, Resident Engineer
D. Daily Diary: Project Manager, Project Engineer, Project Superintendent, Resident Engineer, Owner Representative
E. Telephone Call Diary
F. Foreman Reports

SECTION IV—SPECIFICATIONS & DRAWINGS
A. Contract Drawings: Updated & Each Revision & Control Log
B. Contract Specifications: Updated & Each Revision
C. Shop Drawings & Control Log
D. Sketches
E. Clarifications
F. Schematics
G. Erection Drawings
H. Fabrication Drawings
I. Composite Coordinated Shop Drawings (Electrical, Mechanical, HVAC, Fire Protection)
J. As-Built Drawings

Figure 9.8
Checklist of Project Records

Credit: Avoiding & Resolving Construction Claims, *Copyright RSMeans*

Checklist of Project Records

SECTION V—MEETING MINUTES
A. Pre-Bid
B. Negotiations
C. Pre-Construction
D. Weekly Job Progress
E. Scheduling & Coordination
F. Safety
G. Special Issues
H. Subcontractors

SECTION VI—COST RECORDS
A. Detailed Estimate with Back-up
B. Detailed Bid with Back-up
C. Cost Reports (internal), Coded
D. Cost Status & Projection Reports, Budget Analysis
E. Certified Payroll with Daily Time Records
F. EEO Reports
G. Progress Payment Requisitions (Monthly & with Back-up)
H. Purchase Orders
I. Material Requisitions
J. Time & Material Tickets
K. Invoices
L. Delivery Tickets
M. Change Orders, Request for Quotations, Change Estimates with Back-up
N. Extra and Additional Work Costs

SECTION VII—SCHEDULES
(Logic Networks, Bar Charts, I-J Sorts, Narratives, Procurement,
Status Reports)
A. Pre-Bid and Preliminary (60-Day, 90-Day)
B. Original and "Accepted" if not the original
C. Updates and Mark-up Schedules Used in Field
D. Performance Analysis Studies: "S" Curves, Productivity Analysis,
   Projections, etc.
E. Supplementary Schedules:
   1. Concrete Pour
   2. Finish Work
   3. Daily (Weekly Look Ahead)
   4. Subcontractor
   5. Supplier (Procurement)
   6. Others
F. Impacted Schedules (Depicting Delays)
G. Master Schedule (if Multiple Phases or Contracts)

SECTION VIII—LOGS
A. Contract Drawing Revisions
B. Submittals
   1. Shop Drawings
   2. Samples
   3. Brochures, Manufacturer Information, Data Sheets, etc.
C. Change Orders
D. Clarification/Discrepancy
E. A/E Bulletins, Addenda
F. As-Built
G. Visitors (site)
H. Correspondence

Figure 9.8
Checklist of Project Records (cont.)

Credit: Avoiding & Resolving Construction Claims, Copyright RSMeans

Checklist of Project Records

SECTION IX—PHOTOGRAPHS

A. Job Progress (Date & Description)
B. Off-Site Storage
C. Specific Problem Areas
D. Videotapes
E. Time Lapse

SECTION X—CERTIFICATES

A. Periodic Progress Reports
B. Inspection Reports/Certificates
C. Test Reports/Certificates
D. Mill Reports (Steel)
E. Concrete Tests
F. Aggregate & Asphalt Tests
G. Soil Reports
H. Occupancy
I. Termination
J. Need
K. Substantial Completion
L. Final Completion

SECTION XI—PERMITS—BUILDING

Zoning, Trucking, Erecting, Hazardous Gas, Plumbing, Electrical, Sewer, Discharge, Water, Gas, Fire, EPA, COE, CG, Other Environmental

SECTION XII—MISCELLANEOUS

A. Weather Reports
B. Trade Union Agreements
C. OSHA & EPA Documents
D. Punch Lists
E. Loan Applications and Agreements
F. Warranties & Guarantees
G. Operating Manuals
H. Waiver of Lien
I. Proposals
J. Stop Notices
K. Delay Notices
L. Outside Consultant Reports
M. Reference Material, Means Cost Data, COE Guides
N. Alternate Proposals or Value Engineering Proposals
O. Subcontractor Bonds
P. Liens (Mechanics', Materialmen's)
Q. Oral Instructions (Noted in File)
R. Field Survey Book
S. QA/QC Reports

Figure 9.8

Checklist of Project Records (cont.)

Credit: Avoiding & Resolving Construction Claims, Copyright RSMeans

Chapter 10

Managing the School Construction/ Renovation Process

Brian C. Murphy

The construction of any building is a complex process. The construction of a school is among the most complex project types due to the number of constituencies that need to be satisfied. Skilled project management is critical so that all constituencies are heard while the project progresses, providing communication among all parties, while maintaining focus on the goal of delivering a quality building on time and within budget.

This chapter will summarize the roles of the three primary project team members—the owner (the school), the architect, and the contractor—and will offer guidelines on the practical workings of the project team—prior to, during, and after construction. The chapter includes a recommendation for and explanation of a Project Expectations Workshop, along with the other regular meetings that involve the project team. Project phasing is another important topic in this chapter, and raises many issues relating to the sequence of construction and the special considerations of student safety and learning, while construction is taking place in or adjacent to an operating school building. The chapter ends with the project team's final activities, including the project turnover and the move into the new space.

The Project Team

The key to a successful construction project is teamwork. Think of the project as being created by a team of all-stars. This all-star team includes three primary members: the owner (in this case, the school building committee, school's "project manager" or other representative, or the school's principal), the architect, and the contractor. Each member of the team plays an integral role in the project and is dependent on the others. Each member will have its own "team" to complete their portion of the work. These separate teams all interact with one another and depend on each other to carry out their respective work.

The Owner (School Project Representative)

The owner—through the school representative(s) or building committee—identifies the school's needs and expectations for the project and conveys that information to the architect. The school representative or building committee will work with a number of people, within the school organization and outside of it, in fulfilling its role as a project team member.

Some large school districts employ a full-time *program manager* who represents various schools within the district when they undertake a new construction or renovation project. In other districts, the school building committee or principal may employ a *project manager* as a consultant, who is experienced with school construction—to oversee the project and protect the school's interests. *(See Chapter 9 for guidance on the selection and range of possible duties of a project manager as a consultant.)* The school representative or committee may also consult directly with individuals (both school staff members and other outside consultants) who specialize in areas such as information technology, transportation, food service, media, and physical education, to ensure that specific requirements are met in the project. The school committee or representative may also assign or contract an individual or team of people to verify that the project meets all state and federal requirements. In addition, the committee may contract with several outside firms for testing materials and testing and balancing the heating, ventilation, and air conditioning system, and relies on an accounting department to handle the project finances. *(See Figure 10.1 for a list of potential consultants for a school project.)*

The Architect

The architectural firm is responsible for the design of the project. To accomplish this, the architect depends on the work of a team of professional consultants, including structural, civil, mechanical, plumbing, fire protection, and electrical engineers, a landscape architect, a food service consultant, and perhaps an acoustical or other consultant.

CONSULTANT ...	RESPONSIBILTY ...
Structural Engineer	Design of building structure (concrete, steel, masonry)
Mechanical Engineer	Design of heating, ventilation, and air conditioning
Plumbing Engineer	Design of plumbing system
Electrical Engineer	Design of electrical system
Fire Protection Engineer	Design of fire protection system
Food Service Consultant	Design of kitchen, serving line, dishwashing room, and food storage
Civil Engineer	Site layout, design of land grades, site utilities, and parking lots
Landscape Architect	Design of landscaping and irrigation, playfields, and site amenities
Acoustical Consultant	Design guidelines for wall systems/spaces to meet desired acoustical requirements

Figure 10.1
Consultants and Their Responsibilities

The architect works with the school building committee or representative and seeks input from the community to develop a program for the project. It is the architect's responsibility to gather all necessary information from the school representative, building codes and officials, and others to accomplish the design of the building.

Upon approval of the design, the architect will prepare the contract documents (plans and specifications) that clearly define the project. The architect is also responsible for preparing a preliminary construction cost estimate and assisting/advising the building committee during the bidding/contract award process. The architect observes the construction of the project to ensure that the construction conforms to the plans and specifications and meets the requirements of all relevant building codes.

The Contractor

The contractor is responsible for the construction of the project as defined in the contract documents. The contractor may serve as an "at risk" construction manager, hiring as many as 30 or 40 subcontractors to perform certain scopes of work. Contractors may also perform certain scopes of work using their own workforces.

Contractors may hire their own consultants, such as waterproofing specialists, to review details prior to construction and advise on specific construction methods. The contractor works closely with the architect to ensure that the project is built according to the contract documents, and the design intent. This may involve a "constructability review" of the documents, where the contractor advises the architect on the practical aspects of getting the design built.

Note: The term, "project manager" may be used by all three of the major project team members—owner, architect, and contractor—to refer to an individual assigned by each of these team members to oversee their team's role in the project. "Project Manager" (PM), used in this chapter, refers to the school's representative, unless otherwise noted. The specific responsibilities of the school's PM vary widely based on the practices of different regions, school districts, and individual schools. The responsibilities of the school's project manager can range from liaison/contact between the school administration or building committee and the contractor and architect, to a more active role in the design, construction, and post-construction activities, as described in Chapter 9.

Project Expectations Workshop

It is critical to establish the concept of teamwork as early as possible in the project. One effective tool for establishing teamwork is to hold a Project Expectations Workshop, usually a 4-6 hour session conducted by a facilitator and involving key members of the project team. The contractor almost always provides the facilitator, who may be a hired consultant or a trained member of the contracting firm. The end product of this workshop is a project mission statement and mutually agreed upon project goals. The result of the workshop will be that teamwork will begin to be established.

Timing is key to a successful Project Expectations Workshop. On the one hand, this workshop should be held at the beginning of the project to establish a high level of teamwork as early as possible and to create a mission statement and goals. On the other hand, it is important to include as many participants as possible, some of whom will not be hired until later in the project. There is a delicate balance to achieve the optimum timing for the workshop. All of the major subcontractors—structural, roofing, exterior wall systems, windows and storefront, mechanical, electrical, and plumbing—should be on board for this event. Following are the most likely workshop participants:

- Owner/Principal/Facilities Manager
- Architect/Engineers/Consultants
- General Contractor
- Subcontractors
- Major Suppliers
- Relocation Specialists

Agenda

The first item on the agenda for the Project Expectations Workshop is the introduction of the team members. Participants introduce themselves and present their roles on the project team. They share a little about their background, their hobbies, and personal interests. This is also a great time to talk about the projects and/or professional experiences of which they are most proud, and why. This is an excellent opportunity for team building, as participants are focused primarily on their successes and on positive contributions.

Following is a typical agenda for the Project Expectations Workshop:

- Introductions
- Owner/Principal Expectations
- Architect/Contractor/Subcontractor Expectations
- Identifying Obstacles to Success
- Establishment of Project Goals
- Strategy for Implementation
- Project Mission Statement

Outcome

All parties in attendance will have come to the workshop with their own individual goals and expectations. The outcome of the Project Expectations Workshop should be a clear understanding by all project team members of the owner/principal's (through the school building committee or representative) needs and expectations. The workshop should also make known the architect's, contractor's, and subcontractors' expectations. During the workshop, the team members will develop a list of issues critical to project success, as well as potential problem areas (such as lack of coordination of construction documents), and establish procedures to prevent or resolve these problems. The team will also create a project mission statement and mutually agreed upon goals for the project.

The Owner's (School's) Role in the Workshop

Getting the school building committee, principal, or representative (as owner) involved early on is crucial to the success of the workshop. The facilitator should meet with the committee or individual in advance of the workshop and discuss its purpose. The building committee should identify the following:

- The school's mission and goals for the project.
- How the project relates to the school's needs.
- How the project fits into the school's long-term plans and goals.
- Expectations for the project—milestone dates, project budget, and quality level.
- Key facility operations personnel and other staff members who will provide input.

Active participation from the school (building committee or representative) is paramount to the success of the workshop.

Role of Other Team Members in the Workshop

The architect must share his/her expectations at the workshop, and get an understanding of the expectations of other team members, including the contractor, subcontractor, and major suppliers. All expectations should align with those of the school building committee. If there is incompatibility in the expectations of the team members, there is a potential problem. For example, if the contractor's and subcontractors' focus is on profit and the ramifications of certain project requirements are not completely clear to them, they might be apt to cut costs and reduce quality, in the process failing to meet the owner's or architect's expectations. To promote a successful project, all team members' expectations should align.

Identifying Obstacles

To identify potential obstacles to success and the project goals, the workshop group should break out into smaller groups with representatives from each project team in each small group. Each group will elect a spokesperson who will later share the findings of their small group when all of the small groups reunite. Each small group should identify possible barriers, discontinuities, inefficiencies, and conflicts that could undermine the success of the project. When the large group gets back together, all obstacles identified by the small groups will be presented, and the group as a whole will have an open discussion on ways to prevent them.

Strategies for Success

Likewise, to develop strategies and goals for success, the team members should again break out into small groups, different from the previous breakout groups. The purpose of changing the small group members is to promote personal interaction with as many different team members as possible, which helps with teambuilding. Strategies for success require identifying goals, as well as ways to prevent or mitigate the previously identified obstacles. These results will also be presented (by different small-group spokespersons this time) to the entire team.

Next, the entire team will review, as a group, all the results from the small breakout groups and align their strategies for success and for meeting the project goals. The hope is that common goals will be identified, and that shared principles will be established. These may include that all parties agree to:

- Complete the project on time, within budget, and to a reasonable standard of quality.
- Keep all lines of communication open.
- Solve problems promptly.
- Provide a safe work environment for all workers and establish a zero accidents plan.

The team should then develop and agree on a project mission statement, another opportunity for team alignment.

Mission Statement Example

We, the New School Project Team, in order to achieve our goals, will strive to be proactive in our pursuit of zero accidents, quality craftsmanship, and expeditious completion of the project through team cohesiveness, while attaining fair and reasonable profits and having fun.

Project Meetings

The Kick-Off Meeting

A kick-off or pre-construction meeting takes place at the beginning of the project and is usually held on the project site. The school's project manager or the architect usually chairs this meeting. The contractor's project manager and site superintendent, major subcontractors, and the clerk of the works are in attendance. The purpose of this meeting is to discuss the project and the logistics of the construction site, the phasing plan, and the construction schedule. *(See Chapter 9 for more on the Project Manager's and Clerk's responsibilities during construction.)*

Regular Meetings

The project team—the school representative(s), architect, and contractor—should be in constant communication. Most projects will have weekly project meetings, typically lasting one to two hours and covering a variety of topics. Standard issues that are addressed at each meeting include work progress to date, a schedule update, review of the RFI log (Requests for Information), submittal log, and contingency log/change order log. Detailed meeting minutes should be kept by the contractor and distributed in a timely manner after the meeting is complete. Good meeting minutes track each action item discussed, list who is responsible for completing each item, and list a completion date for each item. *(See Chapter 9, "The Project Manager," for more on meetings.)*

Schedule Update

A good schedule is an integral part of a successful project. New construction of a school is a long process, but there are definitive completion dates that must be met. Completion dates are frequently tied to the school schedule, so most schools are usually completed over the summer. Missing a target completion date can cause serious problems for the school and the community.

Construction schedules are typically broken out into several categories of activities, such as the structure, exterior closure, and interior finishes of the building(s). Because the construction period for an entirely new school is usually 12-18 months, it is easy to let schedule items slide at the beginning of the project. If so, all tasks that follow may be delayed, and there will be serious consequences at the end of the project that may affect its quality and delay occupancy.

The point is, the schedule is a critical topic at project meetings, and it must constantly be monitored. The contractor should be expected to provide meaningful information on the schedule at all construction meetings and should be prepared to discuss the project schedule in detail. He/she should address where the construction is in the overall process and any upcoming milestones and critical items. The contractor should also provide a plan to make up any time that is lost on critical activities.

Project Logs

Project logs, maintained by the contractor, are typically reviewed in each project meeting. RFIs are sent to the architect to request further information that was not included in the plans and specifications, but is needed to complete the construction project. The architect's timely response to RFIs affects the sequence of work and the project schedule. The RFI log should track each RFI and its status. This log will be reviewed at the meeting, and often responses to RFIs are given at the meeting.

Submittals are provided by subcontractors to the contractor for his or her review and forwarded to the architect for final review and approval. These may include shop drawings (detailed plans illustrating how a system will be installed) and detailed product information including written product data, samples, color charts, and similar details. Since all submittals require approval prior to the installation of the item by the contractor, delay in approvals may cause a delay in the schedule. Thus, the submittal log is reviewed at the weekly project meeting.

Special Meetings

A number of special meetings may be held with the project manager, architect, and contractor in order to meet the needs of specialty users of the building. For example, there may be several meetings to review the documents prior to or during construction with the librarian, the cafeteria manager, the head custodian, an information technology representative, and a physical education staff member.

While it is, of course, best that the building's end users be consulted and involved during the design phase of the project, there may be instances during construction where it becomes evident that the end users' needs were not met in the construction documents. It is during construction, as facility users pay more attention to the evolving features of the project, that they may ask important questions that did not occur to them when they looked at the plans in two dimensions.

If appropriate in the particular project/school district, the project manager, as the school representative responsible for effective communication with all parties, will meet with many groups during construction—to explain or clarify work in progress, or obtain further information as needed. For instance, the maintenance staff should be kept informed about new building systems and should be asked to provide their input on all of the components of the project. This may include the operation and maintenance of the HVAC system, the electrical system, and the communications system.

Phasing Plan for Construction

On many school projects, a major responsibility of a project manager who is serving as the school's representative is to coordinate the school's needs with the design team and the contractor to develop a phasing plan. A phasing plan determines which portions of a project will be constructed in what order. The project manager may rely heavily on input from the architect and contractor to develop the phasing plan.

To develop a phasing plan, one has to begin with the end in mind. If a new building is being constructed on the site of an existing school, or an existing building is being renovated, it is important to know what buildings or areas will be needed first and how they will be used, as well as what other functions or areas they will be displacing. The first thing to remember is that the existing operations of the school must be maintained. Activities such as food service, trash removal, physical education, transportation (busses, parent drop-off of students, pedestrians, and bicyclists) must all be addressed. All existing utilities must remain in operation. Throughout the phasing plan, school program functions must be maintained without disruption, and student safety must be ensured.

New School Construction

In the case of new school construction, a primary factor in developing the phasing plan is the land itself. Has the owner acquired all the land? Has the land been vacated? Are there any liens on the property? Are houses or other structures scheduled to be demolished or moved? Numerous school construction projects have a "squatter," or a house that is scheduled to be moved, but remains on-site in the path of construction. This is a serious issue that can take a long time to resolve.

Proper planning and an understanding that these items may take several months to complete are important. They will affect the project schedule and must be accounted for in the phasing plan.

Another major issue with the construction of new schools is the relocation of utilities. New schools are often located in existing neighborhoods, and utilities must be relocated to facilitate new construction, without interrupting or interfering with services to other users. This involves a lot of planning with the utility companies to allow enough time for them to approve, coordinate, and schedule the work. This process could easily take several months. This item must be addressed early on and included in the phasing plan.

A logical sequence for school construction is a critical part of the phasing plan. In the case of a multi-building campus, construction usually begins on the building that houses the central plant—the main electrical and mechanical plant for the entire school facility. Another area that requires special attention and extra time is the kitchen, a complex area that houses a lot of special equipment and includes additional plumbing, electrical, and mechanical requirements. Kitchen construction should be scheduled early in the project. The administration area also requires early attention. School personnel often need to occupy this area prior to the opening of the rest of the facility. The phasing plan must include identification of systems that must be operational for the occupation of this building.

Renovating an Existing School

Renovating an existing school facility displaces the users of the affected space. This situation must be addressed in the phasing plan. Does the project consist of additions and renovations? Will the additions be able to handle the displaced occupants of the future renovations? Will portable classrooms be required? Will additional space need to be rented?

All building systems must be operational in occupied spaces, and this requires a lot of advance planning. Key systems include plumbing, electrical, HVAC supply and returns, fire alarms, fire sprinklers, roof drains, and voice and data cabling. All of these items must be accounted for in any phasing plan. Student health and safety, access and circulation, noise levels, and air quality all must be considered. Security for the students is also a concern. Background checks, drug testing, and a badging system should be required to ensure the students' safety.

Managing a Project in an Operating School

The overwhelming priority when constructing a project in an existing school or adjacent to an existing school is student safety. A close second is maintaining a proper learning atmosphere for the students. Students have a job to do as well; they must be able to learn. Many factors are involved in maintaining a safe learning environment. The following sections will note safety requirements including barriers, signage, and safe drop-off and pickup areas.

New Construction Adjacent to an Existing School

Constant, open communication between the contractor's project manager and the school administration or its representative is key to the success of a new construction project adjacent to an existing facility. Most activities at the adjacent jobsite affect the operations of the existing school. Transportation, food service, trash removal, physical education, and the media center are all areas that must remain in operation. Activities that cause disruption, excessive noise, or vibration should be scheduled so as not to interfere with important school activities such as standardized tests or exams.

The first priority when building a new construction project adjacent to an existing school in operation is securing the site. The site should be completely fenced. It is strongly recommended that a visual barrier also be in place, especially in cases where students are passing by the fence on a regular basis. The visual barrier could be either a solid wood fence or a screening placed over a chain link fence. Responsibility for the fence is not just a one-time installation. The fence must be checked on a daily basis to ensure that it is still intact and in good condition. Proper signage should also be posted on the fence and should state that the site is a designated construction area, that trespassers will be prosecuted, that hard hats must be worn at all times, and that all visitors must check in at the field office.

New construction adjacent to an existing school is likely to include the relocation of several school functions. New school buildings are often constructed on former playing fields of existing schools, which requires relocating physical education activities, often to indoor gymnasiums or nearby parks. The contractor must keep the principal or designated school representative informed of anticipated dates when construction will begin in these areas, so that all necessary arrangements can be made.

In many cases, existing playing fields may also have been in use by the community. Community members must be properly notified of construction activity there. Most, if not all, schools are located within the residential areas they serve. Neighbors should also be kept informed of construction activities that affect them.

Existing bus loops and parent drop-off areas may also be affected by new construction. Temporary bus loops, if required, should be routed in a counter-clockwise fashion so the students do not cross a line of traffic to enter and exit the bus. Drop-offs for children driven to school should be located in an area separate from the bus loop and also routed in a counter-clockwise manner, for the same reason. Special consideration should be given to students who walk or ride bicycles to school. These students must have a safe path to enter school and should not be routed across vehicular traffic.

Deliveries to the school and trash pickup must be considered as part of the planning for constructing the new school. The kitchen in a school usually receives a delivery every day. Likewise, trash pickup is often scheduled several days a week. Grease traps need to be serviced regularly, so there must be access for service vehicles. Furthermore, access for fire and emergency vehicles must be maintained at all times. In short, there are a number of large vehicles, besides busses, that need regular access to the school to maintain facility operations. It is critical that these needs are identified prior to formulation of the construction phasing plan.

Relocating Utilities

If new construction is planned next to an existing facility, the relocation of utilities is a likely requirement. There are a number of possible utilities to contend with, such as:

- Overhead and/or underground electric
- Telephone
- Cable
- Gas
- Domestic water
- Fire lines
- Sanitary sewer
- Storm water
- Rain leaders from existing buildings

Utility relocations are often accompanied by shut-downs of service and must be accomplished after hours or when classes are not in session (holidays, spring break, or summer). Special consideration must be given when planning these events. The contractor must do a good job of thinking far into the future. One never wants to have to relocate a temporary utility again because of a lack of foresight, which means thinking through the entire schedule and specific construction needs.

Interior Renovations in an Existing School

Working inside an existing school building presents unique challenges. First, the construction zone must be segregated from the rest of the school building. This separation should include a secure visual barrier, typically a temporary drywall partition. This barrier should be lockable and not easily accessible to students. Every attempt must be made to prevent a reasonable person from entering a potentially dangerous construction area. Again, maintenance of student safety is paramount.

The partition must not hinder emergency egress from the school in any way. In other words, if a temporary partition were constructed in a corridor, taking a portion of that corridor away, the corridor must still remain accessible to all students, including handicapped students. The corridor must also continue to maintain all life safety systems, such as fire alarm and fire sprinklers, exit signs, and emergency lighting. In addition, these corridors must empty into an open space outside the construction zone. Students must not be directed into a construction area. Temporary partitions must be dustproof and contain all the dust in the construction zone.

Special consideration should be given to the HVAC system. If the existing system must remain in operation, the returns that are fed into the construction zone should have additional temporary filter material protecting the air handler from the dust generated in the construction zone. If asbestos abatement is required, it should be noted that this work requires special attention and precautions and must be accomplished during periods when the building is not occupied.

Temporary partitions should provide as much noise control as possible. This can be accomplished by a number of methods, such as multiple layers of gypsum board, insulation, and staggered studs with gypsum board on both sides of the wall. Finally, temporary partitions should have proper signage warning occupants that they contain an active construction site, and that trespassing on that site is forbidden.

Project Turnover

All of the project team members have a number of responsibilities at the end of the project, beginning with the *punch list*. The architect and contractor prepare the punch list after the project team members, including the owner (represented by the school building committee or their project manager), walk through all parts of the project, inside and out, to identify any deficiencies or incomplete work in the finished product. The consultants to the architect will also be required to "punch" the project. Typically, there will be an architectural, electrical, fire alarm, mechanical and plumbing, civil, landscape, and food service punch list. These consultants are usually accompanied by a representative of the contractor and sometimes by a representative of the subcontractor who performed the work. The punch list will include all corrections that need to be made to the project. The mechanical, electrical, and plumbing engineers should perform an above-ceiling punch list, which should be completed and signed off by the engineer before ceiling tiles are dropped.

In an ideal world, the overall punch list items are quickly and properly addressed, the project is occupied, and there are no further problems. However, this is usually not the case. While most punch items are typically completed prior to occupancy, it is common for a number of miscellaneous items, not discovered during the punch list process, to pop up later. As a result, construction personnel are often present during initial occupancy.

Many other activities occur during the project turnover. The facility's maintenance personnel will have to be trained on all systems in the building. This training usually includes all of the HVAC systems (all handlers, chillers, pumps, etc.), building controls (thermostats, energy management systems, etc.), electrical equipment, food service equipment, and fire alarm systems. Training school personnel usually takes place over several days and involves many different users. Training must be scheduled and coordinated with the school's administration. Sessions may also be videotaped for future reference and as a training tool for future employees.

The contractor will also provide the end user of the facility with as-built drawings and operations and maintenance manuals, more commonly referred to as *O & M manuals*. The as-built drawings consist of marked-up plans that include any modifications made to the contract documents during construction. The specific requirements for the O & M manuals will be defined in the project specifications. The O & M manuals provide detailed instructions on the operation and maintenance of equipment in the school. Typically all the items covered in the training will be included in the O & M manuals.

The contractor will ensure that all spare parts, service plans, and warranties that are required in the specifications are turned over to the school administration. The maintenance personnel will also receive "attic stock" upon the completion of the project. Attic stock is extra material such as extra flooring, ceiling tiles, and paint that is usually outlined in the specifications.

Managing the Move

Coordination, communication, and establishing the parameters up front are all key to a successful move. Are the contents of an entire school being moved to a new building? Is the new building located on the same site? Will the furniture, kitchen equipment, and physical education equipment be moved? Will any items be stored or disposed of off-site? How much and what kind of furnishings, equipment, books, or other items will be donated or disposed of, and how will it be transported to off-site locations? Does any equipment or furnishings require disassembly prior to the move?

Once the parameters of the move are established, the contractor then must work with the school's project manager and administration to establish dates for the move. (The degree to which the general contractor's project manager, versus the school's project manager, is responsible for overseeing the move will vary from district to district and school to school, but the contractor is likely to be involved to some extent with the move.) These dates include not only the actual dates that items will be moved, but also earlier milestone dates for obtaining packing materials and arranging furniture deliveries, material pickups, and so forth.

In addition to dates, it is necessary to determine what items the teachers and other school staff will be moving, and the destinations of those items within the new building. It is extremely helpful to have reduced-size plans of both the existing facility and the new facility for reference. These plans may be marked up indicating the occupants for each space. The movers will most likely develop a labeling system with various colored labels for corresponding areas.

Staff members should also establish the specific locations (within their room or area) to which the items will be moved. Will all the boxes be placed in the center of the room? The corner? Along the window? There must be enough space allowed for the furniture. All of these factors must be considered in advance.

The contractor, the school's project manager, and the mover will develop a plan and present it to the entire staff of the school after receiving input and approval from the principal. At this meeting, all dates will be discussed, and detailed instructions provided for labeling of items. A helpful prelude to the move is getting staff to purge, purge, purge! This can be a challenge, but it needs to be stressed, and it starts with the principal. Teachers should try to weed out all outdated materials. It makes no sense to pay movers to move items that will not be used.

The contractor, the school's project manager, and the moving company should check the facility once or twice prior to the move date to monitor progress of the packing and ensure that the labeling is being done correctly. Then comes moving day. It is important to establish security for this activity. At this time, the school should have its final keying for the new facility. Typically, these keys cannot be loaned out for security reasons. Therefore a member of the school staff must be present to unlock and lock up the facility. There are thousands of valuable items in school facilities, and there is significant opportunity for theft during a move. It is important to establish guidelines for who is authorized to be on-site during the move. There should be only a couple of faculty members present during the move to help maintain a secure environment, while minimizing confusion. Movers should be wearing some type of uniform.

Conclusion

The construction of every school project is unique. It is a major event in the life of a community. There are multiple stakeholders—parents, students, taxpayers, teachers, and administrators—all with their own high expectations for the project. All will maintain high interest for the duration of construction and for years into the future. Add to this mix the designers, constructors, and the local newspaper, and you have high potential for confusion and conflict.

A key to avoiding conflict is early and continuing commitment to teamwork and effective communication among all members of the project team. This effort could start with a Project Expectations Workshop, where team members, including major subcontractors, can get to know one another while defining the project's goals and anticipated challenges, and the mechanisms the team will use to identify and resolve problems. Proper consideration of project phasing, regular project team meetings, and well-planned procedures for project turnover and the move will all help to keep the job on schedule, on budget, and meeting the needs of the school.

Part III

Case Studies of Completed School Projects

As noted in Chapter 1, an excellent source of inspiration for a new school building or renovation is other recently built schools, such as those shown in this section. Ideas for new technologies, such as those that support green building initiatives, can be gleaned from successful and innovative completed projects. They offer a glimpse into what worked and what did not, where the special challenges lie, and how specific goals, such as a LEED building rating, were met. A review of such projects can also help the school administration and its representatives, and members of the local community, as they envision the possibilities during the early design and planning phase.

Information on completed projects is also a valuable resource for cost estimators, as described in Chapter 6. This is particularly true at the budget estimate stage, when different options are being explored.

The case studies in Part III describe the school systems' needs, the design professionals' solutions, and key challenges and systems. Costs are broken down by major building systems and also include General Requirements items, such as coordination, quality control, commissioning, and close out.

(Note: There are also mini-case studies in Chapters 1, 2, 3, and 6 that show, in actual practice, various design features described in the text.)

St. Anne's Episcopal School

Middletown, Delaware

Architect: Anderson Brown Higley Associates

Instructing pre-kindergarten through eighth grade students, St. Anne's Episcopal School embodies the educational goals of its founders. Its teachers prepare students for secondary education and develop their potential as good members of local and world communities.

The school stands on a knoll overlooking Silver Lake near the small farming community of Middletown, Delaware. It is placed so that existing trees screen it from the main thoroughfare, half a mile away, which preserves this setting for the school and for the community. Crops still grow on the site, a former soybean field, and can be seen from the school, reinforcing lessons in ecology and stewardship of the environment. The school's academic wings gather views of the countryside and combine with the central structure to form a courtyard for outdoor classes and special events.

Reflecting on the rural setting, the school's dominant central structure is based on the style and proportions of a traditional Delaware Victorian manor house. It houses administrative offices as well as the library, dining room, and classrooms for art and music. A central two-story lobby connects all of these spaces and is partially illuminated by borrowed light from each.

Connected to this central structure are the gymnasium and academic wings with building forms reminiscent of a barn and a series of outbuildings. Serving as a multifunctional assembly space for sporting events, meetings and performances, the gymnasium houses basketball courts,

a stage and bleacher seating for the student body.

The two academic wings reach out toward the lake view. One houses the lower school, grades pre-kindergarten through fourth; the other houses the middle school, grades fifth through eighth. The wings are divided into pods, each of which supports two grades. Central common spaces within these groupings provide opportunities for students to work together in cooperative learning teams. Each wing has its own entrance lobby to relieve congestion at times of arrival and departure.

The desire for an abundance of natural light and fresh air is accommodated through large operable windows in classrooms and at key locations throughout the common areas. Views through these openings maintain a connection between

the students' studies and the outdoor environment. Academic common spaces borrow light from classrooms via clerestory windows, and throughout the building, indirect lighting supplements natural light.

Most windows are semi-custom wood insulated units with true divided lights. Glazed entrances are a custom color aluminum storefront system. Structural steel costs were minimized by the use of steel stud bearing walls and cold-formed metal roof trusses on the single story portions of the building. Exterior walls are of brick and cement fiber siding.

Helping to reinforce connections to the surrounding environment, natural materials used inside are oak, cork, linoleum, rubber and ceramic tile. High-grade residential oak cabinets, substantially less expensive than custom units, were installed in all of the classrooms and science rooms.

St. Anne's Episcopal School building supplements the work of its teachers. Through natural materials and natural daylight, plus numerous framed views of its surroundings, it helps students see the connections among what they learn, how they live, and the world outside.

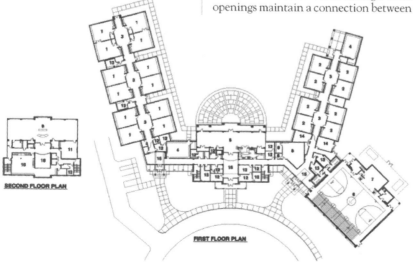

SECOND FLOOR PLAN

FIRST FLOOR PLAN

MANUFACTURERS/SUPPLIERS

DIV 06:	*Cement Plank Siding:* HardiPlank®.
DIV 07:	*Shingles:* Elk.
DIV 08:	*Entrance Doors:* Adams Rite; *Windows:* Pella.
DIV 09:	*Carpet:* Mannington; *VCT:* **Armstrong**; *Cork:* Expanko; *Drywall:* Georgia Pacific.

ARCHITECT
ANDERSON BROWN HIGLEY ASSOCIATES
1621 North Lincoln Street
Wilmington, DE 19806
www.abha.com

CONSTRUCTION MANAGER
EDIS COMPANY
110 S. Poplar Street, #400
Wilmington, DE 19801
www.ediscompany.com

CONSTRUCTION TEAM

LZA Technology
105 S. 12th Street,
Philadelphia, PA 19107

ELECTRICAL & MECHANICAL ENGINEER:
Paul H. Yeomans, Inc.
718 Arch Street, #200S,
Philadelphia, PA 19106

COST ESTIMATOR:
EDiS Company
110 S. Poplar Street, #400,
Wilmington, DE 19801

Photo Courtesy of Gregory Benson Photography

GENERAL DESCRIPTION

SITE: 120 acres.
NUMBER OF BUILDINGS: Two; School and pre-fabricated storage building.
BUILDING SIZES: Garage, 2,000; first floor, 46,160; second floor, 7,840; total, 56,000 square feet.
BUILDING HEIGHT: First floor, 14'; second floor, 12'; total, 44'.
BASIC CONSTRUCTION TYPE: New.
FOUNDATION: Spread footings.
EXTERIOR WALLS: Brick, cement board siding.
ROOF: Shingle.
FLOORS: Carpet, ceramic tile, VCT, cork.
INTERIOR WALLS: Drywall.

ST. ANNE'S EPISCOPAL SCHOOL

Date Bid: June 2001 • Construction Period: June 2001 to Aug 2002 • Total Square Feet: 56,000

C.S.I. Divisions (1 through 16)	COST	% OF COST	SQ.FT. COST		SPECIFICATIONS
BIDDING REQUIREMENTS	340,000	3.40	6.07		—
1. GENERAL REQUIREMENTS	458,000	4.58	8.18	1	Summary of work, coordination, field engineering, project meetings, submittals, quality control, construction facilities & temporary controls, facility startup/commissioning, contract closeout.
3. CONCRETE	215,000	2.15	3.84	3	Formwork, reinforcement, accessories, cast-in-place, curing, grout, mass.
4. MASONRY	410,000	4.10	7.32	4	Masonry & grout, accessories, unit.
5. METALS	325,000	3.25	5.80	5	Structural metal framing, joists, decking, fabrications, ornamental.
6. WOOD & PLASTICS	1,800,000	18.01	32.14	6	Fasteners & adhesives, rough carpentry, wood & metal systems, finish carpentry, wood treatment, architectural woodwork.
7. THERMAL & MOIST. PROTECT	265,000	2.65	4.73	7	Insulation, shingles & roof tiles, manufactured roofing & siding, membrane roofing, flashing & sheet metal.
8. DOORS & WINDOWS	740,000	7.40	13.21	8	Metal doors & frames, wood & plastic doors, entrances & storefronts, hardware, glazing.
9. FINISHES	1,540,000	15.41	27.50	9	Metal support systems, gypsum, tile, acoustical treatment, resilient flooring, carpet, special flooring, special coatings, painting.
10. SPECIALTIES	259,000	2.59	4.63	10	Visual display board, wall & corner guards, flagpoles, lockers, storage shelving.
11. EQUIPMENT	1,300,000	13.01	23.21	11	Theatre & stage, water supply & treatment, food service, laboratory, office.
12. FURNISHING	450,000	4.50	8.04	12	—
13. SPECIAL CONSTRUCTIONS	45,000	0.45	0.80	13	Pre-engineered structure.
14. CONVEYING SYSTEMS	48,000	0.48	0.86	14	Elevators (1).
15. MECHANICAL	1,200,000	12.01	21.43	15	Basic materials & methods, insulation, fire protection, plumbing, HVAC, heat generation, refrigeration, controls, testing, adjusting & balancing.
16. ELECTRICAL	600,000	6.01	10.72	16	—
TOTAL BUILDING COST	**9,995,000**	**100%**	**$178.48**		
2. SITE WORK	1,005,000			2	Preparation, dewatering, excavation support systems, paving & surfacing, water distribution, sewerage & drainage, ponds & reservoirs, improvements, landscaping.
LANDSCAPING & OFFSITE WORK	—				Included in Site Work.
TOTAL PROJECT COST	**11,000,000**		*(Excluding architectural and engineering fees)*		

Pioneer Ridge Center

Chaska, Minnesota

Architect: KKE Architects, Inc.

Photo Courtesy of KKE Architects

Bringing together students from diverse middle schools, Pioneer Ridge Freshmen Center fosters a strong social and academic bond among all district 9th graders allowing the students to nurture relationships and grow together for one significant, transitional year.

The school is designed as a cool place that freshmen would want to spend time. Its distinctive colors, textures and shapes create a memorable learning context, especially the elliptically shaped media center that serves as the eye of knowledge with classrooms spiraling from it.

Another gathering place, The Commons, offers a vortex of social interaction. The openness and connectedness of The Commons allows for a constant sense of community in both sight and sound. It also offers an outdoor courtyard overlooking a grove of trees and adjacent wetland.

Sensitive to the environment, the project was constructed using sustainable practices such as sourcing the majority of materials from local quarries, and

building with long-lasting brick, precast concrete, metal panels and glass.

The building is situated tightly against the site's western edge to make the most

of its natural landscape. Through careful siting and approach, the center is presented as a gateway to the community, both in structure and in spirit.

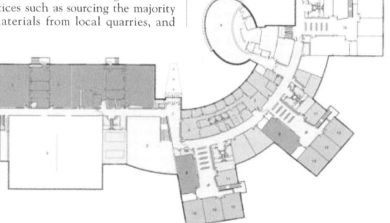

MANUFACTURERS/SUPPLIERS

DIV 03: *Block:* Anchor Block.

DIV 07: *Metal Panels:* Centria; *Membrane Roofing:* Firestone.

DIV 08: *Curtainwall:* **EFCO Corporation**; *Doors:* Curries Manufacturing; *Windows:* Wausau Window & Wall Systems; *Glass:* Oldcastle Glass.

DIV 09: *Carpet:* Collins & Aikman; *Acoustical Treatment:* Armstrong; *Drywall:* National Gypsum; *Paint:* Pratt & Lambert.

DIV 10: *Toilet Partitions:* Santana; *Baby Changers:* Koala.

EXTENDED PRODUCT INFORMATION

Curtainwall: **EFCO Corporation**.
See advertisement on page 5.

ARCHITECT
KKE ARCHITECTS, INC.
300 First Avenue North
Minneapolis, MN 55401
www.kke.com

CONSTRUCTION TEAM

GENERAL CONTRACTOR:
CM Construction Company, Inc.
12215 Nicollet Avenue South, Burnsville, MN 55337
STRUCTURAL ENGINEER:
Ericksen Roed & Associates
2550 University Avenue, #201-S, St. Paul, MN 55114

ELECTRICAL & MECHANICAL ENGINEER:
Dunham Associates
8200 Normandale Blvd., #500,
Minneapolis, MN 55437

LANDSCAPE ARCHITECT:
Dahlgren, Shardlow & Uban, Inc.
300 First Avenue North, #210,
Minneapolis, MN 55401

COST ESTIMATOR: PPM
1858 East Shore Drive, St. Paul, MN 55109

GENERAL DESCRIPTION

SITE: 27 acres.
NUMBER OF BUILDINGS: One; 9th grade center, 35 classrooms with a maximum of 32 seating capacity each; gymnasium seating capacity of 604.
BUILDING SIZES: Lower level, 68,588; main level, 55,525; penthouse, 5,171; total, 129,284 square feet.
BUILDING HEIGHT: First floor, 15'4"; second floor, 15'4"; total, 32'.
BASIC CONSTRUCTION TYPE: New.
FOUNDATION: Concrete.
EXTERIOR WALLS: Block, metal.
ROOF: Membrane.
FLOORS: Wood, resilient, carpet.
INTERIOR WALLS: Metal studs, gypsum.

PIONEER RIDGE CENTER

Date Bid: Mar 2001 • Construction Period: Mar 2001 to Sept 2002 • Total Square Feet: 129,284

	C.S.I. Divisions (1 through 16)	COST	% OF COST	SQ.FT. COST		SPECIFICATIONS
	BIDDING REQUIREMENTS	481,915	3.60	3.73		—
1.	GENERAL REQUIREMENTS	70,000	0.52	0.54	1	—
3.	CONCRETE	1,188,725	8.88	9.19	3	Formwork, reinforcement, cast-in-place, curing, precast, cementitious decks & toppings, grout.
4.	MASONRY	696,430	5.21	5.39	4	Masonry & grout, accessories, unit, simulated masonry.
5.	METALS	1,788,410	13.37	13.83	5	Materials, fastening, structural metal framing, joists, decking, cold formed metal framing, fabrications, ornamental, expansion control.
6.	WOOD & PLASTICS	236,000	1.76	1.83	6	Fasteners & adhesives, rough carpentry, finish carpentry, architectural woodwork.
7.	THERMAL & MOIST. PROTECT	788,100	5.89	6.10	7	Waterproofing, vapor retarders, air barriers, insulation, fireproofing, firestopping, manufactured roofing & siding, membrane roofing, flashing & sheet metal, roof specialties & accessories.
8.	DOORS & WINDOWS	1,010,975	7.56	7.82	8	Metal doors & frames, wood & plastic doors, door opening assemblies, special doors, entrances & storefronts, metal windows, wood & plastic windows, special windows, hardware, glazing, glazed curtainwalls.
9.	FINISHES	1,554,320	11.62	12.02	9	Gypsum, tile, acoustical treatment, wood flooring, resilient flooring, carpet, special coatings, painting.
10.	SPECIALTIES	218,835	1.64	1.69	10	Visual display board, louvers & vents, grilles & screens, wall & corner guards, flagpoles, pedestrian control devices, lockers, fire protection, protective covers, operable partitions, storage shelving, toilet & bath accessories.
11.	EQUIPMENT	464,150	3.47	3.59	11	Audio-visual, loading dock, food service, athletic, recreational & therapeutic.
12.	FURNISHING	379,260	2.83	2.93	12	Window treatment, furniture & accessories, rugs & mats, multiple seating.
13.	SPECIAL CONSTRUCTIONS	—	—	—	13	—
14.	CONVEYING SYSTEMS	37,400	0.28	0.29	14	Elevators (1).
15.	MECHANICAL	3,304,770	24.70	25.56	15	Basic materials & methods, insulation, fire protection, plumbing, HVAC, heat generation, refrigeration, heat transfer, air distribution, controls, testing, adjusting & balancing.
16.	ELECTRICAL	1,160,585	8.67	8.98	16	Basic materials & methods, medium voltage distribution, service & distribution, lighting, communications, controls, testing.
	TOTAL BUILDING COST	**10,070,075**	**100%**	**$100.40**		
2.	SITE WORK	1,627,125			2	Preparation, earthwork, paving & surfacing, utility piping materials, water distribution, sewerage & drainage, landscaping.
	LANDSCAPING & OFFSITE WORK	—				Included in Site Work.
	TOTAL PROJECT COST	**15,007,000**				*(Excluding architectural and engineering fees)*

Tooele Elementary Schools

Tooele, Utah

Architect: MHTN Architects, Inc.

Photos Courtesy of Brian Griffin Photography

MHTN Architects took on the task of designing an elementary school that would take advantage of spectacular mountain and lake settings as well as using an abundance of natural daylighting. The schools, Overlake, Middle Canyon and Willow Elementary in Tooele, Utah are the result of MHTN's work.

The schools are organized around a primary circulation spine. The "Main Street" plan organization provides small, identifiable neighborhoods for grade school children, allowing for closer age matches within each pod. The central "Main Street" corridor acts as the central organizing element within the school. The corridor is filled with light, color, and expansive views to the outside. It is a stimulating transition space between the classrooms, Media Center, Cafetorium and support spaces. The "Main Street" features high ceilings, clerestory windows, large walls for display of student work and large windows that open to landscaped courts and scenic views.

Separate entries for automobile drop-off are provided for the kindergarten and upper level grades. The Administration/Reception area, located between these two entries, uses full height windows to convey a sense of openness while providing security to monitor all visitors. The Media Center and Cafetorium make use of natural light through the use of clerestory windows.

These schools demonstrate the team approach to school design. The Design Team worked closely with the school district, patrons, administrators, and faculty in developing their program, establishing goals and developing a Mission Statement that aided the decision making process from inception to completion.

The need to put in place three new elementary schools as well as a new high school, a large addition and remodel of another high school within a short time period with tight budget constraints required a cooperative effort of the Design Team. This team included the construction manager, architects, engineers, school district facilities personnel and administrators. Weekly meetings with all team members helped to monitor construction methods, material selections, cost estimating and schedule impacts.

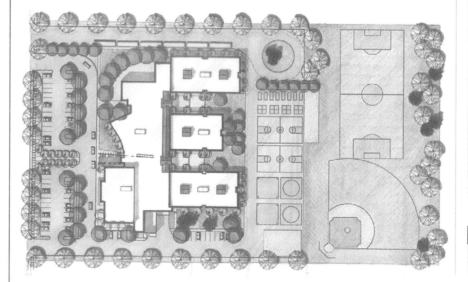

Reprinted with permission from *Design Cost Data*, Nov-Dec 2003, Copyright 2003 DC&D Technologies, Inc.

ARCHITECT

MHTN ARCHITECTS, INC.
420 East South Temple, #100
Salt Lake City, UT 84111
www.mhtn.com

CONSTRUCTION TEAM

GENERAL CONTRACTOR/CONSTRUCTION MANAGER:
  Hughes General Contractors, Inc.
  900 N. Redwood Road, North Salt Lake City, UT 84054

STRUCTURAL ENGINEER:
  Reaveley Engineers & Associates
  1515 S. 1100 East, Salt Lake City, UT 84105

ELECTRICAL ENGINEER: Spectrum Engineers
  175 South Main Street, #300, Salt Lake City, UT 84111

MECHANICAL ENGINEER:
  Olsen & Peterson Consulting Engineers, Inc.
  14 East 2700 South, Salt Lake City, UT 84115

COST ESTIMATOR: Hughes General Contractors, Inc.
  900 N. Redwood Road, North Salt Lake City, UT 84054

GENERAL DESCRIPTION

SITE: 9.3 acres.
NUMBER OF BUILDINGS: One.
BUILDING SIZES: First floor, 54,150; total, 54,150 total square feet.

BUILDING HEIGHT: First floor, 22'; total, 22'.
BASIC CONSTRUCTION TYPE: Type IIN/Type II 1-Hour/NEW.
FOUNDATION: Concrete.
EXTERIOR WALLS: CMU.
ROOF: Single-ply membrane.
FLOORS: Carpet, VCT.
INTERIOR WALLS: Drywall.

TOOELE ELEMENTARY SCHOOLS

Date Bid: Apr 2001 • Construction Period: May 2001 to July 2002 • Total Square Feet: 54,150

C.S.I. Divisions (1 through 16)	COST	% OF COST	SQ.FT. COST		SPECIFICATIONS
BIDDING REQUIREMENTS	290,000	5.92	5.36		Pre-bid information, instruction to bidders, bonds & certificates, general conditions, supplementary conditions.
1. GENERAL REQUIREMENTS	190,000	3.88	3.51	1	Allowances, alternates/alternatives, quality control, facility startup/commissioning, contract closeout.
3. CONCRETE	517,500	10.56	9.56	3	Formwork, reinforcement, accessories, cast-in-place, precast.
4. MASONRY	628,000	12.81	11.60	4	Masonry & grout, accessories, unit.
5. METALS	250,250	5.11	4.62	5	Materials, fastening, structural metal framing, joists, decking, fabrications, ornamental.
6. WOOD & PLASTICS	155,500	3.17	2.87	6	Rough carpentry, finish carpentry, architectural woodwork.
7. THERMAL & MOIST. PROTECT	197,500	4.03	3.65	7	Waterproofing, insulation, EIFS, firestopping, membrane roofing, flashing & sheet metal, joint sealers.
8. DOORS & WINDOWS	217,000	4.43	4.01	8	Metal doors & frames, wood & plastic doors, special doors, entrances & storefronts, hardware, glazing, glazed curtainwalls.
9. FINISHES	275,137	5.61	5.08	9	Metal support systems, gypsum, tile, acoustical treatment, resilient flooring, carpet, special flooring, painting.
10. SPECIALTIES	58,000	1.19	1.07	10	Visual display board, compartments & cubicles, flagpoles, identifying devices, lockers, toilet & bath accessories.
11. EQUIPMENT	202,000	4.12	3.73	11	Theatre & stage, loading dock, athletic, recreational & therapeutic.
12. FURNISHING	—	—	—	12	—
13. SPECIAL CONSTRUCTIONS	—	—	—	13	—
14. CONVEYING SYSTEMS	—	—	—	14	—
15. MECHANICAL	1,313,000	26.79	24.24	15	Basic materials & methods, insulation, fire protection, plumbing, HVAC, air distribution, controls, testing, adjusting & balancing.
16. ELECTRICAL	606,750	12.38	11.20	16	Basic materials & methods, medium voltage distribution, service & distribution, lighting, communications.
TOTAL BUILDING COST	**4,900,637**	**100%**	**$90.50**		
2. SITE WORK	1,084,500			2	Preparation, earthwork, paving & surfacing, utility piping materials, water distribution, sewerage & drainage, improvements, landscaping.
LANDSCAPING & OFFSITE WORK	—				Included in Site Work.
TOTAL PROJECT COST	**5,985,137***				*(Excluding architectural and engineering fees)*

Otter Creek Elementary School

Elgin, Illinois

Architect: Dahlquist and Lutzow Architects, Ltd.
General Contractor: BABCO Construction, Inc.

Otter Creek Elementary School was a competitively bid project for school district U46 and Dahlquist and Lutzow Architects. The two-story, masonry bearing structural steel building was started in June of 2001. It took a dedicated project team to complete the project approximately two months ahead of schedule and under budget.

The complex electrical and low voltage systems along with the heating and ventilation, plumbing and elevator were a few of the trades that took close coordination between all parties to ensure the schedule, quality and costs were staying on track.

The facade was comprised of face brick, curtain wall, and aluminum windows. The building was enclosed before winter, thus allowing work on the interior to proceed through the winter months.

Completed in July 2002, Otter Creek Elementary School has been well received by the students and administration.

Photos Courtesy of Brian Fritz Photography

MANUFACTURERS/SUPPLIERS

DIV 04: *Masonry:* Glen-Gery Corp., Souix City Brick.

DIV 07: *Membrane:* Seaman Corporation, Fibertite Roofing System.

DIV 08: *Curtainwall, Glass, Glazing, Aluminum Windows:* Arcadia Products, United States Aluminum.

DIV 09: *Carpet:* Patcraft; *Resilient Tile,* Armstrong; *Resilient Base, Stair Treads:* Johnsonite.

DIV 10: *Marker & Tack Boards:* Claridge; *Gypsum:* National Gypsum; *Carpet:* Lees; *VCT:* Armstrong.

DIV 14: *Elevator:* KONE.

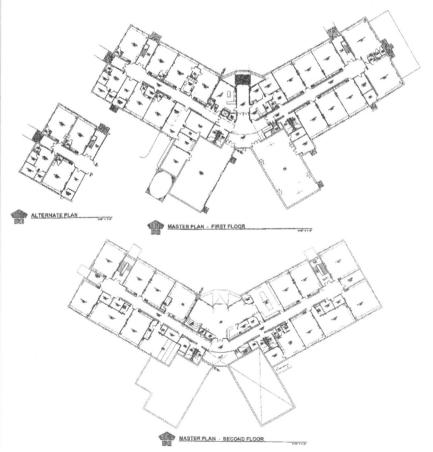

ALTERNATE PLAN

MASTER PLAN - FIRST FLOOR

MASTER PLAN - SECOND FLOOR

ARCHITECT
DAHLQUIST AND LUTZOW
ARCHITECTS, LTD.
462 N. McLean Blvd.
Elgin, IL 60123
www.dla-ltd.com

GENERAL CONTRACTOR
BABCO Construction, Inc.
1723 Howard Street
Evanston, IL 60202
www.babcoinc.com

CONSTRUCTION TEAM

STRUCTURAL ENGINEER:
Pease Borst & Associates, LLC
110 W. Higgins Road, Park Ridge, IL 60068

ELECTRICAL & MECHANICAL ENGINEER:
Mechanical Services Associates Corp.
780 McArdle Drive, #A, Crystal Lake, IL 60014

CONSULTING ENGINEER: Rynear & Son, Inc.
595 Buttonwood Circle, Naperville, IL 60540

LANDSCAPE ARCHITECT:
Dahlquist And Lutzow Architects, Ltd.
462 N. McLean Boulevard, Elgin, IL 60123

GENERAL DESCRIPTION

SITE: —

NUMBER OF BUILDINGS: One.

BUILDING SIZES: First floor, 34,825; second floor, 25,325; total, 60,150 total square feet.

BUILDING HEIGHT: First floor, 13'4"; second floor, 28'8"; total, 41'.

BASIC CONSTRUCTION TYPE: NEW.

FOUNDATION: Concrete.

EXTERIOR WALLS: Masonry.

ROOF: Membrane.

FLOORS: Carpet, VCT.

INTERIOR WALLS: Drywall.

OTTER CREEK ELEMENTARY SCHOOL

Date Bid: June 2001 • Construction Period: Aug 2001 to July 2002 • Total Square Feet: 60,150

C.S.I. Divisions (1 through 16)	COST	% OF COST	SQ.FT. COST		SPECIFICATIONS
BIDDING REQUIREMENTS	531,054	9.13	8.83		Bonds & certificates, general conditions.
1. GENERAL REQUIREMENTS	—	—	—	1	—
3. CONCRETE	277,000	4.76	4.61	3	Cast-in-place, cementitious decks & toppings, grout.
4. MASONRY	956,000	16.43	15.89	4	Masonry & grout.
5. METALS	483,827	8.31	8.04	5	Metal panels, structural metal framing.
6. WOOD & PLASTICS	265,360	4.56	4.41	6	Rough carpentry, architectural woodwork.
7. THERMAL & MOIST. PROTECT	161,945	2.78	2.69	7	Firestopping, membrane roofing, joint sealers.
8. DOORS & WINDOWS	391,000	6.72	6.50	8	Metal doors & frames, special doors, entrances & storefronts, metal windows.
9. FINISHES	409,300	7.03	6.80	9	Drywall, acoustical ceiling, resilient flooring, carpet, painting.
10. SPECIALTIES	87,150	1.50	1.45	10	Visual display board, signage, fire protection, toilet & bath accessories.
11. EQUIPMENT	23,000	0.40	0.38	11	Athletic, recreational, and therapeutic.
12. FURNISHING	5,400	0.09	0.09	12	Window treatment.
13. SPECIAL CONSTRUCTIONS	—	—	—	13	—
14. CONVEYING SYSTEMS	34,000	0.58	0.57	14	Elevator (1).
15. MECHANICAL	1,294,171	22.24	21.52	15	Plumbing, HVAC, heat generation.
16. ELECTRICAL	000,000	15.17	14.56	16	Basic materials & methods.
TOTAL BUILDING COST	**5,819,207**	**100%**	**$96.74**		
2. SITE WORK	324,936			2	Earthwork, paving & surfacing, fencing.
LANDSCAPING & OFFSITE WORK	43,022				Landscaping.
TOTAL PROJECT COST	**6,187,165**				*(Excluding architectural and engineering fees)*

McWillie Elementary School

Jackson, Mississippi

Architect: Dale and Associates Architects, P.A.

Photos Courtesy of Winstead Photography

The McWillie Elementary School was built to relieve overcrowding for the Jackson Public School District. The facility was built on the site of an existing school building, which was no longer used. The existing building was removed to provide space for outdoor play areas.

A committee comprised of educators and community members was created to envision a flagship, prototype school designed to support the educational philosophy of "activity based learning."

The primary components of this 625 student capacity school are the Learning Houses, which divide the students into "families" of learners. Each house consists of five classrooms, a common family room with an adjacent group porch area, a project lab, and a shared teacher's office. A Montessori program housed in the facility occupies one of the Learning Houses, and the qualities of this specific learning experience provide defining architectural strategies for the entire school. Some of these features include expansive exterior views, ample natural light, multiple learning opportunities, and the vibrant use of color. From each classroom students can move freely outside onto a learning porch located in learning gardens. These gardens extend the learning environment to outdoor areas, and help define the overall mass of the facility. The use of color and professional artist installations are employed at prominent loca-

tions throughout the building, and student artwork is mixed with this professional art on display space along the Central Hall.

A dynamic exterior is created by the individual expression of each Learning House, as well as the Dining Hall and Administration/Discovery Center area. The masonry screen walls at each Learning Garden help to create a layered exterior of building forms, exterior spaces, and subtle material changes. The building strives to instill a passion for learning and teaching through its varied and stimulating environments.

MANUFACTURERS/SUPPLIERS

DIV 07: *Manufactured Roofing & Siding:* Architectural Building Components; *Built-Up:* Johns Manville.

DIV 08: *Aluminum Storefront Windows:* Vistawall; *Hollow Metal Windows, Hollow Metal Doors & Frames:* CECO; *Wood Doors:* Oshkosh; *Hardware:* **Corbin Russwin.**

DIV 09: *Metal Studs:* Clark; *Gypsum:* National Gypsum; *Carpet:* Lees; *VCT:* Armstrong.

DIV 10: *Operable Partitions:* Hufcor.

EXTENDED PRODUCT INFORMATION

Hardware — Yale.
See advertisement on page 13.

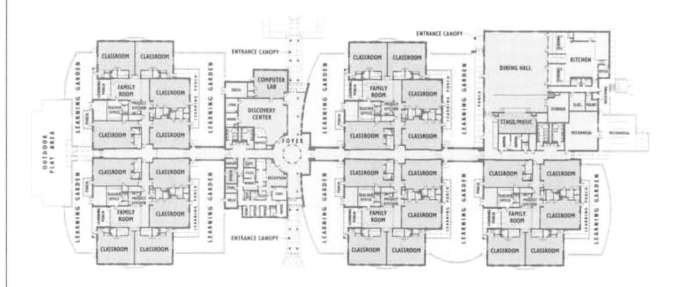

DALE AND ASSOCIATES ARCHITECTS, P.A.
120 North Congress Street, #110
Jackson, MS 39201
www.dalearch.com

CONSTRUCTION TEAM

GENERAL CONTRACTOR: Harrell Construction Group, LLC
368 Highland Colony Parkway, Ridgeland, MS 39157

STRUCTURAL ENGINEER:
Structural Design Group
220 Great Circle Road, #106, Nashville, TN 37228

CIVIL ENGINEER: CivilTech, Inc.
5430 Executive Place, #2B, Jackson, MS 39206

ELECTRICAL ENGINEER:
Andy Covington Engineering, PLLC
7 Lakeland Circle, Jackson, MS 39216

MECHANICAL ENGINEER: Gordin McCool, P.E.
P.O. Box 16488, Jackson, MS 39236

FOOD SERVICE CONSULTANT:
Fisher and Associates
1685 Galloway Avenue, Memphis, TN 38112

GENERAL DESCRIPTION

SITE: 14 acres.

NUMBER OF BUILDINGS: One; elementary school, 25 classrooms seating capacity of 30 each; auditorium seating 625.

BUILDING SIZES: First floor, 69,700; total, 69,700 total square feet.

BUILDING HEIGHT: Classrooms, 16'; dining hall, 20'.

BASIC CONSTRUCTION TYPE: NEW.

FOUNDATION: Concrete.

EXTERIOR WALLS: Masonry.

ROOF: Built-up, metal.

FLOORS: Carpet, VCT, tile.

INTERIOR WALLS: CMU, gypsum.

MCWILLIE ELEMENTARY SCHOOL

Date Bid: June 2001 • Construction Period: July 2001 to Jan 2003 • Total Square Feet: 69,700

C.S.I. Divisions (1 through 16)	COST	% OF COST	SQ.FT. COST	SPECIFICATIONS
BIDDING REQUIREMENTS	—	—	—	
1. GENERAL REQUIREMENTS	759,082	10.79	10.89	1 Allowances, measurement & payment, coordination, regulatory requirements, quality control, construction facilities & temporary controls, contract closeout, maintenance.
3. CONCRETE	661,500	9.40	9.49	3 Formwork, reinforcement, accessories, cast-in-place, cementitious decks & toppings, grout.
4. MASONRY	1,041,400	14.80	14.94	4 Masonry & grout, accessories, unit.
5. METALS	665,046	9.45	9.54	5 Materials, structural framing, joists, decking, fabrications, expansion control.
6. WOOD & PLASTICS	270,010	3.84	3.87	6 Rough carpentry, finish carpentry, architectural woodwork.
7. THERMAL & MOIST. PROTECT	469,768	6.68	6.74	7 Waterproofing, dampproofing, vapor retarders, firestopping, manufactured roofing & siding, membrane roofing, flashing & sheet metal, joint sealers.
8. DOORS & WINDOWS	264,624	3.76	3.80	8 Metal doors & frames, wood & plastic doors, entrances & storefronts, metal windows, hardware, glazing.
9. FINISHES	481,756	6.85	6.91	9 Metal support systems, gypsum, tile, acoustical treatment, special wall surfaces, unit masonry flooring, carpet, painting, wall coverings.
10. SPECIALTIES	76,545	1.09	1.10	10 Visual display board, louvers & vents, wall & corner guards, flagpoles, identifying devices, operable partitions, toilet & bath accessories.
11. EQUIPMENT	335,375	4.77	4.81	11 Theatre & stage, audio-visual, loading dock, food service.
12. FURNISHING	11,200	0.16	0.16	12 Window treatment, rugs & mats.
13. SPECIAL CONSTRUCTIONS	—	—	—	13 —
14. CONVEYING SYSTEMS	—	—	—	14 —
15. MECHANICAL	1,340,000	19.04	19.23	15 Basic materials & methods, insulation, fire protection, plumbing, HVAC, air distribution, controls, testing, adjusting & balancing.
16. ELECTRICAL	660,000	9.37	9.47	16 Basic materials & methods, medium voltage distribution, service & distribution, lighting, controls, testing.
TOTAL BUILDING COST	**7,036,306**	**100%**	**$100.95**	
2. SITE WORK	680,052			2 Demolition, preparation, shoring & underpinning, excavation support systems, earthwork, piles & caissons, paving & surfacing, utility piping materials, water distribution, sewerage & drainage, power & communications, improvements, landscaping.
LANDSCAPING & OFFSITE WORK	—			Included in Site Work.
TOTAL PROJECT COST	**7,716,358**		*(Excluding architectural and engineering fees)*	

Part IV

School Construction Costs

During the planning and design process, when early budgeting is taking place, current cost data is needed to arrive at rough costs for the school project's planned (and potential) new buildings, additions, or systems. The case studies in Part III provide a glimpse into such costs in recently completed projects. Part IV provides "generic" building models with square foot costs for elementary, junior high, and high schools. Cost models are also included for free-standing school buildings, such as athletic facilities, auditoriums, and libraries. These national-average costs have been compiled by RSMeans. They can be adjusted to over 900 specific locations in the United States and Canada, using the Location Factors provided at the end of this section.

School Construction Costs

T his section consists of square foot cost data for school facilities, including related building types that may be found on a school campus. These costs are derived from a larger set of building models, which are updated and published annually as *Means Square Foot Costs*. The data represent national-average, probable costs for the various building types. The estimates, developed by RSMeans' engineering staff, assume typical construction methods and average-quality materials. The building models are designed to be used for budgeting purposes during the early phases of a project, when the project design is not yet complete. Actual costs for any project will vary depending on the final design and product selection. *(For a discussion of square foot cost estimating applications and the range of accuracy to be anticipated using square foot modeling techniques, see Chapter 6.)*

Overview

Each cost model includes a table of square foot costs for combinations of exterior wall and framing systems. This table is supplemented by a list of common additives and their unit costs. A breakdown of the component costs used to develop the base cost for each model can be found on its opposite page. These cost models may be used directly to estimate the construction cost of most types of buildings, provided the floor area, exterior wall construction, and framing (or structural) systems are known.

The costs derived from the models in this book are effective as of January 1, 2004. An escalation factor should be added to these model costs to adjust them from January 1, 2004 to the midpoint of the anticipated construction period. (RSMeans annual cost publications include Historical Cost Indexes with such factors. *Engineering News Record* magazine also publishes escalation rates for specific cities.) Since the model costs represent national averages, they must also be adjusted for project location. This can be done by multiplying total project cost by the factor designated for a particular location in the *Location Factor section* that follows the cost models. The next several pages explain in more detail how to use the models.

Building Identification and Model Selection

The building models in this section are classified according to their use, or *occupancy*. Occupancy, however, does not always best identify the type of building construction. In all instances, the building should be described and identified by its own physical characteristics. Models should be selected by comparing them to whatever specifications are available for the project at the time the budget estimate is being developed. If a building cost model is selected because it best matches the desired building size and type of construction, even though the model is identified for a different use (or occupancy), it will likely require some modifications to suit its actual, intended use. In such cases, data from one model may be used to supplement data from another.

Adjustments

The base cost tables represent the base cost per square foot of floor area for buildings without a basement and without unusual or special features. Basement costs and other common additives are listed below each base cost table.

Dimensions

Areas are calculated from exterior dimensions ("out-to-out"), and story heights are measured from the top surface of one floor to the top surface of the floor above (from the top of one sub-floor to the top of the next sub-floor above). Roof areas are measured by horizontal area covered, and costs related to inclines are converted with appropriate factors. The precision of measurement is a matter of the user's choice and discretion. *(See Chapter 6, "Calculating Area for Square Foot Estimates," for more on how different spaces within a proposed building are classified for estimating purposes.)*

Floor Area

The expression "floor area," as used in this section, includes the sum of the floor plate at grade level and above. This dimension is measured from the outside face of the foundation wall. Basement costs are calculated separately. The user must exercise judgment when the lowest level floor is slightly below grade and decide whether to consider it a grade level or make the basement adjustment. Basement costs shown in the models are for "unfinished" space.

Table
of Contents

The following is a list of the school model building types and related free-standing buildings, as well as the other elements in the cost section.

How to Use the Square Foot Cost Models

The following is a detailed explanation of a sample entry in the Square Foot Cost Section. Each bold number below corresponds to the item being described on the following page with the appropriate component or cost of the sample entry following in parentheses.

Prices listed include overhead and profit of the installing contractor and additional mark-ups for General Conditions and Architects' Fees.

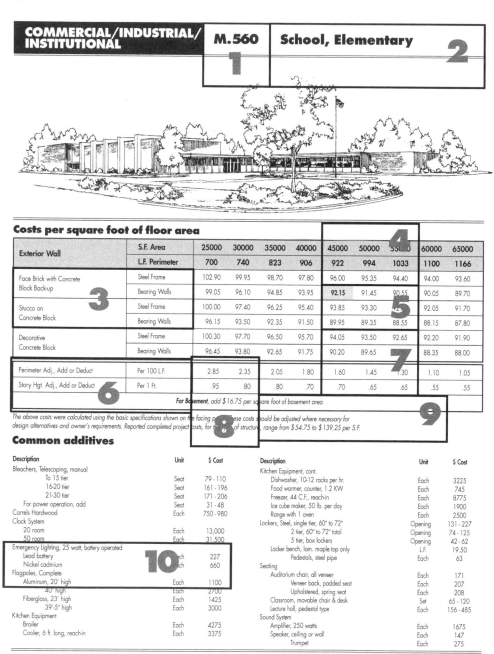

COMMERCIAL/INDUSTRIAL/INSTITUTIONAL	M.560	School, Elementary

Costs per square foot of floor area

Exterior Wall	S.F. Area	25000	30000	35000	40000	45000	50000	55000	60000	65000
	L.F. Perimeter	700	740	823	906	922	994	1033	1100	1166
Face Brick with Concrete Block Back-up	Steel Frame	102.90	99.95	98.70	97.80	96.00	95.35	94.40	94.00	93.60
	Bearing Walls	99.05	96.10	94.85	93.95	92.15	91.45	90.55	90.05	89.70
Stucco on Concrete Block	Steel Frame	100.00	97.40	96.25	95.40	93.85	93.30	92.75	92.05	91.70
	Bearing Walls	96.15	93.50	92.35	91.50	89.95	89.35	88.55	88.15	87.80
Decorative Concrete Block	Steel Frame	100.30	97.70	96.50	95.70	94.05	93.50	92.65	92.20	91.90
	Bearing Walls	96.45	93.80	92.65	91.75	90.20	89.65	88.55	88.35	88.00
Perimeter Adj., Add or Deduct	Per 100 L.F.	2.85	2.35	2.05	1.80	1.60	1.45	1.30	1.10	1.05
Story Hgt. Adj., Add or Deduct	Per 1 Ft.	.95	.80	.80	.70	.70	.65	.65	.55	.55
	For Basement, add $16.75 per square foot of basement area									

The above costs were calculated using the basic specifications shown on the facing page. These costs should be adjusted where necessary for design alternatives and owner's requirements. Reported completed project costs, for this type of structure, range from $54.75 to $139.25 per S.F.

Common additives

Description	Unit	$ Cost
Bleachers, Telescoping, manual		
To 15 tier	Seat	79 - 110
16-20 tier	Seat	161 - 196
21-30 tier	Seat	171 - 206
For power operation, add	Seat	31 - 48
Carrels Hardwood	Each	750 - 980
Clock System		
20 room	Each	13,000
50 room	Each	31,500
Emergency Lighting, 25 watt, battery operated		
Lead battery	Each	227
Nickel cadmium	Each	660
Flagpoles, Complete		
Aluminum, 20' high	Each	1100
40' high	Each	2700
Fiberglass, 23' high	Each	1425
39'-5" high	Each	3000
Kitchen Equipment		
Broiler	Each	4275
Cooler, 6 ft. long, reach-in	Each	3375

Description	Unit	$ Cost
Kitchen Equipment, cont.		
Dishwasher, 10-12 racks per hr.	Each	3225
Food warmer, counter, 1.2 KW	Each	745
Freezer, 44 C.F., reach-in	Each	8775
Ice cube maker, 50 lb. per day	Each	1900
Range with 1 oven	Each	2500
Lockers, Steel, single tier, 60" to 72"	Opening	131 - 227
2 tier, 60" to 72" total	Opening	74 - 125
5 tier, box lockers	Opening	42 - 62
Locker bench, lam. maple top only	L.F.	19.50
Pedestals, steel pipe	Each	63
Seating		
Auditorium chair, all veneer	Each	171
Veneer back, padded seat	Each	207
Upholstered, spring seat	Each	208
Classroom, movable chair & desk	Set	65 - 120
Lecture hall, pedestal type	Each	156 - 485
Sound System		
Amplifier, 250 watts	Each	1675
Speaker, ceiling or wall	Each	147
Trumpet	Each	275

1 **Model Number (M.560)**

"M" distinguishes this section of the book and stands for model. The number designation is a sequential number.

2 **Type of Building (School, Elementary)**

There are 12 different buildings highlighted in this section.

3 **Exterior Wall Construction and Building Framing Options (Face Brick with Concrete Block Back-up and Bearing Walls)**

Three or more commonly used exterior walls, and in most cases, two typical building framing systems are presented for each type of building. The model selected should be based on the actual characteristics of the building being estimated.

4 **Total Square Foot of Floor Area and Base Perimeter Used to Compute Base Costs (45,000 Square Feet and 922 Linear Feet)**

Square foot of floor area is the total gross area of all floors at grade, and above, and does not include a basement. The perimeter in linear feet used for the base cost is for a generally rectangular economical building shape.

5 **Cost per Square Foot of Floor Area ($92.15)**

The highlighted cost is for a building of the selected exterior wall and framing system and floor area. Costs for buildings with floor areas other than those calculated may be interpolated between the costs shown.

6 **Building Perimeter and Story Height Adjustments**

Square foot costs for a building with a perimeter or floor to floor story height significantly different from the model used to calculate the base cost may be adjusted, add or deduct, to reflect the actual building geometry.

7 **Cost per Square Foot of Floor Area for the Perimeter and/or Height Adjustment ($1.60 for Perimeter Difference and $.70 for Story Height Difference)**

Add (or deduct) $1.60 to the base square foot cost for each 100 feet of perimeter difference between the model and the actual building. Add (or deduct) $.70 to the base square foot cost for each 1 foot of story height difference between the model and the actual building.

8 **Optional Cost per Square Foot of Basement Floor Area ($16.75)**

The cost of an unfinished basement for the building being estimated is $16.75 times the gross floor area of the basement.

9 **Range of Cost per Square Foot of Floor Area for Similar Buildings ($54.75 to $139.25)**

Many different buildings of the same type have been built using similar materials and systems. Means historical cost data of actual construction projects indicates a range of $54.75 to $139.25 for this type of building.

10 **Common Additives**

Common components and/or systems used in this type of building are listed. These costs should be added to the total building cost.

How to Use the Square Foot Cost Models *(Continued)*

The following is a detailed explanation of a specification and costs for a model building in the Square Foot Cost Section. Each bold number below corresponds to the item being described on the following page with the appropriate component of the sample entry following in parentheses.

Prices listed include overhead and profit of the installing contractor.

Model costs calculated for a 1 story building with 12' story height and 45,000 square feet of floor area **1**

2

School, Elementary

				Unit	Unit Cost	Cost Per S.F.	% Of Sub-Total
A. SUBSTRUCTURE							
1010	Standard Foundations	Poured concrete; strip and spread footings		S.F. Ground	2.13	2.13	
1030	Slab on Grade	4" reinforced concrete with vapor barrier and granular base		S.F. Slab	3.65	3.65	11.5%
2010	Basement Excavation	Site preparation for slab and trench for foundation wall and footing		S.F. Ground	.14	.14	
2020	Basement Walls	4' foundation wall		L.F. Wall	57	2.00	
B. SHELL							
	B10 Superstructure						
1010	Floor Construction	N/A		—	—	—	3.5%
1020	Roof Construction	Metal deck on open web steel joists		S.F. Roof	2.41	2.41	
	B20 Exterior Enclosure						
2010	Exterior Walls	Face brick with concrete block backup	70% of wall	S.F. Wall	22	3.92	
2020	Exterior Windows	Steel outward projecting	25% of wall	Each	540	1.73	8.8%
2030	Exterior Doors	Metal and glass	5% of wall	Each	2334	.42	
	B30 Roofing						
3010	Roof Coverings	Built-up tar and gravel with flashing; perlite/EPS composite insulation		S.F. Roof	3.76	3.76	5.5%
3020	Roof Openings	N/A		—	—	—	
C. INTERIORS							**6**
1010	Partitions	Concrete block	20 S.F. Floor/L.F. Partition	S.F. Partition	6.98	3.49	
1020	Interior Doors **3**	Single leaf kalamein fire doors **4**	700 S.F. Floor/Door	Each	572	.82	
1030	Fittings	Toilet partitions		S.F. Floor	1.65		
2010	Stair Construction	N/A		—	—	—	26.0%
3010	Wall Finishes **5**	75% paint, 15% glazed coating, 10% ceramic tile		S.F. Surface			**8**
3020	Floor Finishes	65% vinyl composition tile, 25% carpet, 10% terrazzo		S.F. Floor		3.45	
3030	Ceiling Finishes	Mineral fiber tile on concealed zee bars **7**		S.F. Ceiling		3.52	**9**
D. SERVICES							
	D10 Conveying						
1010	Elevators & Lifts	N/A		—	—	—	0.0%
1020	Escalators & Moving Walks	N/A		—	—	—	
	D20 Plumbing						
2010	Plumbing Fixtures	Kitchen, bathroom and service fixtures, supply and drainage	1 Fixture/625 S.F. Floor	Each	2287	3.66	
2020	Domestic Water Distribution	Gas fired water heater		S.F. Floor	.33	.33	6.3%
2040	Rain Water Drainage	Roof drains		S.F. Roof	.33	.33	
	D30 HVAC						
3010	Energy Supply	Oil fired hot water, wall fin radiation		S.F. Floor	6.43	6.43	
3020	Heat Generating Systems	N/A		—	—	—	
3030	Cooling Generating Systems	N/A		—	—	—	21.5%
3050	Terminal & Package Units	Split systems with air cooled condensing units		S.F. Floor	8.35	8.35	
3090	Other HVAC Sys. & Equipment			—	—	—	
	D40 Fire Protection						
4010	Sprinklers	Sprinklers, light hazard		S.F. Floor	1.67	1.67	2.4%
4020	Standpipes	N/A		—	—	—	
	D50 Electrical						
5010	Electrical Service/Distribution	800 ampere service, panel board and feeders		S.F. Floor	.91	.91	
5020	Lighting & Branch Wiring	Fluorescent fixtures, receptacles, switches, A.C. and misc. power		S.F. Floor	7.65	7.65	14.4%
5030	Communications & Security	Alarm systems, communications systems and emergency lighting		S.F. Floor	1.29	1.29	
5090	Other Electrical Systems	Emergency generator, 15 kW		S.F. Floor	.07	.07	
E. EQUIPMENT & FURNISHINGS							
1010	Commercial Equipment	N/A		—	—	—	
1020	Institutional Equipment	Chalkboards		S.F. Floor	.10	.10	0.1%
1030	Vehicular Equipment	N/A		—	—	—	
1090	Other Equipment	N/A		—	—	—	
F. SPECIAL CONSTRUCTION							
1020	Integrated Construction	N/A		—			0.0%
1040	Special Facilities	N/A		—	**10**		
G. BUILDING SITEWORK	**N/A**						
				Sub-Total		68.88	100%
	CONTRACTOR FEES (General Requirements: 10%, Overhead: 5%, Profit: 10%) **11**		**12**		25%	17.24	
	ARCHITECT FEES				7%	6.03	
				Total Building Cost		**92.15**	

1
**Building Description
(Model costs are calculated for a one-story elementary school with 12' story height and 45,000 square feet of floor area)**

The model highlighted is described in terms of building type, number of stories, typical story height and square footage.

2
**Type of Building
(School, Elementary)**

3
**Division C Interiors
(C1020 Interior Doors)**

System costs are presented in divisions according to the 7-division UNIFORMAT II classifications. Each of the component systems is listed.

4
**Specification Highlights
(Single leaf kalamein fire doors)**

All systems in each subdivision are described with the material and proportions used.

5
**Quality Criteria
(700 S.F. Floor/Door)**

The criteria used to determine quantities for the calculations.

6
Unit (Each)

The unit of measure of the particular system that corresponds to the unit cost.

7
Unit Cost ($572)

The cost per unit of measure of the selected system or item, in this case, one installed single-leaf kalamein fire door.

8
Cost per Square Foot ($.82)

The cost per square foot for each system is the unit cost of the system times the total number of units, divided by the total square feet of building area. In this case, the door represents $.82 of the total $92.15 per square foot cost for this building model.

9
% of Sub-Total (26.0%)

The percent of sub-total is the total cost per square foot of all systems in the division divided by the sub-total cost per square foot of the building. In this case, the door is part of Interior Systems, which together represent 26% of the total building cost.

10
Sub-Total ($68.88)

The sub-total is the total of all the system costs per square foot.

11
**Project Fees
(Contractor Fees 25%)
(Architect Fees 7%)**

Contractor Fees to cover the general requirements, overhead and profit of the General Contractor are added as a percentage of the sub-total. Architect Fees, also as a percentage of the sub-total, are also added. These values vary with the building type.

12
Total Building Cost ($92.15)

The total building cost per square foot of building area is the sum of the square foot costs of all the systems plus the General Contractor's general requirements, overhead and profit, and the Architect fees. The total building cost is the amount which appears shaded in the Cost per Square Foot of Floor Area table shown previously.

Costs per square foot of floor area

Exterior Wall	S.F. Area	25000	30000	35000	40000	45000	50000	55000	60000	65000
	L.F. Perimeter	700	740	823	906	922	994	1033	1100	1166
Face Brick with Concrete Block Back-up	Steel Frame	102.90	99.95	98.70	97.80	96.00	95.35	94.40	94.00	93.60
	Bearing Walls	99.05	96.10	94.85	93.95	92.15	91.45	90.55	90.05	89.70
Stucco on Concrete Block	Steel Frame	100.00	97.40	96.25	95.40	93.85	93.30	92.40	92.05	91.70
	Bearing Walls	96.15	93.50	92.35	91.50	89.95	89.35	88.55	88.15	87.80
Decorative Concrete Block	Steel Frame	100.30	97.70	96.50	95.70	94.05	93.50	92.65	92.20	91.90
	Bearing Walls	96.45	93.80	92.65	91.75	90.20	89.65	88.75	88.35	88.00
Perimeter Adj., Add or Deduct	Per 100 L.F.	2.85	2.35	2.05	1.80	1.60	1.45	1.30	1.10	1.05
Story Hgt. Adj., Add or Deduct	Per 1 Ft.	.95	.80	.80	.70	.70	.65	.65	.55	.55
For Basement, add $16.75 per square foot of basement area										

The above costs were calculated using the basic specifications shown on the facing page. These costs should be adjusted where necessary for design alternatives and owner's requirements. Reported completed project costs, for this type of structure, range from $54.75 to $139.25 per S.F.

Common additives

Description	Unit	$ Cost	Description	Unit	$ Cost
Bleachers, Telescoping, manual			Kitchen Equipment, cont.		
To 15 tier	Seat	79 - 110	Dishwasher, 10-12 racks per hr.	Each	3225
16-20 tier	Seat	161 - 196	Food warmer, counter, 1.2 KW	Each	745
21-30 tier	Seat	171 - 206	Freezer, 44 C.F., reach-in	Each	8775
For power operation, add	Seat	31 - 48	Ice cube maker, 50 lb. per day	Each	1900
Carrels Hardwood	Each	750 - 980	Range with 1 oven	Each	2500
Clock System			Lockers, Steel, single tier, 60" to 72"	Opening	131 - 227
20 room	Each	13,000	2 tier, 60" to 72" total	Opening	74 - 125
50 room	Each	31,500	5 tier, box lockers	Opening	42 - 62
Emergency Lighting, 25 watt, battery operated			Locker bench, lam. maple top only	L.F.	19.50
Lead battery	Each	227	Pedestals, steel pipe	Each	63
Nickel cadmium	Each	660	Seating		
Flagpoles, Complete			Auditorium chair, all veneer	Each	171
Aluminum, 20' high	Each	1100	Veneer back, padded seat	Each	207
40' high	Each	2700	Upholstered, spring seat	Each	208
Fiberglass, 23' high	Each	1425	Classroom, movable chair & desk	Set	65 - 120
39'-5" high	Each	3000	Lecture hall, pedestal type	Each	156 - 485
Kitchen Equipment			Sound System		
Broiler	Each	4275	Amplifier, 250 watts	Each	1675
Cooler, 6 ft. long, reach-in	Each	3375	Speaker, ceiling or wall	Each	147
			Trumpet	Each	275

Model costs calculated for a 1 story building with 12' story height and 45,000 square feet of floor area

School, Elementary

				Unit	Unit Cost	Cost Per S.F.	% Of Sub-Total
A.	**SUBSTRUCTURE**						
1010	Standard Foundations	Poured concrete; strip and spread footings		S.F. Ground	2.13	2.13	
1030	Slab on Grade	4" reinforced concrete with vapor barrier and granular base		S.F. Slab	3.65	3.65	11.5%
2010	Basement Excavation	Site preparation for slab and trench for foundation wall and footing		S.F. Ground	.14	.14	
2020	Basement Walls	4' foundation wall		L.F. Wall	57	2.00	
B.	**SHELL**						
	B10 Superstructure						
1010	Floor Construction	N/A		—	—	—	3.5%
1020	Roof Construction	Metal deck on open web steel joists		S.F. Roof	2.41	2.41	
	B20 Exterior Enclosure						
2010	Exterior Walls	Face brick with concrete block backup	70% of wall	S.F. Wall	22	3.92	
2020	Exterior Windows	Steel outward projecting	25% of wall	Each	540	1.73	8.8%
2030	Exterior Doors	Metal and glass	5% of wall	Each	2334	.42	
	B30 Roofing						
3010	Roof Coverings	Built-up tar and gravel with flashing; perlite/EPS composite insulation		S.F. Roof	3.76	3.76	5.5%
3020	Roof Openings	N/A		—	—	—	
C.	**INTERIORS**						
1010	Partitions	Concrete block	20 S.F. Floor/L.F. Partition	S.F. Partition	6.98	3.49	
1020	Interior Doors	Single leaf kalamein fire doors	700 S.F. Floor/Door	Each	572	.82	
1030	Fittings	Toilet partitions		S.F. Floor	1.65	1.65	
2010	Stair Construction	N/A		—	—	—	26.0%
3010	Wall Finishes	75% paint, 15% glazed coating, 10% ceramic tile		S.F. Surface	6.00	3.00	
3020	Floor Finishes	65% vinyl composition tile, 25% carpet, 10% terrazzo		S.F. Floor	5.45	5.45	
3030	Ceiling Finishes	Mineral fiber tile on concealed zee bars		S.F. Ceiling	4.00	3.52	
D.	**SERVICES**						
	D10 Conveying						
1010	Elevators & Lifts	N/A		—	—	—	0.0%
1020	Escalators & Moving Walks	N/A		—	—	—	
	D20 Plumbing						
2010	Plumbing Fixtures	Kitchen, bathroom and service fixtures, supply and drainage	1 Fixture/625 S.F. Floor	Each	2287	3.66	
2020	Domestic Water Distribution	Gas fired water heater		S.F. Floor	.33	.33	6.3%
2040	Rain Water Drainage	Roof drains		S.F. Roof	.33	.33	
	D30 HVAC						
3010	Energy Supply	Oil fired hot water, wall fin radiation		S.F. Floor	6.43	6.43	
3020	Heat Generating Systems	N/A		—	—	—	
3030	Cooling Generating Systems	N/A		—	—	—	21.5%
3050	Terminal & Package Units	Split systems with air cooled condensing units		S.F. Floor	8.35	8.35	
3090	Other HVAC Sys. & Equipment	N/A		—	—	—	
	D40 Fire Protection						
4010	Sprinklers	Sprinklers, light hazard		S.F. Floor	1.67	1.67	2.4%
4020	Standpipes	N/A		—	—	—	
	D50 Electrical						
5010	Electrical Service/Distribution	800 ampere service, panel board and feeders		S.F. Floor	.91	.91	
5020	Lighting & Branch Wiring	Fluorescent fixtures, receptacles, switches, A.C. and misc. power		S.F. Floor	7.65	7.65	14.4%
5030	Communications & Security	Alarm systems, communications systems and emergency lighting		S.F. Floor	1.29	1.29	
5090	Other Electrical Systems	Emergency generator, 15 kW		S.F. Floor	.07	.07	
E.	**EQUIPMENT & FURNISHINGS**						
1010	Commercial Equipment	N/A		—	—	—	
1020	Institutional Equipment	Chalkboards		S.F. Floor	.10	.10	0.1%
1030	Vehicular Equipment	N/A		—	—	—	
1090	Other Equipment	N/A		—	—	—	
F.	**SPECIAL CONSTRUCTION**						
1020	Integrated Construction	N/A		—	—	—	0.0%
1040	Special Facilities	N/A		—	—	—	
G.	**BUILDING SITEWORK**	**N/A**					

		Sub-Total	68.88	100%
CONTRACTOR FEES (General Requirements: 10%, Overhead: 5%, Profit: 10%)		25%	17.24	
ARCHITECT FEES		7%	6.03	
	Total Building Cost		**92.15**	

Costs per square foot of floor area

Exterior Wall	S.F. Area	50000	65000	80000	95000	110000	125000	140000	155000	170000
	L.F. Perimeter	816	1016	1000	1150	1250	1400	1450	1500	1600
Face Brick with Concrete Block Back-up	Steel Frame	105.50	104.35	100.80	100.30	99.35	99.10	98.15	97.40	97.05
	Bearing Walls	101.40	100.25	96.70	96.15	95.25	95.00	94.00	93.30	92.95
Concrete Block Stucco Face	Steel Frame	101.60	100.65	97.85	97.40	96.65	96.40	95.65	95.10	94.85
	Bearing Walls	97.50	96.55	93.75	93.25	92.55	92.30	91.60	90.95	90.70
Decorative Concrete Block	Steel Frame	102.10	101.15	98.20	97.75	96.95	96.70	95.95	95.35	95.05
	Bearing Walls	97.50	96.55	93.60	93.15	92.30	92.15	91.35	90.75	90.50
Perimeter Adj., Add or Deduct	Per 100 L.F.	2.10	1.65	1.35	1.05	1.00	.85	.75	.65	.65
Story Hgt. Adj., Add or Deduct	Per 1 Ft.	1.20	1.20	.95	.90	.85	.80	.75	.70	.70

For Basement, add $22.85 per square foot of basement area

The above costs were calculated using the basic specifications shown on the facing page. These costs should be adjusted where necessary for design alternatives and owner's requirements. Reported completed project costs, for this type of structure, range from $60.10 to $141.10 per S.F.

Common additives

Description	Unit	$ Cost
Bleachers, Telescoping, manual		
To 15 tier	Seat	79 - 110
16-20 tier	Seat	161 - 196
21-30 tier	Seat	171 - 206
For power operation, add	Seat	31 - 48
Carrels Hardwood	Each	750 - 980
Clock System		
20 room	Each	13,000
50 room	Each	31,500
Elevators, Hydraulic passenger, 2 stops		
1500# capacity	Each	43,425
2500# capacity	Each	44,625
Emergency Lighting, 25 watt, battery operated		
Lead battery	Each	227
Nickel cadmium	Each	660
Flagpoles, Complete		
Aluminum, 20' high	Each	1100
40' high	Each	2700
Fiberglass, 23' high	Each	1425
39'-5" high	Each	3000

Description	Unit	$ Cost
Kitchen Equipment		
Broiler	Each	4275
Cooler, 6 ft. long, reach-in	Each	3375
Dishwasher, 10-12 racks per hr.	Each	3225
Food warmer, counter, 1.2 KW	Each	745
Freezer, 44 C.F., reach-in	Each	8775
Lockers, Steel, single tier, 60" to 72"	Opening	131 - 227
2 tier, 60" to 72" total	Opening	74 - 125
5 tier, box lockers	Opening	42 - 62
Locker bench, lam. maple top only	L.F.	19.50
Pedestals, steel pipe	Each	63
Seating		
Auditorium chair, all veneer	Each	171
Veneer back, padded seat	Each	207
Upholstered, spring seat	Each	208
Classroom, movable chair & desk	Set	65 - 120
Lecture hall, pedestal type	Each	156 - 485
Sound System		
Amplifier, 250 watts	Each	1675
Speaker, ceiling or wall	Each	147
Trumpet	Each	275

Model costs calculated for a 2 story building with 12' story height and 110,000 square feet of floor area

School, Jr High, 2-3 Story

				Unit	Unit Cost	Cost Per S.F.	% Of Sub-Total
A. SUBSTRUCTURE							
1010	Standard Foundations	Poured concrete; strip and spread footings		S.F. Ground	1.46	.73	
1030	Slab on Grade	4" reinforced concrete with vapor barrier and granular base		S.F. Slab	3.65	1.83	4.4%
2010	Basement Excavation	Site preparation for slab and trench for foundation wall and footing		S.F. Ground	.14	.07	
2020	Basement Walls	4' foundation wall		L.F. Wall	57	.65	
B. SHELL							
	B10 Superstructure						
1010	Floor Construction	Open web steel joists, slab form, concrete, columns		S.F. Floor	16.58	8.29	15.5%
1020	Roof Construction	Metal deck, open web steel joists, columns		S.F. Roof	6.44	3.22	
	B20 Exterior Enclosure						
2010	Exterior Walls	Face brick with concrete block backup	75% of wall	S.F. Wall	22	4.66	
2020	Exterior Windows	Window wall	25% of wall	Each	36	2.47	10.1%
2030	Exterior Doors	Double aluminum & glass		Each	1512	.39	
	B30 Roofing						
3010	Roof Coverings	Built-up tar and gravel with flashing; perlite/EPS composite insulation		S.F. Roof	3.82	1.91	2.6%
3020	Roof Openings	Roof hatches		S.F. Roof	.02	.01	
C. INTERIORS							
1010	Partitions	Concrete block	20 S.F. Floor/L.F. Partition	S.F. Partition	6.52	3.26	
1020	Interior Doors	Single leaf kalamein fire doors	750 S.F. Floor/Door	Each	572	.77	
1030	Fittings	Toilet partitions, chalkboards		S.F. Floor	1.24	1.24	
2010	Stair Construction	Concrete filled metal pan		Flight	5375	.29	26.0%
3010	Wall Finishes	50% paint, 40% glazed coatings, 10% ceramic tile		S.F. Surface	5.86	2.93	
3020	Floor Finishes	50% vinyl composition tile, 30% carpet, 20% terrrazzo		S.F. Floor	7.29	7.29	
3030	Ceiling Finishes	Mineral fiberboard on concealed zee bars		S.F. Ceiling	4.00	3.52	
D. SERVICES							
	D10 Conveying						
1010	Elevators & Lifts	One hydraulic passenger elevator		Each	56,100	.51	0.7%
1020	Escalators & Moving Walks	N/A		—	—	—	
	D20 Plumbing						
2010	Plumbing Fixtures	Kitchen, toilet and service fixtures, supply and drainage	1 Fixture/1170 S.F. Floor	Each	2585	2.21	
2020	Domestic Water Distribution	Gas fired water heater		S.F. Floor	.33	.33	3.8%
2040	Rain Water Drainage	Roof drains		S.F. Roof	.54	.27	
	D30 HVAC						
3010	Energy Supply	N/A		—	—	—	
3020	Heat Generating Systems	Included in D3050		—	—	—	
3030	Cooling Generating Systems	N/A		—	—	—	20.9%
3050	Terminal & Package Units	Multizone unit, gas heating, electric cooling		S.F. Floor	15.50	15.50	
3090	Other HVAC Sys. & Equipment	N/A		—	—	—	
	D40 Fire Protection						
4010	Sprinklers	Sprinklers, light hazard	10% of area	S.F. Floor	.29	.29	0.4%
4020	Standpipes	N/A		—	—	—	
	D50 Electrical						
5010	Electrical Service/Distribution	1600 ampere service, panel board and feeders		S.F. Floor	.88	.88	
5020	Lighting & Branch Wiring	Fluorescent fixtures, receptacles, switches, A.C. and misc. power		S.F. Floor	7.68	7.68	15.6%
5030	Communications & Security	Alarm systems, communications systems and emergency lighting		S.F. Floor	2.67	2.67	
5090	Other Electrical Systems	Emergency generator, 100 kW		S.F. Floor	.33	.33	
E. EQUIPMENT & FURNISHINGS							
1010	Commercial Equipment	N/A		—	—	—	
1020	Institutional Equipment	Laboratory counters		S.F. Floor	.08	.08	0.1%
1030	Vehicular Equipment	N/A		—	—	—	
1090	Other Equipment	N/A		—	—	—	
F. SPECIAL CONSTRUCTION							
1020	Integrated Construction	N/A		—	—	—	0.0%
1040	Special Facilities	N/A		—	—	—	
G. BUILDING SITEWORK	N/A						

			Sub-Total	74.28	100%
CONTRACTOR FEES (General Requirements: 10%, Overhead: 5%, Profit: 10%)		25%	18.57		
ARCHITECT FEES		7%	6.50		
	Total Building Cost		**99.35**		

Costs per square foot of floor area

Exterior Wall	S.F. Area	50000	70000	90000	110000	130000	150000	170000	190000	210000
	L.F. Perimeter	816	1083	1100	1300	1290	1450	1433	1566	1700
Face Brick with Concrete Block Back-up	Steel Frame	105.50	102.55	97.70	96.50	93.80	93.15	91.50	91.00	90.65
	R/Conc. Frame	109.85	107.10	102.45	101.35	98.70	98.10	96.50	96.05	95.75
Decorative Concrete Block	Steel Frame	101.30	98.75	94.70	93.70	91.40	90.85	89.55	89.10	88.85
	R/Conc. Frame	106.65	104.10	100.00	99.00	96.80	96.25	94.90	94.45	94.15
Limestone with Concrete Block Back-up	Steel Frame	109.60	106.60	100.90	99.70	96.45	95.80	93.80	93.25	92.95
	R/Conc. Frame	115.50	112.55	106.85	105.60	102.40	101.70	99.70	99.20	98.85
Perimeter Adj., Add or Deduct	Per 100 L.F.	2.25	1.60	1.25	1.05	.85	.75	.65	.60	.60
Story Hgt. Adj., Add or Deduct	Per 1 Ft.	1.30	1.30	1.00	1.00	.80	.80	.70	.75	.65
For Basement, add $21.90 per square foot of basement area										

The above costs were calculated using the basic specifications shown on the facing page. These costs should be adjusted where necessary for design alternatives and owner's requirements. Reported completed project costs, for this type of structure, range from $63.65 to $149.85 per S.F.

Common additives

Description	Unit	$ Cost	Description	Unit	$ Cost
Bleachers, Telescoping, manual			Kitchen Equipment		
To 15 tier	Seat	79 - 110	Broiler	Each	4275
16-20 tier	Seat	161 - 196	Cooler, 6 ft. long, reach-in	Each	3375
21-30 tier	Seat	171 - 206	Dishwasher, 10-12 racks per hr.	Each	3225
For power operation, add	Seat	31 - 48	Food warmer, counter, 1.2 KW	Each	745
Carrels Hardwood	Each	750 - 980	Freezer, 44 C.F., reach-in	Each	8775
Clock System			Lockers, Steel, single tier, 60" or 72"	Opening	131 - 227
20 room	Each	13,000	2 tier, 60" or 72" total	Opening	74 - 125
50 room	Each	31,500	5 tier, box lockers	Opening	42 - 62
Elevators, Hydraulic passenger, 2 stops			Locker bench, lam. maple top only	L.F.	19.50
1500# capacity	Each	43,425	Pedestals, steel pipe	Each	63
2500# capacity	Each	44,625	Seating		
Emergency Lighting, 25 watt, battery operated			Auditorium chair, all veneer	Each	171
Lead battery	Each	227	Veneer back, padded seat	Each	207
Nickel cadmium	Each	660	Upholstered, spring seat	Each	208
Flagpoles, Complete			Classroom, movable chair & desk	Set	65 - 120
Aluminum, 20' high	Each	1100	Lecture hall, pedestal type	Each	156 - 485
40' high	Each	2700	Sound System		
Fiberglass, 23' high	Each	1425	Amplifier, 250 watts	Each	1675
39'-5" high	Each	3000	Speaker, ceiling or wall	Each	147
			Trumpet	Each	275

Model costs calculated for a 2 story building with 12' story height and 130,000 square feet of floor area

School, High, 2-3 Story

					Unit	Unit Cost	Cost Per S.F.	% Of Sub-Total
A. SUBSTRUCTURE								
1010	Standard Foundations	Poured concrete; strip and spread footings			S.F. Ground	1.56	.78	
1030	Slab on Grade	4" reinforced concrete with vapor barrier and granular base			S.F. Slab	3.65	1.83	
2010	Basement Excavation	Site preparation for slab and trench for foundation wall and footing			S.F. Ground	.14	.07	4.4%
2020	Basement Walls	4' foundation wall			L.F. Wall	57	.57	
B. SHELL								
	B10 Superstructure							
1010	Floor Construction	Concrete slab without drop panel, concrete columns			S.F. Floor	15.58	7.79	
1020	Roof Construction	Concrete slab without drop panel			S.F. Roof	10.84	5.42	17.9%
	B20 Exterior Enclosure							
2010	Exterior Walls	Face brick with concrete block backup	75% of wall		S.F. Wall	22	4.07	
2020	Exterior Windows	Window wall	25% of wall		Each	47	2.83	9.8%
2030	Exterior Doors	Metal and glass			Each	1376	.32	
	B30 Roofing							
3010	Roof Coverings	Built-up tar and gravel with flashing; perlite/EPS composite insulation			S.F. Roof	3.68	1.84	
3020	Roof Openings	Roof hatches			S.F. Roof	.06	.03	2.5%
C. INTERIORS								
1010	Partitions	Concrete block	25 S.F. Floor/L.F. Partition		S.F. Partition	7.93	3.17	
1020	Interior Doors	Single leaf kalamein fire doors	700 S.F. Floor/Door		Each	572	.82	
1030	Fittings	Toilet partitions, chalkboards			S.F. Floor	1.15	1.15	
2010	Stair Construction	Concrete filled metal pan			Flight	5375	.25	22.0%
3010	Wall Finishes	75% paint, 15% glazed coating, 10% ceramic tile			S.F. Surface	4.16	2.08	
3020	Floor Finishes	70% vinyl composition tile, 20% carpet, 10% terrazzo			S.F. Floor	5.25	5.25	
3030	Ceiling Finishes	Mineral fiber tile on concealed zee bars			S.F. Ceiling	4.00	3.52	
D. SERVICES								
	D10 Conveying							
1010	Elevators & Lifts	One hydraulic passenger elevator			Each	55,900	.43	
1020	Escalators & Moving Walks	N/A			—	—	—	0.6%
	D20 Plumbing							
2010	Plumbing Fixtures	Kitchen, bathroom and service fixtures, supply and drainage	1 Fixture/860 S.F. Floor		Each	2597	3.02	
2020	Domestic Water Distribution	Gas fired water heater			S.F. Floor	.39	.39	5.2%
2040	Rain Water Drainage	Roof drains			S.F. Roof	.82	.41	
	D30 HVAC							
3010	Energy Supply	Oil fired hot water, wall fin radiation			S.F. Floor	3.27	3.27	
3020	Heat Generating Systems	N/A			—	—	—	
3030	Cooling Generating Systems	Chilled water, cooling tower systems			S.F. Floor	11.46	11.46	20.0%
3050	Terminal & Package Units	N/A			—	—	—	
3090	Other HVAC Sys. & Equipment	N/A			—	—	—	
	D40 Fire Protection							
4010	Sprinklers	Sprinklers, light hazard			S.F. Floor	1.48	1.48	
4020	Standpipes	N/A			—	—	—	2.0%
	D50 Electrical							
5010	Electrical Service/Distribution	2000 ampere service, panel board and feeders			S.F. Floor	.90	.90	
5020	Lighting & Branch Wiring	Fluorescent fixtures, receptacles, switches, A.C. and misc. power			S.F. Floor	7.59	7.59	
5030	Communications & Security	Alarm systems, communications systems and emergency lighting			S.F. Floor	2.46	2.46	15.4%
5090	Other Electrical Systems	Emergency generator, 250 kW			S.F. Floor	.42	.42	
E. EQUIPMENT & FURNISHINGS								
1010	Commercial Equipment	N/A			—	—	—	
1020	Institutional Equipment	Laboratory counters			S.F. Floor	.07	.07	
1030	Vehicular Equipment	N/A			—	—	—	0.2%
1090	Other Equipment	Built-in athletic equipment			S.F. Floor	.09	.09	
F. SPECIAL CONSTRUCTION								
1020	Integrated Construction	N/A			—	—	—	
1040	Special Facilities	N/A			—	—	—	0.0%
G. BUILDING SITEWORK	**N/A**							

			Sub-Total	73.78	100%
CONTRACTOR FEES (General Requirements: 10%, Overhead: 5%, Profit: 10%)			25%	18.46	
ARCHITECT FEES			7%	6.46	
		Total Building Cost		**98.70**	

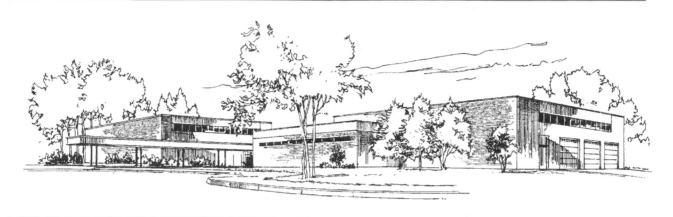

Costs per square foot of floor area

Exterior Wall	S.F. Area	20000	30000	40000	50000	60000	70000	80000	90000	100000
	L.F. Perimeter	400	500	685	700	800	900	1000	1100	1200
Face Brick with Concrete Block Back-up	Steel Frame	108.85	104.75	104.85	101.50	100.60	100.00	99.55	99.25	98.95
	Bearing Walls	105.80	101.60	**101.75**	98.35	97.55	96.90	96.50	96.15	95.85
Decorative Concrete Block	Steel Frame	102.75	99.65	99.65	97.20	96.55	96.15	95.75	95.50	95.25
	Bearing Walls	99.65	96.55	96.60	94.10	93.50	93.00	92.65	92.40	92.20
Steel Siding on Steel Studs	Steel Frame	99.75	97.15	97.10	95.10	94.55	94.15	93.90	93.65	93.50
Metal Sandwich Panel	Steel Frame	99.65	97.05	97.00	95.05	94.45	94.10	93.80	93.60	93.45
Perimeter Adj., Add or Deduct	Per 100 L.F.	5.10	3.30	2.50	1.95	1.70	1.45	1.30	1.10	1.00
Story Hgt. Adj., Add or Deduct	Per 1 Ft.	1.45	1.15	1.20	.95	.95	.95	.95	.85	.85

For Basement, add $22.15 per square foot of basement area

The above costs were calculated using the basic specifications shown on the facing page. These costs should be adjusted where necessary for design alternatives and owner's requirements. Reported completed project costs, for this type of structure, range from $53.90 to $154.00 per S.F.

Common additives

Description	Unit	$ Cost
Carrels Hardwood	Each	750 - 980
Clock System		
20 room	Each	13,000
50 room	Each	31,500
Directory Boards, Plastic, glass covered		
30" x 20"	Each	575
36" x 48"	Each	1075
Aluminum, 24" x 18"	Each	440
36" x 24"	Each	555
48" x 32"	Each	780
48" x 60"	Each	1675
Elevators, Hydraulic passenger, 2 stops		
1500# capacity	Each	43,425
2500# capacity	Each	44,625
3500# capacity	Each	48,525
Emergency Lighting, 25 watt, battery operated		
Lead battery	Each	227
Nickel cadmium	Each	660

Description	Unit	$ Cost
Flagpoles, Complete		
Aluminum, 20' high	Each	1100
40' high	Each	2700
Fiberglass, 23' high	Each	1425
39'-5" high	Each	3000
Seating		
Auditorium chair, all veneer	Each	171
Veneer back, padded seat	Each	207
Upholstered, spring seat	Each	208
Classroom, movable chair & desk	Set	65 - 120
Lecture hall, pedestal type	Each	156 - 485
Shops & Workroom:		
Benches, metal	Each	405
Parts bins 6'-3" high, 3' wide, 12" deep, 72 bins	Each	505
Shelving, metal 1' x 3'	S.F.	13.85
Wide span 6' wide x 24" deep	S.F.	9.00
Sound System		
Amplifier, 250 watts	Each	1675
Speaker, ceiling or wall	Each	147
Trumpet	Each	275

Model costs calculated for a 2 story building with 12' story height and 40,000 square feet of floor area

School, Vocational

				Unit	Unit Cost	Cost Per S.F.	% Of Sub-Total
A. SUBSTRUCTURE							
1010	Standard Foundations	Poured concrete; strip and spread footings		S.F. Ground	1.92	.96	
1030	Slab on Grade	5" reinforced concrete with vapor barrier and granular base		S.F. Slab	8.92	4.46	8.5%
2010	Basement Excavation	Site preparation for slab and trench for foundation wall and footing		S.F. Ground	.14	.07	
2020	Basement Walls	4' foundation wall		L.F. Wall	57	.98	
B. SHELL							
	B10 Superstructure						
1010	Floor Construction	Open web steel joists, slab form, concrete, beams, columns		S.F. Floor	10.82	5.41	9.4%
1020	Roof Construction	Metal deck, open web steel joists, beams, columns		S.F. Roof	3.56	1.78	
	B20 Exterior Enclosure						
2010	Exterior Walls	Face brick with concrete block backup	85% of wall	S.F. Wall	22	7.95	
2020	Exterior Windows	Steel outward projecting	15% of wall	Each	36	2.24	13.9%
2030	Exterior Doors	Metal and glass doors		Each	1897	.39	
	B30 Roofing						
3010	Roof Coverings	Built-up tar and gravel with flashing; perlite/EPS composite insulation		S.F. Roof	4.18	2.09	2.9%
3020	Roof Openings	Roof hatches		S.F. Roof	.20	.10	
C. INTERIORS							
1010	Partitions	Concrete block	20 S.F. Floor/L.F. Partition	S.F. Partition	6.52	3.26	
1020	Interior Doors	Single leaf kalamein fire doors	600 S.F. Floor/Door	Each	572	.95	
1030	Fittings	Toilet partitions, chalkboards		S.F. Floor	1.37	1.37	
2010	Stair Construction	Concrete filled metal pan		Flight	5375	.54	22.0%
3010	Wall Finishes	50% paint, 40% glazed coating, 10% ceramic tile		S.F. Surface	6.56	3.28	
3020	Floor Finishes	70% vinyl composition tile, 20% carpet, 10% terrazzo		S.F. Floor	5.25	5.25	
3030	Ceiling Finishes	Mineral fiber tile on concealed zee bars	60% of area	S.F. Ceiling	3.52	2.11	
D. SERVICES							
	D10 Conveying						
1010	Elevators & Lifts	One hydraulic passenger elevator		Each	56,000	1.40	1.8%
1020	Escalators & Moving Walks	N/A		—	—	—	
	D20 Plumbing						
2010	Plumbing Fixtures	Toilet and service fixtures, supply and drainage	1 Fixture/700 S.F. Floor	Each	2170	3.10	
2020	Domestic Water Distribution	Gas fired water heater		S.F. Floor	.52	.52	5.2%
2040	Rain Water Drainage	Roof drains		S.F. Roof	.72	.36	
	D30 HVAC						
3010	Energy Supply	Oil fired hot water, wall fin radiation		S.F. Floor	6.06	6.06	
3020	Heat Generating Systems	N/A		—	—	—	
3030	Cooling Generating Systems	Chilled water, cooling tower systems		S.F. Floor	9.97	9.97	21.1%
3050	Terminal & Package Units	N/A		—	—	—	
3090	Other HVAC Sys. & Equipment	N/A		—	—	—	
	D40 Fire Protection						
4010	Sprinklers	Sprinklers, light hazard		S.F. Floor	.96	.96	1.3%
4020	Standpipes	N/A		—	—	—	
	D50 Electrical						
5010	Electrical Service/Distribution	800 ampere service, panel board and feeders		S.F. Floor	1.04	1.04	
5020	Lighting & Branch Wiring	Fluorescent fixtures, receptacles, switches, A.C. and misc. power		S.F. Floor	7.70	7.70	13.7%
5030	Communications & Security	Alarm systems, communications systems and emergency lighting		S.F. Floor	1.63	1.63	
5090	Other Electrical Systems	Emergency generator, 11/5 kW		S.F. Floor	.08	.08	
E. EQUIPMENT & FURNISHINGS							
1010	Commercial Equipment	N/A		—	—	—	
1020	Institutional Equipment	Stainless steel countertops		S.F. Floor	.09	.09	0.1%
1030	Vehicular Equipment	N/A		—	—	—	
1090	Other Equipment	N/A		—	—	—	
F. SPECIAL CONSTRUCTION							
1020	Integrated Construction	N/A		—	—	—	0.0%
1040	Special Facilities	N/A		—	—	—	
G. BUILDING SITEWORK	**N/A**						

			Sub-Total	76.10	100%
CONTRACTOR FEES (General Requirements: 10%, Overhead: 5%, Profit: 10%)			25%	18.99	
ARCHITECT FEES			7%	6.66	
		Total Building Cost		**101.75**	

Costs per square foot of floor area

Exterior Wall	S.F. Area	12000	15000	18000	21000	24000	27000	30000	33000	36000
	L.F. Perimeter	440	500	540	590	640	665	700	732	770
Face Brick with Concrete Block Back-up	Steel Frame	131.60	127.30	123.20	120.80	119.00	116.60	115.00	113.60	112.60
	Bearing Wall	127.10	123.15	119.50	117.35	115.70	113.50	112.10	110.85	109.95
Precast Concrete	Steel Frame	122.45	119.00	115.80	113.90	112.45	110.50	109.30	108.20	107.45
Decorative Concrete Block	Bearing Wall	114.75	111.95	109.35	107.80	106.65	105.15	104.10	103.25	102.60
Concrete Block	Steel Frame	118.10	115.85	113.80	112.55	111.65	110.45	109.65	109.00	108.50
	Bearing Wall	111.15	108.70	106.40	105.00	104.00	102.65	101.80	101.05	100.55
Perimeter Adj., Add or Deduct	Per 100 L.F.	9.50	7.65	6.35	5.45	4.70	4.20	3.80	3.45	3.20
Story Hgt. Adj., Add or Deduct	Per 1 Ft.	1.50	1.35	1.25	1.15	1.05	.95	.90	.90	.90
For Basement, add $18.75 per square foot of basement area										

The above costs were calculated using the basic specifications shown on the facing page. These costs should be adjusted where necessary for design alternatives and owner's requirements. Reported completed project costs, for this type of structure, range from $56.35 to $147.65 per S.F.

Common additives

Description	Unit	$ Cost
Closed Circuit Surveillance, One station		
Camera and monitor	Each	1375
For additional camera stations, add	Each	750
Emergency Lighting, 25 watt, battery operated		
Lead battery	Each	227
Nickel cadmium	Each	660
Seating		
Auditorium chair, all veneer	Each	171
Veneer back, padded seat	Each	207
Upholstered, spring seat	Each	208
Classroom, movable chair & desk	Set	65 - 120
Lecture hall, pedestal type	Each	156 - 485
Smoke Detectors		
Ceiling type	Each	151
Duct type	Each	405
Sound System		
Amplifier, 250 watts	Each	1675
Speaker, ceiling or wall	Each	147
Trumpet	Each	275

Model costs calculated for a 1 story building with 24' story height and 24,000 square feet of floor area

Auditorium

				Unit	Unit Cost	Cost Per S.F.	% Of Sub-Total

A. SUBSTRUCTURE

Code	Item	Description		Unit	Unit Cost	Cost Per S.F.	% Of Sub-Total
1010	Standard Foundations	Poured concrete; strip and spread footings		S.F. Ground	1.01	1.01	
1030	Slab on Grade	6" reinforced concrete with vapor barrier and granular base		S.F. Slab	4.37	4.37	
2010	Basement Excavation	Site preparation for slab and trench for foundation wall and footing		S.F. Ground	.14	.14	8.6%
2020	Basement Walls	4" foundation wall		L.F. Wall	63	1.69	

B. SHELL

B10 Superstructure

Code	Item	Description		Unit	Unit Cost	Cost Per S.F.	% Of Sub-Total
1010	Floor Construction	Open web steel joists, slab form, concrete	(balcony)	S.F. Floor	14.80	1.85	8.8%
1020	Roof Construction	Metal deck on steel truss		S.F. Roof	5.53	5.53	

B20 Exterior Enclosure

Code	Item	Description		Unit	Unit Cost	Cost Per S.F.	% Of Sub-Total
2010	Exterior Walls	Precast concrete panel	80% of wall (adjusted for end walls)	S.F. Wall	17.36	8.89	
2020	Exterior Windows	Glass curtain wall	20% of wall	Each	31	4.07	17.0%
2030	Exterior Doors	Double aluminum and glass and hollow metal		Each	2728	1.37	

B30 Roofing

Code	Item	Description		Unit	Unit Cost	Cost Per S.F.	% Of Sub-Total
3010	Roof Coverings	Built-up tar and gravel with flashing; perlite/EPS composite insulation		S.F. Roof	3.93	3.93	4.8%
3020	Roof Openings	Roof hatches		S.F. Roof	.11	.11	

C. INTERIORS

Code	Item	Description		Unit	Unit Cost	Cost Per S.F.	% Of Sub-Total
1010	Partitions	Concrete Block and toilet partitions	40 S.F. Floor/L.F. Partition	S.F. Partition	6.50	2.60	
1020	Interior Doors	Single leaf hollow metal	400 S.F. Floor/Door	Each	572	1.44	
1030	Fittings	Toilet partitions		S.F. Floor	—	—	
2010	Stair Construction	Concrete filled metal pan		Flight	6425	.80	21.9%
3010	Wall Finishes	70% paint, 30% epoxy coating		S.F. Surface	6.50	3.25	
3020	Floor Finishes	70% vinyl tile, 30% carpet		S.F. Floor	7.37	7.37	
3030	Ceiling Finishes	Fiberglass board, suspended		S.F. Ceiling	3.00	2.92	

D. SERVICES

D10 Conveying

Code	Item	Description		Unit	Unit Cost	Cost Per S.F.	% Of Sub-Total
1010	Elevators & Lifts	One hydraulic passenger elevator		Each	61,920	2.58	3.1%
1020	Escalators & Moving Walks	N/A		—	—	—	

D20 Plumbing

Code	Item	Description		Unit	Unit Cost	Cost Per S.F.	% Of Sub-Total
2010	Plumbing Fixtures	Toilet and service fixtures, supply and drainage	1 Fixture/800 S.F. Floor	Each	2480	3.10	
2020	Domestic Water Distribution	Gas fired water heater		S.F. Floor	.25	.25	4.8%
2040	Rain Water Drainage	Roof drains		S.F. Roof	.66	.66	

D30 HVAC

Code	Item	Description		Unit	Unit Cost	Cost Per S.F.	% Of Sub-Total
3010	Energy Supply	N/A		—	—	—	
3020	Heat Generating Systems	Included in D3050		—	—	—	
3030	Cooling Generating Systems	N/A		—	—	—	12.3%
3050	Terminal & Package Units	Single zone rooftop unit, gas heating, electric cooling		S.F. Floor	10.30	10.30	
3090	Other HVAC Sys. & Equipment	N/A		—	—	—	

D40 Fire Protection

Code	Item	Description		Unit	Unit Cost	Cost Per S.F.	% Of Sub-Total
4010	Sprinklers	Wet pipe sprinkler system		S.F. Floor	1.95	1.95	2.3%
4020	Standpipes	N/A		—	—	—	

D50 Electrical

Code	Item	Description		Unit	Unit Cost	Cost Per S.F.	% Of Sub-Total
5010	Electrical Service/Distribution	800 ampere service, panel board and feeders		S.F. Floor	1.57	1.57	
5020	Lighting & Branch Wiring	Fluorescent fixtures, receptacles, switches, A.C. and misc. power		S.F. Floor	8.78	8.78	
5030	Communications & Security	Alarm systems and emergency lighting, and public address system		S.F. Floor	2.52	2.52	16.5%
5090	Other Electrical Systems	Emergency generator, 100KW		S.F. Floor	1.02	1.02	

E. EQUIPMENT & FURNISHINGS

Code	Item	Description		Unit	Unit Cost	Cost Per S.F.	% Of Sub-Total
1010	Commercial Equipment	N/A		—	—	—	
1020	Institutional Equipment	N/A		—	—	—	
1030	Vehicular Equipment	N/A		—	—	—	0.0%
1090	Other Equipment	N/A		—	—	—	

F. SPECIAL CONSTRUCTION

Code	Item	Description		Unit	Unit Cost	Cost Per S.F.	% Of Sub-Total
1020	Integrated Construction	N/A		—	—	—	0.0%
1040	Special Facilities	N/A		—	—	—	

G. BUILDING SITEWORK   N/A

		Sub-Total	84.07	100%
CONTRACTOR FEES (General Requirements: 10%, Overhead: 5%, Profit: 10%)			25%	21.02
ARCHITECT FEES			7%	7.36

Total Building Cost	**112.45**

Costs per square foot of floor area

Exterior Wall	S.F. Area	10000	15000	25000	40000	55000	70000	80000	90000	100000
	L.F. Perimeter	260	320	400	476	575	628	684	721	772
Face Brick with Concrete Block Back-up	R/Conc. Frame	149.80	138.55	127.40	119.65	116.65	114.05	113.30	112.35	111.75
	Steel Frame	154.40	143.10	131.95	124.25	121.20	118.65	117.85	116.90	116.35
Decorative Concrete Block	R/Conc. Frame	139.15	129.95	121.05	115.10	112.75	110.80	110.20	109.45	109.00
	Steel Frame	143.15	133.95	125.05	119.05	116.70	114.75	114.15	113.45	113.00
Precast Concrete Panels	R/Conc. Frame	142.85	132.85	123.20	116.55	113.95	111.75	111.10	110.25	109.75
	Steel Frame	147.30	137.30	127.65	120.95	118.35	116.20	115.55	114.70	114.20
Perimeter Adj., Add or Deduct	Per 100 L.F.	13.40	8.95	5.35	3.30	2.45	1.90	1.70	1.45	1.30
Story Hgt. Adj., Add or Deduct	Per 1 Ft.	2.60	2.10	1.60	1.15	1.05	.90	.85	.75	.70
For Basement, add $22.65 per square foot of basement area										

The above costs were calculated using the basic specifications shown on the facing page. These costs should be adjusted where necessary for design alternatives and owner's requirements. Reported completed project costs, for this type of structure, range from $51.20 to $150.85 per S.F.

Common additives

Description	Unit	$ Cost		Description	Unit	$ Cost
Carrels Hardwood	Each	750-980		Kitchen Equipment		
Closed Circuit Surveillance, One station				Broiler	Each	4275
Camera and monitor	Each	1375		Coffee urn, twin 6 gallon	Each	7375
For additional camera stations, add	Each	750		Cooler, 6 ft. long	Each	3375
Elevators, Hydraulic passenger, 2 stops				Dishwasher, 10-12 racks per hr.	Each	3225
2000# capacity	Each	43,925		Food warmer	Each	745
2500# capacity	Each	44,625		Freezer, 44 C.F., reach-in	Each	8775
3500# capacity	Each	48,525		Ice cube maker, 50 lb. per day	Each	1900
Additional stop, add	Each	3800		Range with 1 oven	Each	2500
Emergency Lighting, 25 watt, battery operated				Laundry Equipment		
Lead battery	Each	227		Dryer, gas, 16 lb. capacity	Each	725
Nickel cadmium	Each	660		30 lb. capacity	Each	2800
Furniture	Student	1900-3600		Washer, 4 cycle	Each	810
Intercom System, 25 station capacity				Commercial	Each	1225
Master station	Each	2025		Smoke Detectors		
Intercom outlets	Each	128		Ceiling type	Each	151
Handset	Each	335		Duct type	Each	405
				TV Antenna, Master system, 12 outlet	Outlet	238
				30 outlet	Outlet	153
				100 outlet	Outlet	145

Model costs calculated for a 3 story building with 12' story height and 25,000 square feet of floor area

				Unit	Unit Cost	Cost Per S.F.	% Of Sub-Total

A. SUBSTRUCTURE

1010	Standard Foundations	Poured concrete; strip and spread footings		S.F. Ground	4.47	1.49	
1030	Slab on Grade	4" reinforced concrete with vapor barrier and granular base		S.F. Slab	3.65	1.21	3.9%
2010	Basement Excavation	Site preparation for slab and trench for foundation wall and footing		S.F. Ground	.14	.05	
2020	Basement Walls	4' Foundation wall		L.F. Wall	57	.92	

B. SHELL

B10 Superstructure

1010	Floor Construction	Concrete flat plate		S.F. Floor	17.43	11.62	15.6%
1020	Roof Construction	Concrete flat plate		S.F. Roof	9.72	3.24	

B20 Exterior Enclosure

2010	Exterior Walls	Face brick with concrete block backup	80% of wall	S.F. Wall	22	10.48	
2020	Exterior Windows	Aluminum horizontal sliding	20% of wall	Each	540	2.70	14.9%
2030	Exterior Doors	Double glass & aluminum doors		Each	4150	.99	

B30 Roofing

3010	Roof Coverings	Single ply membrane, loose laid and ballasted; perlite/EPS composite insulation		S.F. Roof	3.84	1.28	1.3%
3020	Roof Openings	N/A		—	—	—	

C. INTERIORS

1010	Partitions	Gypsum board on metal studs, concrete block	9 S.F. Floor/L.F. Partition	S.F. Partition	4.44	4.93	
1020	Interior Doors	Single leaf wood	90 S.F. Floor/Door	Each	469	5.21	
1030	Fittings	Closet shelving, mirrors, bathroom accessories		S.F. Floor	1.61	1.61	
2010	Stair Construction	Cast in place concrete		Flight	3650	1.90	24.9%
3010	Wall Finishes	95% paint, 5% ceramic tile		S.F. Surface	2.80	3.11	
3020	Floor Finishes	80% carpet, 10% vinyl composition tile, 10% ceramic tile		S.F. Floor	6.28	6.28	
3030	Ceiling Finishes	90% paint, 10% suspended fiberglass board		S.F. Ceiling	1.00	.70	

D. SERVICES

D10 Conveying

1010	Elevators & Lifts	One hydraulic passenger elevator		Each	73,750	2.95	3.1%
1020	Escalators & Moving Walks	N/A		—	—	—	

D20 Plumbing

2010	Plumbing Fixtures	Toilet and service fixtures, supply and drainage	1 Fixture/455 S.F. Floor	Each	3016	6.63	
2020	Domestic Water Distribution	Electric water heater		S.F. Floor	1.83	1.83	9.2%
2040	Rain Water Drainage	Roof drains		S.F. Roof	.78	.26	

D30 HVAC

3010	Energy Supply	N/A		—	—	—	
3020	Heat Generating Systems	Included in D3050		—	—	—	
3030	Cooling Generating Systems	N/A		—	—	—	10.1%
3050	Terminal & Package Units	Rooftop multizone unit system		S.F. Floor	9.65	9.65	
3090	Other HVAC Sys. & Equipment	N/A		—	—	—	

D40 Fire Protection

4010	Sprinklers	Wet pipe sprinkler system		S.F. Floor	1.69	1.69	1.8%
4020	Standpipes	N/A		—	—	—	

D50 Electrical

5010	Electrical Service/Distribution	800 ampere service, panel board and feeders		S.F. Floor	1.63	1.63	
5020	Lighting & Branch Wiring	Fluorescent fixtures, receptacles, switches, A.C. and misc. power		S.F. Floor	7.08	7.08	12.0%
5030	Communications & Security	Alarm systems, communications systems and emergency lighting		S.F. Floor	2.66	2.66	
5090	Other Electrical Systems	Emergency generator, 7.5KW		S.F. Floor	.06	.06	

E. EQUIPMENT & FURNISHINGS

1010	Commercial Equipment	N/A		—	—	—	
1020	Institutional Equipment	N/A		—	—	—	3.2%
1030	Vehicular Equipment	N/A		—	—	—	
2020	Other Equipment	Dormitory furniture		S.F. Floor	673	3.09	

F. SPECIAL CONSTRUCTION

1020	Integrated Construction	N/A		—	—	—	0.0%
1040	Special Facilities	N/A		—	—	—	

G. BUILDING SITEWORK   N/A

	Sub-Total	95.25	**100%**

CONTRACTOR FEES (General Requirements: 10%, Overhead: 5%, Profit: 10%)	25%	23.82	
ARCHITECT FEES	7%	8.33	

Total Building Cost	**127.40**	

Costs per square foot of floor area

Exterior Wall	S.F. Area	2000	5000	7000	10000	12000	15000	18000	21000	25000
	L.F. Perimeter	200	310	360	440	480	520	560	600	660
Tiltup Concrete Panel	Steel Joists	139.95	113.65	107.15	102.60	100.15	97.35	95.45	94.00	92.90
Decorative Concrete Block	Bearing Walls	133.65	108.90	102.85	98.50	96.30	93.65	91.90	90.55	89.50
Brick on Block	Steel Joists	160.80	130.95	123.30	117.90	115.10	111.55	109.25	107.50	106.10
Stucco on Concrete Block	Wood Truss	137.25	112.35	106.30	101.95	99.80	97.15	95.35	94.10	93.00
Brick Veneer	Wood Frame	143.65	117.35	110.85	106.15	103.75	100.75	98.80	97.35	96.15
Wood Siding	Wood Frame	127.95	108.50	103.85	100.45	98.80	96.70	95.35	94.35	93.50
Perimeter Adj., Add or Deduct	Per 100 L.F.	21.95	8.80	6.25	4.40	3.75	2.95	2.50	2.20	1.75
Story Hgt. Adj., Add or Deduct	Per 1 Ft.	2.40	1.45	1.30	.95	1.00	.90	.75	.75	.60
For Basement, add $19.95 per square foot of basement area										

The above costs were calculated using the basic specifications shown on the facing page. These costs should be adjusted where necessary for design alternatives and owner's requirements. Reported completed project costs, for this type of structure, range from $40.00 to $145.60 per S.F.

Common additives

Description	Unit	$ Cost
Emergency Lighting, 25 watt, battery operated		
Lead battery	Each	227
Nickel cadmium	Each	660
Flagpoles, Complete		
Aluminum, 20' high	Each	1100
40' high	Each	2700
70' high	Each	8350
Fiberglass, 23' high	Each	1425
39'-5" high	Each	3000
59' high	Each	7425
Gym Floor, Incl. sleepers and finish, maple	S.F.	9.85
Intercom System, 25 Station capacity		
Master station	Each	2025
Intercom outlets	Each	128
Handset	Each	335

Description	Unit	$ Cost
Lockers, Steel, single tier, 60" to 72"	Opening	131 - 227
2 tier, 60" to 72" total	Opening	74 - 125
5 tier, box lockers	Opening	42 - 62
Locker bench, lam. maple top only	L.F.	19.50
Pedestals, steel pipe	Each	63
Smoke Detectors		
Ceiling type	Each	151
Duct type	Each	405
Sound System		
Amplifier, 250 watts	Each	1675
Speaker, ceiling or wall	Each	147
Trumpet	Each	275

Model costs calculated for a 1 story building with 12' story height and 10,000 square feet of floor area

Day Care Center/Preschool

				Unit	Unit Cost	Cost Per S.F.	% Of Sub-Total
A. SUBSTRUCTURE							
1010	Standard Foundations	Poured concrete; strip and spread footings		S.F. Ground	1.48	1.48	
1030	Slab on Grade	4" concrete with vapor barrier and granular base		S.F. Slab	3.29	3.29	9.7%
2010	Basement Excavation	Site preparation for slab and trench for foundation wall and footing		S.F. Ground	.23	.23	
2020	Basement Walls	4' foundation wall		L.F. Wall	57	2.53	
B. SHELL							
	B10 Superstructure						
1010	Floor Construction	Wood beams on columns		S.F. Floor	.14	.14	8.2%
1020	Roof Construction	Wood trusses		S.F. Roof	6.27	6.27	
	B20 Exterior Enclosure						
2010	Exterior Walls	Brick veneer on wood studs	85% of wall	S.F. Wall	17.76	7.97	
2020	Exterior Windows	Window wall	15% of wall	Each	36	2.86	17.4%
2030	Exterior Doors	Aluminum and glass; steel		Each	1435	2.72	
	B30 Roofing						
3010	Roof Coverings	Asphalt shingles, 9" fiberglass batt insulation, gutters and downspouts		S.F. Roof	2.61	2.61	3.4%
3020	Roof Openings	N/A		—	—	—	
C. INTERIORS							
1010	Partitions	Gypsum board on wood studs	8 S.F. Floor/S.F. Partition	S.F. Partition	5.61	3.74	
1020	Interior Doors	Single leaf hollow metal	700 S.F. Floor/Door	Each	572	1.52	
1030	Fittings	Toilet partitions		S.F. Floor	.41	.41	
2010	Stair Construction	N/A		—	—	—	15.5%
3010	Wall Finishes	Paint		S.F. Surface	1.57	1.57	
3020	Floor Finishes	5% quarry tile, 95% vinyl composition tile		S.F. Floor	1.89	1.89	
3030	Ceiling Finishes	Fiberglass tile on tee grid		S.F. Ceiling	3.00	2.92	
D. SERVICES							
	D10 Conveying						
1010	Elevators & Lifts	N/A		—	—	—	0.0%
1020	Escalators & Moving Walks	N/A		—	—	—	
	D20 Plumbing						
2010	Plumbing Fixtures	Toilet and service fixtures, supply and drainage	1 Fixture/455 S.F. Floor	Each	1009	5.67	
2020	Domestic Water Distribution	Electric water heater		S.F. Floor	1.21	1.21	8.8%
2040	Rain Water Drainage	N/A		—	—	—	
	D30 HVAC						
3010	Energy Supply	Oil fired hot water, wall fin radiation		S.F. Floor	7.08	7.08	
3020	Heat Generating Systems	N/A		—	—	—	
3030	Cooling Generating Systems	N/A		—	—	—	20.7%
3050	Terminal & Package Units	Split systems with air cooled condensing units		S.F. Floor	9.02	9.02	
3090	Other HVAC Sys. & Equipment	N/A		—	—	—	
	D40 Fire Protection						
4010	Sprinklers	Sprinkler, light hazard		S.F. Floor	1.95	1.95	2.5%
4020	Standpipes	N/A		—	—	—	
	D50 Electrical						
5010	Electrical Service/Distribution	200 ampere service, panel board and feeders		S.F. Floor	.72	.72	
5020	Lighting & Branch Wiring	Fluorescent fixtures, receptacles, switches, A.C. and misc. power		S.F. Floor	6.87	6.87	10.2%
5030	Communications & Security	Alarm systems and emergency lighting		S.F. Floor	.32	.32	
5090	Other Electrical Systems	Emergency generator, 15 kW		S.F. Floor	.07	.07	
E. EQUIPMENT & FURNISHINGS							
1010	Commercial Equipment	N/A		—	—	—	
1020	Institutional Equipment	Cabinets and countertop		S.F. Floor	2.85	2.85	3.7%
1030	Vehicular Equipment	N/A		—	—	—	
1090	Other Equipment	N/A		—	—	—	
F. SPECIAL CONSTRUCTION							
1020	Integrated Construction	N/A		—	—	—	0.0%
1040	Special Facilities	N/A		—	—	—	
G. BUILDING SITEWORK	**N/A**						
				Sub-Total		77.91	**100%**
	CONTRACTOR FEES (General Requirements: 10%, Overhead: 5%, Profit: 10%)				25%	19.47	
	ARCHITECT FEES				9%	8.77	
				Total Building Cost		**106.15**	

Costs per square foot of floor area

Exterior Wall	S.F. Area	7000	10000	13000	16000	19000	22000	25000	28000	31000
	L.F. Perimeter	240	300	336	386	411	435	472	510	524
Face Brick with Concrete Block Back-up	R/Conc. Frame	136.65	129.25	123.10	120.25	116.85	114.25	112.90	111.90	110.15
	Steel Frame	128.10	120.75	114.65	111.80	108.40	105.75	104.45	103.45	101.65
Limestone with Concrete Block	R/Conc. Frame	150.00	140.95	133.20	129.70	125.30	122.05	120.30	119.05	116.80
	Steel Frame	141.50	132.50	124.75	121.25	116.80	113.55	111.80	110.55	108.30
Precast Concrete Panels	R/Conc. Frame	128.10	121.80	116.70	114.30	111.45	109.35	108.25	107.45	105.95
	Steel Frame	119.60	113.35	108.20	105.85	102.95	100.85	99.75	98.90	97.50
Perimeter Adj., Add or Deduct	Per 100 L.F.	16.80	11.75	9.05	7.35	6.20	5.40	4.80	4.25	3.80
Story Hgt. Adj., Add or Deduct	Per 1 Ft.	2.50	2.25	1.90	1.80	1.60	1.50	1.45	1.40	1.30
For Basement, add $30.55 per square foot of basement area										

The above costs were calculated using the basic specifications shown on the facing page. These costs should be adjusted where necessary for design alternatives and owner's requirements. Reported completed project costs, for this type of structure, range from $65.20 to $167.35 per S.F.

Common additives

Description	Unit	$ Cost
Carrels Hardwood	Each	750 - 980
Closed Circuit Surveillance, One station		
Camera and monitor	Each	1375
For additional camera stations, add	Each	750
Elevators, Hydraulic passenger, 2 stops		
1500# capacity	Each	43,425
2500# capacity	Each	44,625
3500# capacity	Each	48,525
Emergency Lighting, 25 watt, battery operated		
Lead battery	Each	227
Nickel cadmium	Each	660
Flagpoles, Complete		
Aluminum, 20' high	Each	1100
40' high	Each	2700
70' high	Each	8350
Fiberglass, 23' high	Each	1425
39'-5" high	Each	3000
59' high	Each	7425

Description	Unit	$ Cost
Library Furnishings		
Bookshelf, 90" high, 10" shelf double face	L.F.	140
single face	L.F.	203
Charging desk, built-in with counter		
Plastic laminated top	L.F.	530
Reading table, laminated		
top 60" x 36"	Each	720

Model costs calculated for a 2 story building with 14' story height and 22,000 square feet of floor area

Library

					Unit	Unit Cost	Cost Per S.F.	% Of Sub-Total
A.	**SUBSTRUCTURE**							
1010	Standard Foundations	Poured concrete; strip and spread footings			S.F. Ground	2.78	1.39	
1030	Slab on Grade	4" reinforced concrete with vapor barrier and granular base			S.F. Slab	3.65	1.83	5.3%
2010	Basement Excavation	Site preparation for slab and trench for foundation wall and footing			S.F. Ground	.23	.12	
2020	Basement Walls	4' foundation wall			L.F. Wall	57	1.14	
B.	**SHELL**							
	B10 Superstructure							
1010	Floor Construction	Concrete waffle slab			S.F. Floor	21	10.72	22.4%
1020	Roof Construction	Concrete waffle slab			S.F. Roof	16.40	8.20	
	B20 Exterior Enclosure							
2010	Exterior Walls	Face brick with concrete block backup	90% of wall		S.F. Wall	22	11.43	
2020	Exterior Windows	Window wall	10% of wall		Each	39	2.18	16.5%
2030	Exterior Doors	Double aluminum and glass, single leaf hollow metal			Each	3525	.32	
	B30 Roofing							
3010	Roof Coverings	Single ply membrane, EPDM, fully adhered; perlite/EPS composite insulation			S.F. Roof	3.66	1.83	2.2%
3020	Roof Openings	Roof hatches			S.F. Roof	.06	.03	
C.	**INTERIORS**							
1010	Partitions	Gypsum board on metal studs	30 S.F. Floor/L.F. Partition		S.F. Partition	8.28	3.31	
1020	Interior Doors	Single leaf wood	300 S.F. Floor/Door		Each	469	1.56	
1030	Fittings	N/A			—	—	—	
2010	Stair Construction	Concrete filled metal pan			Flight	6600	.60	15.7%
3010	Wall Finishes	Paint			S.F. Surface	1.00	.50	
3020	Floor Finishes	50% carpet, 50% vinyl tile			S.F. Floor	3.76	3.76	
3030	Ceiling Finishes	Mineral fiber on concealed zee bars			S.F. Ceiling	4.00	3.52	
D.	**SERVICES**							
	D10 Conveying							
1010	Elevators & Lifts	One hydraulic passenger elevator			Each	58,740	2.67	3.2%
1020	Escalators & Moving Walks	N/A			—	—	—	
	D20 Plumbing							
2010	Plumbing Fixtures	Toilet and service fixtures, supply and drainage	1 Fixture/1835 S.F. Floor		Each	1761	.96	
2020	Domestic Water Distribution	Gas fired water heater			S.F. Floor	.68	.68	2.2%
2040	Rain Water Drainage	Roof drains			S.F. Roof	.52	.26	
	D30 HVAC							
3010	Energy Supply	N/A			—	—	—	
3020	Heat Generating Systems	Included in D3050			—	—	—	
3030	Cooling Generating Systems	N/A			—	—	—	19.3%
3050	Terminal & Package Units	Multizone unit, gas heating, electric cooling			S.F. Floor	16.30	16.30	
3090	Other HVAC Sys. & Equipment	N/A			—	—	—	
	D40 Fire Protection							
4010	Sprinklers	Wet pipe sprinkler system			S.F. Floor	1.77	1.77	2.1%
4020	Standpipes	N/A			—	—	—	
	D50 Electrical							
5010	Electrical Service/Distribution	400 ampere service, panel board and feeders			S.F. Floor	.77	.77	
5020	Lighting & Branch Wiring	Fluorescent fixtures, receptacles, switches, A.C. and misc. power			S.F. Floor	8.17	8.17	11.3%
5030	Communications & Security	Alarm systems and emergency lighting			S.F. Floor	.55	.55	
5090	Other Electrical Systems	Emergency generator, 7.5 kW			S.F. Floor	.07	.07	
E.	**EQUIPMENT & FURNISHINGS**							
1010	Commercial Equipment	N/A			—	—	—	
1020	Institutional Equipment	N/A			—	—	—	0.0%
1030	Vehicular Equipment	N/A			—	—	—	
1090	Other Equipment	N/A			—	—	—	
F.	**SPECIAL CONSTRUCTION**							
1020	Integrated Construction	N/A			—	—	—	0.0%
1040	Special Facilities	N/A			—	—	—	
G.	**BUILDING SITEWORK**	**N/A**						

			Sub-Total	84.64	100%
CONTRACTOR FEES (General Requirements: 10%, Overhead: 5%, Profit: 10%)			25%	21.15	
ARCHITECT FEES			8%	8.46	
		Total Building Cost		**114.25**	

Costs per square foot of floor area

Exterior Wall	S.F. Area	2000	3000	5000	7000	9000	12000	15000	20000	25000
	L.F. Perimeter	220	260	320	360	420	480	520	640	700
Wood Siding	Wood Truss	142.35	126.25	111.90	104.65	101.50	97.85	95.05	93.35	91.40
Brick Veneer	Wood Truss	179.80	159.60	141.70	132.70	128.75	124.15	120.75	118.55	116.20
Brick on Block	Wood Truss	168.20	147.25	128.45	118.85	114.70	109.80	106.05	103.80	101.20
	Steel Roof Deck	173.85	150.10	128.95	118.35	113.60	108.10	104.05	101.50	98.60
EIFS on Metal Studs	Steel Roof Deck	163.00	142.20	123.75	114.60	110.50	105.75	102.30	100.05	97.65
Tiltup Concrete Panel	Steel Roof Deck	160.30	140.25	122.50	113.65	109.65	105.15	101.75	99.60	97.25
Perimeter Adj., Add or Deduct	Per 100 L.F.	18.25	12.10	7.25	5.20	4.00	2.95	2.45	1.80	1.50
Story Hgt. Adj., Add or Deduct	Per 1 Ft.	2.30	1.70	1.30	1.10	.95	.80	.75	.65	.60

For Basement, add $20.95 per square foot of basement area

The above costs were calculated using the basic specifications shown on the facing page. These costs should be adjusted where necessary for design alternatives and owner's requirements. Reported completed project costs, for this type of structure, range from $44.00 to $170.00 per S.F.

Common additives

Description	Unit	$ Cost
Clock System		
20 room	Each	13,000
50 room	Each	31,500
Closed Circuit Surveillance, One station		
Camera and monitor	Each	1375
For additional camera stations, add	Each	750
Directory Boards, Plastic, glass covered		
30" x 20"	Each	575
36" x 48"	Each	1075
Aluminum, 24" x 18"	Each	440
36" x 24"	Each	555
48" x 32"	Each	780
48" x 60"	Each	1675
Emergency Lighting, 25 watt, battery operated		
Lead battery	Each	227
Nickel cadmium	Each	660

Description	Unit	$ Cost
Smoke Detectors		
Ceiling type	Each	151
Duct type	Each	405
Sound System		
Amplifier, 250 watts	Each	1675
Speaker, ceiling or wall	Each	147
Trumpet	Each	275
TV Antenna, Master system, 12 outlet	Outlet	238
30 outlet	Outlet	153
100 outlet	Outlet	145

Model costs calculated for a 1 story building with 12' story height and 7,000 square feet of floor area

Administration Building

				Unit	Unit Cost	Cost Per S.F.	% Of Sub-Total
A. SUBSTRUCTURE							
1010	Standard Foundations	Poured concrete; strip and spread footings		S.F. Ground	1.98	1.98	
1030	Slab on Grade	4" reinforced concrete with vapor barrier and granular base		S.F. Slab	3.65	3.65	
2010	Basement Excavation	Site preparation for slab and trench for foundation wall and footing		S.F. Ground	.23	.23	10.5%
2020	Basement Walls	4' foundation wall		L.F. Wall	108	3.11	
B. SHELL							
	B10 Superstructure						
1010	Floor Construction	N/A		—	—	—	
1020	Roof Construction	Steel joists, girders & deck on columns		S.F. Roof	5.54	5.54	6.5%
	B20 Exterior Enclosure						
2010	Exterior Walls	E.I.F.S. on metal studs		S.F. Wall	14.46	7.14	
2020	Exterior Windows	Aluminum outward projecting	20% of wall	Each	540	2.90	13.9%
2030	Exterior Doors	Aluminum and glass, hollow metal		Each	2194	1.87	
	B30 Roofing						
3010	Roof Coverings	Single ply membrane, loose laid and ballasted		S.F. Roof	6.02	6.02	7.2%
3020	Roof Openings	Roof hatch		S.F. Roof	.12	.12	
C. INTERIORS							
1010	Partitions	Gypsum board on metal studs	20 S.F. Floor/L.F. Partition	S.F. Partition	6.24	3.12	
1020	Interior Doors	Single leaf hollow metal	200 S.F. Floor/Door	Each	572	2.86	
1030	Fittings	Toilet partitions		S.F. Floor	.48	.48	
2010	Stair Construction	N/A		—	—	—	19.5%
3010	Wall Finishes	60% vinyl wall covering, 40% paint		S.F. Surface	2.32	1.16	
3020	Floor Finishes	60% carpet, 30% vinyl composition tile, 10% ceramic tile		S.F. Floor	5.58	5.58	
3030	Ceiling Finishes	Mineral fiber tile on concealed zee bars		S.F. Ceiling	4.00	3.52	
D. SERVICES							
	D10 Conveying						
1010	Elevators & Lifts	N/A		—	—	—	0.0%
1020	Escalators & Moving Walks	N/A		—	—	—	
	D20 Plumbing						
2010	Plumbing Fixtures	Toilet and service fixtures, supply and drainage	1 Fixture/1320 S.F. Floor	Each	2798	2.12	
2020	Domestic Water Distribution	Gas fired water heater		S.F. Floor	.59	.59	3.8%
2040	Rain Water Drainage	Roof drains		S.F. Roof	.54	.54	
	D30 HVAC						
3010	Energy Supply	N/A		—	—	—	
3020	Heat Generating Systems	Included in D3050		—	—	—	
3030	Cooling Generating Systems	N/A		—	—	—	20.5%
3050	Terminal & Package Units	Multizone unit gas heating, electric cooling		S.F. Floor	17.55	17.55	
3090	Other HVAC Sys. & Equipment	N/A		—	—	—	
	D40 Fire Protection						
4010	Sprinklers	N/A		—	—	—	0.8%
4020	Standpipes	Standpipes and hose systems		S.F. Floor	.66	.66	
	D50 Electrical						
5010	Electrical Service/Distribution	400 ampere service, panel board and feeders		S.F. Floor	4.00	4.00	
5020	Lighting & Branch Wiring	Fluorescent fixtures, receptacles, switches, A.C. and misc. power		S.F. Floor	9.01	9.01	17.4%
5030	Communications & Security	Alarm systems and emergency lighting		S.F. Floor	1.77	1.77	
5090	Other Electrical Systems	Emergency generator, 7.5 kW		S.F. Floor	.16	.16	
E. EQUIPMENT & FURNISHINGS							
1010	Commercial Equipment	N/A		—	—	—	
1020	Institutional Equipment	N/A		—	—	—	
1030	Vehicular Equipment	N/A		—	—	—	0.0%
1090	Other Equipment	N/A		—	—	—	
F. SPECIAL CONSTRUCTION							
1020	Integrated Construction	N/A		—	—	—	0.0%
1040	Special Facilities	N/A		—	—	—	
G. BUILDING SITEWORK	**N/A**						

		Sub-Total	85.68	100%
CONTRACTOR FEES (General Requirements: 10%, Overhead: 5%, Profit: 10%)		25%	21.42	
ARCHITECT FEES		7%	7.50	

Total Building Cost	**114.60**

Costs per square foot of floor area

Exterior Wall	S.F. Area	12000	16000	20000	25000	30000	35000	40000	45000	50000
	L.F. Perimeter	440	520	600	700	708	780	841	910	979
Reinforced Concrete Block	Lam. Wood Arches	111.70	107.20	104.60	102.50	99.30	98.00	97.00	96.25	95.65
	Rigid Steel Frame	106.90	102.45	99.90	97.75	94.55	93.25	92.25	91.50	90.90
Face Brick with Concrete Block Back-up	Lam. Wood Arches	130.25	123.65	119.80	116.65	111.25	109.30	107.65	106.45	105.60
	Rigid Steel Frame	125.55	118.95	115.10	111.95	106.55	104.50	102.85	101.75	100.80
Metal Sandwich Panels	Lam. Wood Arches	107.50	103.55	101.20	99.35	96.65	95.50	94.60	94.00	93.40
	Rigid Steel Frame	102.80	98.80	96.45	94.60	91.90	90.70	89.85	89.20	88.65
Perimeter Adj., Add or Deduct	Per 100 L.F.	4.85	3.70	2.95	2.35	1.90	1.70	1.45	1.30	1.10
Story Hgt. Adj., Add or Deduct	Per 1 Ft.	.65	.60	.55	.50	.40	.45	.40	.40	.30
Basement—Not Applicable										

The above costs were calculated using the basic specifications shown on the facing page. These costs should be adjusted where necessary for design alternatives and owner's requirements. Reported completed project costs, for this type of structure, range from $50.70 to $151.40 per S.F.

Common additives

Description	Unit	$ Cost
Bleachers, Telescoping, manual		
To 15 tier	Seat	79 - 110
16-20 tier	Seat	161 - 196
21-30 tier	Seat	171 - 206
For power operation, add	Seat	31 - 48
Gym Divider Curtain, Mesh top		
Manual roll-up	S.F.	9.45
Gym Mats		
2" naugahyde covered	S.F.	3.45
2" nylon	S.F.	5.15
1-1/2" wall pads	S.F.	6.80
1" wrestling mats	S.F.	4.62
Scoreboard		
Basketball, one side	Each	2775 - 17,500
Basketball Backstop		
Wall mtd., 6' extended, fixed	Each	1675 - 2150
Swing up, wall mtd.	Each	1875 - 2825

Description	Unit	$ Cost
Lockers, Steel, single tier, 60" or 72"	Opening	131 - 227
2 tier, 60" or 72" total	Opening	74 - 125
5 tier, box lockers	Opening	42 - 62
Locker bench, lam. maple top only	L.F.	19.50
Pedestals, steel pipe	Each	63
Sound System		
Amplifier, 250 watts	Each	1675
Speaker, ceiling or wall	Each	147
Trumpet	Each	275
Emergency Lighting, 25 watt, battery operated		
Lead battery	Each	227
Nickel cadmium	Each	660

Model costs calculated for a 1 story building with 25' story height and 20,000 square feet of floor area

Gymnasium

			Unit	Unit Cost	Cost Per S.F.	% Of Sub-Total
A. SUBSTRUCTURE						
1010	Standard Foundations	Poured concrete; strip and spread footings	S.F. Ground	1.24	1.24	
1030	Slab on Grade	4" reinforced concrete with vapor barrier and granular base	S.F. Slab	3.65	3.65	8.7%
2010	Basement Excavation	Site preparation for slab and trench for foundation wall and footing	S.F. Ground	.14	.14	
2020	Basement Walls	4' foundation wall	L.F. Wall	50	1.79	
B. SHELL						
	B10 Superstructure					
1010	Floor Construction	N/A	—	—	—	18.8%
1020	Roof Construction	Wood deck on laminated wood arches	S.F. Roof	14.68	14.68	
	B20 Exterior Enclosure					
2010	Exterior Walls	Reinforced concrete block (end walls included) 90% of wall	S.F. Wall	9.47	6.39	
2020	Exterior Windows	Metal horizontal pivoted 10% of wall	Each	329	2.47	11.9%
2030	Exterior Doors	Aluminum and glass, hollow metal, steel overhead	Each	1384	.42	
	B30 Roofing					
3010	Roof Coverings	EPDM, 60 mils, fully adhered; polyisocyanurate insulation	S.F. Roof	2.91	2.91	3.7%
3020	Roof Openings	N/A	—	—	—	
C. INTERIORS						
1010	Partitions	Concrete block 50 S.F. Floor/L.F. Partition	S.F. Partition	6.55	1.31	
1020	Interior Doors	Single leaf hollow metal 500 S.F. Floor/Door	Each	572	1.14	
1030	Fittings	Toilet partitions	S.F. Floor	.28	.28	
2010	Stair Construction	N/A	—	—	—	21.4%
3010	Wall Finishes	50% paint, 50% ceramic tile	S.F. Surface	14.90	2.98	
3020	Floor Finishes	90% hardwood, 10% ceramic tile	S.F. Floor	10.50	10.50	
3030	Ceiling Finishes	Mineral fiber tile on concealed zee bars 15% of area	S.F. Ceiling	3.52	.53	
D. SERVICES						
	D10 Conveying					
1010	Elevators & Lifts	N/A	—	—	—	0.0%
1020	Escalators & Moving Walks	N/A	—	—	—	
	D20 Plumbing					
2010	Plumbing Fixtures	Toilet and service fixtures, supply and drainage 1 Fixture/515 S.F. Floor	Each	2152	4.18	
2020	Domestic Water Distribution	Electric water heater	S.F. Floor	2.54	2.54	8.6%
2040	Rain Water Drainage	N/A	—	—	—	
	D30 HVAC					
3010	Energy Supply	N/A	—	—	—	
3020	Heat Generating Systems	Included in D3050	—	—	—	
3030	Cooling Generating Systems	N/A	—	—	—	11.4%
3050	Terminal & Package Units	Single zone rooftop unit, gas heating, electric cooling	S.F. Floor	8.95	8.95	
3090	Other HVAC Sys. & Equipment	N/A	—	—	—	
	D40 Fire Protection					
4010	Sprinklers	Wet pipe sprinkler system	S.F. Floor	1.95	1.95	2.5%
4020	Standpipes	N/A	—	—	—	
	D50 Electrical					
5010	Electrical Service/Distribution	400 ampere service, panel board and feeders	S.F. Floor	.72	.72	
5020	Lighting & Branch Wiring	Fluorescent fixtures, receptacles, switches, A.C. and misc. power	S.F. Floor	6.69	6.69	11.5%
5030	Communications & Security	Alarm systems, sound system and emergency lighting	S.F. Floor	1.44	1.44	
5090	Other Electrical Systems	Emergency generator, 7.5 kW	S.F. Floor	.15	.15	
E. EQUIPMENT & FURNISHINGS						
1010	Commercial Equipment	N/A	—	—	—	
1020	Institutional Equipment	N/A	—	—	—	
1030	Vehicular Equipment	N/A	—	—	—	1.5%
1090	Other Equipment	Bleachers, sauna, weight room	S.F. Floor	1.16	1.16	
F. SPECIAL CONSTRUCTION						
1020	Integrated Construction	N/A	—	—	—	0.0%
1040	Special Facilities	N/A	—	—	—	
G. BUILDING SITEWORK	N/A					

		Sub-Total	78.21	100%
CONTRACTOR FEES (General Requirements: 10%, Overhead: 5%, Profit: 10%)		25%	19.55	
ARCHITECT FEES		7%	6.84	

Total Building Cost | **104.60**

Costs per square foot of floor area

Exterior Wall	S.F. Area	10000	16000	20000	22000	24000	26000	28000	30000	32000
	L.F. Perimeter	420	510	600	640	680	673	706	740	737
Face Brick with Concrete Block Back-up	Wood Truss	183.75	168.50	165.25	163.80	162.60	159.30	158.30	157.50	155.30
	Precast Conc.	211.00	192.80	189.05	187.30	185.95	181.90	180.70	179.75	177.05
Metal Sandwich Panel	Wood Truss	182.25	170.85	168.30	167.20	166.30	163.90	163.15	162.55	160.95
Precast Concrete Panel	Precast Conc.	191.90	178.25	175.30	174.00	172.95	170.00	169.15	168.35	166.45
Painted Concrete Block	Wood Frame	183.15	171.80	169.30	168.15	167.30	164.95	164.15	163.60	162.05
	Precast Conc.	194.70	180.45	177.40	176.00	174.95	171.90	170.95	170.20	168.15
Perimeter Adj., Add or Deduct	Per 100 L.F.	12.30	7.70	6.20	5.65	5.15	4.75	4.45	4.10	3.85
Story Hgt. Adj., Add or Deduct	Per 1 Ft.	1.50	1.15	1.10	1.05	1.05	.95	.95	.90	.90
For Basement, add $24.90 per square foot of basement area										

The above costs were calculated using the basic specifications shown on the facing page. These costs should be adjusted where necessary for design alternatives and owner's requirements. Reported completed project costs, for this type of structure, range from $71.70 to $210.80 per S.F.

Common additives

Description	Unit	$ Cost
Bleachers, Telescoping, manual		
To 15 tier	Seat	79 - 110
16-20 tier	Seat	161 - 196
21-30 tier	Seat	171 - 206
For power operation, add	Seat	31 - 48
Emergency Lighting, 25 watt, battery operated		
Lead battery	Each	227
Nickel cadmium	Each	660
Lockers, Steel, single tier, 60" or 72"	Opening	131 - 227
2 tier, 60" or 72" total	Opening	74 - 125
5 tier, box lockers	Opening	42 - 62
Locker bench, lam. maple top only	L.F.	19.50
Pedestal, steel pipe	Each	63
Pool Equipment		
Diving stand, 3 meter	Each	6975
1 meter	Each	4425
Diving board, 16' aluminum	Each	1875
Fiberglass	Each	1475
Lifeguard chair, fixed	Each	1675
Portable	Each	1900
Lights, underwater, 12 volt, 300 watt	Each	1175

Description	Unit	$ Cost
Sauna, Prefabricated, complete		
6' x 4'	Each	4825
6' x 6'	Each	5625
6' x 9'	Each	5550
8' x 8'	Each	6525
8' x 10'	Each	7225
10' x 12'	Each	9475
Sound System		
Amplifier, 250 watts	Each	1675
Speaker, ceiling or wall	Each	147
Trumpet	Each	275
Steam Bath, Complete, to 140 C.F.	Each	1325
To 300 C.F.	Each	1500
To 800 C.F.	Each	4825
To 2500 C.F.	Each	5125

Model costs calculated for a 1 story building with 24' story height and 20,000 square feet of floor area

Swimming Pool, Enclosed

				Unit	Unit Cost	Cost Per S.F.	% Of Sub-Total
A. SUBSTRUCTURE							
1010	Standard Foundations	Poured concrete; strip and spread footings		S.F. Ground	1.15	1.15	
1030	Slab on Grade	4" reinforced concrete with vapor barrier and granular base		S.F. Slab	3.65	3.65	15.7%
2010	Basement Excavation	Site preparation for slab and trench for foundation wall and footing		S.F. Ground	7.60	7.60	
2020	Basement Walls	4' foundation wall		L.F. Wall	114	6.87	
B. SHELL							
	B10 Superstructure						
1010	Floor Construction	N/A		—	—	—	11.2%
1020	Roof Construction	Wood deck on laminated wood truss		S.F. Roof	13.65	13.65	
	B20 Exterior Enclosure						
2010	Exterior Walls	Face brick with concrete block backup	80% of wall	S.F. Wall	22	13.22	
2020	Exterior Windows	Outward projecting steel	20% of wall	Each	34	5.02	15.2%
2030	Exterior Doors	Double aluminum and glass, hollow metal		Each	1619	.41	
	B30 Roofing						
3010	Roof Coverings	Asphalt shingles with flashing; perlite/EPS composite insulation		S.F. Roof	1.41	1.41	1.2%
3020	Roof Openings	N/A		—	—	—	
C. INTERIORS							
1010	Partitions	Concrete block	100 S.F. Floor/L.F. Partition	S.F. Partition	6.50	.65	
1020	Interior Doors	Single leaf hollow metal	1000 S.F. Floor/Door	Each	572	.57	
1030	Fittings	Toilet partitions		S.F. Floor	.17	.17	
2010	Stair Construction	N/A		—	—	—	15.9%
3010	Wall Finishes	Acrylic glazed coating		S.F. Surface	16.80	1.68	
3020	Floor Finishes	70% terrazzo, 30% ceramic tile		S.F. Floor	15.99	15.99	
3030	Ceiling Finishes	Mineral fiber tile on concealed zee bars	20% of area	S.F. Ceiling	1.75	.35	
D. SERVICES							
	D10 Conveying						
1010	Elevators & Lifts	N/A		—	—	—	0.0%
1020	Escalators & Moving Walks	N/A		—	—	—	
	D20 Plumbing						
2010	Plumbing Fixtures	Toilet and service fixtures, supply and drainage	1 Fixture/210 S.F. Floor	Each	1906	9.08	
2020	Domestic Water Distribution	Gas fired water heater		S.F. Floor	1.94	1.94	9.0%
2040	Rain Water Drainage	N/A		—	—	—	
	D30 HVAC						
3010	Energy Supply	Terminal unit heaters	10% of area	S.F. Floor	.55	.55	
3020	Heat Generating Systems	N/A		—	—	—	
3030	Cooling Generating Systems	N/A		—	—	—	9.0%
3050	Terminal & Package Units	Single zone unit gas heating, electric cooling		S.F. Floor	10.44	10.44	
3090	Other HVAC Sys. & Equipment	N/A		—	—	—	
	D40 Fire Protection						
4010	Sprinklers	Sprinklers, light hazard		S.F. Floor	.98	.98	0.8%
4020	Standpipes	N/A		—	—	—	
	D50 Electrical						
5010	Electrical Service/Distribution	400 ampere service, panel board and feeders		S.F. Floor	.75	.75	
5020	Lighting & Branch Wiring	Fluorescent fixtures, receptacles, switches, A.C. and misc. power		S.F. Floor	6.74	6.74	6.4%
5030	Communications & Security	Alarm systems and emergency lighting		S.F. Floor	.25	.25	
5090	Other Electrical Systems	Emergency generator, 15 kW		S.F. Floor	.07	.07	
E. EQUIPMENT & FURNISHINGS							
1010	Commercial Equipment	N/A		—	—	—	
1020	Institutional Equipment	N/A		—	—	—	15.7%
1030	Vehicular Equipment	N/A		—	—	—	
1090	Other Equipment	Swimming pool		S.F. Floor	19.23	19.23	
F. SPECIAL CONSTRUCTION							
1020	Integrated Construction	N/A		—	—	—	0.0%
1040	Special Facilities	N/A		—	—	—	
G. BUILDING SITEWORK	**N/A**						
				Sub-Total		122.42	100%
	CONTRACTOR FEES (General Requirements: 10%, Overhead: 5%, Profit: 10%)				25%	30.59	
	ARCHITECT FEES				8%	12.24	
				Total Building Cost		**165.25**	

Costs per square foot of floor area

Exterior Wall	S.F. Area	10000	15000	20000	25000	30000	35000	40000	45000	50000
	L.F. Perimeter	450	500	600	700	740	822	890	920	966
Face Brick with Concrete Block Back-up	Steel Frame	136.85	123.35	119.10	116.55	112.85	111.35	109.95	108.00	106.75
	Lam. Wood Truss	141.25	128.30	124.20	121.70	118.20	116.75	115.40	113.55	112.30
Concrete Block	Steel Frame	134.60	126.60	123.95	122.25	120.20	119.30	118.50	117.35	116.65
	Lam. Wood Truss	123.95	116.00	113.30	111.65	109.55	108.70	107.85	106.75	106.05
Galvanized Steel Siding	Steel Frame	130.35	122.35	119.65	118.00	115.90	115.00	114.15	113.10	112.35
Metal Sandwich Panel	Steel Joists	136.35	126.80	123.65	121.75	119.15	118.10	117.15	115.80	114.90
Perimeter Adj., Add or Deduct	Per 100 L.F.	9.95	6.70	4.95	3.90	3.30	2.90	2.50	2.20	2.00
Story Hgt. Adj., Add or Deduct	Per 1 Ft.	1.55	1.15	1.00	.90	.80	.85	.70	.70	.65
Basement—Not Applicable										

The above costs were calculated using the basic specifications shown on the facing page. These costs should be adjusted where necessary for design alternatives and owner's requirements. Reported completed project costs, for this type of structure, range from $46.90 to $145.80 per S.F.

Common additives

Description	Unit	$ Cost
Bar, Front Bar	L.F.	287
Back bar	L.F.	229
Booth, Upholstered, custom straight	L.F.	145 - 265
"L" or "U" shaped	L.F.	150 - 252
Bleachers, Telescoping, manual		
To 15 tier	Seat	79 - 110
16-20 tier	Seat	161 - 196
21-30 tier	Seat	171 - 206
For power operation, add	Seat	31 - 48
Emergency Lighting, 25 watt, battery operated		
Lead battery	Each	227
Nickel cadmium	Each	660
Lockers, Steel, single tier, 60" or 72"	Opening	131 - 227
2 tier, 60" or 72" total	Opening	74 - 125
5 tier, box lockers	Opening	42 - 62
Locker bench, lam. maple top only	L.F.	19.50
Pedestals, steel pipe	Each	63

Description	Unit	$ Cost
Rink		
Dasher boards & top guard	Each	152,000
Mats, rubber	S.F.	16.70
Score Board	Each	11,000 - 32,100

Model costs calculated for a 1 story building with 24' story height and 30,000 square feet of floor area

Rink, Hockey/Indoor Soccer

				Unit	Unit Cost	Cost Per S.F.	% Of Sub-Total
A. SUBSTRUCTURE							
1010	Standard Foundations	Poured concrete; strip and spread footings		S.F. Ground	1.26	1.26	
1030	Slab on Grade	6" reinforced concrete with vapor barrier and granular base		S.F. Slab	4.37	4.37	8.5%
2010	Basement Excavation	Site preparation for slab and trench for foundation wall and footing		S.F. Ground	.14	.14	
2020	Basement Walls	4' foundation wall		L.F. Wall	108	1.85	
B. SHELL							
	B10 Superstructure						
1010	Floor Construction	Wide flange beams and columns		S.F. Floor	20	14.69	27.0%
1020	Roof Construction	Metal deck on steel joist		S.F. Roof	9.58	9.58	
	B20 Exterior Enclosure						
2010	Exterior Walls	Concrete block	95% of wall	S.F. Wall	8.73	4.91	
2020	Exterior Windows	Store front	5% of wall	Each	35	1.06	7.3%
2030	Exterior Doors	Aluminum and glass, hollow metal, overhead		Each	2155	.57	
	B30 Roofing						
3010	Roof Coverings	Elastomeric neoprene membrane with flashing; perlite/EPS composite insulation		S.F. Roof	3.35	3.35	3.9%
3020	Roof Openings	Roof hatches		S.F. Roof	.15	.15	
C. INTERIORS							
1010	Partitions	Concrete block	140 S.F. Floor/L.F. Partition	S.F. Partition	6.53	.56	
1020	Interior Doors	Hollow metal	2500 S.F. Floor/Door	Each	572	.22	
1030	Fittings	N/A		—	—	—	
2010	Stair Construction	N/A		—	—	—	5.8%
3010	Wall Finishes	Paint		S.F. Surface	16.83	1.53	
3020	Floor Finishes	80% rubber mat, 20% paint	50% of floor area	S.F. Floor	5.10	2.55	
3030	Ceiling Finishes	Mineral fiber tile on concealed zee bar	10% of area	S.F. Ceiling	3.52	.35	
D. SERVICES							
	D10 Conveying						
1010	Elevators & Lifts	N/A		—	—	—	0.0%
1020	Escalators & Moving Walks	N/A		—	—	—	
	D20 Plumbing						
2010	Plumbing Fixtures	Toilet and service fixtures, supply and drainage	1 Fixture/1070 S.F. Floor	Each	2428	2.27	
2020	Domestic Water Distribution	Oil fired water heater		S.F. Floor	1.41	1.41	4.1%
2040	Rain Water Drainage	N/A		—	—	—	
	D30 HVAC						
3010	Energy Supply	Oil fired hot water, unit heaters	10% of area	S.F. Floor	.55	.55	
3020	Heat Generating Systems	N/A		—	—	—	
3030	Cooling Generating Systems	N/A		—	—	—	12.2%
3050	Terminal & Package Units	Single zone, electric cooling	90% of area	S.F. Floor	10.44	10.44	
3090	Other HVAC Sys. & Equipment	N/A		—	—	—	
	D40 Fire Protection						
4010	Sprinklers	N/A		—	—	—	0.0%
4020	Standpipes	N/A		—	—	—	
	D50 Electrical						
5010	Electrical Service/Distribution	600 ampere service, panel board and feeders		S.F. Floor	1.24	1.24	
5020	Lighting & Branch Wiring	High intensity discharge and fluorescent fixtures, receptacles, switches, A.C. and misc. power		S.F. Floor	5.68	5.68	8.8%
5030	Communications & Security	Alarm systems, emergency lighting and public address		S.F. Floor	.82	.82	
5090	Other Electrical Systems	Emergency generator		S.F. Floor	.15	.15	
E. EQUIPMENT & FURNISHINGS							
1010	Commercial Equipment	N/A		—	—	—	
1020	Institutional Equipment	N/A		—	—	—	0.0%
1030	Vehicular Equipment	N/A		—	—	—	
1090	Other Equipment	N/A		—	—	—	
F. SPECIAL CONSTRUCTION							
1020	Integrated Construction	N/A		—	—	—	22.5%
1040	Special Facilities	Dasher boards and rink (including ice making system)		S.F. Floor	20	20.18	
G. BUILDING SITEWORK	**N/A**						

		Sub-Total	89.88	100%
CONTRACTOR FEES (General Requirements: 10%, Overhead: 5%, Profit: 10%)		25%	22.46	
ARCHITECT FEES		7%	7.86	

Total Building Cost	**120.20**

General Conditions, Overhead & Profit, Architectural Fees

General Conditions, Overhead & Profit

The total building costs in the Square Foot Models section include a 10% allowance for general conditions and a 15% allowance for the general contractor's overhead and profit and contingencies.

General contractor overhead includes indirect costs such as permits, Workers' Compensation, insurances, supervision and bonding fees. Overhead will vary with the size of project, the contractor's operating procedures and location. Profits will vary with economic activity and local conditions.

Contingencies provide for unforeseen construction difficulties which include material shortages and weather. In all situations, the appraiser should give consideration to possible adjustment of the 25% factor used in developing the Square Foot Models.

Architectural Fees

Tabulated below are typical percentage fees by project size, for good professional architectural service. Fees may vary from those listed depending upon degree of design difficulty and economic conditions in any particular area.

Rates can be interpolated horizontally and vertically. Various portions of the same project requiring different rates should be adjusted proportionately. For alterations, add 50% to the fee for the first $500,000 of project cost and add 25% to the fee for project cost over $500,000.

Architectural fees tabulated below include Engineering fees.

Insurance Exclusions

Many insurance companies exclude from coverage such items as architect's fees, excavation, foundations below grade, underground piping and site preparation. Since exclusions vary among insurance companies, it is recommended that for greatest accuracy each exclusion be priced separately using the unit-in-place section.

As a rule of thumb, exclusions can be calculated at 9% of total building cost plus the appropriate allowance for architect's fees.

Building Types	Total Project Size in Thousands of Dollars						
	100	250	500	1,000	5,000	10,000	50,000
Factories, garages, warehouses, repetitive housing	9.0%	8.0%	7.0%	6.2%	5.3%	4.9%	4.5%
Apartments, banks, schools, libraries, offices, municipal buildings	12.2	12.3	9.2	8.0	7.0	6.6	6.2
Churches, hospitals, homes, laboratories, museums, research	15.0	13.6	12.7	11.9	9.5	8.8	8.0
Memorials, monumental work, decorative furnishings	—	16.0	14.5	13.1	10.0	9.0	8.3

Historical Cost Indexes

The table below lists both the Means Historical Cost Index based on Jan. 1, 1993 = 100 as well as the computed value of an index based on Jan. 1, 2004 costs. Since the Jan. 1, 2004 figure is estimated, space is left to write in the actual index figures as they become available through either the quarterly "Means Construction Cost Indexes" or as printed in the "Engineering News-Record." To compute the actual index based on Jan. 1, 2004 = 100, divide the Historical Cost Index for a particular year by the actual Jan. 1, 2004 Construction Cost Index. Space has been left to advance the index figures as the year progresses.

Year	Historical Cost Index Jan. 1, 1993 = 100		Current Index Based on Jan. 1, 2004 = 100		Year	Historical Cost Index Jan. 1, 1993 = 100	Current Index Based on Jan. 1, 2004 = 100		Year	Historical Cost Index Jan. 1, 1993 = 100	Current Index Based on Jan. 1, 2004 = 100	
	Est.	Actual	Est.	Actual		Actual	Est.	Actual		Actual	Est.	Actual
Oct 2004					July 1989	92.1	69.3		July 1971	32.1	24.1	
July 2004					1988	89.9	67.6		1970	28.7	21.6	
April 2004					1987	87.7	65.9		1969	26.9	20.2	
Jan 2004	133.0		100.0	100.0	1986	84.2	63.3		1968	24.9	18.7	
July 2003		132.0	99.2		1985	82.6	62.1		1967	23.5	17.7	
2002		128.7	96.8		1984	82.0	61.6		1966	22.7	17.1	
2001		125.1	94.1		1983	80.2	60.3		1965	21.7	16.3	
2000		120.9	90.9		1982	76.1	57.3		1964	21.2	15.9	
1999		117.6	88.4		1981	70.0	52.6		1963	20.7	15.6	
1998		115.1	86.5		1980	62.9	47.3		1962	20.2	15.2	
1997		112.8	84.8		1979	57.8	43.5		1961	19.8	14.9	
1996		110.2	82.9		1978	53.5	40.2		1960	19.7	14.8	
1995		107.6	80.9		1977	49.5	37.2		1959	19.3	14.5	
1994		104.4	78.5		1976	46.9	35.3		1958	18.8	14.1	
1993		101.7	76.5		1975	44.8	33.7		1957	18.4	13.8	
1992		99.4	74.8		1974	41.4	31.1		1956	17.6	13.2	
1991		96.8	72.8		1973	37.7	28.3		1955	16.6	12.5	
1990		94.3	70.9		1972	34.8	26.2		1954	16.0	12.0	

Adjustments to Costs

The Historical Cost Index can be used to convert National Average building costs at a particular time to the approximate building costs for some other time. For example, the index can be used to arrive at approximate project costs based on existing completed projects by allowing easy price escalation to the current year.

Example:

Estimate and compare construction costs for different years in the same city.

To estimate the National Average construction cost of a building in 1970, knowing that it cost $900,000 in 2004:

INDEX in 1970 = 28.7

INDEX in 2004 = 133.0

Note: The City Cost Indexes for Canada can be used to convert U.S. National averages to local costs in Canadian dollars.

Time Adjustment using the Historical Cost Indexes:

$$\frac{\text{Index for Year A}}{\text{Index for Year B}} \times \text{Cost in Year B} = \text{Cost in Year A}$$

$$\frac{\text{INDEX 1970}}{\text{INDEX 2004}} \times \text{Cost 2004} = \text{Cost 1970}$$

$$\frac{28.7}{133.0} \times \$900,000 = .216 \times \$900,000 = \$194,400$$

The construction cost of the building in 1970 is $194,400.

Costs shown in *Means cost data publications* are based on National Averages for materials and installation. To adjust these costs to a specific location, simply multiply the base cost by the factor for that city. The data is arranged alphabetically by state and postal zip code numbers. For a city not listed, use the factor for a nearby city with similar economic characteristics.

STATE/ZIP	CITY	Residential	Commercial
ALABAMA			
350-352	Birmingham	.86	.87
354	Tuscaloosa	.73	.78
355	Jasper	.70	.77
356	Decatur	.76	.79
357-358	Huntsville	.84	.85
359	Gadsden	.73	.80
360-361	Montgomery	.75	.79
362	Anniston	.68	.74
363	Dothan	.74	.75
364	Evergreen	.71	.76
365-366	Mobile	.79	.81
367	Selma	.72	.76
368	Phenix City	.73	.78
369	Butler	.71	.75
ALASKA			
995-996	Anchorage	1.28	1.26
997	Fairbanks	1.30	1.25
998	Juneau	1.28	1.25
999	Ketchikan	1.30	1.31
ARIZONA			
850,853	Phoenix	.87	.88
852	Mesa/Tempe	.85	.85
855	Globe	.81	.83
856-857	Tucson	.85	.86
859	Show Low	.84	.84
860	Flagstaff	.85	.86
863	Prescott	.82	.84
864	Kingman	.82	.84
865	Chambers	.82	.82
ARKANSAS			
716	Pine Bluff	.77	.80
717	Camden	.66	.69
718	Texarkana	.71	.72
719	Hot Springs	.64	.68
720-722	Little Rock	.82	.82
723	West Memphis	.75	.77
724	Jonesboro	.73	.77
725	Batesville	.72	.74
726	Harrison	.73	.74
727	Fayetteville	.62	.66
728	Russellville	.71	.73
729	Fort Smith	.77	.78
CALIFORNIA			
900-902	Los Angeles	1.07	1.08
903-905	Inglewood	1.04	1.04
906-908	Long Beach	1.03	1.04
910-912	Pasadena	1.04	1.05
913-916	Van Nuys	1.07	1.07
917-918	Alhambra	1.08	1.06
919-921	San Diego	1.03	1.05
922	Palm Springs	1.00	1.03
923-924	San Bernardino	1.01	1.02
925	Riverside	1.07	1.08
926-927	Santa Ana	1.05	1.04
928	Anaheim	1.08	1.08
930	Oxnard	1.08	1.08
931	Santa Barbara	1.07	1.08
932-933	Bakersfield	1.05	1.06
934	San Luis Obispo	1.07	1.06
935	Mojave	1.04	1.03
936-938	Fresno	1.11	1.09
939	Salinas	1.12	1.11
940-941	San Francisco	1.22	1.24
942,956-958	Sacramento	1.12	1.11
943	Palo Alto	1.17	1.16
944	San Mateo	1.21	1.18
945	Vallejo	1.14	1.12
946	Oakland	1.19	1.18
947	Berkeley	1.22	1.17
948	Richmond	1.23	1.17
949	San Rafael	1.21	1.18
950	Santa Cruz	1.15	1.14
951	San Jose	1.20	1.19
952	Stockton	1.10	1.09
953	Modesto	1.09	1.09

STATE/ZIP	CITY	Residential	Commercial
CALIFORNIA (CONT'D)			
954	Santa Rosa	1.15	1.15
955	Eureka	1.11	1.07
959	Marysville	1.11	1.10
960	Redding	1.12	1.10
961	Susanville	1.11	1.10
COLORADO			
800-802	Denver	.95	.96
803	Boulder	.94	.93
804	Golden	.91	.94
805	Fort Collins	.90	.93
806	Greeley	.79	.86
807	Fort Morgan	.94	.93
808-809	Colorado Springs	.92	.95
810	Pueblo	.93	.93
811	Alamosa	.90	.93
812	Salida	.92	.93
813	Durango	.94	.93
814	Montrose	.89	.92
815	Grand Junction	.93	.93
816	Glenwood Springs	.92	.95
CONNECTICUT			
060	New Britain	1.08	1.08
061	Hartford	1.07	1.08
062	Willimantic	1.07	1.08
063	New London	1.07	1.06
064	Meriden	1.07	1.08
065	New Haven	1.08	1.09
066	Bridgeport	1.08	1.08
067	Waterbury	1.08	1.08
068	Norwalk	1.08	1.09
069	Stamford	1.09	1.11
D.C.			
200-205	Washington	.92	.95
DELAWARE			
197	Newark	1.01	1.03
198	Wilmington	1.01	1.03
199	Dover	1.01	1.03
FLORIDA			
320,322	Jacksonville	.78	.81
321	Daytona Beach	.85	.87
323	Tallahassee	.72	.76
324	Panama City	.66	.71
325	Pensacola	.76	.80
326,344	Gainesville	.76	.80
327-328,347	Orlando	.79	.83
329	Melbourne	.86	.90
330-332,340	Miami	.83	.87
333	Fort Lauderdale	.84	.86
334,349	West Palm Beach	.83	.84
335-336,346	Tampa	.87	.88
337	St. Petersburg	.76	.81
338	Lakeland	.84	.87
339,341	Fort Myers	.81	.83
342	Sarasota	.85	.85
GEORGIA			
300-303,399	Atlanta	.89	.90
304	Statesboro	.67	.73
305	Gainesville	.73	.78
306	Athens	.74	.80
307	Dalton	.70	.76
308-309	Augusta	.76	.79
310-312	Macon	.77	.79
313-314	Savannah	.79	.80
315	Waycross	.71	.77
316	Valdosta	.71	.75
317	Albany	.73	.77
318-319	Columbus	.76	.77
HAWAII			
967	Hilo	1.23	1.21
968	Honolulu	1.24	1.22

Location Factors

STATE/ZIP	CITY	Residential	Commercial
STATES & POSS.			
969	Guam	1.60	1.29
IDAHO			
832	Pocatello	.89	.91
833	Twin Falls	.73	.76
834	Idaho Falls	.72	.80
835	Lewiston	.99	.99
836-837	Boise	.90	.92
838	Coeur d'Alene	.85	.86
ILLINOIS			
600-603	North Suburban	1.11	1.09
604	Joliet	1.13	1.09
605	South Suburban	1.10	1.08
606	Chicago	1.15	1.13
609	Kankakee	1.03	1.02
610-611	Rockford	1.04	1.04
612	Rock Island	.97	.97
613	La Salle	1.02	.99
614	Galesburg	.99	.99
615-616	Peoria	1.02	1.01
617	Bloomington	.98	.99
618-619	Champaign	.99	1.01
620-622	East St. Louis	.99	.99
623	Quincy	.98	.96
624	Effingham	.99	.97
625	Decatur	.99	.98
626-627	Springfield	.99	.98
628	Centralia	.97	.97
629	Carbondale	.96	.95
INDIANA			
460	Anderson	.92	.91
461-462	Indianapolis	.96	.94
463-464	Gary	1.02	1.00
465-466	South Bend	.92	.91
467-468	Fort Wayne	.92	.91
469	Kokomo	.94	.91
470	Lawrenceburg	.88	.88
471	New Albany	.86	.86
472	Columbus	.93	.90
473	Muncie	.92	.91
474	Bloomington	.96	.92
475	Washington	.91	.92
476-477	Evansville	.91	.93
478	Terre Haute	.91	.93
479	Lafayette	.92	.90
IOWA			
500-503, 509	Des Moines	.93	.92
504	Mason City	.78	.82
505	Fort Dodge	.77	.80
506-507	Waterloo	.81	.82
508	Creston	.83	.84
510-511	Sioux City	.87	.88
512	Sibley	.74	.77
513	Spencer	.76	.77
514	Carroll	.76	.78
515	Council Bluffs	.82	.88
516	Shenandoah	.74	.76
520	Dubuque	.86	.89
521	Decorah	.77	.78
522-524	Cedar Rapids	.94	.93
525	Ottumwa	.84	.86
526	Burlington	.88	.87
527-528	Davenport	.98	.97
KANSAS			
660-662	Kansas City	.95	.96
664-666	Topeka	.78	.84
667	Fort Scott	.85	.83
668	Emporia	.73	.80
669	Belleville	.74	.79
670-672	Wichita	.81	.85
673	Independence	.74	.77
674	Salina	.73	.80
675	Hutchinson	.68	.74
676	Hays	.74	.78
677	Colby	.76	.79
678	Dodge City	.74	.79
679	Liberal	.68	.74
KENTUCKY			
400-402	Louisville	.92	.91
403-405	Lexington	.84	.83

STATE/ZIP	CITY	Residential	Commercial
KENTUCKY (CONT'D)			
406	Frankfort	.82	.84
407-409	Corbin	.67	.71
410	Covington	.95	.95
411-412	Ashland	.93	.96
413-414	Campton	.68	.72
415-416	Pikeville	.78	.81
417-418	Hazard	.67	.72
420	Paducah	.89	.91
421-422	Bowling Green	.89	.89
423	Owensboro	.83	.86
424	Henderson	.92	.93
425-426	Somerset	.67	.71
427	Elizabethtown	.88	.89
LOUISIANA			
700-701	New Orleans	.86	.86
703	Thibodaux	.82	.85
704	Hammond	.80	.83
705	Lafayette	.78	.80
706	Lake Charles	.80	.82
707-708	Baton Rouge	.80	.80
710-711	Shreveport	.79	.80
712	Monroe	.75	.79
713-714	Alexandria	.74	.77
MAINE			
039	Kittery	.81	.87
040-041	Portland	.89	.90
042	Lewiston	.89	.90
043	Augusta	.84	.88
044	Bangor	.87	.90
045	Bath	.82	.87
046	Machias	.82	.87
047	Houlton	.87	.89
048	Rockland	.80	.86
049	Waterville	.76	.85
MARYLAND			
206	Waldorf	.84	.87
207-208	College Park	.85	.90
209	Silver Spring	.85	.89
210-212	Baltimore	.90	.91
214	Annapolis	.86	.89
215	Cumberland	.85	.87
216	Easton	.69	.72
217	Hagerstown	.86	.88
218	Salisbury	.75	.77
219	Elkton	.83	.82
MASSACHUSETTS			
010-011	Springfield	1.05	1.03
012	Pittsfield	1.00	1.00
013	Greenfield	1.00	1.00
014	Fitchburg	1.09	1.06
015-016	Worcester	1.10	1.08
017	Framingham	1.11	1.09
018	Lowell	1.12	1.10
019	Lawrence	1.12	1.10
020-022, 024	Boston	1.17	1.15
023	Brockton	1.11	1.09
025	Buzzards Bay	1.09	1.06
026	Hyannis	1.08	1.07
027	New Bedford	1.11	1.08
MICHIGAN			
480, 483	Royal Oak	1.05	1.02
481	Ann Arbor	1.05	1.03
482	Detroit	1.10	1.07
484-485	Flint	.99	.98
486	Saginaw	.96	.96
487	Bay City	.96	.96
488-489	Lansing	.98	.98
490	Battle Creek	.94	.94
491	Kalamazoo	.93	.92
492	Jackson	.94	.95
493, 495	Grand Rapids	.84	.85
494	Muskegon	.90	.91
496	Traverse City	.83	.86
497	Gaylord	.81	.84
498-499	Iron Mountain	.92	.94
MINNESOTA			
550-551	Saint Paul	1.14	1.12
553-555	Minneapolis	1.18	1.13

STATE/ZIP	CITY	Residential	Commercial
MINNESOTA (CONT'D)			
556-558	Duluth	1.10	1.05
559	Rochester	1.05	1.03
560	Mankato	1.02	1.01
561	Windom	.85	.90
562	Willmar	.86	.93
563	St. Cloud	1.10	1.09
564	Brainerd	.98	1.00
565	Detroit Lakes	.99	1.00
566	Bemidji	.96	.99
567	Thief River Falls	.94	.97
MISSISSIPPI			
386	Clarksdale	.60	.66
387	Greenville	.69	.75
388	Tupelo	.63	.70
389	Greenwood	.63	.67
390-392	Jackson	.72	.75
393	Meridian	.66	.74
394	Laurel	.62	.68
395	Biloxi	.75	.78
396	McComb	.73	.76
397	Columbus	.64	.70
MISSOURI			
630-631	St. Louis	1.01	1.02
633	Bowling Green	.91	.94
634	Hannibal	.88	.91
635	Kirksville	.81	.89
636	Flat River	.94	.97
637	Cape Girardeau	.87	.94
638	Sikeston	.84	.91
639	Poplar Bluff	.85	.91
640-641	Kansas City	1.01	1.02
644-645	St. Joseph	.95	.96
646	Chillicothe	.86	.85
647	Harrisonville	.96	.98
648	Joplin	.83	.85
650-651	Jefferson City	.89	.92
652	Columbia	.89	.94
653	Sedalia	.87	.92
654-655	Rolla	.89	.88
656-658	Springfield	.85	.88
MONTANA			
590-591	Billings	.88	.89
592	Wolf Point	.85	.88
593	Miles City	.87	.87
594	Great Falls	.89	.89
595	Havre	.82	.87
596	Helena	.89	.88
597	Butte	.84	.88
598	Missoula	.84	.86
599	Kalispell	.83	.86
NEBRASKA			
680-681	Omaha	.90	.90
683-685	Lincoln	.79	.85
686	Columbus	.69	.76
687	Norfolk	.78	.83
688	Grand Island	.78	.84
689	Hastings	.76	.80
690	Mccook	.69	.75
691	North Platte	.75	.80
692	Valentine	.66	.72
693	Alliance	.65	.71
NEVADA			
889-891	Las Vegas	1.01	1.04
893	Ely	.92	.93
894-895	Reno	.97	.99
897	Carson City	.97	.98
898	Elko	.93	.92
NEW HAMPSHIRE			
030	Nashua	.91	.94
031	Manchester	.91	.94
032-033	Concord	.88	.93
034	Keene	.73	.77
035	Littleton	.81	.82
036	Charleston	.71	.75
037	Claremont	.72	.75
038	Portsmouth	.85	.90

STATE/ZIP	CITY	Residential	Commercial
NEW JERSEY			
070-071	Newark	1.13	1.11
072	Elizabeth	1.15	1.10
073	Jersey City	1.12	1.10
074-075	Paterson	1.13	1.11
076	Hackensack	1.12	1.10
077	Long Branch	1.12	1.09
078	Dover	1.12	1.09
079	Summit	1.12	1.10
080,083	Vineland	1.10	1.08
081	Camden	1.11	1.08
082,084	Atlantic City	1.14	1.08
085-086	Trenton	1.12	1.10
087	Point Pleasant	1.11	1.09
088-089	New Brunswick	1.12	1.09
NEW MEXICO			
870-872	Albuquerque	.86	.89
873	Gallup	.86	.90
874	Farmington	.86	.90
875	Santa Fe	.86	.89
877	Las Vegas	.86	.89
878	Socorro	.86	.89
879	Truth/Consequences	.84	.86
880	Las Cruces	.83	.84
881	Clovis	.85	.89
882	Roswell	.86	.89
883	Carrizozo	.86	.90
884	Tucumcari	.86	.89
NEW YORK			
100-102	New York	1.37	1.34
103	Staten Island	1.30	1.30
104	Bronx	1.32	1.29
105	Mount Vernon	1.18	1.19
106	White Plains	1.21	1.19
107	Yonkers	1.22	1.21
108	New Rochelle	1.23	1.19
109	Suffern	1.15	1.14
110	Queens	1.30	1.30
111	Long Island City	1.33	1.31
112	Brooklyn	1.34	1.31
113	Flushing	1.32	1.31
114	Jamaica	1.32	1.30
115,117,118	Hicksville	1.22	1.24
116	Far Rockaway	1.31	1.31
119	Riverhead	1.23	1.25
120-122	Albany	.96	.97
123	Schenectady	.96	.97
124	Kingston	1.04	1.09
125-126	Poughkeepsie	1.08	1.11
127	Monticello	1.05	1.08
128	Glens Falls	.88	.92
129	Plattsburgh	.93	.92
130-132	Syracuse	.96	.96
133-135	Utica	.93	.94
136	Watertown	.92	.95
137-139	Binghamton	.92	.93
140-142	Buffalo	1.06	1.02
143	Niagara Falls	1.04	1.02
144-146	Rochester	.99	.99
147	Jamestown	.91	.93
148-149	Elmira	.89	.92
NORTH CAROLINA			
270,272-274	Greensboro	.74	.75
271	Winston-Salem	.74	.75
275-276	Raleigh	.75	.76
277	Durham	.74	.75
278	Rocky Mount	.64	.68
279	Elizabeth City	.62	.69
280	Gastonia	.74	.74
281-282	Charlotte	.75	.75
283	Fayetteville	.72	.75
284	Wilmington	.72	.74
285	Kinston	.62	.67
286	Hickory	.62	.67
287-288	Asheville	.72	.74
289	Murphy	.66	.67
NORTH DAKOTA			
580-581	Fargo	.81	.85
582	Grand Forks	.76	.82
583	Devils Lake	.81	.83
584	Jamestown	.75	.80
585	Bismarck	.81	.85

Location Factors

STATE/ZIP	CITY	Residential	Commercial
NORTH DAKOTA (CONT'D)			
586	Dickinson	.78	.84
587	Minot	.81	.86
588	Williston	.78	.83
OHIO			
430-432	Columbus	.96	.95
433	Marion	.94	.93
434-436	Toledo	1.02	1.00
437-438	Zanesville	.91	.91
439	Steubenville	.96	.96
440	Lorain	1.03	1.00
441	Cleveland	1.03	1.02
442-443	Akron	1.00	.99
444-445	Youngstown	.97	.97
446-447	Canton	.95	.95
448-449	Mansfield	.97	.95
450	Hamilton	.96	.93
451-452	Cincinnati	.96	.94
453-454	Dayton	.93	.91
455	Springfield	.94	.92
456	Chillicothe	.97	.95
457	Athens	.88	.89
458	Lima	.91	.94
OKLAHOMA			
730-731	Oklahoma City	.81	.83
734	Ardmore	.79	.81
735	Lawton	.83	.83
736	Clinton	.78	.81
737	Enid	.78	.81
738	Woodward	.77	.80
739	Guymon	.67	.67
740-741	Tulsa	.80	.81
743	Miami	.83	.82
744	Muskogee	.72	.72
745	Mcalester	.75	.76
746	Ponca City	.78	.80
747	Durant	.77	.80
748	Shawnee	.77	.80
749	Poteau	.78	.80
OREGON			
970-972	Portland	1.02	1.04
973	Salem	1.02	1.04
974	Eugene	1.01	1.03
975	Medford	1.00	1.03
976	Klamath Falls	1.00	1.04
977	Bend	1.02	1.04
978	Pendleton	.99	1.00
979	Vale	.98	.95
PENNSYLVANIA			
150-152	Pittsburgh	.98	1.01
153	Washington	.94	.99
154	Uniontown	.92	.97
155	Bedford	.88	.94
156	Greensburg	.95	.98
157	Indiana	.91	.96
158	Dubois	.90	.96
159	Johnstown	.91	.96
160	Butler	.94	.97
161	New Castle	.94	.97
162	Kittanning	.95	.98
163	Oil City	.91	.95
164-165	Erie	.97	.96
166	Altoona	.90	.94
167	Bradford	.90	.96
168	State College	.93	.95
169	Wellsboro	.89	.94
170-171	Harrisburg	.93	.95
172	Chambersburg	.89	.93
173-174	York	.89	.93
175-176	Lancaster	.91	.92
177	Williamsport	.86	.89
178	Sunbury	.90	.93
179	Pottsville	.90	.94
180	Lehigh Valley	.99	1.01
181	Allentown	1.02	1.00
182	Hazleton	.90	.96
183	Stroudsburg	.93	.97
184-185	Scranton	.96	.97
186-187	Wilkes-Barre	.92	.94
188	Montrose	.90	.95
189	Doylestown	1.04	1.05

STATE/ZIP	CITY	Residential	Commercial
PENNSYLVANIA (CONT'D)			
190-191	Philadelphia	1.13	1.12
193	Westchester	1.07	1.06
194	Norristown	1.06	1.07
195-196	Reading	.95	.97
PUERTO RICO			
009	San Juan	.84	.86
RHODE ISLAND			
028	Newport	1.07	1.04
029	Providence	1.07	1.05
SOUTH CAROLINA			
290-292	Columbia	.73	.74
293	Spartanburg	.72	.72
294	Charleston	.72	.75
295	Florence	.67	.72
296	Greenville	.71	.72
297	Rock Hill	.65	.66
298	Aiken	.84	.85
299	Beaufort	.67	.69
SOUTH DAKOTA			
570-571	Sioux Falls	.77	.81
572	Watertown	.73	.78
573	Mitchell	.75	.77
574	Aberdeen	.76	.80
575	Pierre	.76	.79
576	Mobridge	.74	.77
577	Rapid City	.76	.78
TENNESSEE			
370-372	Nashville	.84	.87
373-374	Chattanooga	.77	.79
375,380-381	Memphis	.83	.87
376	Johnson City	.72	.80
377-379	Knoxville	.74	.79
382	Mckenzie	.70	.75
383	Jackson	.71	.78
384	Columbia	.73	.78
385	Cookeville	.68	.76
TEXAS			
750	Mckinney	.77	.80
751	Waxahackie	.78	.80
752-753	Dallas	.84	.84
754	Greenville	.70	.73
755	Texarkana	.75	.78
756	Longview	.69	.73
757	Tyler	.76	.80
758	Palestine	.69	.72
759	Lufkin	.74	.74
760-761	Fort Worth	.84	.82
762	Denton	.77	.77
763	Wichita Falls	.80	.79
764	Eastland	.73	.72
765	Temple	.76	.75
766-767	Waco	.78	.79
768	Brownwood	.69	.71
769	San Angelo	.73	.75
770-772	Houston	.86	.87
773	Huntsville	.69	.72
774	Wharton	.71	.75
775	Galveston	.84	.85
776-777	Beaumont	.83	.82
778	Bryan	.74	.81
779	Victoria	.75	.76
780	Laredo	.73	.76
781-782	San Antonio	.79	.81
783-784	Corpus Christi	.78	.78
785	Mc Allen	.76	.75
786-787	Austin	.80	.80
788	Del Rio	.66	.68
789	Giddings	.69	.71
790-791	Amarillo	.79	.80
792	Childress	.76	.77
793-794	Lubbock	.77	.79
795-796	Abilene	.76	.78
797	Midland	.77	.78
798-799,885	El Paso	.76	.77
UTAH			
840-841	Salt Lake City	.84	.89
842,844	Ogden	.82	.87

STATE/ZIP	CITY	Residential	Commercial
UTAH (CONT'D)			
843	Logan	.83	.88
845	Price	.73	.78
846-847	Provo	.84	.88
VERMONT			
050	White River Jct.	.74	.76
051	Bellows Falls	.75	.76
052	Bennington	.74	.76
053	Brattleboro	.75	.77
054	Burlington	.80	.85
056	Montpelier	.81	.84
057	Rutland	.82	.85
058	St. Johnsbury	.75	.77
059	Guildhall	.74	.76
VIRGINIA			
220-221	Fairfax	.86	.90
222	Arlington	.87	.90
223	Alexandria	.90	.91
224-225	Fredericksburg	.76	.83
226	Winchester	.72	.78
227	Culpeper	.78	.79
228	Harrisonburg	.68	.75
229	Charlottesville	.73	.81
230-232	Richmond	.82	.84
233-235	Norfolk	.79	.82
236	Newport News	.77	.81
237	Portsmouth	.75	.81
238	Petersburg	.80	.83
239	Farmville	.69	.72
240-241	Roanoke	.73	.75
242	Bristol	.68	.75
243	Pulaski	.66	.72
244	Staunton	.69	.74
245	Lynchburg	.70	.76
246	Grundy	.68	.73
WASHINGTON			
980-981,987	Seattle	1.01	1.04
982	Everett	1.03	1.02
983-984	Tacoma	.99	1.02
985	Olympia	.99	1.01
986	Vancouver	.98	1.02
988	Wenatchee	.92	.95
989	Yakima	.95	.97
990-992	Spokane	1.00	.96
993	Richland	.99	.97
994	Clarkston	.98	.96
WEST VIRGINIA			
247-248	Bluefield	.89	.88
249	Lewisburg	.89	.91
250-253	Charleston	.97	.94
254	Martinsburg	.85	.88
255-257	Huntington	.96	.95
258-259	Beckley	.90	.92
260	Wheeling	.92	.95
261	Parkersburg	.92	.94
262	Buckhannon	.91	.94
263-264	Clarksburg	.91	.94
265	Morgantown	.92	.94
266	Gassaway	.92	.94
267	Romney	.87	.91
268	Petersburg	.89	.93
WISCONSIN			
530,532	Milwaukee	1.06	1.01
531	Kenosha	1.06	1.00
534	Racine	1.04	1.00
535	Beloit	1.02	.99
537	Madison	1.01	.98
538	Lancaster	1.00	.96
539	Portage	.98	.95
540	New Richmond	1.00	.97
541-543	Green Bay	1.03	.97
544	Wausau	.96	.94
545	Rhinelander	.97	.96
546	La Crosse	.96	.96
547	Eau Claire	1.00	.97
548	Superior	.99	.97
549	Oshkosh	.96	.94
WYOMING			
820	Cheyenne	.76	.79
821	Yellowstone Nat. Pk.	.71	.76

STATE/ZIP	CITY	Residential	Commercial
WYOMING (CONT'D)			
822	Wheatland	.72	.76
823	Rawlins	.70	.75
824	Worland	.69	.74
825	Riverton	.70	.76
826	Casper	.77	.82
827	Newcastle	.69	.74
828	Sheridan	.74	.79
829-831	Rock Springs	.74	.77
CANADIAN FACTORS (reflect Canadian currency)			
ALBERTA			
	Calgary	1.05	1.05
	Edmonton	1.05	1.05
	Fort McMurray	1.03	1.01
	Lethbridge	1.04	1.01
	Lloydminster	1.03	1.01
	Medicine Hat	1.03	1.01
	Red Deer	1.03	1.01
BRITISH COLUMBIA			
	Kamloops	1.01	1.03
	Prince George	1.02	1.04
	Vancouver	1.07	1.07
	Victoria	1.02	1.04
MANITOBA			
	Brandon	.99	.96
	Portage la Prairie	.99	.96
	Winnipeg	.99	.98
NEW BRUNSWICK			
	Bathurst	.91	.91
	Dalhousie	.91	.91
	Fredericton	.97	.93
	Moncton	.91	.91
	Newcastle	.91	.91
	Saint John	.97	.94
NEWFOUNDLAND			
	Corner Brook	.92	.94
	St. John's	.93	.94
NORTHWEST TERRITORIES			
	Yellowknife	.99	.99
NOVA SCOTIA			
	Dartmouth	.93	.95
	Halifax	.94	.95
	New Glasgow	.93	.95
	Sydney	.92	.93
	Yarmouth	.93	.95
ONTARIO			
	Barrie	1.10	1.05
	Brantford	1.11	1.07
	Cornwall	1.10	1.05
	Hamilton	1.11	1.08
	Kingston	1.11	1.06
	Kitchener	1.05	1.02
	London	1.09	1.06
	North Bay	1.08	1.04
	Oshawa	1.10	1.06
	Ottawa	1.11	1.06
	Owen Sound	1.08	1.05
	Peterborough	1.09	1.05
	Sarnia	1.12	1.07
	St. Catharines	1.05	1.01
	Sudbury	1.03	1.01
	Thunder Bay	1.07	1.02
	Toronto	1.14	1.10
	Windsor	1.08	1.03
PRINCE EDWARD ISLAND			
	Charlottetown	.88	.91
	Summerside	.88	.91
QUEBEC			
	Cap-de-la-Madeleine	1.10	1.01
	Charlesbourg	1.10	1.01
	Chicoutimi	1.10	1.00
	Gatineau	1.09	1.00
	Laval	1.09	1.00

Location Factors

STATE/ZIP	CITY	Residential	Commercial
QUEBEC (CONT'D)			
	Montreal	1.09	1.02
	Quebec	1.11	1.02
	Sherbrooke	1.09	1.01
	Trois Rivieres	1.10	1.01
SASKATCHEWAN			
	Moose Jaw	.91	.92
	Prince Albert	.90	.91
	Regina	.91	.92
	Saskatoon	.90	.91
YUKON			
	Whitehorse	.89	.91

Glossary, Resources, Index

Glossary

The following is a glossary of terms used throughout the book. *(Note: Consult the "Key Terms" at the end of Chapter 3, "Integration of Technology," and Chapter 7, "Scheduling a School Construction Project," for terms and definitions specific to those topics.)*

activity-based layout
A classroom layout that features work stations, large and small presentation areas, work tables, and project/research areas that allow for simultaneous independent and group activities.

adjacency requirements
The requirements for each space in relation to other spaces in terms of operational efficiency, convenient proximity, acoustics, security, or other factors.

aggregate bonding capacity
The maximum total contract value that a bonding company will cover (in performance bonds) for all of a construction company's current contracts.

bar chart   An early scheduling method, also known as a *Gantt chart*, that lists construction activities on the left-hand side of a page with a scaled, horizontal bar to the right showing the duration of the corresponding activity.

building orientation
An important factor in green design, it involves locating a building on a site to take advantage of views, while maximizing energy conservation through the building's relationship to the sun, wind, trees, and surrounding structures.

change order cost estimates
An accounting of the costs resulting from modifications to project scope after the project has been awarded and after the start of construction. These changes will affect individual construction contract costs and the overall construction budget.

clerk of the works   A full-time, on-site representative who reports to the project manager.

closed-circuit television (CCTV)
A television circuit with no broadcasting facilities and a limited number of reception stations. Can be used as a surveillance device where output is recorded onto videotape for review.

commissioning agent   A member of the project team who ensures the proper installation and operation of technical building systems. Normally, the commissioning agent is hired directly by the owner and works independently of both the designer and contractor.

construction contingency   An amount included in a construction budget to cover the cost of unforeseen construction work or expenses that are likely to be incurred, but are difficult or impossible to precisely predict. The two major categories are *costs due to design changes,* and *costs due to unforeseen construction conditions,* such as removal of underground storage tanks or large rock ledges. Typically the contingency is 5%-10% of total construction costs for most new school projects.

construction manager (CM)   One who directs the construction process as an agent of an owner or a contractor.

consultant   A person (or firm) with particular expertise who is contracted to perform a service.

contract   An agreement between two parties to perform work or provide goods, including an agreement or order for the procurement of supplies or services.

contract documents   All the written and graphic documents concerning execution of a particular construction contract. These include the agreement between the owner and contractor, all conditions of the contract, the specifications and drawings, any changes to the original contract, and any other items specifically itemized as being part of the contract documents.

critical path   The order of events (each of a particular duration) that results in the least amount of time required to complete a project.

critical path method (CPM)   A scheduling technique that shows the relationships of all construction activities to the other activities, the duration of each activity, and the activities that require the most time and are therefore critical to the project's completion time.

daylighting   Maximizing the use of natural light in the design of a space to achieve energy and cost savings and improve the quality of indoor light.

design/build project delivery   A construction delivery method in which one entity provides both design and construction services to an owner.

design contingency   An amount included in a construction budget to cover additional costs for possible design changes. The amount of contingency varies with the stages of design. As the design is finalized, the contingency should be reduced to near zero for most school projects.

design development (DD)   The process by which the design team prepares a detailed schematic design for a project, incorporating feedback gathered from the school building team and other project stakeholders. The design development documents will provide product specifications (including specific manufacturers, models, and quantities) and detailed cost estimates.

design charettes   Meetings, often public (for public schools with community involvement), in which the architect presents potential design concepts.

digital video recording (DVR)   A video recording system used as a surveillance device that is capable of retaining voluminous records for long periods of time, limited only by the digital storage device.

duration   In scheduling, the amount of time estimated to complete an activity based on the scope of work and the resources being used.

educational design specialists   Architectural firms that specialize in the design of educational environments and have knowledge of building materials and furnishings suitable to schools.

energy-efficient design   Design that emphasizes highly effective space conditioning equipment and controls, a tight building envelope, and an efficient ventilation system.

estimate   The anticipated cost of materials, labor, equipment, and other expenses for a proposed construction project.

facilities planning   The process of identifying the needs of facility users in order to create a project design that meets those needs.

"fast-tracked" projects   Projects whose various segments are in progress simultaneously. Portions of the building, called "bid packages," are constructed while others are still being designed. Although fast-tracking reduces overall project time, it requires more careful scheduling and monitoring, as construction delays can reduce anticipated time savings.

float   In scheduling, the amount of time that each construction activity in a project (not on the critical path) can fall behind before it starts delaying the rest of the project.

fuel cell   Cell that uses hydrogen as a fuel source through a catalytic process, producing electricity and giving off heat and small amounts of hot water as by-products. The heat can be captured for space heating needs, and the electricity generated can provide for power needs (referred to as co-generation).

Gantt chart See *bar chart.*

green design Attention to environmental concerns in all aspects of construction to create a building that is healthy for users and energy- and resource-efficient.

high-performance design An integrated design approach that emphasizes the latest technologies to achieve optimal conservation of resources.

holistic design An approach that emphasizes the functional relationship between the various building parts and the facility as a whole. May include protection of the Earth's resources, as well as an element of spirituality, aiming to create spaces that enrich the quality of the environment *and* the lives of those who use the building.

"house" or "cluster" design
Also referred to as a "school within a school," a design approach that subdivides a large facility into a number of smaller, clustered spaces. Each "house" or clustered area is equivalent to the size of a small school, so that students have the feel of a small school, yet there is an economy of scale in the construction.

incidence history The statistical measurement of the number of times a particular event occurs in a facility over a specific period of time (such as the number of security breaches). An analysis of incidence history can identify patterns and trends in incident types, locations, and affected individuals.

instructional-based layout
A classroom layout that features a horseshoe configuration locating each individual work station along three of the peripheral walls, with the teacher stationed along the fourth.

instructional media center (IMC) A combined library and media area that includes traditional printed materials, in addition to electronic media, such as DVDs, videos, compact disks, and Internet access.

integrated networking Computer networking where traffic from dissimilar applications and networks converges onto a single telecommunications network infrastructure.

intelligent building A facility with a network infrastructure that enables occupants to control or program building functions, from computers to building automation systems (e.g., HVAC, life safety, and security).

intrusion alarms Sensors that detect break-ins or forced entries into a facility. They have two principal functions: to detect intruders after-hours or in controlled areas, and to signal monitoring personnel when a security event is occurring.

IT security Security that focuses on user authorization to access network and associated IT services.

kick-off meeting A meeting that takes place at the beginning of a project. Its purpose is to introduce the project team members, review the overall project, and to discuss items such as construction site logistics, the phasing plan, and the schedule.

Leadership in Energy and Environmental Design (LEED) A U.S. Green Building Council rating system for commercial, institutional, and high-rise residential buildings used to evaluate environmental performance from a "whole building" perspective over a building's life cycle. Widely recognized as a standard for green design in schools.

life cycle costing An economic assessment of an item, system, or facility. Considers design alternatives in terms of cost of ownership over the life of the facility or item being evaluated.

light shelves Reflective horizontal surfaces adjacent to windows positioned to "bounce" daylight deep into buildings and produce a uniform light level.

line item In budgeting and estimating, refers to the description and costs associated with a particular building item. (The word *line* is used because these costs are usually represented on a single row or line in a budget or estimate.) Line items can be as broad as the foundation, walls, or roof in preliminary estimates, or as specific as rebar ties, drywall taping, or snow guards in detailed estimates.

"living roof" A green design system consisting of a suitable support structure, waterproofing, earth, and plant materials. This type of roof eliminates or reduces run-off and can help minimize temperature fluctuation inside a building, particularly in sunnier climates.

local area network (LAN)
A computer network that spans a relatively small geographic area, such as a school or group of adjacent buildings on a campus. LANs reside on private premises and do not use public common carrier transmission facilities.

low-emissivity (low-E) coatings
Coatings applied to glass that allow the transmission of short-wave (visible light), but have low emissivity to long-wave infrared radiation (heat). The result is a reduction in a facility's net heating and cooling requirements.

master schedule The most complete schedule for a project, it covers not only the construction portions, but also items that are not strictly construction-related, such as financing deadlines and community board reviews. The master schedule includes all the details of the project, but can be presented in a summary or executive-level format, with the ability to "drill down" into specific parts to get more detailed information, as needed.

metropolitan area network (MAN)
A popular network choice for a town or a city that spans a geographic area larger than a local area network (LAN). School districts, local libraries, and municipalities often use a MAN to connect to citizens and local business enterprises.

milestone A measurable event that is expected to be accomplished by a certain date. In scheduling, it is usually graphically designated on the schedule by a small diamond shape. An example of a milestone is, "finish final plans."

modular buildings Buildings that are constructed in sections, or "boxes," in a factory and then moved to the final site. Material costs are reduced because large quantities can be purchased in advance for several projects, taking advantage of discounts. Productivity is increased, because the module is moved assembly-line style to workers with all tools, materials, and supplies.

network Two or more computers linked in order to share resources, exchange files, or allow electronic communications. The computers on a network may be linked by cables, wires, radio waves, infrared light beams, or satellites.

occupant unit cost estimate
An early-stage planning estimate based on the projected number of facility users. Costs are expressed per common unit, which may be desks for schools, seats for auditoriums, beds for hospitals, or rental rooms for hotels. Also referred to as *end product unit, end unit,* or *capacity* estimates.

owner's contingency An amount included in an estimate and construction budget to cover costs directly attributed to the owner over and above the base budget for which the owner is responsible.

owner-controlled insurance program (OCIP) With "wrap-up" insurance plans, the owner or its contracting agency purchases a large insurance policy that covers the insurance needs of all contractors working on all of the projects in the owner's building program. School construction projects are often covered by OCIPs, since public agencies and large non-profit organizations have the financial backing to purchase such large policies.

owner's representative
An individual or entity acting as an owner's representative during the construction process. This individual, who might be a project management consultant or construction manager, should have the authority to make decisions consistent with the owner's goals.

payment bond A guarantee by a surety company that the contractor will pay all material, labor, equipment suppliers, and subcontractors. This helps ensure that the project will be lien-free.

performance bond A surety company's guarantee to the owner that the contractor will complete a project under the terms of the contract.

phasing Working on a construction project in parts and at specified intervals. Usually phasing is required when construction activity is not permitted at certain locations or on particular dates during the project.

photovoltaic (PV) systems Systems that produce electrical energy directly from the sun. PVs generate power without noise, pollution, or fuel consumption. Maximum energy production (hot summer days) directly offsets maximum energy demand (air-conditioning) on the typical grid.

physical security Security that focuses not only on the protection of people and properties against potential assessed risks, but also on managing the flow of people and moveable properties into, out of, or within a facility. Managing areas, perimeter intrusion, occupancy, access methods, internal and external facility monitoring, and containment are all issues that must be addressed.

post-construction schedules
A schedule that incorporates all changes, and shows actual work and the durations and dates of all activities as they were completed on the project. These schedules provide important documentation for use in any claims that may come about after the project.

power drops Electrical power outlets to serve specific pieces of equipment.

pre-bid schedule A summary-level schedule developed by the design professional.

pre-design The early action stage of a school design project, it establishes parameters that will be the basis for architectural design solutions and construction. Also referred to as *planning* or *facility planning.*

program manager
An individual who manages multiple projects for the same owner.

program/space program (for schools)
A comprehensive list identifying every space required within a school facility. Normally includes current space needs, as well as projected needs (often five to ten years out, depending on the scope of the project). The program identifies requirements of each space, including size and configuration, number of users, special electrical and mechanical requirements, special servicing needs, security issues, public and private access requirements, adjacency requirements, and other special needs.

programming See *pre-design.*

programming and pre-design studies (for schools) Studies that are conducted when there is an existing or anticipated need (such as enrollment changes or deteriorating building systems). Studies may be system-wide *comprehensive master plans* for school districts, or *facility master plans* for individual schools (new stand-alone facilities, renovation or addition to existing facilities, or a combination).

project cost Defined in terms of total "hard" and "soft" costs. Hard cost is the cost of construction including the contractor's overhead and profit and any modifications to the contract for construction. Soft cost is the cost of land, professional fees, owner's contingencies, and other incidental costs.

project expectations workshop A workshop conducted prior to the start of construction involving key members of the project team. The end product of this workshop is a project mission statement and mutually agreed upon project goals.

project input sessions In a school project, meetings that occur early in the planning process (before design) to allow parents, neighbors, and other community members (as well as trustees/board members and potential donors in the case of private schools) to express their views of the project and raise issues that the design team may not have considered.

project manager (PM) The main point of contact and facilitator among the architect, general contractor, and Clerk of the Works (on-site representative). The PM may be a consultant hired by the owner, or may be an employee of the general contractor. This term may also be used by a design firm and by major suppliers to refer to their own team member who is responsible for their firm's contribution to a particular project.

project room Sometimes called a *project lab* or *multi-purpose classroom,* a fairly new concept for classroom layout that allows space for students to work on group projects.

protective night lighting A constant level of light provided on a facility's grounds after dark, ensuring reasonably good visibility. In particular, high-risk areas and those that could conceal a potential intruder should be illuminated, and bright spots and shadows should be avoided.

punch list A list of items within a *substantially complete* project that need to be corrected or completed. The punch list is prepared by the owner and the owner's representative(s) after a walk-through inspection, and confirmed by the contractor.

quality A combination of attributes, properties, value, and other characteristics of a particular design, material, system, equipment, or other element, according to comparative excellence and degree of perfection in workmanship, manufacture, performance, longevity, or attractiveness.

request for information (RFI) A formal request for preliminary information for the purpose of evaluating potential bids for design services, construction services, or both. This request does not usually signify a firm commitment by an owner, but it provides information on potential bidders and their capabilities. The information gathered by RFIs is sometimes used to develop a list of architects, engineers, or contractors who will eventually receive a Request for Proposal (RFP).

request for proposal (RFP) A document provided to potential contractors to communicate building project requirements and to solicit proposals.

request for qualifications (RFQ) A formal request used to solicit information regarding bids from architects, engineers, project managers, and developers. An RFQ may or may not ask for an actual price for delivering the services. *(Note: RFQ can also be used to designate a Request for Quotation.)*

risk probability A concept applied to assess a facility's security needs based on consideration of factors such as incidence history, trends in the surrounding environment, warnings or threats, and similar events occurring at other comparable schools.

schematic design (SD) A design phase in a construction project that sets the tone by defining system components, locations, quantities, schedule, and costs that meet the goals stipulated in the facility's plan.

single bonding capacity The maximum contract value that the firm's bonding company will extend to a contractor in performance bonds for an individual contract.

sound isolation Attenuating sound transmission between adjacent spaces. In schools, sound isolation is particularly important between classrooms and areas of varying purposes, and in construction that uses gypsum wallboard and metal stud classroom walls.

substantial completion The point at which the project is substantially complete and ready for owner acceptance and occupancy. Any items remaining to be completed should, at this time, be noted or stipulated in writing, as the *punch list.*

sustainable design Selecting technologies and materials and using them in a manner that avoids depleting natural resources. Considers material durability and sustainability, which involves not only the energy and environmental costs to replace the material, but availability and rate of regeneration.

swing space A space temporarily occupied by building users away from areas that are undergoing renovation. Swing space can be new space built before renovations or existing space that has already been renovated.

target hardening Prohibiting entry or access to a facility by installing security hardware such as keyed or tamper-proof window locks, deadbolts for doors, interior door hinges, and rock-guard shields for windows.

technology integration In school design, this term refers to the assimilation of technology resources and technology-based practices into the daily teaching, learning, and administration of schools.

temporary classrooms Space that may be required as a stopgap measure to meet enrollment needs before school construction or expansion can be completed. These facilities may also be used in a phasing strategy for expansion projects, or on constricted sites where a swing-space addition may not be appropriate.

value engineering Optimizing the life cycle costs and performance of a facility by examining a project's required functions, proposed design elements, and construction costs. The focus of a VE study is to provide for the facility's essential functions, while exploring cost savings through modification or elimination of nonessential design elements.

volatile organic compounds (VOCs) Organic chemicals that are harmful when released (off-gassed from building materials) after construction. Most paints, coatings, flooring and wall covering adhesives off-gas VOCs that can aggravate chemical sensitivity in occupants. Many low- or zero-VOC products are available.

white roof systems Roofing systems that reflect heat and have proven to reduce the net cooling requirements of a facility by as much as 20%.

work breakdown structure (WBS) A hierarchical breakdown of a project that contains successive levels of detail. Provides a way to incorporate project details as they become available without having to prepare an entirely new estimate or budget at each new level.

working schedule A schedule that is prepared after a construction project is awarded. It should include enough detail to allow tracking of construction, and serves as the realistic basis on which the project will be built.

xeriscaping The practice of using drought-tolerant, slow-growing, native species of plants as part of a green design approach and water conservation. Xeriscaping also minimizes pest and disease problems, reduces or eliminates fertilization requirements, and reduces landscaping maintenance.

zoned building design Separating areas of a facility by establishing a series of clearly discernible zones to control access by the public and, to a lesser extent, by school personnel. In schools, four zones may be applicable.

Resources

The following pages list professional associations, private and government agencies, and services that can be contacted for additional information on school facility design and planning, construction, and specialty topics, such as green building, technology, safety, and security.

Professional Organizations

The following organizations are listed in two main categories:

- *School Organizations and Agencies*
- *Architecture, Engineering, Construction, and Facility Management Organizations*

Following those two lists is an additional "Other Resources by Topic" section, which includes Web sites, publications, and services that may be helpful.

School Organizations and Agencies
(See "Other Resources by Topic" later in this section for additional school organizations.)

American School and University
9800 Metcalf Street
Overland Park, KS 66212
913-341-1300
www.asumag.com

The Association of Higher Education Facilities Officers (APPA)
1643 Prince Street
Alexandria, VA 22314
703-684-1446
www.appa.org

National Private Schools Association Group (NPSAG)
8815 Conroy-Windermere Road
Suite 413
Orlando, FL 32835
800-840-0939
www.npsag.com

National Program for Playground Safety
University of Northern Iowa
School for Health, Physical Education, and Leisure Services
WRC 205
Cedar Falls, IA 50614
888-544-PLAY
www.uni.edu/playground

National School Plant Management Association (NSPMA)
P.O. Box 8010
Lexington, KY 40533
423-434-5200
www.nspma.com

National School Supply and Equipment Association (NSSEA)
8380 Colesville Road
Suite 250
Silver Spring, MD 20910
800-395-5550
www.nssea.org

School Construction News
1241 Andersen Drive
Suite N
San Rafael, CA 94901
415-460-6185
www.schoolconstruction.org

Architecture, Engineering, Construction, and Facility Management Organizations

(See "Other Resources by Topic" later in this section for additional school organizations.)

American Association of Cost Engineers
209 Prairie Avenue
Suite 100
Morgantown, WV 25501
800-858-COST
www.aacei.org

American Council of Engineering Companies (ACEC)
Environmental Business Committee
1015 Fifteenth Street, N.W.
Washington, D.C. 20005
202-347-7474
www.acec.org

American Public Works Association (APWA)
2345 Grand Boulevard
Suite 500
Kansas City, MO 64108
816-472-6100
www.apwa.net

American Society of Civil Engineers (ASCE)
1801 Alexander Bell Drive
Reston, VA 20191
800-548-2723
www.asce.org

American Society of Heating, Refrigeration, and Air-Conditioning Engineers (ASHRAE)
1791 Tullie Circle, N.E.
Atlanta, GA 30329
800-527-4723
www.ashrae.org

American Subcontractors Association
1004 Duke Street
Alexandria, VA 22314
703-684-3450
www.asaonline.com

American Society of Professional Estimators (ASPE)
11141 Georgia Avenue
Suite 412
Wheaton, MD 20902
888-EST-MATE
www.aspenational.com

Associated Builders and Contractors, Inc. (ABC)
4250 N. Fairfax Drive
9th Floor
Arlington, VA 22203
703-812-2000
www.abc.org

Associated General Contractors of America
333 John Carlyle Street
Suite 200
Alexandria, VA 22314
703-548-3118
www.agc.org

Association for Facilities Engineering (AFE)
8180 Corporate Park Drive
Suite 125
Cincinnati, OH 45242
513-489-2473
www.afe.org

Building Owners and Managers Association (BOMA)
1201 New York Avenue, N.W.
Suite 300
Washington, D.C. 20005
202-408-2662
www.boma.org

Construction Financial Management Association (CFMA)
29 Emmons Drive
Suite F-50
Princeton, NJ 08540
609-452-8000
www.cfma.org

Construction Specifications Institute (CSI)
99 Canal Center Plaza
Suite 300
Alexandria, VA 22314
800-689-2900
www.csinet.org

DesignShare, Inc.
4937 Morgan Avenue, S.
Minneapolis, MN 55409
612-925-6897
www.designshare.com

Engineers Joint Contract Documents Committee (EJCDC)
www.ejcdc.org
The EJCDC publishes the *Standard Conditions of the Construction Contract,* widely used in the industry as a standard for contract conditions.

FacilitiesNet
www.facilitiesnet.com
Internet resource for building designers,
contractors, and managers.

FacilityManagement.com
www.facilitymanagement.com
Online site of *American School and
Hospital Magazine.*

FMLink
FMLink Group, LLC
P.O. Box 59557
Potomac, MD 20859
301-365-1600
www.fmlink.com

**International Facility
Management Association (IFMA)**
1 E. Greenway Plaza
Suite 1100
Houston, TX 77046
713-623-4362
www.ifma.org

National Safety Council
1121 Spring Lake Drive
Itasca, IL 60143
630 285 1121
www.nsc.org

**National Society of Professional
Engineers**
1420 King Street
Alexandria, VA 22314
703-684-2800
www.nspe.org

**Professional Construction
Estimators Association (PCEA)**
P.O. Box 680336
Charlotte, NC 28216
704-987-9978
www.pcea.org

*Other Resources,
by Topic*

Programming and
Pre-Design

**American Association of School
Administrators (AASA)**
801 N. Quincy Street
Suite 700
Arlington, VA 22203
703-528-0700
www.aasa.org

**American Institute of Architects
(AIA) Committee on Architecture
for Education (CAE)**
1735 New York Avenue, N.W.
Washington, D.C. 20006
800-AIA-3837
www.aia.org/cae

**Council of Educational Facility
Planners (CEFPI)**
9180 E. Desert Cove
Suite 104
Scottsdale, AZ 85260
480-391-0840
www.cefpi.org

**Education Commission of
the States**
700 Broadway
Suite 1200
Denver, CO 80203
303-299-3600
www.ecs.org

> *State of the States* (Governors'
> addresses on educational issues)
> www.ecs.org/ecsmain.asp?page=
> /html/statesTerritories/
> state_map.htm?am=2

> *Summary of Policy Initiatives in State
> Legislatures*
> www.ecs.org/ecs/ecscat.nsf/
> Web2003All?OpenView&Count=-1

**National Association of State
Boards of Education (NASBE)**
277 S. Washington Street
Suite 100
Alexandria, VA 22314
703-684-4000
www.nasbe.org

**National School Boards
Association (NSBA)**
1680 Duke Street
Alexandria, VA 22314
703-838-6722
www.nsba.org

U.S. Department of Education
400 Maryland Avenue, S.W.
Washington, D.C. 20202
800-USA-LEARN
www.ed.gov/index.jhtml

> *No Child Left Behind Act of 2002*
> www.ed.gov/nclb/
> landing.jhtml?src=pb

> *(Note: A state-by-state list of
> Departments of Education follows these
> Resources.)*

Funding Resources

**Carnegie Foundation for the
Advancement of Teaching**
51 Vista Lane
Stanford, CA 94305
650-566-5100
www.carnegiefoundation.org
Policy and research center aimed at
strengthening teaching and learning.

Michael & Susan Dell Foundation
www.msdf.org/about/Default.aspx
Funds programs to improve college
readiness skills.

Bill & Melinda Gates Foundation
P.O. Box 23350
Seattle, WA 98102
206-709-3607
www.gatesfoundation.org/Education
Provides grants for creation of small high
schools and for the reduction of financial
barriers to higher education.

Green Design

**American Institute of Architects
(AIA)**
Committee on the Environment:
www.aia.org/cote
Building Performance: www.aia.org/bp
1735 New York Avenue, N.W.
Washington, D.C. 20006
800-AIA-3837
www.aia.org

Collaboration for High Performance Schools
c/o Eley Associates
142 Minna Street
San Francisco, CA 94105
877-642-CHPS
www.chps.net/index.htm

> *See publication:* **The CHPS Manual/ Best Practices Manual,** *Volumes 1, 2, and 3.*

Environmental Law Institute
1616 P Street, N.W.,
Suite 200
Washington, D.C. 20036
202-939-3800
www.eli.org

Environmental Protection Agency (EPA)
Ariel Rios Building
1200 Pennsylvania Avenue
Washington, D.C. 20460
202-272-0167
www.epa.gov

Green Building Council
1015 18th Street, N.W.
Suite 805
Washington, D.C. 20036
202-82-USGBC
www.usgbc.org

National Council of Architectural Registration Boards
1801 K Street, N.W.
Washington, D.C. 20006
202-783-6500
www.ncarb.org
> See publication: *Sustainable Design, 2001*
> http://www.ncarb.org/publications/ titles/sd.htm

Sustainable Buildings Industry Council (SBIC)
1331 H Street, N.W.
Suite 1000
Washington, D.C. 20005
202-628-7400
www.sbicouncil.org

> See publication: *High Performance School Buildings (HPSB)*
> www.buildingmedia.com/sbic

U.S. Department of Energy (DOE) Office of Energy Efficiency and Renewable Energy
www.eere.energy.gov/EE/buildings.html
1000 Independence Avenue, S.W.
Washington, D.C. 20585
800-DIAL-DOE
www.energy.gov

Recommended Reading

Building Healthy, High Performance Schools: A Review of Selected State and Local Initiatives
Environmental Law Institute,
September 2003
www.elistore.org/reports_detail.asp?ID=10925

E Magazine
Earth Action Network, Inc.
28 Knight Street
Norwalk, CT 06851
203-854-5559
www.emagazine.com
> *(Note: Jan/Feb 2003 issue on hydrogen)*

Environmental Design and Construction Magazine
755 W. Big Beaver Road
Suite 1000
Troy, MI 48084
248-244-1280
www.edcmag.com

Green Building: Project Planning and Cost Estimating. Kingston, MA: RSMeans, 2002.
www.rsmeans.com/bookstore/ detail.asp?sku=67338

Technology Integration

Association for the Advancement of Computing in Education (AACE)
P.O. Box 3728
Norfolk, VA 22902
757-623-7588
www.aace.org

Building Industry Consulting Service International, Inc. (BICSI)
8610 Hidden River Parkway
Tampa, FL 33637
813-979-1991
www.bicsi.org

Center for Children and Technology
96 Morton Street
7th Floor
New York, NY 10014
212-807-4200
www2.edc.org/CCT/cctweb

Center for Technology in Learning
SRI International
333 Ravenswood Avenue
Menlo Park, CA 93025
650-859-2000
www.sri.com/policy/ctl

Classroom Connect
8000 Marina Boulevard
Suite 400
Brisbane, CA 94005
650-351-5100
www.classroom.com
Delivers professional development programs and online instructional materials for K-12 school districts nationwide.

Computer-Using Educators (CUE)
1210 Marina Village Parkway
Suite 100
Alameda, CA 94501
510-814-6630
www.cue.org

Consortium for School Networking (CoSN)
1555 Connecticut Avenue, N.W.
Suite 200
Washington, D.C. 20036
202-462-9600
www.cosn.org

Focus on Technology
National Education Association
1202 16th Street, N.W.
Washington, D.C. 20036
202-822-7360
www.nea.org/cet

Global Engineering Documents
15 Inverness Way, E.
Englewood, CO 80112
800-854-7179
www.global.ihs.com

Institute of Electrical and Electronics Engineers (IEEE)
Operations Center
445 Hoes Lane
P.O. Box 1331
Piscataway, NJ 08855
800-678-4333
www.ieee.org

Institute for the Transfer of Technology to Education (ITTE)
National School Boards Association
1680 Duke Street
Alexandria, VA 22314
703-838-6722
www.nsba.org/itte

International Society for Technology in Education (ISTE)
480 Charnelton Street
Eugene, OR 97403
800-336-5191
www.iste.org

International Technology Education Association (ITEA)
1914 Association Drive
Suite 201
Reston, VA 20191
703-860-2100
www.iteawww.org

National Center for Education Statistics
1990 K Street, N.W.
Washington, D.C. 20006
202-502-7300
www.nces.ed.gov/pubs2003/
tech_schools/index.asp

> See Publication: *Technology in Schools: Suggestions, Tools, and Guidelines for Assessing Technology in Elementary and Secondary Education.*

Office of Educational Technology
U.S. Department of Education
400 Maryland Avenue, S.W.
Washington, D.C. 20202
800-872-5327
www.ed.gov/technology

State of the States
www.ccrpyramid.com/states.htm
Provides current educational status of technology in every state. Also offers links and contact information to resources within each state.

Security Integration

American Society for Industrial Security (ASIS)
1625 Prince Street
Alexandria, VA 22314
703-522-5800
www.asisonline.org

Campus Safety Association
1121 Spring Lake Drive
Itasca, IL 60143
708-775-2026

Center for the Prevention of School Violence
20 Enterprise Street
Suite 2
Raleigh, NC 27607
800-299-6054
www.ncdjjdp.org/cpsv

Education Resources Information Center (ERIC)
2277 Research Boulevard
Suite 6M
Rockville, MD 20850
800-538-3742
www.eric.ed.gov

International Association of Campus Law Enforcement Administrators
638 Prospect Avenue
Hartford, CT 06105
860-586-7517
www.iaclea.org

International Association of Professional Security Consultants (IAPSC)
1444 I Street
Suite 700
Washington, D.C. 20005
202-712-9043
www.iapsc.org

International CPTED Association (ICA)
Crime Prevention Through Environmental Design
www.cpted.net

Keep Schools Safe
www.keepschoolssafe.org

National Alliance for Safe Schools (NASS)
P.O. Box 1068
College Park, MD 20741
301-935-6063
www.safeschools.org

National Association of School Safety and Law Enforcement Officers
P.O. Box 118
Catlett, VA 20119
540-788-4966
www.nassleo.org

National Clearinghouse for Educational Facilities (NCEF)
National Institute of Building Sciences
1090 Vermont Avenue, N.W.
Suite 700
Washington, D.C. 20005
888-552-0624
www.edfacilities.org

National Crime Prevention Council
1700 K Street, N.W.
Second Floor
Washington, D.C. 20006
202-466-6272
www.ncpc.org

National Criminal Justice Reference Service (NCJRS)
P.O. Box 6000
Rockville, MD 20849
800-851-4320
www.ncjrs.org

National School Safety Center (NSSC)
4165 Thousand Oaks Boulevard
Suite 290
Westlake Village, CA 91362
805-373-9977
www.nssc1.org

National School Safety and
Security Services (NSSSS)
P.O. Box 110123
Cleveland, OH 44111
216-251-3067
www.schoolsecurity.org

**Safe and Drug-Free Schools
Program**
Office of Elementary and
Secondary Education
U.S. Department of Education
600 Independence Avenue, N.W.
Washington, D.C. 20202
202-260-3954
www.ed.gov/offices/OESE/SDFS

Recommended Reading

Building Security: Strategies and Costs.
David D. Owen. Kingston, MA:
RSMeans, 2003.
www.rsmeans.com/bookstore/
detail.asp?sku=67339

Specialty Spaces

Coalition for Community Schools
c/o Institute for Educational Leadership
1001 Connecticut Avenue, N.W.
Suite 310
Washington, D.C. 20036
202-822-8405
www.communityschools.org

Art Classrooms
Recommended Reading

*Design Standards for School Art
Facilities.*
Reston, VA: National Art Education
Association, 1993.

*Art Safety Procedures for Art Schools
and Art Departments.*
McCann, Michael. Center for Safety
in the Arts, 1998.
www.uic.edu/sph/glakes/harts/
HARTS_library/Artdept0.txt

Computer and Language Labs

**Association for the Advancement
of Computing in Education
(AACE)**
P.O. Box 3728
Norfolk, VA 22902
757-623-7588
www.aace.org

Focus on Technology
National Education Association
1202 16th Street, N.W.
Washington, D.C. 20036
202-822-7360
www.nea.org/cet

Office of Educational Technology
U.S. Department of Education
400 Maryland Avenue, S.W.
Washington, D.C. 20202
800-872-5327
www.ed.gov/Technology

Library/Media Centers
Recommended Reading

*Designing a School Library Media
Center for the Future.* Rolf Erikson and
Carolyn Markuson. Chicago: American
Library Association, 2001.

*Checklist of Library Building Design
Considerations, Fourth Edition.*
William W. Sannwald. Chicago: Library
Administration and Management
Association, 2001.

Performing Arts Centers

**Janis A. Barlow & Associates
Theater Consulting**
44 Charles Street, W.
Toronto, ON M4Y 1R8
Canada
416-921-0208
www.barlowandassociates.com

Recommended Reading

Theater Design, Second Edition.
George C. Izenour, Vern Oliver Knudsen,
and Robert B. Newman. New Haven: Yale
University Press, 1996.

Science Classrooms
Labplan
www.labplan.org
Interactive Web site for a study on
developing criteria and standards for
planning prototype labs and support
spaces for secondary school instruction.

National Academy of Sciences
500 Fifth Street
Washington, D.C. 20001
202-334-2000
www4.nationalacademies.org/nas/
nashome.nsf

National Science Foundation
4201 Wilson Boulevard
Arlington, VA
703-292-5111
www.nsf.gov

**National Science Teachers
Association**
1840 Wilson Boulevard
Arlington, VA 22201
703-243-7100
www.nsta.org

Recommended Reading

*National Science Education Standards
(NSES),* 1997 Washington, D.C.:
National Academy Press.
http://lab.nap.edu/
catalog/5704.html

Science Facilities. National
Clearinghouse for Educational Facilities,
Washington, D.C.
www.edfacilities.org

Sports Facilities
**National Federation of State High
School Associations**
NFSH Court and Field Diagram Guide, 2000
P.O. Box 690
Indianapolis, IN 46206
317-972-6900
www.nths.org

Vocational-Technical Education

National Automotive Technicians Education Foundation (NATEF)
101 Blue Seal Drive
Suite 101
Leesburg, VA 20175
703-669-6650
www.natef.org

Office of Vocational and Adult Education
U.S. Department of Education
400 Maryland Avenue, S.W.
Washington, D.C. 20202
800-USA-LEARN
www.ed.gov/about/offices/list/ovae/index.html

Estimating Building Construction Costs

RSMeans.com
Construction cost data and software, estimating and other construction and facility management references, seminars, and consulting.
www.rsmeans.com

School Construction Costs
National Clearinghouse for Educational Facilities
www.edfacilities.org/rl/construction_costs.cfm
Resource list of books, articles, and links on school building construction costs.

Recommended Reading

Historic Preservation: Project Planning and Estimating. Kingston, MA: RSMeans, 2000.
http://www.rsmeans.com/bookstore/detail.asp?sku=67323

Life Cycle Costing for Facilities. Alphonse J. Dell'Isola, PE, CVS and Stephen J. Kirk, FAIA, CVS. Kingston, MA: RSMeans, 2003.
http://www.rsmeans.com/bookstore/detail.asp?sku=67341

Square Foot & Assemblies Estimating Methods, Third Edition. Bill J. Cox and William F. Horsley. Kingston, MA: RSMeans, 2001.
www.rsmeans.com/bookstore/detail.asp?sku=67145B

Square Foot Costs
Kingston, MA: RSMeans, 2004.
www.rsmeans.com/bookstore/detail.asp?sku=60054

Successful Estimating Methods. John D. Bledsoe, PhD, PE. Kingston, MA: RSMeans, 1992.
www.rsmeans.com/bookstore/detail.asp?sku=67287

Value Engineering: Practical Applications for Design, Construction, Maintenance, and Operations. Alphonse Dell'Isola, PE, CVS. Kingston, MA: RSMeans, 1997.
http://www.rsmeans.com/bookstore/detail.asp?sku=67319

Scheduling a School Construction Project

Recommended Reading

"Cost Estimating and Scheduling Integration." Phillip D. Larson, *Cost Engineer.*

Means Scheduling Manual, Third Edition. William F. Horsley. Kingston, MA: RSMeans, 2004.

Owner's Reviews of Schedules: How Far Should They Go? Donald J. Fredlund, Jr., and Fred King. AACE Transactions, 1992.

Project Controls in the Pre-Construction Phase. Joseph W. Wallwork and Ian A. Street.
http://www.greyhawk.com/publications-bulletinboard/articles/Default.asp

Project Scheduling and Management for Construction, Third Edition. David R. Pierce, Jr. Kingston, MA: RSMeans, 2004.
www.rsmeans.com/bookstore/detail.asp?sku=67247B

"Using Earned Value Management." Quentin W. Fleming and Joel Koppelman. *Cost Engineering,* Vol. 44/No. 9, September, 2002.

Contracts and Bidding

Recommended Reading

The Building Professional's Guide to Contract Documents. Waller S. Poage. Kingston, MA: RSMeans, 2000.
www.rsmeans.com/bookstore/detail.asp?sku=67261A

Successful Interior Projects Through Effective Contract Documents. Joel Downey, RA and Patricia J. Gilbert. Kingston, MA: RSMeans, 1995.
www.rsmeans.com/bookstore/detail.asp?sku=67313

Project Management

Recommended Reading

Builder's Essentials: Plan Reading and Material Takeoff. Wayne J. DelPico, CPE. Kingston, MA: RSMeans, 1994.
www.rsmeans.com/bookstore/detail.asp?sku=67307

Facilities Planning and Relocation. David D. Owen. Kingston, MA: RSMeans, 1993.
www.rsmeans.com/bookstore/detail.asp?sku=67301

Means Illustrated Construction Dictionary, Unabridged Third Edition. Kingston, MA: RSMeans, 2000.
www.rsmeans.com/bookstore/detail.asp?sku=67292A

Planning and Managing Interior Projects. Carol E. Farren, CFM, IFMA Fellow. Kingston, MA: RSMeans, 1999.
www.rsmeans.com/bookstore/detail.asp?sku=67245A

The Project Team

Recommended Reading

Fundamentals of the Construction Process. Kweku K. Bentil, AIC. Kingston, MA: RSMeans, 1989.
www.rsmeans.com/bookstore/detail.asp?sku=67260

State-by-State Resources

Contact information for each U.S. state's Department of Education, Facilities/Construction Unit, and Green Funding source is listed in the following section. It should be noted that, although the listing is comprehensive, information for each category may not be available for all states.

At the onset of a school project, be sure to contact the appropriate state resource for detailed information on utility-based rebates. Funding and eligibility requirements change frequently and should be reviewed regularly.

State	Department of Education	Facilities/Construction Unit	Green Funding Sources
Alabama	**Department of Education** 50 North Ripley Street P.O. Box 302101 Montgomery, AL 36104 (334) 242-9700 http://www.alsde.edu	**School Architect and School Facilities** (334) 242-9731 http://www.alsde.edu (click "Sections" / "School Architect and School Facilities")	**Alabama Department of Economic and Community Affairs (ADECA)** Science Technology and Energy Division P.O. Box 5690 Montgomery, AL 36103-5690 (334) 353-5951 www.adeca.alabama.gov
Alaska	**Department of Education and Early Development** 801 West 10th Street Juneau, AK 99801 (907) 465-2802 http://www.eed.state.ak.us	**Facilities** 801 West 10th Street Juneau, AK 99801 (907) 465-1858 http://www.eed.state.ak.us/facilities	**Alaska Energy Authority/AIDEA** 813 West Northern Lights Boulevard Anchorage, AK 99503 (907) 269-4541 www.aidea.org/energyconservation.htm
Arizona	**Department of Education** 1525 West Jefferson Street Phoenix, AZ 85007 (602) 542-5072 http://www.ade.state.az.us	**School Facilities Board** 1700 West Washington Street, Suite 230 Phoenix, AZ 85007 (602) 542-6501 http://www.sfb.state.az.us (click "Site map" / "Architecture" / "Design")	**Arizona Department of Commerce** Energy Office 1700 W. Washington Street Executive Tower, Suite 600 Phoenix, AZ 85007 (602) 771-1100 www.commerce.state.az.us *Also, for Scottsdale:* Green Building Program http://www.scottsdaleaz.gov/greenbuilding/default.asp?catID=5
Arkansas	**Department of Education** #4 Capitol Mall Little Rock, AR 72201 (501) 682-4475 http://arkedu.state.ar.us	**School Plant Services** (501) 682-4261 http://arkedu.state.ar.us/directory/publicschool_finance.html (click "School Plant Services")	**Arkansas Energy Office** One State Capitol Mall, Suite 4B-215 Little Rock, AR 72201 (501) 682-8065 www.1-800-arkansas.com/energy

State	Department of Education	Facilities/Construction Unit	Green Funding Sources
California	**Department of Education** P.O. Box 944272 Sacramento, CA 94244-2720 (916) 319-0791 http://www.cde.ca.gov	**Office of Public School Construction** 1130 K Street, Suite 400 Sacramento, CA 95814-2928 (916) 445-3160 http://www.opsc.dgs.ca.gov	*Sustainability Incentives:* **Division of the State Architect (DSA) Headquarter's Office** 1130 K Street Suite 101 Sacramento, CA 95814 (916) 445-8100 http://www.sustainableschools.dgs.ca.gov/ SustainableSchools/financing/incentives.html *Energy Programs:* **Office of Public School Construction** 1130 K Street Suite 400 Sacramento, CA 95814-2928 (916) 445-3160 http://www.opsc.dgs.ca.gov/School+Energy+ Programs/Default.htm
Colorado	**Department of Education** 201 East Colfax Avenue Denver, CO 80203-1799 (303) 866-6600 http://www.cde.state.co.us	**Capital Construction Grants** http://www.cde.state.co.us/cdefinance/ CapConstMain.htm	**Governor's Office of Energy Management and Conservation** 225 E. 16th Avenue, Suite 650 Denver, CO 80203 (303) 894-2383 (800) 632-6662 www.state.co.us/oemc *See also:* **Built Green® Colorado Home Builders Assoc. of Metro Denver** 1400 South Emerson Street Denver, CO 80210 (303) 778-1400 http://www.builtgreen.org/default.htm

State	Department of Education	Facilities/Construction Unit	Green Funding Sources
Connecticut	**Department of Education** 165 Capitol Avenue Hartford, CT 06145 http://www.state.ct.us/sde	**Grants Management – School Construction** (860) 713-6450 http://www.state.ct.us/sde/dgm/sfu/index.htm	**Connecticut Clean Energy Fund (CCEF)** 999 West Street Rocky Hill, CT 06067 (860) 563-0015 www.ctcleanenergy.com
Delaware	**Department of Education** 401 Federal Street P.O. Box 1402 Dover, DE 19903-1402 (302) 739-4601 http://www.doe.state.de.us	**Division of Facilities Management** 540 South Dupont Highway Suite 1 Dover, DE 19901 (302) 739-5644 http://www2.state.de.us/dfm/profsrv/psstands.asp	**Delaware State Energy Office** Department of Natural Resources and Environmental Control 146 S. Governor's Avenue Dover, DE 19901 (302) 739-1530 www.delaware-energy.com
Florida	**Department of Education** Turlington Building Suite 1514 325 West Gaines Street Tallahassee, FL 32399 (850) 245-0505 http://www.fldoe.org	**Office of Educational Facilities** Turlington Building, Suite 1054 325 West Gaines Street Tallahassee, FL 32399-0400 (850) 245-0494 http://www.firn.edu/doe/edfacil	**Department of Environmental Protection** Florida Energy Office Energy Conservation Assistance Program 3900 Commonwealth Boulevard MS-19 Tallahassee, FL 32399-3000 (850) 245-2940 www.dep.state.fl.us/energy
Georgia	**Department of Education** 2054 Twin Towers East Atlanta, GA 30334 (404) 656-2800 http://www.doe.k12.ga.us	**Facilities Services** 1670 Twin Towers East Atlanta, GA 30334 (404) 656-2454 http://www.doe.k12.ga.us./schools/facilities/index.asp	**Georgia Environmental Facilities Authority (GEFA)** 100 Peachtree Street, N.W. Suite 2090 Atlanta, GA 30303-1911 (404) 656-0938 www.gefa.org
Hawaii	**Department of Education** P.O. Box 2360 Honolulu, HI 96804 (808) 586-3336 http://doe.k12.hi.us/index.html	**Facilities and Support Services Branch** Capital Improvement Program http://fssb.k12.hi.us/cip_overview.htm	**State of Hawaii** **Department of Business, Economic Development, and Tourism** Strategic Industry Division Strategic Technology Industry Development Branch P.O. Box 2359 Honolulu, HI 96804 (808) 587-3807 www.hawaii.gov/dbedt/ert/stid.html

State	Department of Education	Facilities/Construction Unit	Green Funding Sources
Idaho	**State Department of Education** 650 West State Street P.O. Box 83720 Boise, ID 83720-0027 (208) 332-6800 http://www.sde.state.id.us	**Idaho State Board of Education** Policies and Procedures http://www.idahoboardofed.org/policies/v/k.asp	**Idaho Energy Authority** 140 South Capitol Avenue Idaho Falls, ID 83402 (208) 529-1443 www.rebuild.org/partnerships/communityview.asp?OrganizationID=2781
Illinois	**State Board of Education** 100 North 1st Street Springfield, IL 62777 (866) 262-6663 or 100 West Randolph Suite 14-300 Chicago, IL 60602 (312) 814-2220 http://www.isbe.state.il.us	**School Construction Program** School Business and Support Services Division (217) 785-8779 http://www.isbe.state.il.us/construction/Default.htm	**Illinois Clean Energy Community Foundation (ICECF)** 2 North LaSalle Street Suite 950 Chicago, IL 60602 (312) 372-5191 www.illinoiscleanenergy.org
Indiana	**Department of Education** State House Room 229 Indianapolis, IN 46204-2798 (317) 232-6610 http://www.doe.state.in.us	**Indiana State Board of Education** School Facility Guidelines http://www.doe.state.in.us/stateboard/constguide.html	**Public Facility Energy Efficiency Program** Indiana Department of Commerce Energy Policy Division One North Capitol, Suite 700 Indianapolis, IN 46204 (317) 232-8940 www.in.gov/doc/businesses/EP_Basics.html
Iowa	**Department of Education** Grimes State Office Building 400 East 14th Street Des Moines, IA 50319-0146 (515) 281-5294 http://www.state.ia.us/educate/index.html	**Bureau of Administration and School Improvement Services** School Facility Unit http://www.state.ia.us/educate/ecese/asis/si/index.html	**Alternate Energy Revolving Loan Program (AERLP)** Iowa Energy Center 2521 Elwood Drive Suite 124 Ames, IA 50010-8229 (515) 294-8819 www.energy.iastate.edu

State	Department of Education	Facilities/Construction Unit	Green Funding Sources
Kansas	**State Department of Education** 120 S.E. 10th Avenue Topeka, KS 66612-1182 (785) 296-3204 http://www.ksbe.state.ks.us/ Welcome.html	**School Facilities Office** 120 S.E. 10th Avenue Topeka, KS 66612-1182 (785) 296-2627	**Kansas Institutional Conservation Program (ICP)** Kansas Corporation Commission Energy Programs Section 1500 S.W. Arrowhead Road Topeka, KS 66604-4027 (785) 271-3184 http://www.kcc.state.ks.us/energy/index. htm
Kentucky	**Department of Education** 500 Mero Street 19th Floor Frankfort, KY 40601 (502) 564-3421 http://www.kde.state.ky.us	**Division of Facilities Management** 500 Mero Street, 15th Floor Frankfort, KY 40601 (502) 564-4326 http://www.kde.state.ky.us/KDE/Adminis trative+Resources/Facilities/default.htm	
Louisiana	**Department of Education** 626 North 4th Street P.O. Box 94064 Baton Rouge, LA 70804-9064 (877) 453-2721 http://www.doe.state.la.us/ DOE/asps/home.asp	Handled at the local level.	**Louisiana Department of Natural Resources** Technology Assessment Division Institutional Energy Programs 617 N. 3rd Street P.O. Box 44156 Baton Rouge, LA 70804-4156 (225) 342-1399 www.dnr.state.la.us/SEC/EXECDIV/ TECHASMT/index.htm
Maine	**State Department of Education** 23 State House Station Augusta, ME 04333-0023 http://www.state.me.us/ education	**School Facilities Services** Cross Office Building, 5th Floor 111 Sewall Street Augusta, ME 04330 http://www.state.me.us/education/const/ homepage.htm#Topic%20List	**Maine Public Utilities Commission** 242 State Street 18 State House Station Augusta, ME 04333-0018 (207) 287-3831 http://www.efficiencymaine.com/school_ efficiency_program.htm

State	Department of Education	Facilities/Construction Unit	Green Funding Sources
Maryland	**State Department of Education** 200 West Baltimore Street Baltimore, MD 21201 (410) 767-0100 http://www.msde.state.md.us	**Public School Construction Program** Interagency Committee on School Construction 200 West Baltimore Street Baltimore, MD 21201 http://www.pscp.state.md.us	**Maryland Department of Natural Resources** 580 Taylor Avenue Annapolis, MD 21401 (410) 260-8100 http://www.dnr.state.md.us/ed/funding/html
Massachusetts	**Department of Education** 350 Main Street Malden, MA 02148-5023 (781) 338-3000 http://www.doe.mass.edu	**School Building Assistance** 17 Pleasant Street Malden, MA 02148 http://finance1.doe.mass.edu/sbuilding	**Massachusetts Technology Collaborative (MTC)** 75 North Drive Westborough, MA 01581 (508) 870-0312 http://www.mtpc.org/Grants_and_Awards/index.htm
Michigan	**Department of Education** 608 W. Allegan Lansing, MI 48933 http://www.michigan.gov/mde	**Michigan Public Educational Facilities Authority** Treasury Building 430 W. Allegan P.O. Box 15128 Lansing, MI 48922 (517) 373-3199 http://www.michigan.gov/treasury/0,1607,7-121-1751_2217_22686---,00.html	**Michigan Consumer and Industry Services** Energy Office 525 W. Ottawa P.O. Box 30004 Lansing, MI 48909 (517) 373-1820 http://www.michigan.gov/cis
Minnesota	**Department of Education** 1500 Highway 36 West Roseville, MN 55113-4266 (651) 582-8200 http://education.state.mn.us/html/mde_home.htm	**Department of Administration** Minnesota Building Codes and Standards Division http://www.buildingcodes.admin.state.mn.us	**Minnesota Office of Environmental Assistance (OEA)** 520 Lafayette Road, North Floor 2 St. Paul, MN 55155-4100 (651) 296-3417 (800) 657-3843 http://www.moea.state.mn.us/index.html
Mississippi	**Department of Education** Central High School P.O. Box 771 359 North West Street Jackson, MS 39205 (601) 359-3513 http://www.mde.k12.ms.us	**Office of School Building** P.O. Box 771 Jackson, MS 39205-0771 (601) 359-1028 http://www.mde.k12.ms.us/lead/osos/webpage.htm	**Mississippi Development Authority** Energy Division P.O. Box 849 Jackson, MS 39205-0849 (601) 359-6600 http://www.mississippi.org/index.html

State	Department of Education	Facilities/Construction Unit	Green Funding Sources
Missouri	**Department of Elementary and Secondary Education** P.O. Box 480 Jefferson City, MO 65102 (573) 751-4212 http://www.dese.state.mo.us	**Division of Administrative and Financial Services: School Governance and Facilities** (573) 526-6949 http://www.dese.mo.gov/divadm/govern/schfacility.html	**Missouri Department of Natural Resources** Energy Center P.O. Box 176 Jefferson City, MO 65102 (573) 751-3443 (800) 361-4827 http://www.dnr.state.mo.us/energy
Montana	**Office of Public Instruction** P.O. Box 202501 Helena, MT 59620-2501 (406) 444-3095 http://www.opi.state.mt.us	**Department of Labor and Industry** Building Codes Bureau Plan Review Services (406) 841-2040 http://discoveringmontana.com/dli/bsd/bc/index.htm	**Montana Department of Environmental Quality** 1520 E. Sixth Avenue P.O. Box 200901 Helena, MT 59620 (406) 444-2544 http://www.deq.state.mt.us/index.asp
Nebraska	**Department of Education** 301 Centennial Mall South Lincoln, NE 68509 (402) 471-2295 http://www.nde.state.ne.us	Handled at the local level.	**Nebraska Energy Office** P.O. Box 95085 Lincoln, NE 68509-5085 (402) 471-2867 http://www.nol.org/home/NEO
Nevada	**Department of Education** Carson City Main Location 700 East Fifth Street Carson City, NV 89701-5096 (775) 687-9200 and Las Vegas Location 1820 East Sahara Avenue Suite 205 Las Vegas, NV 89104 http://www.nde.state.nv.us	Handled at the local level.	**Nevada State Office of Energy** 727 Fairview Drive, Suite F Carson City, NV 89701 (775) 687-5975 http://energy/state.nv.us/default.htm

State	Department of Education	Facilities/Construction Unit	Green Funding Sources
New Hampshire	**Department of Education** 101 Pleasant Street Concord, NH 03301-3860 (603) 271-3494 http://www.ed.state.nh.us	**Office of School Building Aid** 101 Pleasant Street Concord, NH 03301-3860 (603) 271-2037; (603) 271-3620 http://www.ed.state.nh.us/BuildingAid/building.htm	**Governor's Office of Energy and Community Services** Rebuild New Hampshire Program (603) 271-2676 http://www.ed.state.nh.us/BuildingAid/buildinginfo.htm
New Jersey	**Department of Education** P.O. Box 500 Trenton, NJ 08625 (609) 292-4469 http://www.state.nj.us/education	**Division of Facilities and Transportation** School Facilities 320 West State Street P.O. Box 500 Trenton, NJ 08625 (866) 284-5365 http://www.nj.gov/njded/facilities	**New Jersey Clean Energy Program (NJCEP)** New Jersey Board of Public Utilities Office of Clean Energy 44 South Clinton Avenue P.O. Box 350 Trenton, NJ 08625-0350 (877) 786-5278 www.njcep.com
New Mexico	**Department of Education** 300 Don Gaspar Santa Fe, NM 87501-2786 (505) 827-5800 http://sde.state.nm.us	**Facilities Authority Office** 2019 Gallisteo Street Santa Fe, NM 87505 (505) 988-5989	**New Mexico Energy, Minerals, and Natural Resources Department** Energy Conservation and Management Division 1220 South St. Francis Drive Santa Fe, NM 87505 (505) 476-3310 http://www.emnrd.state.nm.us/ecmd/index.htm
New York	**New York State Education Department** Education Building Albany, NY 12234 (510) 474-3852 http://www.nysed/gov	**Facilities Planning** Room 1060 Education Building Annex The New York State Education Department Washington Avenue Albany, NY 12234 (518) 474-3906 http://www.emsc.nysed.gov/facpian	**New York State Energy Research and Development Authority** (NYSERDA) 17 Columbia Circle Albany, NY 12203-6399 (866) 697-3732 (518) 862-1090 www.nyserda.org
North Carolina	**Department of Public Instruction** 301 N. Wilmington Street Raleigh, NC 27601 (919) 807-3300 http://www.dpi.state.nc.us	**School Planning** 6322 Mail Service Center Raleigh, NC 27699-6322 http://www.schoolclearinghouse.org	**North Carolina Department of Administration** State Energy Office Division 1340 Mail Service Center Raleigh, NC 27699-1340 (919) 733-2230 http://www.energync.net

State	Department of Education	Facilities/Construction Unit	Green Funding Sources
North Dakota	**Department of Public Instruction** 600 E. Boulevard Avenue Dept. 201 Bismarck, ND 58505-0440 (701) 328-2260 http://www.dpi.state.nd.us	**Administrative Rules** http://www.state.nd.us/lr/information/acdata/pdf/67-09-01.pdf	**North Dakota Department of Commerce** Division of Community Services Energy Programs 1600 East Century Avenue Suite 2 P.O. Box 2057 Bismarck, ND 58502-2057 (701) 328-5300 http://www.state.nd.us/dcs/Energy/default.html
Ohio	**Ohio Department of Education** 25 South Front Street Columbus, OH 43215-4183 (877) 644-6338 http://www.ode.state.oh.us	**Ohio School Facilities Commission** 10 West Broad Street Suite 1400 Columbus, OH 43215 (614) 466-6290 http://www.osfc.staste.oh.us	**Ohio Energy Loan Fund** Office of Energy Efficiency 77 S. High Street, 26th Floor P.O. Box 1001 Columbus, OH 43216-1001 (614) 466-6797 www.odod.state.oh.us/cdd/oee
Oklahoma	**Oklahoma State Department of Education** 2500 North Lincoln Boulevard Oklahoma City, OK 73105-4599 (405) 521-3301 http://www.sde.state.ok.us	**Capital Improvement** 2500 North Lincoln Boulevard Oklahoma City, OK 73105-4599 (405) 521-3812	**Oklahoma Department of Commerce** State Energy Program 900 North Stiles Oklahoma City, OK 73126-0980 (405) 815-6552 (800) 879-6552 http://busdev3.odoc5.odoc.state.ok.us
Oregon	**Department of Education** 255 Capitol Street, N.E. Salem, OR 97310-0203 (503) 378-3569 http://www.ode.state.or.us	**School Finance, Data & Analysis** Oregon Department of Education 255 Capitol Street, N.E. Salem, OR 97310-0203 (503) 378-3600 *School Fund Grants* http://www.ode.state.or.us/sfda/grants/grants.aspx See "Facility Grants"	**Oregon Office of Energy** 625 Marion Street, N.E. Salem, OR 97301 (503) 378-4040 (800) 221-8035 http://www.energy.state.or.us/sb1149/schools/index.htm

State	Department of Education	Facilities/Construction Unit	Green Funding Sources
Pennsylvania	**Pennsylvania Department of Education** 333 Market Street Harrisburg, PA 17126 (717) 783-6788 http://www.pde.state.pa.us	**School Facilities and Construction** (717) 787-5480 http://www.pde/state.pa us/constr_facil/ site/default.asp	**Governor's Green Government Council** (717) 772-5161 http://www.gggc.state.pa.us/schools
Rhode Island	**Department of Elementary and Secondary Education** 255 Westminster Street Providence, RI 02903 (401) 222-4600 http://www.ridoe.net	**Department of Elementary and Secondary Education** School Construction Aid http://www.ridoe.net/funding/construction	**Rhode Island State Energy Office** Department of Administration Division of Central Services One Capitol Hill Providence, RI 02903 (401) 222-3370 (401) 222-6920 http://www.riseo.state.ri.us
South Carolina	**Department of Education** 1429 Senate Street Columbia, SC 29201 (803) 734-8815 http://www.myscschools.com	**Office of School Facilities** 3710 Landmark Drive Suite 205 Columbia, SC 29204 (803) 734-4837 http://www.myscschools.com/offices/sf	**South Carolina Energy Office** 1201 Main Street Suite 1010 Columbia, SC 29211 (803) 737-8030 (800) 851-8899 http://www.state.sc.us/energy/index.htm
South Dakota	**Department of Education** 700 Governors Drive Pierre, SD 57501 (605) 773-5669 http://www.state.sd.us/deca	**State Fire Marshal's Office** 118 West Capitol Avenue Pierre, SD 57501 (605) 773-3562 Code Compliance http://legis.state.sd.us/rules/rules/6115. htm#61:15:02	**Energy Management Office** 523 E. Capitol Avenue Pierre, SD 57501-3182 (605) 773-3899 http://www.state.sd.us/boa/EnergyMgt.htm
Tennessee	**Department of Education** Andrew Johnson Tower 6th Floor Nashville, TN 37243-0375 (615) 741-2731 http://www.state.tn.us/ education	**Office of the State Architect** 3128th Avenue, North Suite 2100 William R. Snodgrass Tennessee Tower Nashville, TN 37243-0300 (615) 741-2388 http://www.state.tn.us/finance/cpm/regs. pdf	**Department of Economic and Community Development** Energy Division 3128th Avenue, North Nashville, TN 37243-0405 (615) 741-1888 http://www.state.tn.us/ecd/energy_loans. htm

State	Department of Education	Facilities/Construction Unit	Green Funding Sources
Texas	**Texas Education Agency** 1701 North Congress Avenue Austin, TX 78701 (512) 463-9734 http://www.tea.state.tx.us	**School Facilities** 1701 North Congress Avenue Austin, TX 78701 (512) 463-9190 http://www.tea.state.tx.us/school.finance/facilities/stg.html	**Green Building Program** (Austin only) Austin Energy 721 Barton Springs Road Austin, Texas 78704 (512) 974-7217 http://www.ci.austin.tx.us/greenbuilder/programs_mun.htm
Utah	**Utah State Office of Education** 250 East 500 South P.O. Box 144200 Salt Lake City, UT 84114-4200 (801) 538-7500 http://www.usoe.k12.ut.us	**School Finance and Statistics** 250 East 500 South P.O. Box 144200 Salt Lake City, UT 84114-4200 (801) 538-7669 http://www.usoe.k12.ut.us/data/uasbo.htm	**Utah Department of Natural Resources** Energy Office (800) 538-5428 http://www.energy.utah.gov
Vermont	**Department of Education** 120 State Street Montpelier, VT 05620-2501 http://www.state.vt.us/educ	**Vermont Department of Education** School Construction 120 State Street Montpelier, VT 05620-2501 (802) 828-5402 http://www.state.vt.us/educ/new/html/pgm_construction.html	**Vermont Department of Education** School Construction 120 State Street Montpelier, VT 05620-2501 (802) 828-5402 http://www.state.vt.us/educ/new/html/pgm_construction.html
Virginia	**Department of Education** James Monroe Building 101 North 14th Street Richmond, VA 23219 (804) 225-2023 http://www.pen.k12.va.us	**Facilities Services** (804) 225-2035 http://www.pen.k12.va.us/VDOE/Finance/Facilities	**Virginia Department of Mines, Minerals, and Energy** Division of Energy 202 North Ninth Street 8th Floor Richmond, VA 23219 (804) 692-3216 http://www.mme.state.va.us/de
Washington	**State Board of Education** P.O. Box 47206 600 South Washington Street Olympia, WA 98504-47206 (360) 725-6025 http://www.sbe.wa.gov	**School Facilities** Old Capitol Building P.O. Box 47200 Olympia, WA 98504-7200 (360) 725-6261 (360) 725-6000 http://www.k12.wa.us/facilities	**Seattle Sustainable Building** http://www.cityofseattle.net/sustainablebuilding

State	Department of Education	Facilities/Construction Unit	Green Funding Sources
West Virginia	**Department of Education** 1900 Kanawha Boulevard, East Charleston, WV 25305 (304) 558-2699 http://wvde.state.wv.us	**School Facilities Office** 1900 Kanawha Boulevard East Charleston, WV 25305 (304) 558-2969 http://wvde.state.wv.us/policies (Article VI)	**West Virginia Development Office** Energy Efficiency Program Capital Complex Building 6, Room 553 1900 Kanawha Boulevard East Charleston, WV 25305-0311 (304) 558-2234 (800) 982-3386 http://www.wvdo.org/community/eep.html
Wisconsin	**Department of Public Instruction** 125 South Webster Street P.O. Box 7841 Madison, WI 53707-7841 (800) 441-4563 http://www.dpi.state.wi.us	**School Management Services** 125 South Webster Street P.O. Box 7841 Madison, WI 53707-7841 (608) 266-2803 http://www.dpi.state.wi.us/dpi/dfm/sms/index.html	**Wisconsin Focus on Energy (WFE)** (800) 762-7077 www.wifocusonenergy.com
Wyoming	**Department of Education** 2300 Capitol Avenue Hathaway Building 2nd Floor Cheyenne, WY 82002-0500 (307) 777-7673 http://www.k12.wy.us	**School Facilities Commission** 1920 Thones Street, Suite 300 Cheyenne, WY 82002 (307) 777-8670 http://sfc.state.wy.us	**Wyoming Business Council** Minerals, Energy and Transportation Division 214 West 15th Street Cheyenne, WY 82002 (307) 777-2800 (800) 262-3425 http://www.wyomingbusiness.org
American Samoa	**American Samoa Government Department of Education** P.O. Box 186 Pago Pago, AS 96799 011 (684) 633-5237 http://www.doe.as		**American Samoa Territorial Energy Office** Office of the Governor American Samoa Government Pago Pago, AS 96799 011 (684) 699-1101
District of Columbia	**District of Columbia Public Schools** 825 North Capitol Street, North East 7th Floor Washington, D.C. 20002 (202) 724-4222 http://www.k12.dc.us/dcps/home.html	**Office of Facilities Management** DCPS - Penn Center 1709 3rd Street, N.E. Washington, D.C., 20002 (202) 576-7718 http://www.k12.dc.us/dcps/OFM/dcofmhome.html	**District of Columbia Energy Office** Government of the District of Columbia 2000 14th Street, N.W. 300 East Washington, D.C. 20009 (202) 673-6700 http://www.dcenergy.org/inside.htm

State	Department of Education	Facilities/Construction Unit	Green Funding Sources
Guam	**Guam Department of Education** P.O. Box DE Hagåtña, GU 96932 011 (671) 475-0461 http://www.doe.edu.gu		**Guam Energy Office** 548 North Marine Drive P.O. Box 2950 Tamuning, GU 96913 011 (671) 646-4361 http://www.guamenergy.com
Northern Mariana Islands	**CNMI-Public School System (PSS)** P.O. Box 501370 Saipan, MP 96950 011 (670) 664-3721 /24 http://net.saipan.com/cftemplates/pss/index.cfm		**Northern Mariana Islands Division of Energy** Office of the Secretary of Public Works Saipan, MP 96950 011 (670) 644-4480 http://www.naseo.org/members/states.asp?vcStateNm=northern%20mariana%20islands
Puerto Rico	Ave. Tnte. César González Esq. Calle Calaf Tres Monjitas Hato Rey, P.R. 00917 (787) 759-2000 http://www.de.gobierno.pr/EDUPortal/default.htm		**Energy Affairs Administration** Department of Natural and Environmental Resources Puerta de Tierra Station P.O. Box 9066600 San Juan, PR 00906-6600 (787) 724-8777 http://www.naseo.org/members/states.asp?vcStateNm=puerto%20rico
Tribal Governments	**Office of Indian Education** 400 Maryland Avenue, S.W. Washington, D.C. 20202-6335 (202) 260-3774 http://www.ed.gov/about/offices/list/ous/oie		
U.S. Virgin Islands	**United States Virgin Islands Dept. of Education** No. 44-46 Kongens Gade Charlotte Amalie, U.S. Virgin Islands 00802 (340) 774-0100 http://www.networkvi.com/education		**Virgin Islands Energy Office** Oscar E. Henry Customs House 200 Strand Street Frederiksted, St. Croix, VI 00840 (340) 772-2616 http://www.vienergy.org

Index